DO NOT REMOVE
CARDS FROM POCKET

6/93

BOOKS BY HERSHEL SHANKS

The City of David: A Guide to Biblical Jerusalem

Judaism in Stone: The Archaeology of Ancient Synagogues

The Dead Sea Scrolls After Forty Years (with James C. VanderKam, P. Kyle
McCarter, Jr., and James A. Sanders)

BOOKS EDITED BY HERSHEL SHANKS

The Art and Craft of Judging: The Opinions of Judge Learned Hand

*Ancient Israel: A Short History from Abraham to the Roman
Destruction of the Temple*

*Christianity and Rabbinic Judaism: A Parallel History
for the First Six Centuries*

Recent Archaeology in the Land of Israel (with Benjamin Mazar)

Archaeology and the Bible: The Best of BAR (two volumes)
(with Dan P. Cole)

UNDERSTANDING
THE DEAD SEA
SCROLLS

UNDERSTANDING THE DEAD SEA SCROLLS

A Reader from the
Biblical Archaeology Review
Edited by

HERSHEL SHANKS

Random House New York

Grateful acknowledgment is made to Jonathan Cape for
permission to reprint excerpts from *The Dead Sea Scrolls
Deception* by Michael Baigent and Richard Leigh
(published in the United States by Simon and Schuster).
Reprinted by permission.

Library of Congress Cataloging-in-Publication Data
Understanding the Dead Sea scrolls : a reader from the *Biblical
Archaeology Review* / edited by Hershel Shanks.—1st ed.
p. cm.
ISBN 0-679-41448-7
1. Dead Sea scrolls. I. Shanks, Hershel. II. Biblical
archaeology review.
BM487.U49 1992 296.1′55—dc20 91-45727

Manufactured in the United States of America
Book design by J. K. Lambert
4 6 8 9 7 5 3

Acknowledgments

This book is truly a collective effort. It is a pleasure to express the gratitude of the Biblical Archaeology Society for the contributions so many people have made to this book.

First and foremost, our thanks go to the authors of the various chapters and to the photographers of the illustrations.

Two of the authors have died—my friend Yigael Yadin and Harry Thomas Frank. I wish they were here to see their words reprinted in this form.

Only someone who has coordinated a project like this and seen it through to fruition can appreciate the contribution of the publisher of *Biblical Archaeology Review* and *Bible Review,* Susan Laden—a tireless worker of infallible judgment.

The managing editor of *Biblical Archaeology Review* and *Bible Review,* Suzanne F. Singer, organized the pictures and gave her final approval to the editorial product. She was ably assisted by Nita Sue Kent and Carol Andrews, who copyedited the entire text.

The charts and maps were prepared by Auras Design.

A special expression of thanks goes to Professor James C. VanderKam of the University of Notre Dame and Professor Lawrence H. Schiffman of New York University for serving as informal consultants and technical advisors. That there are remaining errors is, as I express below, my fault, not theirs. There is no way to record, however, the many errors from which they saved us.

Is there more? Yes, people had to search for the best photographs that could be found. The text had to be input and proofed, biographies of the authors had to be prepared, citations had to be checked. It is with great gratitude that we thank Janet Bowman, Coleta M. A. Campanale, Jennifer Horn, Cheryl R. W. McGowan, Katherine Munro, and Judith Wohlberg.

My experience is that few authors are satisfied with their publisher. We are an exception. We are grateful for the work of our Random House editor Jason Epstein (whom Norman Mailer has accurately called the "bona fide mandarin of American letters") and his assistant editor Maryam Mohit.

Robert B. Barnett, Esq., handled our formal relations with Random House—not only successfully but amiably.

To all, we express our thanks.

I have elsewhere written that it is impossible to write about the Dead Sea Scrolls without making errors. I have no doubt that that is the case here. I can only record that the responsibility for the errors is mine and apologize in advance. If the readers of *Biblical Archaeology Review* and *Bible Review* are any indication of what I can expect, I will hear in no uncertain terms from readers of this volume. I hope we have an opportunity to correct these errors in future printings.

Hershel Shanks
Editor, *Biblical Archaeology Review* and *Bible Review*
February 1, 1992
Washington, D.C.

Contents

IX | CONTROVERSY AND THE SCROLLS

Illustrations and Charts

Of Caves and Scholars: An Overview

HERSHEL SHANKS

The Dead Sea Scrolls are the greatest manuscript discovery of the twentieth century, certainly as concerns biblical studies. Amidst confusion and speculation, they have ignited the imagination of nonscholar and scholar alike. It is easy to understand why. A library of over eight hundred texts, they cast a direct light on the critical period more than two thousand years ago out of which both Christianity and rabbinic Judaism emerged.

In 70 A.D., the Romans destroyed Jerusalem and its Temple. That year has functioned as a kind of impenetrable wall to students of rabbinic Judaism and early Christianity: It has been extremely difficult to go behind it. Out of the variety of Judaisms that vied for influence while the Temple still stood, after 70 there emerged the single normative Judaism we call rabbinic, the Judaism we know today. The only other form of "Judaism" to survive the tragedy of 70 was Christianity, which, as transformed of course, came to dominate the Western world.

Yet the earliest post-70 document of rabbinic Judaism, the Mishnah, dates to about 200 A.D. While Paul's letters were written before the Roman destruction of Jerusalem, other Christian literature, except perhaps the gospel of Mark, was not. This is why it has been difficult for scholars to understand how these two major movements—rabbinic Judaism and Christianity—emerged out of the extraordinary varieties of pre-70 Judaism. How did rabbinic Judaism and Christianity develop from the soil, the same soil, of pre-70 Judaism?

Suddenly, in our time, the Dead Sea Scrolls provide scholars with a vast library of over eight hundred volumes that sheds a direct light—undistorted by later editors with their own ideologies and biases—on pre-70 Judaism. The promise—by no means yet fully realized—is a clearer understanding of how these two major religious movements developed in their formative stages.

The term *Dead Sea Scrolls* is imprecise. In a narrow sense, Dead Sea Scrolls refers to the inscriptional materials found in eleven caves in the Wadi* Qumran on the northwest shore of the Dead Sea. But scholars often include manuscripts found in other nearby sites along the Dead Sea—Wadi Murabba 'at, Nahal† Hever, Khirbet Mird, and even Masada. On occasion, the term also includes documents found in the Wadi Daliyeh north of Jericho. For the most part, however, this book will discuss the Dead Sea Scrolls in the narrow sense—that is, the documents found in eleven caves in the Wadi Qumran. The documents from nearby sites (except Masada) date from different periods than the documents found in the Wadi Qumran and therefore raise entirely different problems. Dealing with the Wadi Qumran finds is enough for one book.

Another problem is the meaning of the word *scroll*. The first seven scrolls plus fragments of others were found in a cave in 1947 by a Bedouin shepherd. Thereafter, the Bedouin and archaeologists scoured other caves looking for other manuscripts. Between 1952 and 1956, ten other caves were found in the Wadi Qumran containing inscriptional materials (I say "inscriptional materials" because one of the eleven caves contained only a small inscription on a piece of pottery—an ostracon). In these caves, which were subsequently numbered 1 through 11, hundreds of other manuscripts were found. But only a handful were intact scrolls. Depending on what one means by intact, between three and five intact scrolls, in addition to the seven intact scrolls found in Cave 1, were eventually recovered. The rest were mere fragments. So it can be a little misleading, unless you understand their fragmentary nature, to describe these documents as scrolls. They were once scrolls, but all that is left are mere scraps, pieces often no bigger than a fingernail.

Of the over eight hundred different manuscripts scholars have identi-

---

Wadi is an Arabic word for a dry riverbed or valley that flows occasionally after a winter rain.

†*Nahal* is the Hebrew equivalent of the Arabic *wadi*.

1. *The Dead Sea Scroll caves
are in the cliffs at center. At
right is the Wadi Qumran
leading to the Dead Sea to the
east. Beyond is ancient Moab,
now Jordan.*

2. *The settlement at Qumran as excavated.*
Some of the caves where scrolls were found
are located in the spur at left.

fied from the eleven caves, some consist of only a single fragment. In others, there are many pieces. In some cases, the fragments are large. In others, they are very small. Yet even the scraps can tell us a great deal.

Clearly these are the remains of an important library in antiquity, but where the library came from and who wrote the documents is a matter of dispute. Some scholars say they were written in a nearby settlement the remains of which is called Qumran. Others say that the library must have come from Jerusalem, brought here for safekeeping when the Romans attacked the city, ultimately destroying it in 70 A.D. In either event, it is clear that the Qumran manuscripts constituted a vast and varied library for its time.

The documents were written between about 250 B.C. and 68 A.D., when, according to its excavator, the nearby settlement of Qumran was destroyed by the Roman army in anticipation of its attack on Jerusalem. Although that is when the documents were written, some may have been composed much earlier. Indeed, the earliest documents among the Dead Sea Scrolls were actually written before the establishment of the nearby settlement with which they are often associated.

The period of Jewish history in which the Dead Sea Scrolls were written is one of extreme complexity, documented only in ambiguous sources. Governments were unstable and often failed to insure social tranquility. Violence erupted frequently. Religious politics played a major role in securing social stability—or in destroying it. In the second century B.C. the Maccabees, a family of Jews from Modi'in in central Palestine rebelled against the Assyrian (Seleucid*) overlord Antiochus IV Epiphanes who then ruled the land of the Jews. The ultimately successful Maccabean-led liberation of the Jerusalem Temple is still celebrated in the Jewish festival of Hanukkah. In fact, the struggle for an independent Jewish state lasted for a quarter of a century, finally culminating in the establishment of the Hasmonean dynasty of Jewish rulers. Even before the Maccabean revolt, bribery had led to the appointment of high priests who were not of the Zadokite line established by King Solomon. This usurpation, it was charged, continued under the Hasmoneans. The Hasmonean rulers combined both political and religious authority and were bitterly opposed by various religious segments of the population, not only for what was regarded as a usurpation of the high priesthood, but

---

*After the death of Alexander the Great in 323 B.C., his kingdom was divided between the Ptolemies and the Seleucids. Palestine was at various times ruled by one or the other of these two ruling houses.

also for the unique synthesis of Hellenism and Judaism they espoused. The Hasmonean dynasty was followed in the mid-first century B.C. by the Herodian period, named for its most illustrious figure, Herod the Great (37–4 B.C.).

In the Hasmonean period, numerous, often competing Jewish religious groups, sometimes referred to as sects, had begun to form. They continued to vie for influence in the Herodian period. The best known of these were the Pharisees, the only group (other than the Christians) to survive the Roman destruction of Jerusalem in 70 A.D. Thus, Pharisaic thought became the foundation of rabbinic Judaism, the Judaism that has survived to this day. But numerous other Jewish groups jostled one another in the pre-70 period. These included the Sadducees and Essenes, described by the Jewish historian Josephus (c. 37–100 A.D.).

The Sadducees were a priestly, aristocratic party commanding significant wealth and political prominence. They served as diplomats as well as military leaders. They also claimed to be the only legitimate priests, apparently taking a stricter approach to many legal matters than the Pharisees. Unfortunately, the Sadducees left no literature of their own— unless it is reflected in the Dead Sea Scrolls. Thus we don't know how the Sadducees would have described themselves. All our descriptions— the most important come from the Jewish historian Josephus and the New Testament—are mildly or intensely antagonistic.

The Pharisees are better known. It is they who ultimately shaped Jewish life to our own day. The name appears to derive from the Hebrew word *parush,* meaning "separated" or "standing apart." Most of what we know about the Pharisees, however, comes from later rabbinic references. The references to them in the New Testament are obviously antagonistic—and biased. The Pharisees appear to have been the most popular Jewish group among the populace. Although it is commonly thought that their determinations of religious laws were more moderate and lenient than those of the Sadducees, this is by no means invariably the case. Thus it is difficult to characterize the difference in their beliefs in a sentence or two. The Pharisees did, however, accept the Oral Law as the authentic amplification of the Written Law of Moses, unlike their rival Sadducees.

The Essenes were, by comparison with the Pharisees, a smaller group. Oddly, however, Josephus describes them in greater detail than either the Pharisees or the Sadducees—perhaps because he thought his readers would be fascinated by a group exhibiting such curious and exotic behavior. The sect was governed by a tight organization with rigorous rules for acceptance and clearly defined penalties. Although Essene groups lived all over the country, including Jerusalem, a small subgroup of them lived in a settlement in the desert by the Dead Sea. Their lives were dedicated to strict observance of the law. We shall learn a great deal more about them in the discussion of the sectarian documents found among the Dead Sea Scrolls.

These three groups were not the only ones active in Jewish life. There were numerous others—the Hasidim, the Zealots, the Sicarii, the Boethusians, and toward the end of this period, the early Christians.

— · —

The Dead Sea Scrolls can be divided into two groups: biblical texts and nonbiblical texts. Between 20 and 25 percent of the documents are biblical texts. Every book of the Hebrew Bible is represented, at least by a fragment, except the book of Esther. Whether by coincidence or not, Esther is the only book of the Hebrew Bible that does not mention the name of God.

The biblical texts are easier for scholars to deal with than the nonbiblical texts even though only small fragments of a book may have survived. The biblical text is known from later copies that provide a kind of template on which to fit the Qumran fragments. This is also true of some of the nonbiblical texts, such as the books of Enoch and Jubilees, that were previously known to us.

But many of the nonbiblical texts were entirely unknown to us before they were found in the Qumran caves and it is often difficult to arrange the fragments of these texts in any meaningful order.

The nonbiblical texts are remarkably varied and can be subdivided in several ways, for example, by genre: hymns and psalms, biblical commentaries, wisdom literature, legal texts, a letter, pseudepigrapha,* a designation of hidden treasure. Another way to subdivide them is by whether a text is a so-called sectarian text or not—that is, does it represent the concepts and ideas of the particular religious group that collected this library?

Some texts—the sectarian ones—seem to reflect the rules and beliefs of a unique sect or group of Jews. Scholars refer to this group as the Qumran sect. But what was this sect? The usual answer is that it was the Essenes, mentioned not only by Josephus but also by Pliny the Elder (23–79 A.D.) and Philo (c. 20 B.C.–50 A.D.). But other scholars question

---

*A Bible-like text, often falsely ascribed to an ancient worthy like Enoch or Noah.

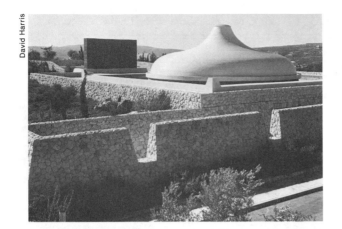

3. *The Shrine of the Book,
Jerusalem, where the
seven intact scrolls from
Cave 1 are housed.*

4. *The Shrine of the Book,
interior. The great Isaiah
Scroll is wound around
the lighted drum in the center
of the upper floor.*

5. *The great Isaiah Scroll in
the Shrine of the Book.*

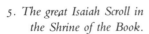

this identification. Two chapters in this book vigorously debate the issue.* Those who challenge the Essene identification argue that the so-called sectarian texts often seem inconsistent with Essene doctrine as reflected in independent sources and are even inconsistent among themselves. For example, how do the militant, even warlike, statements in some Qumran texts square with the commonly held view that the Essenes were pacifists?

Other questions concern the Qumran settlement itself. What is its relationship to the scrolls? Were the scrolls written there? Did the library belong to the settlement? Or were the scrolls brought to the caves by others who may or may not have had some relationship to the settlement? Qumran was excavated between 1951 and 1956 by Père Roland de Vaux of the École Biblique et Archéologique Française in Jerusalem who died in 1971 without writing a final report on his excavation. De Vaux, a Dominican father, regarded the settlement as a kind of monastery. Professor Norman Golb of the University of Chicago believes it was a military fort. Scholars now preparing the final excavation report on the basis of records left by de Vaux suggest the site may have been a winter residence, a kind of desert plantation, for wealthy, and perhaps powerful, Jerusalemites.

The site contained a great many water installations. But were they all drinking water cisterns? Or were some for bathing? And if so, were some for ritual bathing?

De Vaux excavated part of a large cemetery adjacent to the site and found among the nearly one thousand graves the remains of two females and a child. Were they simply female servants or does this destroy the theory that the monks who lived here were celibate and that Qumran was entirely male?

The seven large intact scrolls from Cave 1 were published reasonably soon after they came into scholarly hands—by Israeli and American scholars. Over the years, the fragmentary texts from other caves (as well as from Cave 1) were also published—with the exception of the fragmentary texts from Cave 4. But problems with the Cave 4 texts would eventually discredit the entire publication enterprise.

Cave 4 presented a special problem from the outset. Like most of the finds, Cave 4 was discovered by the Bedouin. It proved to be the richest of all the caves, with over five hundred different manuscripts—but all in tatters. Not a single intact scroll was recovered from this jumbled mess.

*See Chapters 3 and 4.

Yet this cache represented over five-eighths of the Qumran texts—approximately five hundred of a total of approximately eight hundred manuscripts.

While the number of discrete manuscripts found in Cave 4 is approximately five hundred, the number of fragments is much larger. Estimates range from ten thousand to one hundred thousand, the most common being about fifteen thousand fragments from this cache. In effect, the fragments constitute a giant jigsaw puzzle—or more accurately, five hundred different jigsaw puzzles with 90 percent of the pieces missing.

But this was not the worst of it. If the Bedouin who discovered Cave 4 sold the fragments on the antiquities market to various dealers, it would be impossible ever to assemble the fragments in one place, and scholars would never have been able to work on the surviving pieces of the jigsaw puzzles.

To avoid this, an arrangement was made with the Bedouin in the early 1950s to purchase the fragments from Cave 4 for one Jordanian dinar per centimeter (then $5.60). The money to purchase the fragments was provided by a group of so-called national schools—that is, foreign schools in east Jerusalem devoted to archaeological and biblical research. Among those participating were the French, the Americans, the English, and the Germans. The Vatican was also a source of funds. It was agreed that after the fragments had been assembled into discrete documents and then published, the originals would be divided among the various national schools that provided the funds to purchase them. In this way, the cache was kept together and assembled in what was then a private museum in Jerusalem, the Palestine Archaeological Museum (now the Rockefeller Museum).

To work on the texts, an international team of young scholars was assembled under Jordanian auspices since at the time Jordan controlled what is now called the West Bank where the scrolls were found as well as east Jerusalem where the contents of the caves were assembled. The team would include no Jews and the task of assembling it fell to Père de Vaux. The German member of the group, Claus Hunzinger, soon resigned, leaving a seven-man team of young scholars, mainly Catholic clerics, who set to work fitting the pieces of the jigsaw puzzles together.

The work took place in a long museum room that they called the Scrollery. Some of the conditions there would today be regarded as horrendous, but that was then. Little effort was made to prevent deterioration of the fragments. No record was made of the original fragments in their original condition. Pictures show the young scholars working in a room with the windows open and the sun streaming in, holding fragments in their hands while smoking cigarettes. As the young scholars—the oldest was thirty-two—sought to divide the fragments into discrete documents and to look for possible joins, any one of them was free to move fragments around under the glass plates.

By the late 1950s, the team of scholars had substantially completed the task of arranging the fragments. I say substantially completed because the task of arranging the fragments will never be complete; there will always be room for improvement. The next generation of scholars will always find new connections. And indeed today's team of scholars continues to improve the arrangements.

With the fragments thus arranged into discrete documents, the team divided the five hundred different texts among themselves for publication. In hindsight, this was an act of enormous hubris and greed. They clearly took on more work than they could complete in a lifetime. Only one scholar on the team, John M. Allegro of England, published his entire assignment, but his work was so bad that an article correcting it is longer than his original publication. On the other hand, Allegro did get his texts out—which is more than can be said for any of the others.

By the late 1950s the team succeeded in making transcripts of the texts by simply writing down the letters in an easily readable form as one might study a handwritten letter by a poor penman or one written in eighteenth-century style. In the case of the Qumran fragments, the letters are often difficult to read—not so much because they were originally obscure, but because of the ravages of time.

As the transcripts were being completed, arrangements were made to have four other young scholars create a concordance of the nonbiblical texts, listing each word in the text, indicating the document in which it appeared, the column, the line, and the adjacent words.* This concordance would be an invaluable tool for anyone attempting to translate and understand these often obscure Hebrew and Aramaic texts.

This brings the story of the Cave 4 team up to about 1960. In the next thirty years the team managed to publish less than one hundred of their five hundred texts—approximately 20 percent of their assignment. The four hundred unpublished texts comprise approximately half of the total number of Qumran manuscripts.

According to a scholarly convention that is nowhere written or even referred to in writing, a scholar who is assigned to publish a text has

*This concordance includes nonbiblical texts from Caves 1–10.

6. The Scrollery in the 1950s, with fragments from Cave 4 under glass plates and the sun pouring in.

complete control over it. That person may take as long as he or she likes to publish it. It can be seen by others only with the scholar's permission. No one else is permitted to print the text.

The Cave 4 team asserted these "publication rights" with a vengeance. Several of the original team members have died and "bequeathed" their "publication rights" to trusted colleagues, who then themselves exercise the right to exclude others. Requests by outside scholars to see various texts have been turned down. Team members have even "given" texts to their graduate students, while excluding senior scholars.

Over the years, the discontent of excluded scholars mounted. In 1977, Oxford don Geza Vermes, one of the excluded scholars, made his now-famous prediction that the Dead Sea Scrolls publication project would become "the academic scandal par excellence of the twentieth century." Ten years later, Vermes commented that what he had forecast had become a reality.

In 1985, as editor of *Biblical Archaeology Review,* I attended a scholarly conference at New York University at which scroll editor John Strugnell addressed his audience of Qumran scholars. Strugnell was the only member of the team there; he alone had access to the texts. He spoke with an authority only he could command. Morton Smith, a distinguished professor from Columbia University, called the situation "disgusting." Other scholars were obsequiously grateful for whatever Strugnell dribbled out to them; inwardly they were seething with resentment.

That marked the beginning of a six-year campaign by *Biblical Archaeology Review* to free the Dead Sea Scrolls.

In all fairness, it must be recognized that as the pressure mounted, the editing team responded by speeding up the process. After John Strugnell became chief editor in 1987, he expanded the team, adding Jews and Israelis for the first time. He convinced one of the original members of the team, J. T. Milik, to relinquish a major portion of his original hoard for reassignment to younger scholars. In consultation with the other editors, he fixed a "Suggested Timetable" for completion of the work.

At the same time the Israel Antiquities Authority (then the Department of Antiquities) began for the first time to assert itself with regard to the problem of Dead Sea Scroll publication.

Israel obtained physical control of the Cave 4 fragments in the 1967 Six-Day War. Ironically, the Jordanian government itself gave Israel a claim to the scroll fragments from Cave 4 that Israel would otherwise not have had. As indicated earlier, the Cave 4 fragments were purchased with funds provided by the national schools, which presumably could lay claim to ownership of the fragments. However, in 1961 the government of Jordan muddied the waters, to say the least. The background is this: Most of the original editors were Catholic clerics. The only agnostic on the team was John Allegro, whose idiosyncratic views of the scrolls and their contents soon alienated him from the rest of the team. In the ensuing struggle between Allegro and the other members of the team, Allegro attempted to enlist his friends in the Jordanian government. Jordan, he argued, should wrest from these Catholic clerics documents they were using to support their religious beliefs while at the same time suppressing interpretations of the scrolls they feared would undermine their religious doctrine. The full story of this struggle is yet to be told. But in 1961, the Jordanian government nationalized the scrolls. (In November 1966, Jordan nationalized the museum.) The government of Jordan then claimed to own the Cave 4 fragments. (Israel's intact scrolls were of course housed in its own museum—the Shrine of the Book in west Jerusalem.)

When Jerusalem—and the Rockefeller Museum—fell to the Israelis in the 1967 Six-Day War, Jordanian governmental property including the Cave 4 scroll fragments became subject to Israeli administration. Even without the Jordanian nationalization, the Israelis would have had a strong claim to the scrolls not only because Jordanian sovereignty over the West Bank where the scrolls were found was recognized by only two countries—Great Britain and Pakistan—but also because the documents themselves represent Israel's patrimony, not Jordan's.

In any event, when the scroll fragments fell to Israel in 1967, Israel made no effort to gain control of the publication project—perhaps for fear of political fallout if questions of ownership were raised. So Israeli authorities did not even attempt to add Jews to the official publication team. On the contrary, Israel agreed to recognize the "publication rights" of the official team, provided only that the fragments were promptly published.

This of course did not happen. Israel nevertheless made no effort to assert its authority until a former general, Amir Drori, was appointed director of the Antiquities Authority in 1988. Drori introduced numerous reforms and revitalized the agency. His influence was also felt with regard to the Dead Sea Scrolls. Indeed, he claims that the reforms he introduced had nothing to do with *Biblical Archaeology Review*'s campaign to permit free access to the scrolls, and he may well be right.

Under Drori's aegis, a scroll advisory committee was appointed, in effect to represent Israel in connection with the Dead Sea Scroll publication project.

Although Drori, on the recommendation of the scroll advisory committee, ratified Strugnell's appointment as editor in chief, relations between Strugnell and the Antiquities Authority soon deteriorated into a
struggle for control. In late 1990, the Israelis appointed Hebrew University professor Emanuel Tov as co-editor in chief with Strugnell, but,
pointedly, Tov reported not to Strugnell, but to the Israel Antiquities
Authority.

Strugnell reacted with fury to Tov's appointment; he regarded it as a
strongarm move. According to an Associated Press report, "Strugnell
said he would fight Tov's appointment, which he called an 'alarming
attempt' by Israeli scholars to claim credit for the research."

Soon thereafter Strugnell gave a virulently anti-Jewish interview to an
Israeli journalist, which was published first in Hebrew in a Tel Aviv daily
and then in English in the *Biblical Archaeology Review*.* Strugnell was
promptly relieved of his duties as editor in chief, although not removed
from the team. As of this writing, he still holds his hoard of texts.

With Strugnell's removal, Tov became chief editor along with two
other chief editors, Professor Eugene Ulrich of the University of Notre
Dame and Père Émile Puech of the École Biblique.

Since then the team leadership has operated efficiently and harmoni-
ously. They continue to respond to international outrage by expanding
the team, creating deadlines for completion, and urging the various
editors to speed up their work. In addition, they have persuaded some
editors—particularly J. T. Milik—to release more of their hoard to
others.

On the other hand, the team, as well as the Antiquities Authority and
its scroll advisory committee, adamantly defended the cartel, though
insisting that it be expanded. That is, the unpublished texts must remain
secret, subject to allowing other qualified scholars to see them, provided
they agree not to publish them until the *editio princeps* is published by a
team editor.

As part of his effort to speed up the publication process, Strugnell
decided in 1988 to have published for the exclusive use of the team
editors the concordance prepared in the late 1950s. Until 1988, the
concordance had lain in the basement of the Rockefeller, for all practical
purposes inaccessible. A concordance would be an invaluable tool to
anyone working on the texts because it would guide the researcher to all
uses of any particular word, including its context. In 1988, under Strug-

*See Chapter 20.

nell's direction, thirty copies of the concordance were printed and distributed.

The team had refrained from making the concordance available earlier because of fears that someone might reconstruct from the concordance the secret transcripts from which it had been made. Admittedly, this would be a laborious job, but the team editors knew it could be done. By the time Strugnell printed the concordance in 1988, however, the age of the computer had arrived. It was no longer so laborious to reconstruct the secret transcripts from the concordance. What the team had feared was exactly what happened.

Professor Ben Zion Wacholder of Hebrew Union College in Cincinnati, Ohio, is sixty-seven years old, white-haired, and nearly blind. He has devoted much of his professional life to study of the Dead Sea Scrolls and has written a book about them.[1] At a meeting of scholars in November 1990, at which Wacholder gave a paper on a particular Dead Sea Scroll text, one of his fellow scholars raised a question that Wacholder suspected could be answered by an unpublished fragment. Wacholder returned to Cincinnati and then, with the help of Martin G. Abegg, a graduate student who was a computer buff, Wacholder recreated the fragments of the unpublished text from the concordance, using Abegg's computer. Wacholder and Abegg were so pleased with the result that they began generating other transcripts—transcripts that had been prepared by the team editors in the 1950s, but that had been kept secret except insofar as they had provided the basis for the concordance.

After much agonizing, Wacholder and Abegg decided to make the result of their work available to the scholarly world at large. Arrangements were made with the Biblical Archaeology Society to publish the computer-reconstructed transcripts in fascicles, the first of which appeared on September 4, 1991.

The publication of the computer-reconstructed texts was reported the next day on the front page of *The New York Times, The Washington Post,* the *Baltimore Sun,* and other newspapers. Approving editorials soon followed in these and other newspapers. "Mr. Wacholder and Mr. Abegg are to be applauded for their work," said *The New York Times.* "The committee [of official team editors], with its obsessive secrecy and cloak and dagger scholarship, long ago exhausted its credibility with scholars and laymen alike. The two Cincinnatians seem to know what the scroll committee forgot: that the scrolls and what they say about the common roots of Christianity and Rabbinic Judaism belong to civilization, not to a few sequestered professors."[2]

Neither the team editors, the Israel Antiquities Authority, nor its scroll advisory committee agreed with this widely held opinion. Instead they reacted with their customary fury. Strugnell accused Wacholder and Abegg of stealing. A member of the scroll advisory committee characterized the publication as "intellectual thievery." One of the editors in chief charged the publisher with a violation of international law and threatened to sue.

Meanwhile, unbeknownst to the Biblical Archaeology Society, the Huntington Library in San Marino, California, was planning its own surprise. The Huntington possessed a set of photographic negatives of the scroll fragments it had received from a California philanthropist named Elizabeth Hay Bechtel. Mrs. Bechtel had founded the Ancient Biblical Manuscript Center in Claremont, California. More than a decade ago, she arranged to send a photographer to Jerusalem to photograph the scrolls—or, rather, to photograph photographs of the scrolls—for security purposes—so a set of negatives would be available in case something happened to the originals. The Bechtel negatives were intended to be deposited in her Ancient Biblical Manuscript Center. Before this occurred, however, Mrs. Bechtel had a falling out with the director of the center, Professor James A. Sanders. In the ensuing struggle for control of the center, Mrs. Bechtel lost—but she had the negatives. As part of the settlement of the dispute, Mrs. Bechtel gave a set of the negatives to the Ancient Biblical Manuscript Center but kept another for herself. The center agreed in writing with the Israel Antiquity Authority not to allow anyone to see its set of negatives without the express permission of the editor to whom it was assigned for publication. Mrs. Bechtel signed no such agreement. She deposited her set of negatives in the Huntington. In 1987 Mrs. Bechtel died, leaving her negatives of the scrolls to the library.

In 1990, a new director, William A. Moffett, was appointed at the Huntington. Moffett is an independent man with a no-nonsense attitude in favor of intellectual freedom. When he became aware of the Bechtel negatives and the controversy regarding the monopolists' control of the texts, he announced that all scholars could have access to the Huntington archive. The announcement was reported on September 22, 1991, in a three-column head at the top of the front page of the Sunday *New York Times:* "Monopoly Over Dead Sea Scrolls Is Ended."

Again universal applause—except from the Israel Antiquities Authority, its scroll advisory committee, and the official team of editors. From them came the by-now predictable reaction—accusations of breach of agreement, unethical conduct, immoral action, stealing scholars' work, and threats of lawsuit. The Huntington was not to be cowed, however. On the other hand, it was not in a position administratively to respond to the flood of requests for access to its negatives.

The Antiquities Authority and the scroll publication team then proceeded to attempt to reverse the Huntington decision by negotiating a restrictive definition of access. After threatening the Huntington with a lawsuit, the Antiquities Authority and editor in chief Tov called a meeting in Jerusalem for December 4, 1991, to which they invited institutions having negatives of the scrolls. (In addition to the Huntington and the Ancient Biblical Manuscript Center, two other institutions have negatives of unpublished scrolls: Hebrew Union College—whose set is only partial—and the Oxford Centre for Postgraduate Hebrew Studies, which recently obtained a copy in connection with a British foundation's funding the work of the official editing team.) While the Antiquities Authority and the official team editors "agree[d] in principle to facilitate free access to photographs of the Scrolls," they also expressed their concern "that the work of scholars who in recent years have taken upon themselves to publish texts should not be harmed by any new arrangements." In subsequent negotiations with the invitees, it became clear what the monopolists had in mind: they would agree to let otherwise qualified scholars have access, but such access would be conditioned upon an express agreement by outside scholars who were given access that they would not publish what they saw.

When Huntington would not agree to attend the meeting and it became clear that it would not abide by the restrictions that the Antiquities Authority and the official editing team were seeking to impose, the Antiquities Authority and chief editor Emanuel Tov attempted to preempt the situation by cancelling the meeting and announcing at a press conference that they were permitting free access to the scrolls to all scholars. But behind this announcement were the same restrictions. Professor James M. Robinson of Claremont Graduate School and director of the Institute for Antiquity and Christianity called the Israel Antiquities Authority announcement "a smoke screen"; others called it a subterfuge. For behind the announcement was a press release that stated that any scholar applying to see the unpublished text must sign a statement certifying that the inspection was "for personal research only and not for the preparation of a text edition." In other words, you could look, but you could not print what you saw. This announcement by the Israeli authorities clearly did not satisfy the critics.

The drama ended on November 19, 1991, when the Biblical Archaeology Society published a two-volume edition of photographs of the unpublished scrolls. This project had been in the works for over a year. Where the Biblical Archaeology Society obtained its photographs remains a mystery. The introduction to the set of books states that the Huntington Library was not the source.

The edition of photographs of the unpublished texts contains 1,787 plates—all fragments. This is the scholarly raw material. At last it is available. The question of access has now been resolved.

The next startling disclosure is likely to be the terrible conditions under which the fragments have been kept. Just before the 1956 Arab-Israeli war, the fragments were packed up and shipped to Amman where they were stored for safekeeping in the damp basement of the Ottoman Bank. When they were returned to Jerusalem months later, mildew had already formed on some of the fragments. It took several months to clean them. But even in Jerusalem they were not kept in a climate-controlled environment; as a result, many of the fragments are today illegible. That means that the best evidence of the texts in many, if not most, cases is not the fragment itself, but an early photograph.

Fortunately, the fragments in plates were photographed over a period of years by the superb Arab photographer, Najib Albina. He is one of the unsung heroes of the Dead Sea Scroll saga. Many of his photographs were taken with infrared film, thereby enhancing the text. Since the fragments came into Israeli possession, they have never been rephotographed as a whole. The negatives in the various depositories are largely copies of Albina's negatives.

Alas, Albina's negatives were kept under as poor conditions as the fragments and they too have badly deteriorated, some to the point where they have simply been discarded, others to the extent that they have become too buckled to reproduce by placing film on top of them. The combination of the deterioration of the fragments and the deterioration of the Albina negatives accounts for the many illegible and unusable plates in the photographic edition of the scrolls. How much has been lost by this negligence will never be known.

Almost from the outset, the scrolls have been the subject of controversy. In the early days, much of the controversy involved the extent to which Christianity would be "cut down to size" by the contents of the scrolls, a theme made popular by Edmund Wilson's long article in the *New Yorker,* later published as a book, *The Scrolls from the Dead Sea.*[3]

But almost every other aspect of the scrolls was also an occasion for often rancorous debate among scholars—whether the scrolls were medieval forgeries, what was their date, whether references to Jesus, Paul, John the Baptist, or Jesus' brother James could be found there; and whether the gospels or other books of the New Testament were included in the fragments.

Then around 1960, the scrolls almost dropped from sight. For twenty-five years, not only the public but scholars too seemed to forget the scrolls. Little was published in this period by the official team of editors—and no one seemed to care. Then in the mid-1980s Israeli archaeologist Yigael Yadin published the Temple Scroll in English. The latest of the Dead Sea Scrolls to be recovered—Israel confiscated it intact from an Arab antiquities dealer after the 1967 Six-Day War—at twenty-seven feet, it is also the longest. At about the same time, we began to hear of a letter, perhaps from the leader of the Dead Sea Scroll sect himself, the so-called Teacher of Righteousness. It had apparently been discovered among the Cave 4 fragments. If so, this was the only letter (although it was found in multiple copies, emphasizing its significance) to be found at Qumran.

Finally, also in the mid-1980s, the *Biblical Archaeology Review* began complaining about the painfully slow pace of publication and the official editors' obsessive secrecy about the unpublished texts, fully half of which remained inaccessible to scholars more than thirty years after their discovery.

Oddly, the general press took up this arcane cause. How to account for enormous public interest in these abstruse texts? Some have tried to explain it on the ground that the public thought the unpublished texts contained evidence that would undermine the fundamental tenets of either Christianity or Judaism, a speculation fed by the official editors' obsessive secrecy. I do not accept this theory. I believe instead that intelligent men and women who were not part of the controversy realized these tattered fragments would tell them something of the sources of their culture, and knew that a principle of enormous importance was at stake. Public approval for the publication of the scrolls has been in proportion to the outrage that accompanied this suppression.

The essays in this book reflect not only the controversies, but also the drama, surrounding the scrolls—beginning with the initial discovery of seven intact scrolls in Cave 1 and their ultimate acquisition by Israel after four of them were taken to the United States and sold through a classified ad in, of all places, *The Wall Street Journal* (Chapter 1).

By whom, where, and why was this library assembled? This is the subject of a brilliant synthesis by Harvard professor Frank M. Cross (Chapter 2).

In recent years, a new generation of Dead Sea Scroll scholars has matured. Some of them now question conclusions that had been long accepted—for example, Cross's contention that the sectarian texts from Qumran represent the thinking of the Jewish sect of Essenes. In Chapter 3, Professor Lawrence Schiffman of New York University questions the Essene theory and suggests that in fact the Qumran sect finds its origins in the Sadducees, a contention roundly opposed by one of Cross' students, James C. VanderKam of the University of Notre Dame (Chapter 4). More than simply a name is at stake. At issue is the basic philosophy of the sectarian texts.

Strangely, the most important text for tracing the physical origins of the Qumran sect was found not in the Qumran caves—at least it was not found there first. It was found instead in a Cairo synagogue nearly a hundred years ago and has long been available to scholars. Known as the Damascus Document (because the group made a journey, either actually or symbolically, from—or to—Damascus), this text reflects the thought of a Jewish group who, a few prescient scholars long ago speculated, lived before the Roman destruction of the Temple, even though the two copies recovered from the Cairo synagogue date from more than a thousand years later. Imagine the surprise when the scholarly world learned that at least eight copies of this document were in the Qumran library. That is why some have called the two copies of the Damascus Document found in the Cairo synagogue the first Dead Sea Scrolls to be discovered (Chapter 5). Just how this text bears on the origins of the Dead Sea Scroll sect is further explored in Chapter 6.

By 1967 everyone assumed that all the scrolls the Bedouin had discovered had come into scholarly hands—everyone, that is, except Israeli archaeologist Yigael Yadin. For years he had been secretly—and unsuccessfully—negotiating for the purchase of another scroll from a Bethlehem antiquities dealer. The go-between—Bethlehem was then in Jordanian hands—was an American clergyman Yadin would identify only as Mr. Z. When Bethlehem fell into Israeli hands in the 1967 Six-Day War, Yadin immediately went to the home of the antiquities dealer, lifted some floor tiles, and there found the now-famous Temple Scroll—one of the most important and controversial of the scrolls. Both its discovery and its significance are discussed by Yadin himself in Chapter 7. The visionary temple for which this scroll is named is described for us in Chapter 8 by Magen Broshi, the curator of the Shrine of the Book in Jerusalem, which houses the seven intact scrolls from Cave 1 that had been acquired by Israel by the mid-1950s as well as the Temple Scroll acquired in 1967.

Mr. Z, the American clergyman who represented the Bethlehem antiquities dealer in his pre-1967 negotiation with Yadin, first learned of Israel's acquisition of the Temple Scroll from the article by Yadin in *Biblical Archaeology Review*. Mr. Z then told his side of the story of the aborted negotiation—quite different from Yadin's, who had since died in 1984. In Chapter 9 we tell the story of Joe Uhrig, the American television evangelist who tried his best to acquire the scroll for Yadin and was unsuccessful because, he claims, Yadin misled him. This business of the scrolls is, indeed, a cloak and dagger affair, as Yadin had always maintained.

In Chapter 10, a leading German Dead Sea Scroll scholar, Hartmut Stegemann, explains why he believes the Temple Scroll was in fact a long-lost sixth book of the Torah (Pentateuch) that did not make the final cut.

This naturally leads to an examination of the significance of the biblical scrolls from Qumran—about 25 percent of the scrolls are books of the Hebrew Bible—for our understanding of the development of the biblical text. Before the Qumran discoveries our oldest texts of the Hebrew Bible were medieval—tenth century and later. With the Qumran discoveries, we suddenly had texts a thousand years earlier—at a time when the biblical texts had not yet been standardized. In Chapters 11, 12, and 13, we examine what the Dead Sea Scrolls can tell us about the early development of the biblical text, how a passage from the book of Samuel had accidentally been omitted from the Hebrew Bible, and how scholars use the Qumran biblical texts to interpret various difficult passages in the Hebrew Bible.

In Chapter 14, Professor VanderKam discusses the relationship between the Dead Sea Scrolls and Christianity, a subject that must be considered from many aspects. VanderKam's masterful survey, a sober consideration of a complex issue, comes to two somewhat surprising conclusions: (1) Early Christianity is grounded more deeply in Jewish thought than previously supposed; (2) aspects of Christian beliefs previously considered unique were in fact part of the intellectual baggage of the time. Nevertheless, the Christian combination with its unique Messiah remains unparalleled.

An example of a Qumran text with remarkable parallels to a passage in the gospel of Luke is explored in Chapter 15.

In Chapter 16, the eminent German scholar Otto Betz considers whether John the Baptist spent his early years at Qumran and concludes that he probably did, although the Baptist later determined to take his message to a broader public.

What Professor VanderKam does for Christianity in Chapter 14, Professor Schiffman does for rabbinic Judaism in Chapter 17. Schiffman briefly surveys what we can learn from the Dead Sea Scrolls about the Pharisaic origins and development of rabbinic Judaism.

If the earliest Dead Sea Scroll—the Damascus Document—was not found in the Dead Sea caves, but in a Cairo synagogue, then perhaps we may say that the Copper Scroll, although found in Qumran Cave 3, is not really a Dead Sea Scroll. The reason is that in almost every respect the Copper Scroll is different from, and unrelated to, the other Dead Sea Scrolls. It was found tucked away by itself in Cave 3. It was written on copper foil—the only such scroll. It is a "hidden-treasure" map—again unique among the scrolls. Some have speculated that the Copper Scroll is a secret guide to where the treasures of the Jerusalem Temple have been hidden to prevent their capture by the Romans. But will we ever be able to discover the secret code? And is any of the treasure still to be found? Professor P. Kyle McCarter of The Johns Hopkins University in Baltimore, Maryland, is reediting the Copper Scroll (it was originally published thirty years ago) based on remarkable new photographs by Bruce and Kenneth Zuckerman. Chapter 18 provides us with the latest insights of McCarter's new edition of the Copper Scroll.

In Chapter 19 we return to the problems of the fragmentary scrolls—and how to reconstruct them. The author, Hartmut Stegemann, is the world's leading expert on the subject. He has even devised some unique ways of placing fragments that do not join in relation to one another.

In the book's final section, we reprint the anti-Jewish, anti-Israeli interview that led to John Strugnell's dismissal as chief scroll editor (Chapter 20). Then we directly confront an issue that has been widely whispered about, but seldom openly discussed—whether and how anti-Semitism has affected the management and interpretation of the scrolls (Chapter 21). Finally, we consider the widely expressed charge that somehow the Vatican has been suppressing the scrolls, because they undermine church doctrine (Chapter 22).

We have not included a chapter on the contents of the unpublished scrolls for the obvious reason that no one is quite sure yet what they contain. But the likelihood is that they do not contain any great surprises, like a copy of the gospels or a direct mention of Jesus of

Nazareth. Enough of the scrolls have been published so that the general direction of the unpublished texts can be assumed. New insights, yes. Bombshells, no.

Will more scrolls turn up? It's a tantalizing possibility. One source might be the caves themselves. A new, more systematic exploration of the caves is being undertaken, so this remains a possibility.

Another possibility is that more scrolls were found long ago, but are being kept secret by an antiquities dealer or even a canny businessman. Deposed chief editor Strugnell maintains that there are at least four such scrolls. According to Strugnell, Lankester Harding, the last British director of antiquities in Jordan, told him on his deathbed of three such scrolls. Strugnell himself claims to know of two scrolls, one of which overlaps with the three Harding told him about. According to Strugnell these scrolls are in Jordan; some have been purchased by bankers: "They're being kept very carefully, no one need worry about them. They're a better investment than anything on the Israeli or the New York stock exchanges."

Except for this overview, which was written especially for this book, the essays in this book all appeared or, as of this writing, will appear in *Biblical Archaeology Review* or its sister publication *Bible Review*. Each is on the forefront of scholarship. Together they represent the pathbreaking ideas of some of the world's most distinguished experts on the Dead Sea Scrolls.

I

THE FIND

CHAPTER 1

DISCOVERING THE SCROLLS

HARRY THOMAS FRANK

Numerous, sometimes conflicting, accounts exist of how the Dead Sea Scrolls were discovered and came into scholarly hands. All the details may never be known with certainty. But this account by Professor Harry Thomas Frank is as reliable, as well as dramatic, as any. Frank died in 1980 at the age of forty-seven.

This chapter deals only with the discovery of Cave 1, the first at Qumran found to contain manuscripts, from which seven nearly intact scrolls were recovered. Later, ten other Qumran caves were discovered containing inscriptional material. —ED.

—·—

The most sensational archaeological discovery of the century was made entirely by accident. On a morning in the winter of 1946–1947 three shepherds of the Ta'amireh tribe of Bedouin watched their nimblefooted goats skip across the cliffs just south of an old ruin on the northwest shore of the Dead Sea. The ruin, once thought to be the City of Salt mentioned in the Old Testament (Joshua 15:62), had from time

David Harris

7. *The entrance to Cave 1*
where seven intact scrolls were found
by Bedouin shepherds in 1947.

John Trever

8. *Jum'a Muhammed and*
Muhammed Ahmed el-Hamed,
the Bedouin shepherds who
discovered Cave 1 in 1947.

to time intrigued archaeologists. But from the middle of the nineteenth century, when they first worked in the area, they had said that there was not much at that desolate site. Possibly it was a minor Roman fort. Perhaps, some of the more fanciful said, it was even Gomorrah!

About a mile to the south of the ruin is one of the larger of the numerous freshwater springs that surround the Dead Sea. This place, known as Ein Feshkha, is where these three Bedouin watered their animals. Then it was up the cliffs and into the forbidding wilderness where shepherds, like David, let their flocks wander in search of food. And so on that fateful day the immemorial scene was repeated, with black beasts defying gravity on steep inclines, leaping, stopping to nibble here and there. A seemingly disinterested shepherd moved leisurely below, but his eye missed nothing. Some of the goats were climbing too high up. It was getting late and time to get them down. Jum'a Muhammed—that was the name of the fellow—now showed his own nimbleness in getting up the cliff face. As he climbed something caught his attention. There were two small openings in the rock. They were caves, or maybe two openings into the same cave. But they were so small. A man could not get through the lower one but might just squeeze through the upper one. He threw a rock into the opening. The rock had broken pottery, and what else would be in these remote caves but treasure? Maybe his days of following the sheep were over. He peered into the black depths of the cave but could make out nothing. He yelled down to his two cousins. Khalil Musa was older. Muhammed Ahmed el-Hamed was younger, a teenager. They came up and heard the exciting tale. But it was now getting very late and the goats had to be gathered. Tomorrow would take them to Ein Feshkha. In the afternoon they would return for another look at this intriguing cave.

But they did not visit the cave the next afternoon, returning somewhat later than planned from Ein Feshkha. At dawn of the next morning Muhammed Ahmed el-Hamed, who was nicknamed "The Wolf" (edh-Dhib), woke first. Leaving his two cousins sleeping on the ground, he scaled the 350 or so feet up to the cave Jum'a had found two days before. With effort the slender young man was able to lower himself feet first into the cave. The floor was covered with debris including broken pottery. But along the wall stood a number of narrow jars, some with their bowl-shaped covers still in place. Edh-Dhib scrambled over the floor of the cave and plunged his hand into one of the jars. Nothing. Frantically he tore the cover from another, eagerly exploring the smooth inside of the empty container. Another and yet another with the same

9. Jars in which scrolls were discovered.

result. The ninth was full of dirt. The increasingly desperate young Bedouin at last closed his hand around something wrapped in cloth. He extracted two such bundles and then a third, which had a leather covering but no cloth wrapping. The cloth and the leather were greenish with age. These were all edh-Dhib took from the cave that morning.

He wiggled himself out of the opening and half-ran, half-fell down the hillside to show his sleepy cousins what he had found. Treasure indeed! Scholars who later interviewed edh-Dhib think that this boy had in his hands on that winter morning nothing less than the great Isaiah Scroll, the Habakkuk Commentary, and the Manual of Discipline!

Khalil and Jum'a could not have been less interested in the scrolls edh-Dhib showed them. Where was the treasure? Had he hidden it for himself? Relentless questions. A little roughing-up. But in the end edh-Dhib was able to convince the other two that there was nothing but these worthless rolls. Had he looked carefully? Maybe there were other jars. Maybe one of the broken ones had spilled its valuable contents on the floor of the cave and it was in the debris.

Once more the three made their way up the hill to the cave. Edh-Dhib passed a number of jars out of the opening, but these were left in front of the cave when they proved to be empty, just as he had said. Downcast, the shepherds zigzagged their way down to the makeshift camp. Jum'a crammed the rolls into a bag. When they later returned to the Ta'amireh center near Bethlehem he took them with him. The bag with its "treasure"—so much more vast than the disappointed men ever dreamed!—was hung on a tent pole. How long it was there we do not know for certain. Occasionally its contents were removed and passed around among more curious members of the tribe. The Isaiah Scroll was damaged, but only its cover. The precious text was unhurt. When the Manual of Discipline reached St. Mark's Monastery in Jerusalem some months later it was in two pieces. But no one is sure if this was the fault of the Ta'amireh. The break is such that it could have occurred in ancient times.

A few weeks after the initial discovery of this cave—an orifice that came to be known to scholars as Qumran Cave 1, the cave of the great scrolls—Jum'a returned with other Bedouin and removed several other scrolls that they found there. As nearly as it is possible to reconstruct the story now, they removed seven major manuscripts altogether, the four that ended up at St. Mark's and the three that came into the possession of the Hebrew University.

Such was the discovery of the Dead Sea Scrolls, manuscripts a thousand years older than the then oldest known Hebrew texts of the Bible, manuscripts many of which were written a hundred years before the birth of Jesus and at least one of which may have been written almost three hundred years before the journey of Mary and Joseph to Bethlehem.

How these manuscripts got from a Bedouin tent pole into the scholar's study is as fascinating as their chance discovery. The setting for this part of the story was the last days of the British Mandate in Palestine. His Majesty's Foreign Office had somewhat irresponsibly decided that since the problem of Palestine could not be solved by reason they would withdraw, leaving the two sides to decide the issue by blood. Jewish and Arab families who had lived side by side for generations were being wrenched apart by fear and distrust. Barbed wire appeared in the most unlikely places. Immigrants, legal and illegal, added impetus to the worsening situation. The British were literally besieged by both sides, but particularly by the Jewish underground army. Murders were growing in number. The King David Hotel in Jerusalem was blown up with severe loss of life. In such times the Bedouin youths wondered if they could find a buyer for their greenish rolls.

In early April 1947 Jum'a and Khalil took them to Bethlehem, principal market town of the Ta'amireh. They took three scrolls and two jars to the carpenter shop of Ibrahim 'Ijha who dabbled in antiquities. Faidi Salahi, another dealer in antiquities, was there. He was later to play a large role in the story of the scrolls, but on this occasion he cautioned 'Ijha to be careful. These things might be stolen. There might be serious trouble. The two shepherds moved on carrying their jars and their scrolls.

In the marketplace Jum'a, with the scrolls, ran into George Ishaya Shamoun, who was often in Bethlehem on Saturdays selling cloaks to Bedouin. Jum'a imparted the tale of these worthless scrolls to his friend. Someone suggested that they go to the cobbler's shop of Khalil Iskander Shahin—better known as Kando. Kando was a Syrian Orthodox Christian. He was also serious about the scrolls. For one-third of whatever the sale price might be, Kando and George would handle the disposal of the scrolls. Agreed. Jum'a and Khalil were given five pounds and the scrolls were left in the little shop in Bethlehem.

During Holy Week, George, also Syrian Orthodox, mentioned the manuscripts to Athanasius Yeshue Samuel, Syrian Orthodox Metropolitan, or Archbishop, of Jerusalem. He told the priest they were written in Syriac, wrapped "like mummies," and were from the wilderness near the Dead Sea. Samuel knew that they would have to be very old, if genuine, because that region had not been inhabited since early Christian times. He expressed an interest in the scrolls and urged Kando to bring them to St. Mark's.

Within the week Kando and George were at the monastery with one manuscript, The Manual of Discipline. It was, the Metropolitan Samuel saw at once, not written in Syriac but in Hebrew. Then to the astonishment of his visitors he broke off a piece of the margin and burned it. By this somewhat crude but effective means he determined it was animal skin. Yes, Samuel would buy this scroll and any others the Bedouin might have. Kando, with the manuscript securely in hand, departed but promised to get in touch with his friends from the desert. For several days anxious calls went out from St. Mark's to Kando's shop near Manger Square in Bethlehem. The conversations were fruitless. Weeks went by. Samuel's frustration turned to resignation.

On the first Saturday in July 1947 Kando called. Two Bedouin had brought some scrolls to Bethlehem. Would they risk bringing them to Jerusalem? asked Samuel. Yes. The tide of violence between Jew, Arab, and Briton was swelling. Jewish terrorism, mostly directed against the British, was beginning to be heavily felt in certain Arab areas. The worst was yet to come, but it was already a difficult and dangerous time in and around Jerusalem. In this atmosphere Samuel became anxious when the Bedouin and their scrolls had not appeared by noon. Yet he had not mentioned his appointment to anyone since he was not entirely sure that the whole affair was not some kind of hoax. Hungry, agitated, Samuel sat down to eat. In the idle lunchtime conversation the Metropolitan heard one of the fathers mention that he had turned away some Bedouin from the door earlier in the morning. When questioned he affirmed that they were carrying scrolls. The Syrian monk had even ascertained that they were written in Hebrew. Probably old Torahs from somewhere, but filthy and covered with pitch or something else that smelled equally bad. These he steadfastly refused to allow within the monastery walls, still less into His Grace's presence as the bearers demanded.

Samuel returned to his office to call Kando. As he reached for the telephone, it rang. It was none other than the Bethlehem parishioner himself, deeply offended at the treatment given his friends. Explanations were offered, apologies made. Where were the scrolls now? Thanks entirely to George, said Kando, they were safely back in Bethlehem.

It seems that when the Bedouin along with George, who was the man closest to the shepherds in all this, had been turned away from the monastery, they went to the Jaffa Gate to catch the bus back to Bethlehem. There in discussion with a Jewish merchant an offer was made to buy them. George, however, had correctly guessed what the trouble had been at the door of St. Mark's. He was, furthermore, committed to the Metropolitan. He argued with his friends and finally prevailed. The three boarded the bus for Bethlehem with the manuscripts. Kando reached for his telephone when he heard what had happened. This reported incident at the Jaffa Gate, it should be pointed out, is not well authenticated and may be a part of the considerable legend that has grown up around the Dead Sea Scrolls.

It was two weeks before Kando could make his way to Jerusalem. He was graciously received by the Syrian fathers. Samuel heard the story of the discovery of the cave and its contents. Of greater interest five scrolls, including the one that had been brought previously, were produced from a bag. Two documents were in a delicate state. Two others looked similar and later proved to be the two halves of The Manual of Discipline. The fifth, the largest, was superbly preserved. It could be easily unrolled, revealing graceful Hebrew characters. A deal was quickly made. The Metropolitan gave Kando £24 ($97), of which two-thirds went to Jum'a and Khalil.

Three months after Samuel had first heard of the existence of the scrolls, they were in his possession. Now doubts began to creep in. Were they genuine? Was there such a cave as had been described to him? With George's help Father Yusef, one of the monks from St. Mark's, visited the site and reported to his superior that there was such a cave and indeed it contained scraps of other scrolls as well as a large jar suitable for storing much water.

With his faith in the authenticity of the scrolls revived, the Metropolitan set about to determine their contents and to sustain or destroy his view that they were from early Christian times. One would think that in a city such as Jerusalem, with its multiplicity of religious communities and prestigious scholarly institutions, this would have been a relatively simple matter. But few things are simple in Jerusalem, still less in a time of violence and when the question at hand is so patently improbable as authenticating scrolls two thousand years old. It was fully six months before Samuel's dreams were confirmed.

His first contact was the Palestine Department of Antiquities in the person of Stephen Hanna Stephen, a member of the Syrian Orthodox Church and thus well known to Samuel. There had been reports in Byzantine and earlier times of scrolls having been found near Jericho (Qumran is seven and a half miles south). From the second, third, and fourth Christian centuries came reports of Greek and Hebrew books found in jars in the area. Origen, an early church father, is said to have used some of these in compiling his famous *Hexapla*. In the late eighth century Patriarch Timothy I reported a similar find, noting that the manuscripts were found in caves. These things, common knowledge among scholars, were apparently not known to Stephen. But he did know of numerous incidents of hoaxes involving antiquities. He responded to the Metropolitan by suggesting the embarrassment that might come should his manuscripts turn out to be fake. Would Stephen, asked Samuel, call the documents to the attention of those in the Department of Antiquities who might be able to render proper judgment? Stephen had rather not lest he, too, be held up to ridicule before his colleagues.

The Syrian priest, undaunted by this rebuke, now found his way to the famous École Biblique, the Dominican monastery of St. Stephen and home of the French Biblical and Archaeological School. There he was received by Father Marmardji, a fellow Syrian and friend of long standing, who listened to the story of the finding of the scrolls with some interest. Some days later Father Marmardji came to St. Mark's accompanied by a young Dutch Dominican, Father J. Van der Ploeg. Together they examined the materials. Neither thought the writings were as old as claimed. The Dutchman did, however, immediately recognize the largest scroll as the Book of Isaiah. He was the first to do so. When he returned to the École, Van der Ploeg spoke with some enthusiasm of the documents he had just seen. L.-H. Vincent, the distinguished Dominican scholar and a fixture at the French monastery for forty years, noting that this was the Dutch monk's first visit to Jerusalem, suggested he should not be taken in so easily. Perhaps, thought the learned Vincent, if Samuel could produce pottery from the alleged context where the writings had been found it might help to sustain his claims. When no pottery was forthcoming Van der Ploeg did not pursue the matter further.

The Metropolitan Samuel continued to make attempts to find scholarly help with the scrolls and even attempted to learn Hebrew. At one point a chance business contact resulted in the inspection of the scrolls by two men from the library of Hebrew University. According to Samuel, they said they wished to photograph a few parts for further study. The monastery was placed at their disposal for such purposes, but they never returned, perhaps because of the increasing danger to a Jew in the Old City. A little later an antiquities dealer suggested sending the manuscripts to Europe or America where they could be evaluated. But with postal services breaking down under the weight of civil conflict Samuel thought it not a good idea to place his materials in the mails.

In late January 1948 the St. Mark's manuscripts came temporarily into the hands of E. L. Sukenik, the distinguished archaeologist of the Hebrew University. Unknown to all but a very few, Sukenik had had other scrolls from the Bedouin's discovery in his hands since the previous November. His story illustrates the chaotic conditions and personal danger of those times.

On Sunday, November 23, 1947, Sukenik received a message from an Armenian friend of his, Faidi Salahi, a dealer in antiquities. He had something of interest to show the scholar. The next morning, according to the professor's dramatic account, the two met across one of the barbed wire barricades the British were erecting in an effort to keep violent factions apart. The Armenian held up a scrap of leather. On it were Hebrew characters, which Sukenik immediately recognized as being similar to those he had seen on early Jewish funeral ossuaries. For the briefest moment he thought it must be a forgery of some sort. He had never heard of this kind of script on leather, parchment, or papyrus other than the Nash. But the man holding it was an old and trusted friend, and besides, the fragment had all the appearances of authenticity. There and then he made up his mind to buy the document from which it came. Could other fragments be seen? Yes, said the Armenian, they were in Bethlehem. Could they be brought to Jerusalem? Yes.

On Thursday Sukenik, now armed with a pass that allowed him through the barricades, went to his friend's shop and viewed additional pieces of the manuscript. He was convinced. He must go to Bethlehem and deal directly with the Arab dealer who had the document in his possession. For Sukenik to visit an Arab area involved great personal risk. Moreover, the very next day the United Nations was scheduled to vote on the partition of Palestine. Whichever way the vote went, wholesale hostilities were almost sure to follow. His wife and his son, Yigael (Yadin), then commander of the Jewish armed forces, knew the danger and argued against it. Persuasion put off the fulfillment of an archaeologist's dream. Then the UN delayed its vote. Jerusalem held its breath. It was an opening for Sukenik. The day was November 29, 1948.

There is a good deal of confusion about the events of that day with reference to the Dead Sea Scrolls. According to one story Sukenik risked his life by going to Arab Bethlehem. There, according to this version, he was shown three scrolls and was even allowed to bring them back to Jerusalem. According to another account, an Arab friend of the professor's brought them to him in Jerusalem. No matter. The net result is the same. Sukenik came into possession of three scrolls, which turned out to be the War Scroll, the Thanksgiving Scroll, and another copy of Isaiah in somewhat poorer condition than the magnificent Isaiah manuscript then at St. Mark's.

The day after these ancient Hebrew scrolls came to Hebrew University the United Nations voted to partition Palestine. Much moved by both events Sukenik felt there was something symbolic in the coincidence. Full of joy at the acquisition of the documents, the professor told almost anyone who would listen of his good fortune. About a week later he told one of the university librarians. In astonished silence Sukenik listened to a tale this man had to relate. Some months before, he and another of the library staff had gone to St. Mark's Monastery in the Old City to have a look at some manuscripts. The Syrian Metropolitan wanted to know their content and age and whether Hebrew University might wish to acquire them. They were written in Samaritan, the two librarians decided, and were not very old. A little later he had called St. Mark's with the offer of a Samaritan specialist, but Samuel was away. So the matter was dropped.

Stunned, Sukenik could not believe what he was being told. Those so-called Samaritan manuscripts were part of the collection he now had, he was sure of it. His impulse was to go by St. Mark's on his way home, but the Old City was now securely in Arab hands and no one entered without a pass. This he was not likely to get, since his son was who he was. Even if by some miracle he got a pass he had no money to offer for the scrolls.

Sukenik went home and began work on trying to raise funds. Slowly from various sources a little money began to accumulate. Sukenik thought that about £1,500 (then about $6,075) might be enough. Efforts to reach the Syrian priest and open negotiations came to nothing. Then, near the end of January, a letter came from the Old City, from a man on whose property Sukenik had excavated an early Jewish tomb in 1945. His name was Anton Kiraz. He offered to show some scrolls that were for sale. Kiraz was a parishioner at St. Mark's. He was, in addition, extremely close to Samuel. Because Sukenik excavated on some of Kiraz's property and was personally known to him, Kiraz was admirably situated to act as contact between the priest and the professor.

Kiraz arranged for Sukenik to see the scrolls at the YMCA, which was at that time in neutral territory. As soon as he saw them Sukenik made an offer of £100 for the materials, as Kiraz recalled. Sukenik, in his written recollection of the event, did not mention an offer. However that may have been, Kiraz allowed one scroll to be removed to Hebrew University for further study. The other documents remained in a drawer

John Trever

10. *The Metropolitan Samuel and*
Butrus Sowmy displaying a scroll from Cave 1.
John Trever holds the Isaiah Scroll at right.

at the YMCA. The Isaiah Scroll stayed for about a week at the university during which time a portion (chapters 42 and 43) was hastily and somewhat incorrectly copied. When it was returned Sukenik spoke of the university's interest in purchasing all of the scrolls.

According to Kiraz, the figure of £500 ($2,025) was mentioned. But Kiraz said he would have to talk with the Metropolitan Samuel. Sukenik is said to have increased the offer to £1,000—750 for Kiraz, 250 for Samuel—but Kiraz insisted on talking with the Metropolitan. He would contact Sukenik once he had had a chance to discuss the offer. There the matter was left.

At this juncture, in early February 1948 and fully a year since edh-Dhib had first slithered into the cave, Samuel's lifelong friend and fellow monk, Butros Sowmy, returned to St. Mark's after an absence. He was a learned man and one of good judgment. With increasing concern he heard of Sukenik's offer and of Samuel's apparent readiness to accept it. If Sukenik were so anxious to secure these documents, perhaps, reasoned Sowmy, it would be well to get another opinion before selling. Kiraz wrote to the distraught professor saying they were not going to sell just now, but would wait until the local situation settled a bit and they could perhaps get some international judgments and overseas offers.

Meantime, Sowmy recalled his cordial dealings with the American School of Oriental Research just north of the Old City, quite near the École Biblique. He telephoned and the call was turned over to John Trever, a fellow of the school, who had been left in temporary charge during the absence of Millar Burrows, the director. Sowmy asked if Trever would help date some old manuscripts that had been lying about St. Mark's library for some years. As a precaution the Americans had not gone into the Old City for some time. It was now dangerous in the extreme. Could the materials be brought to the school? In response Sowmy agreed to present himself and the scrolls the next day at 2:30 P.M.

With mounting excitement Trever examined the manuscripts. The writing on the Isaiah Scroll, although clearly Hebrew, was nonetheless strange to his eyes. Yet he had seen a similar script somewhere. A superb and inveterate photographer, Trever was never one to be far away from cameras and their products. On his desk was a series of slides dealing with the background of the English Bible. He extracted a picture of the ninth-century A.D. British Museum Codex. The writing on the scrolls brought by Sowmy was older. Next Trever removed a slide of the Nash Papyrus, a second-century fragment and the then oldest known Biblical Hebrew. The script was similar, but not exactly the same. It was hard to be sure; the slide was much too small for detailed comparison in the hand viewer. His cameras unfortunately at the moment at the Museum of the Department of Antiquities, Trever copied by hand that portion of the manuscript open before him. He then proposed to Sowmy that a complete photographic record be made of all the scrolls. The monk was agreeable but would have to discuss it with his superior.

Sowmy left. Trever soon determined that what he had copied was a portion of chapter 65 of Isaiah. Was the rest of Isaiah on that scroll? Could it be as old as the Nash Papyrus? Early the next morning, after an almost sleepless night, Trever determined to go to St. Mark's in spite of the danger. With the aid of Miss Faris, the Arab secretary of the American School, he secured the necessary permissions and risking life and limb was taken by her through the narrow, hazardous streets to the Syrian monastery. There he met the Metropolitan, who was at length convinced the manuscripts should again be brought to the school where there was photographic equipment and better conditions for obtaining good results than in St. Mark's dim library.

For the rest of the day Trever and William Brownlee culled from the library of the American School all the material they could find about ancient manuscripts. Unfortunately fighting and sabotage interrupted Jerusalem's electric service in the afternoon. After working by kerosene lamps late into the night the two men were convinced that the form of the script on the Isaiah Scroll was as old as or older than the Nash Papyrus.

The next day, a Saturday, dawned bright—on the outside, that is. The lights were still out inside the school. By 9:30 the Metropolitan and Father Sowmy were there with the materials to be photographed. Just as Trever was about to use natural light from a window, the electric lights came on. With Brownlee's help two scrolls, Isaiah and the Habakkuk Commentary, were unrolled and photographed. By late afternoon the task was not complete. Three scrolls remained. But by this time the two young Americans had won the confidence of the Syrians, who gladly left the unrecorded scrolls and a fragment behind as they returned to St. Mark's. Among the many happenstances surrounding the scrolls none was more felicitous than the presence of so fine a photographer as Trever. His record of the contents of the four Dead Sea Scrolls from the Syrian monastery (a fifth was too delicate to be opened then) now constitutes the finest material available for study of these documents. This is especially so since the originals have faded from exposure despite the best of care under controlled conditions.

Subsequent excavations at the caves indicated the scrolls had been damaged when they were removed from their jars and unwrapped. Fragments from the manuscripts were on the floor of the cave. The documents had also been stripped of their linen protection and carried about in sacks, paper bags, and otherwise. But at last the precious scrolls were in loving hands. Before return to St. Mark's they were carefully wrapped. The seriously deteriorated leather scroll was placed in a specially constructed box. While this was going on, Trever sent photographic copies to the doyen of Palestinian archaeologists and the leading expert on ancient forms of writing, W. F. Albright at Johns Hopkins University in Baltimore.

In the following days Trever, sometimes accompanied by Burrows, now returned, made numerous trips to St. Mark's, each journey fraught with its own several perils. Often guards were provided by the monastery to insure safety. At least once the scrolls were returned to the American School. Trever was not pleased with all his initial pictures. Ever a perfectionist in matters photographic he wished to retake the Isaiah Scroll. This involved a difficult search of the shops of the city for proper film. Only outdated portrait film was located. But Trever rejoiced to find even this.

On March 15 a letter from the United States reached the school:

> My heartiest congratulations on the greatest manuscript discovery of modern times! There is no doubt in my mind that the script is more archaic than that of the Nash Papyrus . . . I should prefer a date around 100 B.C.! . . . What an absolutely incredible find! And there can happily not be the slightest doubt in the world about the genuineness of the manuscript.

Albright's practiced eyes had confirmed the Metropolitan's hopes and the scholarly judgment of Trever and Brownlee.

Two weeks later steadily increasing violence forced the abandonment of the American School. Trever was the last to go. He left on April 5. Samuel, under various urgings, sought a safe place for his scrolls. St. Mark's was a particularly vulnerable location. Sowmy suggested a bank vault in Beirut as a safer place. (Shortly thereafter Sowmy was killed by bomb fragments as he stood in the courtyard at St. Mark's.) Beirut became the way station for the manuscripts on their journey to America, where the Metropolitan later took them.

In the end Burrows, Trever, and Brownlee were able to continue their work on the texts and to publish them. Now famous, the Dead Sea Scrolls were displayed at various locations in the United States and seen by thousands. The publicity enhanced their value but the Metropolitan's attempts to sell were clouded by claims to the scrolls by Jordan and the new nation of Israel, as well as by the go-between Anton Kiraz. Confusion over ownership was such that Yale and Duke universities found reasons not to buy the scrolls. Yale bought a Boswell diary for a reported $450,000. Duke built another building. The Library of Congress displayed the scrolls but showed little interest in purchasing them. At last they came to rest in a specially prepared safe in the home of a Syrian Orthodox Christian in Worcester, Massachusetts.

Meanwhile, all scholars did not agree with the judgment of Professor Albright and that of a vast and growing host. Tovia Wechsler, a journalist and something of a Hebraist, who had been one of the first to see the scrolls and who at the time had laughed them away, attacked Trever for his views and stoutly maintained that the story of the find was a hoax. Not only the manuscripts were under attack. Metropolitan Samuel was declared an outlaw in Jordan and found his integrity and reputation a matter of widespread debate. He decided to sell the scrolls by whatever means at hand. One way was a simple newspaper ad. On June 1, 1954, the following appeared in *The Wall Street Journal*.

MISCELLANEOUS FOR SALE

THE FOUR DEAD SEA SCROLLS

Biblical manuscripts dating back to at least 200 B.C. are for sale. This would be an ideal gift to an educational or religious institution by an individual or group. Box F 206 *Wall Street Journal*.

On July 1, after some delicate negotiations, the scrolls, accompanied by the Metropolitan and two others, came to the Waldorf-Astoria Hotel in New York. There they met Mr. Sidney Esteridge, the would-be purchaser, with his lawyers and several experts. The price, $250,000, had been agreed upon in advance. It was a bargain by any realistic standard. After considerable discussion of various details in the bill of sale, the matter was consummated. Three months later the "Archbishop Samuel Trust" to aid Syrian Orthodox churches was considerably enriched. But the legal papers for the trust were not properly drawn. The sum was reported as personal income and the United States Internal Revenue Service got most of the purchase price.

For all the Metropolitan knew the scrolls were in the private collection of a rich American. In February 1955 the Israeli prime minister announced that these four manuscripts were in Israel. How the scrolls came into the possession of the state of Israel remained somewhat of a mystery until Professor Yigael Yadin told the story. He tells how, on a visit to America, his attention was called to the newspaper ad. He knew the value of the materials and remembered the agonizing attempt of his father, Professor Sukenik, to obtain the scrolls in January of 1948. Yadin determined to try to buy the documents for the state of Israel. A direct approach was unwise. Thus a subterfuge was invented. Mr. Esteridge was in fact acting on behalf of Yadin and the Israeli government.

The four scrolls formerly in Metropolitan Samuel's possession thus were returned to Jerusalem to be with other major scrolls from Cave 1 at Qumran. They came to Hebrew University, which Professor Sukenik had honored with his knowledge for so long. But it was too late for Sukenik. He had died a year earlier, writing in his diary that "the Jewish people (had) lost a precious heritage."[1] Thanks to the diligence of his son, the scrolls had come full circle, through the hands of shepherds, clerics, and scholars, Muslims, Christians, and Jews, to their present home in the Shrine of the Book in Jerusalem.

CHAPTER 2

THE HISTORICAL CONTEXT
OF THE SCROLLS

FRANK MOORE CROSS

In this chapter, the eminent Harvard scholar Frank Cross discusses the dating of the scrolls and how the dates were arrived at, introducing us to palaeography, the science—or art—of analyzing ancient writing, and to the excavations at the site adjacent to the caves where the scrolls were found. He also gives his reasons for identifying the inhabitants of Qumran as members of a religious sect called Essenes. Cross is convinced that his identification is correct—and his view still represents the mainstream of scholarship. On the other hand, a number of scholars have more recently questioned this identification. In the next two chapters two younger scholars—Lawrence Schiffman of New York University and James VanderKam of Notre Dame University—vigorously debate this question. In this chapter, Professor Cross describes Essene beliefs, as reflected in the Dead Sea Scrolls. Whether or not he is correct that the Qumran sectarians were Essenes, his views on the contents of the scrolls are beautifully expressed and widely agreed upon. His description of the theological views of the Qumran sectarians is indeed profound. Finally, Cross attempts to place the history of the Essenes (in his view, the Qumran community) in a specific historical context, even identifying the Wicked Priest who is vilified so frequently in the Dead Sea Scrolls.   —ED.

—·—

Aftter a quarter century of discovery and publication, the study of the manuscripts from the desert of Judah has entered a new, more mature phase. True, the heat and noise of the early controversies have not wholly dissipated. One occasionally hears the agonized cry of a scholar pinned beneath a collapsed theory. And in the popular press, no doubt, the so-called battle of the scrolls will continue to be fought with mercenaries for some time to come. However, the initial period of confusion is past. From the burgeoning field of scroll research and the new disciplines it has created, certain coherent patterns of fact and meaning have emerged.

The scrolls and the people who wrote them can be placed within a broad historical framework with relative certainty by virtue of external controls provided by the archaeologist and the palaeographer. Once the scrolls are placed in a particular time period, the historian must begin his difficult task—difficult because internal data from the scrolls pose special historiographic problems resulting from their esoteric language. The usual methods of historical criticism are difficult to apply without excessive subjectivity.

The archaeological context of the community of the Dead Sea—its caves, its community center at Qumran, and its agricultural adjunct at Ein Feshkha—has been established by six major seasons of excavations. The ancient center of Qumran has yielded a clear archaeological stratification, and in turn the strata are closely dated by their yield of artifacts, notably coins. For the era in which we are especially interested, the site exhibits three phases. The first of these, so-called Period Ia, consists of the remains of the earliest communal structures. In Period Ib the settlement was almost completely rebuilt and enlarged. The coins suggest that the buildings of the second phase were constructed no later than the time of Alexander Jannaeus (103–76 B.C.). The dating of the first phase is more difficult. So thoroughly were the structures of the first phase rebuilt that only the barest foundations were left. The problem is further complicated by the relatively short life and small size of the first phase; few coins accumulate in foundations in the first years of occupation. Moreover, coins have a considerable period of currency. When Alexander Jannaeus introduced the new Jewish coinage, coins of the Seleucid kings continued to circulate. The earliest coins of Period Ia appear to be five Seleucid coppers of imprecise date from the reign of Antiochus VII Sidetes (138–129 B.C.). This and other coin evidence indicate that the first buildings were probably constructed at the site in the desert of Qumran sometime in the interval between 140 and 100 B.C.

In the second phase, Period Ib, the community center took its permanent form, though extensions or repairs of a minor sort were introduced before the destruction of its buildings in the earthquake of 31 B.C., reported by the first-century historian Josephus. After a short, but indeterminate period of abandonment, the site—in the third phase—was reoccupied, rebuilt, and repaired precisely on the plan of the old communal complex. It flourished until 68 A.D., when it was stormed and occupied by the forces of the Roman emperor Vespasian in the course of his raid on Jericho.

Theoretically, I suppose, the communities occupying the ruins in each of these phases need not have been related.[1] In fact, the community of the second and third, and no doubt the little known first phase, was one continuing community. It takes more than the historian's normally vivacious imagination to conceive of two communities, following one upon another and leading the peculiar life reflected at Qumran without having a relationship to one another. The very setting of the community requires a special explanation. Only powerful motivations would send a large group of persons into this wasteland. But more difficult to explain than the desolate environment chosen by the desert folk is the special character of the community center. The center was composed of communal facilities for study, writing, eating, domestic industries, and common stores. The members of the community did not live in the buildings (for the most part, at any rate) but in caves and shelters radiating out from the central buildings. Thus, the architectural functions of the rooms and structures require a special mode of religious and communalistic life. We can conclude only that the people of the scrolls founded the community in the second half of the second century B.C. and occupied it, with a brief interruption in the reign of Herod the Great, until the dreadful days of the Jewish Revolt (66–70 A.D.), which culminated in the Roman destruction of the Jewish state. Corroboration of this dating of the archaeological evidence is immediately furnished by the palaeographical analysis of some eight hundred manuscripts recovered from Qumran.

The main lines of the evolution of the late Aramaic and early Jewish book-handwriting had already been fixed on the basis of documents and inscriptions analyzed between the two world wars.[2] Now, thanks to the discoveries in the Judean desert, the science of early Jewish palaeography has grown rich in materials for the typology of scripts.[3] These discoveries include not only the manuscripts of Qumran in Palaeo-Hebrew, Jewish, and Greek bookhands, but also the important discoveries from the Wadi Murabba'at and the Nahal Hever, written in both formal and cursive Jewish hands, as well as in Greek, Latin, and Nabatean. While these discoveries have occupied the center of the stage, other discoveries from the Wadi ed-Daliyeh north of Jericho, from the excavations of Khirbet Qumran, from the tombs of Jerusalem, from Khirbet el-Kom, and from the excavations at Masada, to mention only the most important, have steadily expanded, extending our knowledge of the evolution and relative dating of early Jewish scripts.

Not only do we now possess ample materials for precise typological analysis of the scripts of the Qumran manuscripts, we have also accumulated a series of externally dated scripts by which the relative dates gained by typological study can be turned into absolute dates. Most striking no doubt are the documents bearing date formulae of the late fourth century B.C. (Daliyeh), of the third century (el-Kom), and of the first century and second century of the Christian era (Qumran, Murabba'at, and Hever), which overlap in part and extend the Qumran series backward and forward in time. To these may be added documents from excavations, notably from Qumran itself and Masada, dated by archaeological context to the first century B.C. and later.

The scripts from Qumran belong to three periods of palaeographical development. A very small group of biblical manuscripts belong to an archaic style whose limits are about 250–150 B.C. Next, a large number of Qumran manuscripts, biblical and nonbiblical, were written in a style reflecting the Hasmonean period, that is, between 150 and 30 B.C. However, scrolls of specifically sectarian content, many composed and copied at Qumran, begin only about the middle of the Hasmonean period, that is, about 100 B.C. Finally, there is a relatively large corpus of Herodian manuscripts dating between 30 B.C. and 70 A.D.

The termination of the series with late Herodian hands correlates precisely with the archaeological data. The library was abandoned at the time of the destruction of the community in 68 A.D. We must in turn establish the origins of the community no later than the date of the earliest sectarian compositions, that is, somewhat before 100 B.C. Nonsectarian scrolls, especially the biblical manuscripts, begin in quantity about 150 B.C. Scrolls of the archaic period are exceedingly rare and were probably master scrolls brought into the community at the time of its founding. Extant copies of such characteristic sectarian scrolls as the Rule of the Community and the Damascus Document go back to the beginning of the first century B.C. Sectarian commentaries on Habakkuk,

Nahum, and other biblical works date mostly from the second half of the first century B.C. and contain traditional lore of biblical interpretation developed in the community in its earlier history and precipitated into writing relatively late in the life of the sect.

—— · ——

Extant classical texts that treat the second century B.C. mention four Jewish movements in Judea: the Hasidim, a pious "congregation" that disappeared in the Maccabean/Hasmonean era (175–63 B.C.), and three orders that emerge no later than the early Hasmonean era* and presumably have their roots in the Maccabean period. These are the Essenes, the Pharisees, and the Sadducees. Of these three, only the Essene order can be described as separatist, in the radical sense that they regarded themselves as the only true Israel and separated themselves fully from contact with their fellow Jews. Josephus informs us that the Essenes rejected even the sacrificial service of the Temple as unclean and "offered their sacrifices by themselves." Pliny the Elder (or rather his sources) tells us of their "city" in the wilderness between Jericho and Ein Gedi near the shore of the Dead Sea—where the Qumran ruins are located.

This reference in Pliny is decisive in identifying the sectarians of Qumran with the Essenes, in the absence of strong counterarguments. We know of no other sect arising in the second century B.C. that can be associated with the wilderness community. Surface exploration has turned up no rival settlement in the crucial era. Further, the community at Qumran was organized precisely as a new Israel, a true sect that repudiated the priesthood and cults of Jerusalem. Neither the Pharisees nor the Sadducees can qualify. The Essenes qualify perfectly. There is no reason to belabor the point. A careful examination of the classical references side by side with the texts of Qumran establishes the identification, in my opinion, beyond cavil.

The strongest argument that has been raised against the identification of the Qumran sect with the Essenes is as follows: Since Palestine "swarmed" with obscure sects in the first century of the Christian era, one must exercise caution in assigning the Dead Sea sect to a known group. The argument had plausibility only when a few manuscripts of uncertain date were known.

The Qumran sect was not one of the small, ephemeral groups of the first century of the Common Era. Its substantial community at Qumran

*The rulers of Judea after the Maccabean revolt were the Hasmonean dynasty.

was established in the second century B.C. and flourished some two centuries or more. Moreover, it was not restricted to Qumran, but, like the Essenes of the classical sources, counted its camps and settlements throughout the villages of Judah.

Its own sectarian literature was enormous, exercising a considerable influence upon later sectarian, including Christian, literature. The task, therefore, is to identify a major sect in Judaism. To suppose that a major group in Judaism in this period went unnoticed in our sources is simply incredible.

The scholar who would "exercise caution" in identifying the sect of Qumran with the Essenes places himself in an astonishing position: He must suggest seriously that *two* major parties formed communalistic religious communities in the same district of the desert of the Dead Sea and lived together in effect for two centuries, holding similar bizarre views, performing similar or rather identical lustrations, ritual meals, and ceremonies. He must suppose that one, carefully described by classical authors, disappeared without leaving building remains or even potsherds behind; the other, systematically ignored by the classical sources, left extensive ruins, and indeed a great library. I prefer to be reckless and flatly identify the men of Qumran with their perennial houseguests, the Essenes. At all events, in what follows, I shall assume the identification and draw freely upon both classical and Qumran texts.

— · —

The Essenes of Qumran were a priestly party. Their leader was a priest. The archenemy of the sect was a priest, usually designated the Wicked Priest. In protocols of the Essene community, the priests took precedence, and in the age to come, a messiah priest ranked above the traditional Davidic or royal messiah. There is some reason to believe that the sect conducted a sacrificial system in its community at Qumran. At any rate, the community was preoccupied with priestly lore, ceremonial law, the orders of the priests, and the liturgical calendar; many of their sectarian compositions reflect their almost obsessive interest in priestly orthopraxy (i.e., correct orthodox practice and observance).

The community referred to its priesthood as "sons of Zadok," that is, members of the ancient line of high priests established in Scripture. At the same time, they heaped scorn and bitter condemnation upon the ungodly priests of Jerusalem, who, they argued, were illegitimate. This animosity toward the priests in power in Judah on the part of the priests at Qumran did not stem merely from doctrinal differences. Our texts rather reflect a historical struggle for power between high priestly families. The Essenes withdrew in defeat and formed their community in exile, which was organized as a counter-Israel led by a counterpriesthood, or, viewed with Essene eyes, as the true Israel of God led by the legitimate priesthood. The theocrat of Jerusalem, the so-called Wicked Priest, attacked the Essene priesthood, even in exile, and made an attempt on the life of the Righteous Teacher, the Essene priestly leader. For their part, the Essene priests confidently expected divine intervention to establish their cause. They predicted that the Wicked Priest and his cronies would meet violent death at the hand of God and their enemies; and they searched Scripture for prophecies of the end of days when they, the poor of the desert, would be reestablished in a new, transfigured Jerusalem.

Mention of the Essene hopes of a New Age of glory leads us naturally to some comments on the special theological views of the Essenes that informed their understanding of history and gave to their community its peculiar institutions. The Essenes belong in the center of that movement, which goes under the designation *apocalypticism*. The late visionaries of the Old Testament, notably the author of Daniel, as well as the later Baptist and Christian communities, discovered themselves to be living in the last days of the Old Age, or rather in the days when the Old Age was passing away and the Kingdom of God was dawning. According to apocalypticism, the upsurge of evil powers in history reflected the last defiant outbreak of cosmic Satanic powers. The gifts of the Holy Spirit, manifest in the community of the faithful, adumbrated the age of the Spirit to follow the final war in which the Spirit of Truth and his heavenly armies would put an end to the rule of the powers of darkness.

The constitution of the Essene community was a crystallized apocalyptic vision. Each institution and practice of the community was a preparation for or, by anticipation, a realization of, life in the New Age of God's rule. On the one hand, their communal life was a reenactment of the events of the end time, both the final days of the Old Age and the era of Armageddon. On the other hand, their community, being heir of the kingdom, participated already in the gifts and glories that were the first fruits of the age to come.

For the apocalyptist of Qumran, the key to these future mysteries was at hand. One had only to read biblical prophecies with the understanding given the inspired interpreter (that is, one who reads under the power of the Holy Spirit), because the secrets of events to come in the last days were foretold by God through the mouth of his holy prophets. So the

Essenes searched the Scriptures. They developed a body of traditional exegesis, no doubt inspired by patterns laid down by their founder, which is reflected in most of their works, above all in their biblical commentaries, *pesharim,* in which their common tradition was fixed in writing.

In apocalyptic exegesis, three principles should be kept in mind. Prophecy openly or cryptically refers to the last days. Second, the so-called last days are in fact the present, the days of the sect's life. And, finally, the history of ancient Israel's redemption, her offices and institutions, are prototypes of the events and figures of the new Israel.

On this basis, the Essene camp in the wilderness found its prototype in the Mosaic camp of Numbers (see Numbers 2–4; 9:15–10:28). The Essenes retired to Qumran to "prepare the way of the Lord" in the wilderness. As God established his ancient covenant in the desert, so the Essenes entered into the new covenant on their return to the desert. As Israel in the desert was mustered into army ranks in preparation for the Holy War of conquest, so the Essenes marshaled their community in battle array and wrote liturgies of the Holy Warfare of Armageddon, living for the day of the second conquest when they would march with their messianic leaders to Zion. Meanwhile, they kept the laws of purity laid down in Scripture for soldiers in Holy Warfare, an ascetic regimen that at the same time anticipated life with the holy angels before the throne of God, a situation requiring similar ritual purity.

The offices of the sect reveal this apocalyptic typology. The council of the community was numbered after the princes of Israel and Levi in the desert; at the same time, they prefigured the judges who would rule the tribes of Israel in the New Age. As God sent Moses, Aaron, and David, so they looked for three messiahs—prophet, priest, and prince. The founder of their community bore a biblical sobriquet, the "Righteous Teacher" (from Hosea 10:12 and Joel 2:23), apparently understood as the title of a priestly forerunner of the messianic age. And even the enemies of the sect, the False Oracle, the Wrathful Lion, and so on, all bore designations culled ingeniously from prophecy.

The great external events of history of their times were discovered in the Scriptures, predicted as signs of the last days: the Seleucid rule, the wars of the Hasmoneans, the rise of the Romans, and the conquest of Palestine by Pompey. And the internal events of sectarian life and history were rehearsed even more dramatically in the sayings of the prophets. Here we come upon one of the major difficulties in writing Essene history. Major political events and, from our point of view, minor or private events in the life of the sect are mixed in their expositions of Scripture in dizzying fashion, and as if this were not bad enough, the whole is veiled in the esoteric language of apocalypticism.

To sum up, the Essenes of Qumran were a community formed and guided by a party of Zadokite priests. In the latter half of the second century B.C., having lost hope of regaining their ancient authority in the theocracy of Jerusalem and under active persecution by a new house of reigning priests, they fled to the desert. There, finding new hope in apocalyptic dreams, they readied themselves for the imminent judgment when their enemies would be vanquished and they, God's elect, would be given final victory in accordance with the predictions of the prophets.

— · —

It is not difficult to identify the priestly conflict out of which the dissident Essene party emerged. In the days of Antiochus IV Epiphanes (175–163 B.C.), the orderly succession of Zadokite high priests failed. The high priestly office became a prize dispensed by the Seleucid overlord Antiochus, to be purchased by the highest bidder. The strife between rivals for the theocratic office soon developed into civil war, and in the resulting chaos Antiochus found opportunity to carry out his fearful massacres, terminating in the notorious desecration of the Temple and the Hellenization of Holy Jerusalem. The stage was set for the rise of the Maccabees, whose destiny it was to lead the Jews in a heroic war of independence, and who, having won popularity by freeing Judah from foreign suzerains, themselves usurped the high priestly office. In this way, the ancient Zadokite house gave way to the lusty, if illegitimate, Hasmonean dynasty. Essene origins are to be discovered precisely in the struggle between these priestly houses and their adherents.

Perhaps the historian should say no more. However, historical allusions in Essene biblical commentaries tempt one to reconstruct the origins of the Qumran sect more precisely. We should like to know the identity of the Wicked Priest of Jerusalem and to fix more exactly the occasion for the flight and persecution of the sectarians; and we should like, if possible, to relate the Essene sect to the other Jewish parties, especially to the Pharisees who came into being in the same historical milieu. Perhaps it is too much to ask the identity of the Essene Teacher or of other sectarian figures who, from the standpoint of general history, played insignificant roles.

Scholarly debate on these more precise details of Essene history continues. No consensus has fully emerged. My own views underwent a major change as the archaeological and palaeographical data piled up and narrowed options. Nevertheless, I think it is very likely that the Wicked Priest of Jerusalem can be identified with the High Priest Simon Maccabeus, the last and perhaps the greatest of the five Maccabean brothers. In February of 134 B.C., Simon together with Judas (probably his eldest son) and Mattathias (his youngest) toured the cities of Judah, evidently reviewing fortifications that he had built or that were in the process of construction. On their tour, Simon and his sons descended to Jericho. Jericho was administered under Simon by one Ptolemy, son of Abubos. Ptolemy had ambitions to rule Judea and he organized a plot of considerable proportions.

Ptolemy's opportunity came upon the occasion of Simon's visit to Jericho. Ptolemy held a banquet for his victims in a newly completed fortress guarding Jericho. When Simon and his sons were drunk, Ptolemy's men murdered Simon, and later his two sons. Ultimately Ptolemy's plot failed. John Hyrcanus, Simon's remaining son, who was then in Gezer, eluded assassins sent to slay him and escaped to Jerusalem in time to rally loyal Jews against the forces sent by Ptolemy to take the city. Ptolemy sent to Antiochus VII Sidetes for immediate aid. Although he arrived too late to succor Ptolemy, Antiochus was successful in reducing the country and in forcing Jerusalem to surrender.

These events comport well with certain historical allusions found in the so-called List of Testimonia from Cave 4 at Qumran. One of the Testimonia (the fourth) refers to a "Cursed One," predicted in Joshua 6:26. The passage in Joshua follows the account of the ancient destruction of Jericho and reads this way: "May the Lord's curse light on the man who comes forward to rebuild this city of Jericho: The laying of its foundations shall cost him his eldest son, the setting up of its gates shall cost him his youngest."

The curse was once fulfilled when in the ninth century B.C. Jericho was rebuilt by a certain Hiel with the loss of his sons (see I Kings 16:34). The Essenes chose this particular text, once fulfilled, and reapplied it to their own time. The Testimonia, partly reconstructed, reads in part as follows:

> And behold, a cursed man, a man of Belial, shall come to power to be a trapper's snare and ruin to all his neighbors, and he shall come to power and (his sons) . . . (with him), the two of them becoming violent instruments, and they shall rebuild again the (city . . . and shall set) up a wall and towers for it, to make a stronghold of wickedness (in the land and a great

evil) in Israel and horrors in Ephraim and in Judah . . . (and they shall com)mit sacrilege in the land and great contumely among the children of (Jacob and blo)od (shall be poured out) like water on the battlement of the daughter of Zion and in the district of Jerusalem.

If we follow the pattern of close apocalyptic exegesis that normally obtains in sectarian exposition of Scripture, we must look for an event connected with the fortification of Jericho by a major enemy of the sect when the dreadful curse of Joshua repeated itself. And properly, we must look for a high priest of Jerusalem who associated his sons with him in his rule.

The events concerning the murder of Simon and his two sons in Jericho when they came to inspect the new fortifications at Jericho, as well as the bloody aftermath of their triple assassination, seem to explain adequately the resurrection of the old curse on Jericho by the Essenes. Most of the elements of the prophecy fit strikingly; the association of the cursed man with two sons in the fortification overlooking Jericho, their death at the hands of Ptolemy's henchmen as evidence of the effectiveness of the curse, and the subsequent devastation and bloodshed in Judah and Jerusalem. I find it very difficult not to conclude that Simon is established as the Cursed Man of the Testimonia.

Is this Cursed Man identical with the Wicked Priest? The other Testimonia relate to the messianic prophet, priest, and king, as well as to the priestly forerunner of the New Age who founded the sect. The juxtaposition of the Cursed Man with the other central figures of the sect strongly suggests that the Cursed Man is in fact the Wicked Priest.

Jonathan (162–142 B.C.), the second of the Maccabean brothers, not Simon, was the first to usurp the high priestly office, and some have suggested that it is he who should be identified with the Wicked Priest. Several historical factors, however, make this choice unlikely. Jonathan's position was tenuous throughout his term in the office. Jewish independence was not to be fully won until the reign of Simon. To the end of his days Jonathan struggled to maintain himself against foreign foes. It seems unlikely that he was sufficiently secure to turn upon his fellow Jews and persecute the Zadokites (Essenes); moreover, in view of the de facto nature of his theocratic rule and the uncertainty of the times, the Zadokite priests would not have abandoned hope and fled Jerusalem upon the occasion of Jonathan's donning the high priestly robes. On the contrary, we should expect that move only to *initiate* hostilities between the orthodox and the Maccabean nationalists.

Simon, Jonathan's successor, brought to fulfillment his brothers' national dreams. In the second year of his rule he succeeded in driving out the Syrian garrison from the citadel in Jerusalem. Judea only then became fully free of the Seleucid yoke. Simon ruled in peace and was at liberty to consolidate his realm. In 140 B.C., the third year of his reign, a great assembly was held "of the priests and people and heads of the nation and the elders of the country." The work of the assembly and the significance of its decree for the history of the high priesthood cannot be overestimated. The decree of the assembly was engraved in bronze and set up on stelae on Mount Zion. Simon was made high priest de jure and the high priesthood was given to Simon's house forever, "until a faithful prophet should arise" (I Maccabees 14:30–39). The claim is here made to a legal transference of the high priesthood from the Zadokite dynasty (appointed by David!) to the Hasmonean dynasty. The illegitimacy of Simon's house is admitted tacitly in the phrase "until a faithful prophet arise," that is, until a final arbiter between the rival houses appears in the age to come. Further, the decree warned against any opposition to Simon by layman or priest, prohibited private assembly, and threatened punishment to anyone who acted contrary to the stipulations of the decree.

In this decree we can clearly discern the new high priest's determination to stamp out opposition, to persecute those who refused to recognize the full legitimacy of his office. This program, falling in the early years of Simon, seems to give the appropriate occasion for the crystallization of the Essene sect, its persecution and the persecution of the Righteous Teacher, and the exile in the wilderness of Judah. Simon had the leisure, power, popularity, and inclination to root out Jewish opposition to the ascendancy of his party and his house. Certain texts, especially the Testimonia, give evidence in support of my identification of the Wicked Priest with Simon. Finally, it should not be overlooked that the archaeological evidence for the dating of the foundation of the community fits more easily with a date in Simon's reign than with a date in Jonathan's reign.

I have not dealt, of course, with a large number of texts relating to the Wicked Priest and his relations with the Righteous Teacher and the exiled community. Most fit equally well with Jonathan or Simon, or indeed with a number of other priests. In this era one cannot complain of a shortage of wicked priests. One final text, however, deserves mention. In a passage of the Commentary on Habakkuk, the expositor comments, "This means the priest whose dishonor was greater than his honor. For he . . . walked in the ways of drunkedness in order to quench his thirst. But the cup of God's wrath will swallow him up . . . !" The high priest caroused once too often. In Jericho, at the hands of Ptolemy, the cup of pleasure turned into the cup of wrath and swallowed Simon. So I should interpret the text.

I have been able to fix the general framework of the Essene community's life in the desert. Perhaps I have succeeded also in identifying the villain of the esoteric commentaries. No doubt, I have also illustrated the complexities and frustrations that face the student of the Essene library from Qumran.

II

WHERE THEY
CAME FROM

CHAPTER 3

THE SADDUCEAN ORIGINS
OF THE DEAD SEA SCROLL SECT

LAWRENCE H. SCHIFFMAN

This chapter introduces us to some of the profound disagreements among scholars regarding the Dead Sea Scrolls. Yet whoever is right, we find valuable background here about which all scholars agree.

The author of this chapter is a prominent younger Jewish scholar who looks at the scrolls more from a Jewish perspective than did many earlier scholars.

His principal thesis is that the Qumran sectarians were not Essenes—or if they were, we must radically change our ideas about what it meant to be an Essene. He would identify the Qumran sectarians as Sadducean, if not Sadducees.

In considering his argument, we learn a great deal else about the scrolls. We are introduced for the first time to the Damascus Document, about which we will learn in detail in Chapter 5. We also learn about texts from caves other than Cave 1. Indeed, we also learn about texts from sites other than Qumran—including Masada.

Schiffman here gives us his overall assessment of the significance of the scrolls, how they illuminate Second Temple Judaism, the roots of rabbinic Judaism and early Christianity. He sees rabbinic Judaism and early Christianity as tracing their ideological sources to different strands of Second Temple Judaism. He also explains how, in his view, the Qumran library tells a great deal about Jewish religious movements other than the Qumran sectarians—

about the Pharisees and the Sadducees, as well as the Essenes. Finally, he explains how Hellenistic influence affected the varieties of Second Temple Judaism.

Whether or not one agrees with everything in this chapter, it is a brilliant tour de force. In the chapter that follows it, James VanderKam vigorously disputes Schiffman's effort to distance the Essenes from the Qumran documents. —ED.

— · —

Dead Sea Scroll scholarship is undergoing a virtual revolution. New ideas and perspectives are percolating among the small group of scholars who dedicate themselves to primary research on the content of the scrolls. Recent publications focus on major changes in the way Dead Sea Scroll research affects our understanding of the history of Judaism and Christianity.

What are these new perspectives? How do they differ from the scroll scholarship of the past forty years? What is likely to emerge from the still-unpublished materials? These are the questions we will try to explore here.

In a strange way, Dead Sea Scroll research really began fifty years before the first Dead Sea Scrolls were discovered in 1947.* In 1896, a Cambridge University scholar named Solomon Schechter traveled to Egypt to purchase the remains of the Cairo Genizah, a vast treasure trove of Hebrew manuscripts from the storehouse of a synagogue in Fostat, Old Cairo. Among the many important documents he recovered there were two medieval manuscripts of part of a hitherto unknown work now known to scholars as the Damascus Document (because it mentions an exile to Damascus).

Schechter immediately realized that these manuscripts represented the texts of an ancient Jewish sect far older than the medieval copies in the Cairo Genizah.† Another talmudic scholar, Louis Ginzberg, in a later series of articles on the Damascus Document,[1] was able to outline the

---

*See Chapter 5.

†The word *genizah* in Hebrew refers to a storage area where holy books and other Hebrew writings are "hidden away" *(gnz)* after they are no longer usable, since discarding them otherwise would be an act of disrespect.

nature of this sect—which turned out to be the Dead Sea Scroll sect. Fragments of several copies of the Damascus Document were found in Qumran Cave 4. Ginzberg realized that the Damascus Document found in the Cairo Genizah was the remnant of a sect of Jews that had separated from the dominant patterns of Second Temple Judaism before the Roman destruction of the Temple in 70 C.E.* Ginzberg was able to describe the laws, the theology, and even aspects of the history of this sect. We now know that Ginzberg missed the mark only in regard to his emphasis on the closeness of these sectarians to Pharisaism.

In 1947 in a cave in the cliffs near Wadi Qumran, overlooking the Dead Sea just south of Jericho, a shepherd came upon the first of the documents now known collectively as the Dead Sea Scrolls. Seven scrolls were eventually sold, in two lots, to the Hebrew University and the state of Israel, and they are now housed in the Shrine of the Book of the Israel Museum.

As the British mandate over Palestine drew to a close, and the state of Israel was proclaimed in 1948, action shifted to the kingdom of Jordan, which in the aftermath of Israel's War of Independence held the rocky area where the first scrolls had been found. In the early 1950s the Bedouin—and, to a much lesser extent, professional archaeologists—uncovered enormous numbers of additional fragments and some complete scrolls in ten other caves. Particularly rich was a site known as Cave 4, in which an estimated fifteen thousand fragments—parts of over five hundred different scrolls—were discovered. All of these texts were collected at the Palestine Archaeological Museum (later the Rockefeller Museum) in east Jerusalem, then under Jordanian control.

The manuscripts were carefully sorted by a team of scholars assembled primarily from the American Schools of Oriental Research and the École Biblique, the French Catholic biblical and archaeological school in Jerusalem. The initial achievements of this group were remarkable: They assembled the fragments into larger columns, stored in "plates." They transcribed the texts. They even prepared a concordance of all the words in the nonbiblical texts. It was only later, in the early 1960s, when funds ran out and other factors, both personal and political, intervened, that work came to a virtual standstill for almost twenty years.

The texts in Israel's hands were promptly published. Indeed, three of the scrolls had already been published by the American Schools of Orien-

---

*B.C.E. (Before the Common Era) and C.E. (Common Era) are the alternate designations corresponding to B.C. and A.D.

tal Research before Israeli acquisition. The other four scrolls in Israeli hands were published by Israeli scholars E. L. Sukenik, Nahman Avigad, and Yigael Yadin.

After the Six-Day War in 1967, the Israelis acquired the last of the nearly complete scrolls (as opposed to fragmentary texts), the lengthy Temple Scroll. The crown of Israeli scroll achievement was Yigael Yadin's publication of this important text.*[2]

Yadin's Hebrew publication of the Temple Scroll in 1977 sparked renewed interest in the field. At about the same time, significant publications from the original Jordanian lot, then in Israeli hands, began to appear. Especially important were fragments from the book of Enoch, published by J. T. Milik,[3] and liturgical texts published by Maurice Baillet.[4]

While the first generation of Dead Sea Scroll scholars consisted primarily of specialists in the Hebrew Bible and the New Testament, the scholars now involved in research on the scrolls are, to a large extent, a new generation. These researchers are undertaking the study of particularly Jewish issues in the scrolls—Jewish history, law, theology, and messianism. It is to this generation that I belong, having been occupied almost full time for twenty years in Dead Sea Scroll research (Qumran studies, as it is known in the trade). Not being bound to the original theories of those who first identified the authors of the scrolls, this younger generation of scholars has opened anew all kinds of questions pertaining to the origins of the texts.

The initial battle of the Dead Sea Scrolls involved their date and the identity of the people who wrote them. One group of scholars, collected around Solomon Zeitlin of Dropsie College in Philadelphia, argued that they were medieval documents associated with the Karaites, a Jewish sect that based its laws and customs solely on the Bible and rejected the Talmud.[5]

Another group of scholars argued for a late first-century C.E. date. They connected the scrolls either with the Zealots (militant Jewish rebels in the First Jewish Revolt against Rome, which culminated in the destruction of Jerusalem in 70 C.E.) or with early Christians.

These theories all ultimately failed, resulting in a virtual scholarly consensus that the scrolls are to be dated primarily to the Hasmonean period (152–63 B.C.E.) and the Early Roman period (63 B.C.E.–68 C.E.). Indeed, some material from the Qumran caves is even earlier. This dating

*See Chapter 7.

is supported by archaeological evidence from the Qumran settlement adjacent to the caves where the scrolls were found, by carbon-14 tests of the cloth in which the scrolls were wrapped in ancient times, by more recent carbon-14 tests on the scrolls themselves,[6] by palaeographic evidence (the shape and stance of the letters) and, more generally, by the content of the scrolls thus far published.

As a consensus on the dating of the scrolls developed, so did a consensus on the identity of the sect with whom the scrolls were to be associated—the Essenes. The Essenes were a group or sect of Jews who lived a strictly regulated life of piety and who shared property in common. While their center was located at the Dead Sea, the group was said to have had members spread throughout the cities of Palestine as well. The Essenes are described—unfortunately, only briefly—by the first-century Jewish historian Josephus; by his Alexandrian Jewish contemporary, the philosopher Philo; and by the first-century Roman historian Pliny. That the Qumran texts were associated with the Essenes was first suggested by E. L. Sukenik of the Hebrew University.[7] This position has been most fully elaborated in the works of Frank M. Cross, Millar Burrows, and Andre Dupont-Sommer.[8] The Essene hypothesis quickly became, and still remains, the reigning theory.

The theory has a certain surface attractiveness. Josephus, Philo, and Pliny all describe Essenes at the shore of the Dead Sea, living in a manner not inconsistent with what the remains at the Qumran settlement seemed to reveal. (The excavations were conducted in the mid-1950s. Unfortunately, the director of the excavation, Roland de Vaux of the École Biblique, never succeeded in publishing a final excavation report; only preliminary reports and a survey volume appeared.[9] De Vaux died in 1971.) Furthermore, in many ways, what was known about the Essenes paralleled what was found, or seemed to be implied, in the Qumran texts: initiation rites, organizational patterns, a special calendar. The Essenes were therefore assumed to be the authors of virtually all of the scrolls, except the biblical texts and copies of some previously known apocrypha such as Jubilees.

The Essene theory also had another dimension. Many doctrines of the Essenes, then taken to be synonymous with the Qumran sect, had parallels in early Christianity. The Essenes thus became a kind of precursor to Christianity, perhaps even a harbinger.

Methodologically, the identification of the Essenes with the Qumran sect was often supported with a circular argument: If the sectarian materials in the Dead Sea texts could be identified with the Essenes, then all information in the Greek sources (Philo, Josephus, and Pliny) could be read into and harmonized with the evidence of the scrolls. And if the scrolls were Essene, then they could in turn be used to interpret the material in Philo, Josephus, and Pliny. A similar circularity was used to connect the scrolls with New Testament texts. Material from the New Testament regarding the early Church was read back into the scrolls and vice versa. This approach, the dominant hypothesis for some forty years, yielded the "monks," "monastery," "bishop," "celibacy," and numerous other terminological exaggerations used to describe Qumran texts, behind which lay a distinct set of preconceptions. For the most part, the fallacy of these arguments somehow escaped scholarly scrutiny.

Beginning in 1985 with a conference held at New York University,[10] and continuing to the present, contradictions of the "official" Essene hypothesis were voiced as the field of learning advanced. Gradually a new nonconsensus began to emerge. It calls for postponing definite conclusions on the identity of the sect until the publication of the entire corpus. Further, it strongly challenges the right of the few scholars who had exclusive access to the still-unpublished material to require the adherence of others to their theories. Indeed, it is now understood that the term *Essene* may have designated a variety of sectarian groups that had certain common characteristics.

Accordingly, most scholars now refer to the "Qumran sect," no longer assuming that it is the Essenes. And the character of the "ancient library" is being reevaluated.

The collection of Qumran texts consists of biblical manuscripts, the sect's special texts (generally written according to the linguistic peculiarities of the sect), plus a whole variety of other texts collected by the people who lived at Qumran. The relationship of these other texts to the sect is unclear. Many texts were apparently brought to Qumran from elsewhere and held because they had some affinities with the beliefs of the sectarians. These texts may have emerged from earlier, somewhat different sectarian circles, or perhaps they came from contemporary groups close in their ideology to the Qumran sect. These texts cannot be regarded as representing the Qumran sect itself because they do not include its characteristic themes, polemics, and terminology, nor are they written in the distinctive language and style of the works of the sect.

Very recently several fragmentary texts were published from Masada (Herod's wilderness fortress about thirty-five miles south of Qumran) which was occupied by rebels during the First Jewish Revolt against Rome. In addition, a manuscript of the Sabbath Songs (angelic liturgy), known in several manuscripts from Qumran, was found at Masada. Thus, the Jewish defenders of Masada possessed books of the same kind as those found in the Qumran collection, but that were not directly associated with the sect itself. In other words, many of the works found at Qumran were the common heritage of Second Temple Judaism and did not originate in, and were not confined to, Qumran sectarian circles.

The sectarian documents of the Qumran sect, however, form the core of this varied collection. What was the sect, and what was its origin? An unpublished text known in scholarly circles as MMT (for *Miqsat Ma'aseh ha-Torah*—literally, "Some Rulings Pertaining to the Torah"—abbreviated 4QMMT, 4Q referring to Cave 4 at Qumran) is likely to shed considerable new light on these questions. Also known as the Halakhic Letter, referring to the fact that it appears to be a letter and contains about twenty-two religious laws *(halakhot)*, MMT is essentially a foundation document of the Qumran sect. Although it was discovered in 1952, its contents were made known only in 1984 by the scholar assigned to publish it.[11] The ancient author of MMT asserts that the sect broke away from the Jewish establishment in Jerusalem because of differences involving these religious laws. He asserts that the sect will return if their opponents, who are pictured as knowing that the sectarians were right all along, will recant.

The scholars who are preparing a critical edition of MMT, John Strugnell and Elisha Qimron, were kind enough to make available to me this text and their commentary on it. I have compared the laws in MMT with passages in the rabbinic texts known as the Mishnah and the Talmud, which identify the legal views of the Pharisees and the Sadducees, two Jewish movements that flourished before the Roman destruction of the Temple. From this investigation I have been able to show that the origins of the Qumran sect are Sadducean. The Jewish sect of the Sadducees, best known as the opponents of the Pharisees, broke away from their fellow Jews following the Maccabean revolt (168–164 B.C.E.), in which the Hasmonean Jewish rulers regained control of their land and their Temple from the Seleucid Syrian overlord Antiochus IV. The Hasmoneans took control of the Temple, making common cause with the Pharisees. This situation lasted until the Herodian period, which began with the assumption of power by Herod the Great in 37 B.C.E. Some of the Sadducees bent their principles and adjusted to the new situation. Others did not. For those who were unwilling to adjust to the new reality or to compromise their deeply held legal and exegetical principles, this situation proved intolerable. Although quite technical, the religious laws of the two groups differed very considerably. It is in this context that we must understand MMT.

MMT, which dates to the Hasmonean period, is a letter sent by those unwilling to accept the legal rulings enunciated by the Hasmonean high priests. In its legal sections, MMT argues with those compromising Sadducees, setting forth, on the one hand, what the correct law is and, on the other hand, what the law enunciated by the Hasmoneans is. At the end of the letter, the author addresses the Hasmonean ruler himself, and attempts to sway him to MMT's views by warning him that God blesses only those rulers who follow His ways.[12]

MMT revolutionizes the question of Qumran origins and requires us to reconsider the entire Essene hypothesis. It shows beyond question that either the sect was not Essene, but was Sadducean, or that the Essene movement must be totally redefined as having emerged out of Sadducean beginnings. Such a possibility is in agreement with the basic conclusions of Schechter, reached only on the basis of the Damascus Document before the discovery of the Dead Sea Scrolls. Schechter entitled this text a "Zadokite Work" and outlined its Sadducean connections.

The most likely scenario, based on the entire collection of Qumran documents published so far, but especially on the as-yet-unpublished MMT, is that a process of sectarianism and separatist mentality grew throughout the Hasmonean period and blossomed in the Herodian period. As a result, a group of originally Sadducean priests, under the leadership of the Teacher of Righteousness (who, in my view, came to lead the sect only after MMT was written), developed into the group that left us the sectarian texts found at Qumran.

As more and more scrolls are published, our understanding of the nature of the collection widens. It is now becoming increasingly clear that the scrolls are the primary source for the study of Judaism in all its varieties in the last centuries before the Common Era. In short, this corpus does not simply give us an entry into the sect that inhabited the nearby settlement, but also has an enormous amount to tell us about the widely varying Judaisms of the Hasmonean and Herodian periods. In assessing the importance of the collection, we must remember that almost no other primary Hebrew or Aramaic sources exist for the reconstruction of Judaism during these periods. Thus these documents are providing a critical background for the study of the later emergence both of rabbinic Judaism and of the early Christian Church.

Scholars used to think that the library was entirely the product of the inhabitants of Qumran. Instead, it can now be stated, this hoard of manuscripts includes material representing a variety of Jewish groups as well as polemics against other Jewish groups. As a result of this new understanding, much more can be done with the scrolls.

Specifically, it was believed, until very recently, that we had no contemporary sources for the Pharisees during the Hasmonean period. Because the Pharisees bequeathed their approach to the rabbinic Judaism that emerged after the Roman destruction of Jerusalem, this lack of sources was particularly keenly felt. The situation was much the same with the Sadducees. Nor could we make much sense of the various apocalyptic groups whose existence scholars could only assume.

In the last few years, however, we have come to realize that this evaluation is incorrect. The scrolls inform us not only about the unusual sect that inhabited the ruins of Qumran, but also about the other groups as well.

Let us begin with the Pharisees. This elusive group of lay teachers and expounders of the Torah—previously known only from later accounts in Josephus, the largely polemical treatment in the New Testament, and the scattered references in talmudic literature—is now coming to life before our eyes. So far as we can tell from the published material, the scrolls include material on the Pharisees only in polemical context, but this can still tell us a great deal. And who knows what the unpublished material will reveal?

The polemics against the Pharisees are of two kinds. In the better-known, sectarian texts, the Pharisees are called by various code words, such as "Ephraim."[13] In these texts, the Pharisees are said to be the "builders of the wall,"[14] that is, they built fences around the Torah by legislating additional regulations designed to ensure its observance. These fences were no more acceptable to the Qumran sect than the *halakhot* (laws) of the Pharisees. The sect, using a play on words, derisively called the Pharisees *doreshe halaqot,* best translated as "those who expound false laws."[15] The same text refers to the *talmud* (literally "study") of "Ephraim" as falsehood, no doubt a reference to the Pharisaic method of deriving new, extended laws from expressions of Scripture. In these texts from Qumran we see that Josephus' description of the Pharisees and their traditions—which were the precursor of the concept of oral rabbinic law that became embodied in the Talmud—were already in place in the Hasmonean period.

A second type of anti-Pharisaic polemic is reflected in MMT. In MMT, the author castigates his opponents and then expresses his own view, specifying the legal violation in the opponents' views. In a number of cases, the laws the author(s) of MMT opposes are the same laws that later rabbinic sources attribute to the Pharisees, and the laws the author(s) of MMT espouse match those of the Sadducees as reflected in later rabbinic texts. Accordingly, we now have good reason to believe that in MMT we have *halakhot,* as they were already called in the Hasmonean period, maintained by the Pharisees.

This letter requires that the view of prominent scholars—most notably Jacob Neusner[16]—who doubted the reliability of the rabbis regarding the Pharisees must be reevaluated. The talmudic materials are far more accurate than previously thought. This is true in at least two respects.

First, the Pharisaic view did indeed predominate during much of the Hasmonean period. In short, this is not a later talmudic anachronistic invention. Second, the terminology, and even some of the very laws as recorded in rabbinic sources (some in the name of the Pharisees, and others attributed to anonymous first-century sages), were actually used and espoused by the Pharisees. In other words—and this is extremely important—rabbinic Judaism as embodied in the Talmud is not a postdestruction invention, as some scholars had maintained; on the contrary, the roots of rabbinic Judaism reach back at least to the Hasmonean period.

The Qumran texts also teach us a great deal about the Sadducees. In the *Pesher Nahum* they are termed "Menasseh,"[17] the opponents of "Ephraim" (the code word for the Pharisees). Here the Sadducees are described as aristocratic members of the ruling class. This fits the period at the end of Hasmonean rule, just before the Roman conquest of Palestine in 63 B.C.E., when the Pharisees had fallen out with the Hasmoneans. All this accords perfectly with the description of the Sadducees by Josephus. As with the Pharisees, so with the Sadducees: Josephus' description is generally accurate. Moreover, as previously noted, the twenty-two examples of Sadducean laws in MMT frequently match views attributed to the Sadducees in talmudic sources.

A number of Sadducean laws found in MMT also have parallels in the Temple Scroll.* In some cases the Temple Scroll provides a scriptural basis when MMT cites only the law. Although the final text of the Temple Scroll was edited in the Hasmonean period, some of its sources were apparently earlier—before the emergence of the Qumran sect, in a time when these teachings were indeed Sadducean. The author/editor of the final text of the complete Temple Scroll, whether a member of the

*See Chapter 7.

Qumran sect or of some related or similar group, used these Sadducean sources. In recovering the sources of the Temple Scroll, we get a clearer and clearer picture of the views of the Sadducees. We are finally beginning to understand their brand of literalism—barely suggested by the later references in ancient literature that had previously been known. In short, the Sadducees required that all laws be based on Scripture: They rejected laws unrelated to the Bible.

The Qumran scrolls also tell us about various apocalyptic groups whose teachings are so important for our understanding of the later development of aspects of Jewish mysticism as well as Christian apocalypticism. For these apocalyptic groups, we unfortunately lack all social and historical context—at least so far; but who knows what we may find in still-unpublished Qumran texts? Texts like the book of Noah, as well as the books of Daniel and Enoch, have a common structure: Heavenly secrets of the present and of the end of days are revealed to the hero. These texts often involve heavenly ascents and other journeys of this kind frequently found in later Jewish mysticism. Their notions of immediate messianic fulfillment must have greatly influenced Christian messianism. This influence can also be seen in the messianic pressures for Jewish resistance against Roman rule that were important factors in fueling the two Jewish revolts, the First Revolt of 66–70 C.E. and the Second Revolt, the so-called Bar-Kokhba Revolt, of 132–135 C.E., both of which had messianic overtones.

At this point, I should perhaps comment briefly on the Dead Sea Scroll hypothesis recently put forward by Professor Norman Golb of the University of Chicago. According to him the Qumran scrolls are the library of the Jerusalem Temple, brought from Jerusalem and hidden at Qumran during the First Jewish Revolt against Rome. The Qumran documents, Golb argues, therefore represent a balanced picture of the Judaism of the Second Temple period. Indeed he goes so far as to claim that there was no Qumran sect; the settlement at Qumran was, he says, a military fortress. In his view, the ruins of Qumran have no relation to the scrolls found in the adjacent caves.[18]

Despite the aggressive way in which he has argued for this theory, he has never supported it by a study of, or citations to, the texts themselves. Indeed, he ignores the evidence we have cited from MMT (although, in fairness, at best only a pirated copy of the unpublished texts of MMT has been available to him). Equally important, he has also ignored the clear sectarian emphasis of the collection as a whole insofar as it has been published.

Moreover, the settlement at Qumran was constructed in much too unsturdy a manner to be a fortress. Its water supply was completely open and unprotected, contrary to what we would expect of a fortress. Its location was exposed, with its back and one flank abutting a cliff from which it could be attacked and overwhelmed. The wall that surrounded at least part of the settlement was not the wall of a fortress, but a mere enclosure wall, barely thicker than the walls of the buildings inside. Golb relies on the fact that a building at the site was identified by the excavator as a tower. The only reason this building appears to be a tower is because by coincidence it is the only building preserved to the height of its second story. Golb also calls our attention to the fact that graves of women and children, as well as of men, have been found at the site. He correctly argues that this disproves the claim that the site was the monastery of celibate monks. But these graves of women and children also fly in the face of his argument that Qumran was a fortress. In sum, Golb's hypothesis is not valid. It is put forward despite incontrovertible facts, not in an effort to explain doubtful matters on the basis of known information.[19]

Let us turn now to what the Qumran texts can teach us about early Christianity. It is clear that many expressions, motifs, and concepts found in early Christianity have their background in sectarian Judaism of the Second Temple period, as reflected in the Qumran texts. This has long been observed. I also agree that the use of postdestruction rabbinic literature, which once served as the primary source for establishing and interpreting the background of Christian ideas, turns out to be misguided in light of our current knowledge of the varied character of Judaism in the Greco-Roman period. Such ideas as the dualism of light and darkness, the presentation of the figure of the messiah as combining a variety of leadership roles known from earlier Hebrew sources, the immediate messianism—all these are ideas we can and do trace in the Qumran texts.

Yet the quest for parallels to, and antecedents of, Christian doctrines and ideas should remain secondary. The better way to use the Qumran texts for understanding early Christianity is to understand them as illuminating the full spectrum of Jewish groups in the Hellenistic period in Palestine. When we compensate for the sectarian emphasis of the collection as a whole, it turns out that the contribution the Qumran texts can make to the prehistory of Christianity is even greater.[20]

Second Temple Judaism can now be seen as a transition period in which the sectarianism and apocalypticism of the period gradually gave way to rabbinic Judaism, on the one hand, and Christianity, on the other.

Indeed, it is now clear that the Second Temple period was a kind of sorting out process.

Until the Maccabean revolt (168–164 B.C.E.), the Jewish communities in Palestine and in the Diaspora fiercely debated the extent to which they would partake of and absorb the Hellenistic culture all around them. The successful Maccabean revolt resolved this issue: Extreme Hellenism was overwhelmingly rejected in Palestinian Judaism. While Judaism would therefore not become simply one of the Hellenistic cults, the new cultural environment caused by the contact with Hellenism led nonetheless to a reevaluation of many issues in Judaism. The variety of responses that developed brought about the splitting of the Jewish community into various groups, or perhaps, in some cases, sects, each seeking to dominate the religious scene. The writings of some of these groups and considerable information about others can be gleaned, as we have seen, from the Dead Sea Scrolls.

The competing groups vied with one another throughout the Hasmonean period. This debate finally was resolved only in the aftermath of the Bar-Kokhba Revolt (135 C.E.). Apocalyptic messianic tendencies, now much better understood from the sectarian texts authored by the Qumran group (and from some of the other texts preserved there as well), became more and more pronounced among some groups. This led eventually to the two Jewish revolts against Rome. These same trends led a small group of Jews to conclude that their leader, Jesus of Nazareth, was indeed the "son of man," interpreted by some as a messianic designation. This term is well known from Daniel and also from Enochic writings preserved at Qumran.

Postdestruction rabbinic Judaism based itself, in the main, on Pharisaism, although it also included some aspects of the traditions of the sectarian and apocalyptic groups. Christianity, on the other hand, primarily inherited the immediate apocalypticism of these groups. Christianity also adopted, or adapted, certain dualistic tendencies and a wide variety of motifs found in the doctrines of these groups. In other words, Christianity is to a great extent the continuation of trends within Second Temple Judaism that were rejected by the emerging Pharisaic-rabbinic mainstream.

Finally, let us look at the Qumran texts for the light they can shed on the history of the biblical texts. Here again, more recent study requires the modification of earlier held views. In the early years of Qumran studies, it was thought that the biblical texts found in the caves—at least fragments of every book of the Hebrew Bible except Esther were found—would somehow illuminate the "original" text that emerged from ancient Israel. This entire notion has been proven wrong. We now know that the transmission of the text in the postbiblical period resulted in many textual variants. These variants resulted not only from the copying process itself, but also from interpretation of the text and linguistic updating, phenomena that could not have been understood before the discovery of the scrolls.[21]

Very early in the study of the biblical manuscripts from Qumran, a theory was put forward, first by William F. Albright[22] and then more fully by Frank M. Cross,*[23] that supposedly identified three text types. One of these text types stood behind the Masoretic text, the traditional Jewish Hebrew text adopted by rabbinic Judaism as authoritative; another text type stood behind the Samaritan Pentateuch (before the introduction of certain Samaritan polemical changes); a third text type stood behind the text preserved only in the Greek translation known as the Septuagint. These three textual families were shown to have coexisted at Qumran, and it was widely assumed that they were represented in roughly equivalent numbers of texts, although this assumption was in fact based only on a limited sample.

Recent studies require a modification of this approach. In fact, most of the biblical manuscripts at Qumran indicate that the proto-Masoretic text type in fact predominated: Thus, the process of standardization, whereby this text became authoritative in rabbinic Judaism, may have taken place much earlier than was previously presumed. In short, the proto-Masoretic tradition was in ascendence by the Hasmonean period. It is likely that this text type was the most common because it was the most ancient. The process of standardization was in reality one of eliminating variant texts. This, indeed, is the picture presented in rabbinic literature.

Another modification of Cross's analysis is also required. Most biblical texts at Qumran represent, to some extent, mixtures of text types. The biblical manuscripts commonly share readings with other texts to such an extent that few can be understood as representative purely of a single text type.[24] Indeed, the very notion of text types to a certain extent projects backward in time the textual "witnesses" that have survived in later copies—that is, the Masoretic Hebrew text, the Samaritan Pentateuch, and the Greek Septuagint—which were known to us before the Qumran finds. Had we not had the Septuagint and the Samaritan Bibles, we

*For Cross's views, see Chapter 11.

would never have concluded from the Qumran material itself that three text families existed. A more accurate picture would describe trends reflected in varying degrees in different biblical texts from Qumran. This would explain much better the predominance of the many mixed texts of the Hebrew Bible found at Qumran.

The claim that New Testament manuscripts were found at Qumran can be dealt with in a sentence. None was found—for a very good reason: New Testament texts are later than the Qumran texts.

What we have described here as to the Qumran collection and its implications is based on published documents as well as on a number of unpublished materials that I have been able to inspect—including MMT, which the editors allowed me to study. Further, I have had the use of the concordance to the full lot, including the unpublished texts. There is much more to come, as some four hundred documents, most very fragmentary—about half the documents from the Qumran caves—are yet to be published. At the present time, scholars are updating the old catalogues of the Qumran manuscripts, and a full catalogue is expected to be available soon. When the entire corpus is finally published, students of the varieties of Second Temple Judaism and their relevance to rabbinic Judaism and early Christianity will have a veritable feast.

CHAPTER 4

THE PEOPLE OF THE
DEAD SEA SCROLLS: ESSENES
OR SADDUCEES?

JAMES C. VANDERKAM

In this chapter a distinguished younger scholar, James VanderKam of the University of Notre Dame, takes strong issue with Lawrence Schiffman's views expressed in the preceding chapter. In short, VanderKam believes that the case that the Qumran sectarians were Essenes is well-nigh irrefutable. He makes his argument by closely examining the ancient Greek sources regarding the Essenes and comparing them not only with the archaeological evidence from Qumran but also with the beliefs reflected in the Dead Sea Scrolls. In addition, he compares the beliefs reflected in the Dead Sea Scrolls with the beliefs of the Pharisees and Sadducees. He concludes that the views reflected in the scrolls are far closer to the Essenes than to any other known Jewish group at the time.

In the course of his discussion, VanderKam calls our attention to the difficulty of deciding which of the Qumran documents are in fact sectarian texts, a problem we will return to in Chapter 10. He also discusses the details of the immensely important, but still-unpublished, Qumran document known as MMT. In addition, we get an introduction to the Temple Scroll, which will be a major focus of later chapters. —ED.

—·—

Adjacent to the eleven caves on the northwestern shore of the Dead Sea where the famous Dead Sea Scrolls were found are the remains of an ancient settlement overlooking the Wadi Qumran. It is almost certain that the people who lived in this settlement placed the scrolls in the nearby caves. In two of the caves—Cave 4 and Cave 11—archaeologists found regularly spaced holes in the walls where supports for shelves were once anchored. Before the shelves collapsed or were destroyed, banks of scrolls were no doubt neatly stacked on the shelves.

But who were the people who lived in this settlement and collected these scrolls?

Throughout the history of research on the Dead Sea Scrolls, the dominant position has been that the people who inhabited this settlement were part of a Jewish sect known as the Essenes. True, some scholars questioned this view and preferred to identify the group as Pharisaic, Sadducean, or even Christian, but their views have gained only very modest support.

In the last year, however, a distinguished scholar from New York University, Lawrence H. Schiffman, has argued that certain important, more recently available Qumran (that is, Dead Sea Scroll) texts exhibit traits of the Sadducees. If so, we must raise anew the question of who the people were who lived at Qumran.

Schiffman relies primarily on a still-unpublished document known as 4QMMT,* or MMT for short, and, to a lesser extent, on the famous Temple Scroll.

In the previous chapter, Schiffman sets out his position at some length.† He concludes that "MMT revolutionizes the question of Qumran origins and requires us to consider the entire Essene hypothesis. It shows beyond question that either the sect was not Essene, but was Sadducean, or that the Essene movement must be totally redefined as having emerged out of Sadducean beginnings."

I see no justification for Schiffman's first alternative ("the sect was not Essene, but Sadducean"). His second alternative ("the Essene movement must be totally redefined as having emerged out of Sadducean begin-

---

*The number 4 indicates that it was found in the fourth cave, Q refers to Qumran, and the letters MMT are an abbreviation for the Hebrew words *Miqsat Ma'aseh ha-Torah* (Some of the works of the Torah), which the editors, John Strugnell and Elisha Qimron, have suggested as a title for the work. These words appear near the end of the text.

†See Chapter 3.

nings") is, as he has formulated it, misleading, although it ultimately points in the right direction.

From a variety of texts, such as the writings of the first-century A.D. historian Josephus, the New Testament, and the Mishnah,* we learn that the two leading Jewish groups during the last two centuries B.C. and the first century A.D. were the Sadducees and the Pharisees. But no Sadducean or Pharisaic documents have survived, unless, for the Sadducees, Schiffman is correct about works such as MMT.† Accordingly, we learn about the Sadducees and Pharisees only through the reports of others—reports that are sometimes hostile (the New Testament), sometimes later (the Mishnah and the Talmud), and always biased.

The situation with respect to the Essenes—the third of the three sects or philosophies that Josephus mentions—is even more problematic. There are fewer ancient references to the Essenes than there are to the Pharisees and Sadducees. The Essenes are mentioned by Josephus first in his account of Jewish history during the high priesthood of Jonathan the Maccabee (152–142 B.C.).[1] Apparently these three groups—the Pharisees, the Sadducees, and the Essenes—operated continuously from at least the mid–second century B.C. until the end of the First Jewish Revolt against Rome (66–70 A.D.).

Although the Essenes are mentioned less frequently than the Pharisees and Sadducees, the Essenes may today have won an advantage over their more famous rivals, since, according to most scholars, the authors and copyists of the Dead Sea Scrolls were Essenes. If they were in fact Essenes, we can now learn their views from their own pens, not merely through the reports and distortions of others. Oddly enough, the little-known Essenes may now have emerged into a brighter public light than their more famous coreligionists.

The identification of the Dead Sea Scroll community as Essene has been based primarily on two kinds of data: (1) evidence from the Roman geographer Pliny the Elder, and (2) the contents of the scrolls themselves as compared with Josephus' and others' descriptions of Essene beliefs and practices. (The scrolls themselves, however, do not contain the word *Essene*.)

Pliny the Elder (23–79 A.D.) almost certainly mentions the Qumran

---

*The Mishnah is the code of Jewish Law prepared by Rabbi Judah haNasi about 200 A.D.

†There may be one or two other exceptions. The Psalms of Solomon are thought by some to be Pharisaic.

group, referring to them as Essenes. In his famous *Natural History* he describes Judea and the Dead Sea:

> On the west side of the Dead Sea, but out of range of the exhalations of the coast, is the solitary tribe of the Essenes, which is remarkable beyond all the other tribes in the whole world, as it has no women and has renounced all sexual desire, has no money, and has only palm-trees for company. Day by day the throng of refugees is recruited to an equal number by numerous accessions of persons tired of life and driven thither by the waves of fortune to adopt their manners. Thus through thousands of ages (incredible to relate) a race into which no one is born lives on forever; so prolific for their advantage is other men's weariness of life!
>
> *Lying below the Essenes* [literally: lying below these] was formerly the town of Engedi, second only to *Jerusalem* in the fertility of its land and in its groves of palm-trees, but now like Jerusalem a heap of ashes.[2] [I have italicized two items to be discussed below.]

The only place on the west side of the Dead Sea north of Ein Gedi where archaeological remains of a communal center were found is Qumran, as scholars have been quick to note. And precisely in that location, says Pliny, were to be found those peculiar Essenes about whose manner of life he seems so well informed.

Small objections have been raised to the inference that Pliny is talking about the inhabitants of the settlement at Qumran. Some have suggested that "lying below these" indicates that Pliny located the Essenes on the hills overlooking Ein Gedi. But there was no settlement at that location. Pliny does make a few mistakes—or the extant witnesses to the text of his book do. (They could be copyists' mistakes.) The first mention of *Jerusalem* (italicized above), which was even more fertile than Ein Gedi, should be *Jericho;* Pliny also seems exceedingly optimistic about the antiquity of the Essenes, suggesting that the "tribe" has endured through "thousands of ages." These, however, are only minor matters; they have, quite rightly, played little part in the discussion.

More importantly, some scholars have concluded that, since Pliny refers to the Essenes in the present tense and since his book, dedicated to Titus before he became emperor, was written in about 77 A.D., after the Qumran community had been destroyed in 68 A.D.,[3] he can hardly have been describing Qumran and its residents. This potentially damaging objection is hardly fatal, however. Pliny regularly describes sites in the present tense. Moreover, in this section of his book it is quite likely that he is basing his description on an earlier source. Pliny himself acknowledged his heavy indebtedness to his sources; he names some one hundred of them for *Natural History*. For Book 5 alone, he lists fifty-nine authorities from whom he extracted information. H. Rackham has written about Pliny's own meager contributions to his book: "[T]hey form only a small fraction of the work, which is in the main a second-hand compilation from the works of others."[4] Accordingly, the date when Pliny finished his book does not necessarily, or even probably, specify the time when his description of the Essenes, which he probably draws from another author, was written.

When all is said and done, the result is a pleasant surprise: An ancient Roman author, who would have had no reason to fabricate this report, found a community of Essenes living alone on the northwestern shore of the Dead Sea—precisely where Qumran is. And he apparently took the trouble to discover that this group did not marry, had no private property, and regularly welcomed new recruits.

The second fundamental argument for the claim that the residents of Qumran were Essenes is that the contents *of the specifically sectarian texts* among the scrolls are in remarkably close agreement with what the ancient writers—Pliny, Philo, and especially Josephus—tell us about Essene beliefs and practices. What the sectarian texts have to say coincides much more closely with Essene thought and action than with what the sources say about the Pharisaic and Sadducean views.

The most important Qumran text in these comparisons is the Manual of Discipline—one of the first of the scrolls to be published.[5] The Manual of Discipline (also known as the Community Rule or *Serekh Hay-Yahad*, 1QS) describes, among other topics, some fundamental beliefs of the Qumran group, the initiation process and ceremonies for new members, and the rules that governed their daily life and gatherings.

Consider, for example, the striking harmony in the doctrine of fate or predeterminism as reflected first in Josephus and then in the Manual of Discipline. Josephus tells us that the three Jewish parties held differing opinions on this matter:

> As for the Pharisees, they say that certain events are the work of Fate, but not all; as to other events, it depends upon ourselves whether they shall take place or not. *The sect of the Essenes, however, declares that Fate is mistress of all things,* and that nothing befalls men unless it be in accordance with her decree. *But the Sadducees do away with Fate,* holding that there is no such thing and that human actions are not achieved in accordance with her decree, but that all things lie within our own power, so that we ourselves

are responsible for our well-being, while we suffer misfortune through our own thoughtlessness."[6] [Italics added.]

Compare this with the Manual of Discipline, which articulates a strongly predestinarian theology of world history and human endeavor:

> From the God of Knowledge comes all that is and shall be. Before ever they existed He established their whole design, and when, as ordained for them, they come into being, it is in accord with His glorious design that they accomplish their task without change.[7]

And again:

> The Angel of Darkness leads all the children of righteousness astray, and until his end, all their sin, iniquities, wickedness, and all their unlawful deeds are caused by his dominion in accordance with the mysteries of God.[8]

Sentiments like this place the Qumran sectarians *furthest from the Sadducean position* (as described by Josephus), somewhat nearer the Pharisaic, and clearly closest to the Essenes. To be more precise, the views contained in the Manual of Discipline are identical with Essene thinking as described by Josephus. From theoretical points like this to other more mundane matters, the series of close resemblances continues. Josephus tells us of the Essenes' common ownership of property:

> Riches they despise, and their community of goods is truly admirable; you will not find one among them distinguished by greater opulence than another. They have a law that new members on admission to the sect shall confiscate their property to the order, with the result that you will nowhere see either abject poverty or inordinate wealth; the individual's possessions join the common stock and all, like brothers, enjoy a single patrimony.[9]

Compare this with the Manual of Discipline:

> . . . when (the novice) has completed one year within the Community, the Congregation shall deliberate his case with regard to his understanding and observance of the Law. And if it be his destiny, according to the judgment of the Priests and the multitude of the men of their Covenant,

to enter the company of the Community, his property and earnings shall be handed over to the Bursar of the Congregation who shall register it to his account and shall not spend it for the Congregation. [. . . .] But when the second year has passed, he shall be examined, [. . . .]; his property shall be merged . . .[10] (The dots indicate lacunae in the text.)

True, there are some differences of detail—for example, in precisely how the years of the initiatory period are divided, but, in the end, the extent of agreement is astonishing.

Or take something as trivial as the rule that when the group is assembled, no one may spit. Josephus wrote: "They are careful not to spit into the midst of the company or to the right."[11] The Manual of Discipline prescribes: "Whoever has spat in an Assembly of the Congregation shall do penance for thirty days."[12]

Many more examples could be added, but the point is clear. In a recent analysis of the material in Josephus and in the sectarian scrolls, Todd Beall concluded that there are twenty-seven parallels between Josephus and the scrolls regarding the Essenes, twenty-one probable parallels, ten cases in which Josephus makes claims about the Essenes that have no known parallel among the scrolls, and six discrepancies between them.[13] In two of these six discrepancies, the scrolls are not unanimous, but differ among themselves. And even the discrepancies can be explained. For example, on the issue of common ownership of property: Josephus (and Pliny) and the Manual of Discipline mention it; another sectarian document among the scrolls, the Damascus Document, however, talks about placing the earnings of "at least two days out of every month into the hands of the Guardian and Judges" for charitable distribution.[14] This doesn't sound like common ownership of property. However, the standard theory is that the Damascus Document gives the law for the Essenes living in towns and villages; the Manual of Discipline legislates for the branch of the Essene movement that lived at Qumran. Thus, different Essene groups seem to have had different rules about such matters.

Identifying the residents of Qumran with the Essenes does, thus, have sturdy backing, and most have accepted it.

Before turning to Schiffman's challenge to this thesis, however, I do want to add a few notes. First, as the preceding discussion has hinted, one must initially establish which documents from the caves are specifically sectarian before making comparisons of these kinds. A text cannot be considered sectarian just because it was found in one of the eleven manuscript caves of Qumran. If that alone were sufficient, all the biblical manuscripts would have to be considered Essene and clearly they are not

Essene in origin. Scholars have been surprisingly slow to address this question. The method for determining which of the documents are sectarian must begin with one or two documents that undoubtedly are sectarian—such as the Manual of Discipline, the biblical commentaries, and the Hymn Scroll—and then extrapolate from these to other texts.[15] Although it is sometimes difficult to tell whether a text is a sectarian document—the Temple Scroll is an example—this problem need not detain us here because it is precisely the Manual of Discipline, an un- doubted sectarian document, that displays these numerous and weighty agreements with Josephus' account of the Essenes. This, accordingly, is reassuring support for the identification.

Second, a cautionary note: We can compare the contents of Qumran documents only with what other ancient writers recorded about the parties in reports that have survived. Possibly, if they had recorded more about them or more of these descriptions had survived, additional agree- ments or discrepancies would surface.

Third, it is mildly disturbing that there are some very noticeable traits in the scrolls that neither Josephus nor any other ancient cataloguer of Essene beliefs noted. For example, the peculiar 364-day solar calendar referred to in several Qumran texts is nowhere mentioned by ancient writers. The same is the case with the belief of the Qumran sectarians that two messiahs would appear. It may be thought that Josephus, for one, did not mention these matters in connection with the Essenes because he believed they would be of no interest to his Greco-Roman audience or because he did not reproduce material of this sort for any of the other Jewish parties; but one wonders whether his audience would have been any more interested in the Essenes' avoidance of spitting during commu- nal gatherings. In short, these are some puzzling omissions.

Fourth, where differences exist between Josephus and the Qumran texts, it may be that Josephus merely reflects a later version of Essene beliefs that could have changed over time, or that Josephus is talking about another, non-Qumran wing of the Essene party with which he happened to be familiar. All Essenes surely did not agree on everything, nor did their views remain static over some two hundred years.

In light of all the evidence adduced above, I think most scholars would agree with Frank Cross's forceful statement:*

> The scholar who would "exercise caution" in identifying the sect of
> Qumran with the Essenes places himself in an astonishing position: He

*See Chapter 2.

must suggest seriously that two major parties formed communalistic religious communities in the same district of the desert of the Dead Sea and lived together in effect for two centuries, holding similar bizarre views, performing similar or rather identical lustrations, ritual meals, and ceremonies. He must suppose that one [the Essenes], carefully described by classical authors, disappeared without leaving building remains or even potsherds behind; the other [the inhabitants of Qumran], systematically ignored by the classical sources, left extensive ruins, and indeed a great library. I prefer to be reckless and flatly identify the men of Qumran with their perennial houseguests, the Essenes.[16]

Cross's lecture, from which the above quotation was taken, was first presented in 1966, and much has changed since then. For one thing, the Temple Scroll—the longest document from Qumran—has been published. Its heavily legal content has received intense scrutiny. Some regard it as an extremely important statement of sectarian law; others deny that it is sectarian—either Qumranian or Essene. A second text, although unpublished, is also very much part of the Essene-Sadducee discussion—MMT, which its editors bill as a letter, possibly from the Teacher of Righteousness himself,* to the opponents of the group.[17] In this letter (if that is what it is), the group distinguishes its views from its opponents' views on some twenty-two laws. In the text of MMT, legal statements are listed with phrases such as "you say" and "but we think," so we know what the writer's view of the law is and what the opponents' view is. In one copy of this intriguing text—parts of at least seven copies have survived—the "epistolary" part is preceded by a complete annual calendar of 364 days that dates the various festivals within the year. The document is clearly sectarian.

In Schiffman's view, MMT is a Sadducean document—that is, the legal views that the text defends significantly overlap with positions that later rabbinic literature attributes to the Sadducees. If he is correct and if MMT is a sectarian text that dates from near the beginning of the Qumran writings, it would imply that the sect at its inception was Sadducean or at least exhibited heavy Sadducean influence on its legal positions.[18]

I consider this view implausible.

A critical element in Schiffman's case is a series of disagreements between the Pharisees and Sadducees recorded in the Mishnah (*Yadayim* 4.6–7), where four disputed points are raised. Schiffman finds echoes of

*The Teacher of Righteousness was the early leader and revered teacher of the Qumran group; he is credited with being an inspired interpreter of the prophets.

these four disputed points in MMT. In each case, the Sadducean position, as recorded in the Mishnah, is consistently defended in MMT, while the Pharisees' view is attributed to MMT's opponents. So says Schiffman.

In an appendix to this chapter, I examine these four legal points and compare the Mishnah text with MMT in an effort to determine whether in fact the writer of MMT does agree, in each case, with the position of the Sadducees as recorded in the Mishnah. My conclusion is that the writer of MMT probably agrees with the Sadducean position, as presented in the Mishnah, in three of the four cases. Moreover, there are other instances in which the Sadducean and Qumran positions coincide.

But what is one to make of this evidence? I doubt very much that the far-ranging conclusions Schiffman has drawn actually follow from this meager evidence. Even if the Sadducean views given in the Mishnah and the laws of MMT agreed in twice as many instances, it would be interesting but perhaps not terribly significant. There may well have been many areas in which the Sadducees and the Essenes agreed with one another; to be a Sadducee or an Essene presumably did not mean that they disagreed about everything. Especially in the case of these two groups, one would expect some shared views because both had strong priestly roots. The Qumran group was founded and led by priests, the sons of Zadok; the very name *Sadducees* seems to be derived from this same Zadok, and influential priests are known to have been Sadducees.

Moreover, it is no simple matter to decide how much credence to give to the record of Sadducean-Pharisaic disputes in the Mishnah. The Mishnah may, but may not, preserve a precise recollection of differences between the two groups; the Mishnah was written long after the two parties had ceased to exist (about 200 A.D.). Moreover, the Mishnah regularly sides with the Pharisees and thus sees the disputes from their angle. Indeed, Emil Schürer thought that "[t]he attacks of the Sadducees on the Pharisees mentioned in [this Mishnah passage] can only have been intended as mockery."[19]

Schiffman bases a major conclusion on a few agreements in religious laws *(halakhah):* Because the views in MMT and those attributed much later to the Sadducees correspond for a few individual laws, Schiffman concludes that the Qumran group was Sadducean or had strong Sadducean influences at its inception. In order to reach this conclusion he has to ignore the *contemporary* testimony of Pliny. Schiffman also has to ignore the numerous and fundamental agreements between Josephus' description of Essene thought and practice, on the one hand, and the contents of the sectarian documents from Qumran, on the other.

Equally important, Schiffman ignores the fact that the sectarian texts from Qumran teach such thoroughly non-Sadducean doctrines as the existence of multitudes of angels[20] and the all-controlling power of fate. Schiffman tells us nothing about how the Sadducees are supposed to have developed such teachings—certainly strange ones for Sadducees. The fact that an *early* sectarian document such as the Manual of Discipline enunciates markedly Essene, non-Sadducean positions makes it most improbable that the Qumran residents emerged from Sadducean origins. If they did, they somehow managed to reverse themselves on fundamental theological tenets within a few years—from nonpredestinarians to all-out determinists, to name just one example. Such a scenario is thoroughly implausible. The evidence from people like Josephus and Pliny (or his source), who had actually witnessed the ways and theology of the Essenes, and the data from central Qumran texts can hardly be outweighed by the few legal details on which Schiffman relies—individual laws that may well be just a few of many points on which Sadducees and Essenes agreed (they agreed with Pharisees on others).

The sparse data that Schiffman (and Joseph Baumgarten before him) has uncovered merely evidence something that was already known: Both the Essenes (including those who lived at Qumran) and the Sadducees had similar origins in the priestly class of Judea, and both (in their strict view of the Law) seemed to have opposed the Pharisaic amelioration of some laws and penalties. That Essenes and Sadducees agreed on some points is to be expected; that they disagreed fundamentally on others is why they were identified as different groups. One would have to posit a very strange history for the Qumran group to hold that they began as Sadducees and swiftly evolved into people who held numerous diametrically opposed views. Since we do not know which of the two groups came first—Essenes or Sadducees—it is preferable *not* to speak of strong Sadducean influences on the origins of the Qumran group. What can be said on the basis of the evidence is that both groups shared deep priestly roots but grew from them in rather different ways.

APPENDIX

TRACKING THE LAW IN THE MISHNAH
AND IN A QUMRAN TEXT

In arguing that the Qumran sectarians were Sadducees, at least in their origins, Lawrence Schiffman relies on a comparison of four laws discussed both in a

Qumran sectarian document known as MMT and in a rabbinic text from about 200 A.D. called the Mishnah. The passage in the Mishnah (*Yadayim* 4.6–7) records a dispute between the Pharisees and the Sadducees regarding the law on four rather obscure points. According to Schiffman, MMT defends the same views that are ascribed to the Sadducees in the Mishnah.

The passage from the Mishnah reads as follows:

The Sadducees say, "We cry out against you, O you Pharisees, for you say, 'The Holy Scriptures render the hands unclean,' [and] 'The writings of Hamiram [Homer?] do not render the hands unclean.'"

Rabban Yohanan b.* Zakkai [himself a Pharisee] said [perhaps mockingly], "Have we nothing else against the Pharisees except this? For lo, the [Pharisees say], 'The bones of an ass are [ritually] clean [so cooking implements can be made from them], and the bones of Yohanan the High Priest are unclean.'"

They [Pharisees] said to him, "As is our love for them so is their [the bones] uncleanness [they cannot be made into cooking implements]—that no man may make spoons of the bones of his father or mother."

He [Yohanan] said to them [the Sadducees], "Even so the Holy Scriptures: as is our love for them so is their uncleanness; [whereas] the writings of Hamiram which are held in no account do not render the hands unclean."

The Sadducees say, "We cry out against you, O you Pharisees, for you declare clean an unbroken stream of liquid [that is poured into something ritually unclean; according to the Pharisees, the vessel from which the liquid is poured is not rendered unclean by the unbroken stream of liquid that touches the unclean vessel]." The Pharisees say, "We cry out against you, O you Sadducees, for you declare clean a channel of water that flows from a burial ground."[1]

Four legal issues are involved here. The first is whether the books of Hamiram (Homer?)[2] defile the hands. Schiffman relates this to the fact that the leaves of books are made from parchment, that is, animal skins; whether the animal skin is pure or not may depend on where the animal was slaughtered. The Sadducees, unlike the Pharisees, believed that all books, including Hamiram's, defiled the hands. Books were made from animal skins; if the animals from which the parchment was made had been slaughtered outside the Temple, as was probably the case with Hamiram's books, the books were unclean. At least this was the Saducean view, as expounded by Schiffman. A damaged section of MMT does discuss animal skins and indicates that the skins of animals made unclean the person who carried them. But whether this is in fact what lies behind this first dispute is more of an assumption than a fact.

The next issue deals with the ritual purity of bones. The Pharisaic view as expressed in the Mishnah is that bones, even of an unkosher animal like an ass, can be used to fashion a spoon—or at least the Sadducees accuse the Pharisees of this view.

---

*"b." is the standard rabbinic abbreviation for *ben,* meaning "son of."

The Sadducees would declare all bones of unclean animals impure. Just as they would not make spoons from the bones of their parents, so they would not make spoons from the bones of an animal.

Yohanan then catches the Sadducees in an inconsistency (although an inconsistency that is irrelevant for our purposes): If, as the Sadducees claim, their high regard (or love) for the bones of their parents (and of animals) renders the bones unclean, and their love for Holy Scripture renders these books unclean, how is it that the books of Hamiram (probably Homer), which the text tells us are worthless and therefore certainly unloved, defile the hands?

Putting aside this inconsistency, it is true that in MMT there is a reasonable inference from the preserved words that making handles out of bones and skins for use on containers is prohibited;[3] animal bones, like human bones, render one unclean upon contact. In MMT, the bones of unclean animals are considered unclean. The same position, incidentally, is enunciated in the Temple Scroll. The Mishnah passage implies, through the words of Rabban Yohanan b. Zakkai, that the Sadducees embraced this position.[4] Thus Schiffman has a point in his favor in the second dispute.

The third issue relates to whether a stream of liquid can convey impurity. Imagine a stream of pure (that is, ritually clean) water poured from a pure container into an impure container. On contact with the impure container, the water in the impure container of course becomes impure. But what of the water still in the pure container and the container itself? Does the impurity that attaches to the water when it touches the impure container travel back up the stream of water to contaminate the remaining water in the previously pure container? The Sadducees say the impurity does attach to the stream of liquid, rendering impure both the water in the previously pure container and the container itself. The Pharisees are more liberal and are of the opposite view.

Here MMT clearly agrees with the Sadducees. The form of the word for a stream of liquid is not exactly the same in the two texts, but the legal stance is.[5]

The fourth issue is really a counterexample of the third issue. Despite the strictness of the Sadducean view, they do not stick to it regarding running water that has flowed through a burial ground and that should be, according to Sadducean logic, impure. In short, the Pharisees argue that the Sadducees are being inconsistent because in the case of a stream of water that comes from a burial ground the Sadducees seem not to have applied their principle, enunciated in the previous case, that a liquid stream conveys impurity.

MMT probably agrees with the Sadducean position, as reflected in the Mishnah, in two (the second and third) of the four cases, while in the last case it is claimed that the MMT/Sadducean principle is not practiced.

But this comparison has little significance in identifying the Qumran sectarians as Sadducean. It does, however, allow the reader to appreciate how difficult it is to read and understand the logic in an important and compressed rabbinic text like the Mishnah.—J.C.V.

CHAPTER 5

"FIRST DEAD SEA SCROLL" FOUND IN EGYPT FIFTY YEARS BEFORE QUMRAN DISCOVERIES

RAPHAEL LEVY

We have already heard about the Damascus Document and its importance to the discussion of the origin of the Qumran sectarians. Oddly, two fragmentary copies of this document dating to the medieval period (a thousand years after the scrolls were deposited in the Qumran caves) were found in the last century, not in caves by the Dead Sea, but in the genizah, *or worn manuscript storeroom, of an old synagogue in Cairo. In a sense, these Cairo copies were the first Dead Sea Scrolls to be discovered. Fifty years after they were recovered from the Cairo synagogue, at least nine fragmentary copies of this same document were discovered in the Qumran caves—confirming not only the early date of its composition, but also many of the prescient insights of the Jewish scholar who brought these early copies to Cambridge University in England.*

The drama of this nineteenth-century discovery is the subject of this chapter by Raphael Levy. It provides a fitting background to the later drama of the discovery of the scrolls by the Dead Sea. Levy also describes the content of the Cairo copies of the Damascus Document, which explains why they are so important in ferreting out the origins of the Qumran sectarians.

The fragmentary copies of the Damascus Document found at Qumran have still not been fully published. As this chapter indicates, they were originally assigned for publication to Jozef T. Milik who failed, after more than thirty years, to complete this assignment. Recently, however, the Qumran copies *were reassigned to Professor Joseph Baumgarten of Baltimore Hebrew University. In the meantime, Hebrew transcripts of eight of the Qumran copies prepared in the 1950s by Milik have been released in the computer-generated texts of Professor Ben Zion Wacholder and Martin Abegg of Hebrew Union College in Cincinnati.* These Qumran copies of the Damascus Document double and perhaps triple the amount of text available from the Cairo copies. The implications of the newly available material are not yet clear.*

However, the Cairo copies are themselves extraordinary. They describe a Jewish sect that regarded itself as the True Israel and that was in bitter opposition to the Jewish leaders in Jerusalem from whom they had fled. The sect was led by a Teacher of Righteousness who was "gathered in," but who was expected to return as a Messiah at the end of days.

Like the later Dead Sea Scrolls, early exaggerated claims were made about the connection between the Jewish sect described in the Cairo copies and Jesus, John the Baptist, and Paul. —ED.

— · —

S ome call it the First Dead Sea Scroll—but it was found in Cairo and not in a cave. It was recovered in 1897 in a *genizah,* a synagogue repository for worn-out copies of sacred writings. The gifted scholar who found it, Solomon Schechter, gave it with a hoard of other ancient Hebrew manuscripts to Cambridge University, where it remains today.

Of course no one called it the First Dead Sea Scroll in 1897. That was fifty years before the momentous discovery of the actual Dead Sea Scrolls, in 1947, in the caves of Qumran on the northwestern shore of the Dead Sea. The manuscript Schechter retrieved received its nickname only after Dead Sea Scroll scholars realized that it was a copy of a document that belonged to, and described, the sect whose hidden library had been discovered at Qumran.

Today, the "Damascus Document" (or the "Zadokite Fragments"), as this Genizah manuscript is known to scholars, is considered to be the most important document in existence for understanding the history of the Essenes, the people who produced and subsequently hid the scrolls

---

**A Preliminary Edition of the Unpublished Dead Sea Scrolls: The Hebrew and Aramaic Texts from Cave Four.* Fascicle One. Reconstructed and edited by Ben Zion Wacholder and Martin G. Abegg (Washington: Biblical Archaeology Society, 1991). —ED.

in the Qumran caves. And from its tattered pages, Schechter, who never dreamed of Qumran and died before its discovery, was able to give us our first recognizable portrait of the Qumran sect.

The picture he painted was an astonishing one, and was, for a long time, unexplainable. "The annals of Jewish history," Schechter wrote, "contain no record of a Sect agreeing in all points with the one depicted . . . "[1]

Schechter's account told of a strange, highly structured and unknown Jewish brotherhood of Second Temple times, given to a fierce piety, the communal ownership of property, and a belief in a Messiah. Their doctrinal differences with establishment Judaism, he surmised, "led to a complete separation . . . from the bulk of the Jewish nation."[2]

Schechter's report of the brotherhood's history and laws contained most of the mysterious and intriguing characters, places, and events that give the story of the Dead Sea Scroll sect its special flavor. In his pioneering study of the Cairo Genizah document published in 1910, Schechter told us of the sect's unknown leader, the "Teacher of Righteousness," and his terrible enemy, the "Man of Scoffing."

He told us also of the sect's "Flight to Damascus" (hence the scholarly designation, "Damascus Document") to escape persecution at home, and of its adoption there of a "New Covenant." Finally, he told us that although the Teacher of Righteousness died, the sect believed that by remaining true to his teachings, the Teacher would return as a Messiah.

These, of course, are the very *personae* and occurrences that have emerged from such Dead Sea Scrolls as the Habakkuk Commentary and the Manual of Discipline. Numerous scholars since Schechter's time have sought to date and identify the actual people referred to in the scrolls and to clarify the historical context of the events described. But to Schechter must go the credit for first bringing to the world's attention this intriguing chapter in our common history.

How Solomon Schechter came to the Cairo Genizah is an exciting story in itself. In 1896, when he set out for Cairo, Schechter was Reader in Talmud and rabbinical literature at Cambridge University. Born in a small Jewish community in Rumania, he showed early brilliance as a student and was sent to a series of *yeshivot* (rabbinical seminaries). Later he went to Vienna and Berlin, where he supplemented his rabbinical studies with secular subjects, including the new *Jüdische Wissenschaft,* the scientific study of Jewish history.

In 1882, Claude Goldsmid Montefiore, wealthy scion of two great English-Jewish families, asked Schechter to be his tutor in rabbinics and brought him to London. Schechter was delighted with England and stayed. English Jews enjoyed many freedoms unknown to Jews in Germany, and the famous collections of Hebrew manuscripts and books in the British Museum and the Bodleian Library at Oxford were an additional enticement for Schechter.

In 1890, Schechter was appointed Lecturer in Talmud at Cambridge. By then he had acquired something of a reputation as a scholar and essayist, and at the university his wit and abilities soon brought him warm friends. One of them was Dr. Charles Taylor, mathematician, eminent Christian Hebraist, and Master of St. John's College.

Then two remarkable women entered the story: Mrs. Agnes Smith Lewis and Mrs. Margaret Dunlop Gibson, twin sisters who were "incredibly learned . . . unbelievably eccentric . . . and wholly inseparable."[3] Both women were wealthy Scottish widows who were devoted to biblical scholarship, travel, and the collecting of early manuscripts. Other Victorian women might stay at home as they were expected to, but the "Giblews" had already made three daring trips on camels from Cairo to St. Catherine's Monastery at Mt. Sinai to study and photograph the ancient writings in the library there. In May 1896 they returned to Cambridge from yet another Near Eastern trip, this time to Palestine and Egypt. There they had purchased ancient leaves of Hebrew writings that they asked Schechter to examine.

To his astonishment, Schechter recognized one leaf as part of the long-lost Hebrew text of the book of Ben Sira, a Jewish writing of the second century B.C., also known as Ecclesiasticus. Considered part of the bible by Catholics, and part of the Apocrypha by Protestants and Jews, The Wisdom of Ben Sira had not been seen in its Hebrew version for about a thousand years. It had been dropped from the Old Testament canon by Jews as not truly biblical, but it had been preserved in the Greek and other translations by the early Christian Church.

Schechter's discovery established for the first time that Ecclesiasticus had indeed been written originally in Hebrew. (In 1964, fragments of an original Hebrew text of Ben Sira were found at Masada by Yigael Yadin. They showed that Schechter's leaf, although inscribed in the Middle Ages, was the authentic Hebrew text and not a translation from Greek into Hebrew as some skeptics had suggested.)

Mrs. Lewis now reported Schechter's discovery to the press. This prompted others to search for additional Ben Sira material. Soon two Oxford scholars announced that they had found more Ben Sira leaves among recent acquisitions of the Bodleian. Suddenly a flurry of fresh press reports told of other Bible-related pieces that had been recently acquired by English libraries. As Schechter personally examined many of these, he came to suspect what no one else had yet realized: Most of this new material was coming from a single source, and in all likelihood that source was the *genizah* of the thousand-year-old Ben Ezra Synagogue in Fostat, Old Cairo.

Fostat had once been a major center of Jewry, especially in the eleventh and twelfth centuries, when Egypt, along with much of the Near East, North Africa, and parts of Europe, was under Islamic rule. Its thriving Jewish community had had close connections with sister communities in Babylonia, Palestine, Spain, and other Mediterranean lands. Prominent Jewish scholars and religious leaders, such as Sa'adia ben Joseph (882–942), Yehuda ha-Levi (1075–1141), and the renowned theologian and philosopher Moses Maimonides (1135–1204), either lived in Fostat or stopped off there in their travels.

Schechter hardly dared to dream of what the Fostat synagogue *genizah* might contain. He knew that he must go to Cairo to try to "empty" it and bring the mass of its contents back to Cambridge for scholars to study. Supported by colleagues, he took his plan to the Cambridge authorities and won their approval. His friend, Dr. Taylor, provided the funds for the expedition out of his personal means. In December 1896, Schechter sailed for Egypt armed with an impressive letter of recommendation from Cambridge University to Cairo's Jewish leaders, and another to Cairo's Grand Rabbi from the Chief Rabbi of Britain.

Contrary to popular belief, Schechter did not discover the Cairo Genizah and took pains to disclaim that he had. Its existence, as well as that of other *genizahs* in Europe and Asia, had been known, more or less, to several generations of travelers, manuscript hunters, and scholars. Considerable misfortune, however, supposedly awaited those who attempted to remove its contents. One legend told of a great snake that protected the entrance and attacked would-be collectors. Such stories may have played a part in preserving the Genizah's contents over the centuries.

Still another deterrent may have discouraged would-be collectors: the real difficulties they would encounter in trying to enter and search the Genizah proper. It was a kind of attic chamber—dark, airless, and windowless. The entry was a hole reached by climbing a high, shaky ladder that stood against the end-wall of the synagogue's women's gallery. Jacob Saphir, a nineteenth-century scholar and traveler, entered the Genizah in 1864, but he left after two days without retrieving anything of importance; he was defeated by the dust, the dirt, and the hordes of insects.

From the middle of the nineteenth century, however, despite deterrents, Cairo Genizah material found its way into the hands of individuals and institutions in England, Palestine, and elsewhere. Cambridge University acquired its first manuscript fragment from the Cairo Genizah in 1891. Fragments were generally secured from Cairo's dealers in "antikas," and their real source went unrecognized. As for the dealers, they had discovered that *baksheesh,* liberally extended to the keepers of the synagogue, overcame many obstacles.

At least two visitors to the Ben Ezra Synagogue who preceded Schechter managed to secure significant amounts of Genizah material on their own. Both are remembered as among the most industrious and successful collectors of Hebrew manuscripts of their times.

One was Abraham Firkowitch (1786–1874), who appears to have reached Cairo in the late 1860s. Firkowitch was a Karaite rabbi from the Crimea who was especially interested in finding material that supported the Karaite rejection of talmudic Judaism. Two large collections amassed by Firkowitch are part of the important Hebraica holdings of the Saltykov-Scherin Public State Library in Leningrad. The second collection is reported to hold valuable items that probably came from the Genizah.

The second earlier manuscript hunter was Elkan Nathan Adler (1861–1946), London lawyer, bibliophile, and world traveler, who acquired a vast Hebrew library that included approximately five thousand Hebrew manuscripts and fragments, now owned by the Jewish Theological Seminary of New York. In January 1896, Adler was permitted to take away from the Cairo Genizah as much material as he could carry in an old Torah mantle. Schechter talked briefly with Adler before leaving for Cairo.

It remained for Schechter, however, to penetrate the fabled storeroom and to empty it more or less. This feat required every bit of his considerable persuasive powers, his patience, his scholarship and, important as anything, his sheer physical stamina. It also required considerable *baksheesh* to mollify the synagogue's custodians. After all, with every fragment he took, he was depriving them of their "fringe benefits"—the items they could sell surreptitiously to visitors and dealers.

The incomplete record suggests that Schechter spent six to eight weeks in securing his prize. He left for Egypt in mid-December 1896. By the latter part of January 1897, he wrote from Cairo that the work was done "thoroughly" and that he intended to send the results back to England. He added his frequent complaint: "People steal fragments and sell them to the dealers."[4]

Jews, since ancient times, have buried worn-out or defective copies of

11. Balcony of Cairo synagogue
where two copies of the Damascus Document
were discovered in 1897. The entrance to the
storeroom, *or* genizah, *is at upper center.*

Courtesy Meir Ben-Dov, QADMONIOT XV, No. 1, 1982.

*12. Interior of Cairo synagogue where
Damascus Documents were found in storeroom
off balcony at upper left.*

sacred texts to keep them from desecration. Normally, a *genizah* attached to a synagogue, as in Cairo, served as a temporary storage place until its contents could be buried in consecrated ground. No one knows why the contents of the Cairo Genizah were permitted—fortunately—to accumulate for centuries. But Schechter's proposal to the Grand Rabbi and the lay heads of the Cairo Jewish community to "empty" the Genizah and to take away its "almost" buried works must have struck them at first as an unthinkable profanation.

Here Schechter's vast knowledge of Jewish law and tradition undoubtedly stood him in great stead—and provided the assurances that, on the contrary, the transfer to a great university would mean the respected preservation of the Genizah's manuscripts and texts.

In due time the Grand Rabbi drove with Schechter to the Ben Ezra synagogue and showed him around. Schechter wrote: "The Rabbi introduced me to the beadles of the synagogue, who are at the same time the keepers of the Genizah, and authorized me to take from it what, and as much as, I liked."[5] Armed with this critical endorsement that the keepers could hardly ignore, he was at last able to climb into the storeroom. He described what he found:

> It is a battlefield of books, and the literary productions of many centuries had their share in the battle, and their *disjecta membra* are strewn over the area. Some of the belligerents have perished outright, and are literally ground to dust in the terrible struggle for space, whilst others are squeezed into big, unshapely lumps, which . . . can no longer be separated without serious damage."[6]

Inside the Genizah, Schechter also found a serious threat to his health. Every move stirred up the dust of centuries—dust that got into his eyes, throat, every pore. He felt threatened with suffocation, but he persisted. To get the job done, he reluctantly accepted the help of the synagogue's keepers, who declined regular payment but asked for *baksheesh*. Later, he noted dryly that *baksheesh* "besides being a more dignified kind of remuneration, also has the advantage of being expected for services not rendered."[7] Schechter also bought, from a dealer in "antikas" in Cairo, some items that especially interested him—items that quite apparently had just come from the Genizah.

Schechter more or less confined his search to securing manuscript material. He chose few printed works, dismissing them as "parvenus." In a few weeks he had some thirty large bags crammed with his finds. When he ran into difficulties trying to export his material to Liverpool, he turned for help to the Office of the British Agent. The difficulties promptly vanished. Lord Cromer, the British Agent, was a Greek scholar who could readily appreciate the fact that Schechter's fragments would add to England's cultural treasures. He was also the virtual ruler of Egypt.

By early spring—after his only visit to Palestine—Schechter went back to Cambridge. He plunged at once into the enormous task of examining, classifying, conserving, and storing his great haul. He estimated that he had secured one hundred thousand fragments and texts. But today at Cambridge the collection is counted at one hundred forty thousand pieces. It has taken eight decades to preserve, classify, and house all the pieces so they can be readily studied by scholars.

News of Schechter's scholarly exploit spread quickly. Soon he was something of a celebrity. Learned men came to visit him in his workroom in the university library and to get a glimpse of what he had brought back from Cairo. Dr. Taylor came by almost daily to help look for more Ben Sira leaves and to examine, with considerable enjoyment, any new finds.

In June 1898, the senate of Cambridge University was advised that Dr. Taylor and Dr. Schechter had offered the university on certain conditions, "the valuable collection of manuscripts . . . brought back from the Genizah of Old Cairo with the consent of the heads of the Jewish community."[8] The offer was duly accepted on November 10, 1898, thereby establishing the now-famous Taylor-Schechter Genizah Collection of Cambridge University Library.

Schechter's first hope had been to "empty" the Genizah. He did do a splendid job of taking away its oldest material, but he did not empty it, and others finished the task. Today, though there are other important collections of Genizah material (secured both before and after Schechter's expedition) in Oxford, London, New York, Leningrad, and other centers, none matches the collection at Cambridge either in size or in the volume of significant findings.

Until the discovery of the Dead Sea Scrolls, the Taylor-Schechter Genizah collection easily represented the most important recovery of ancient Hebrew manuscript material in modern times. For some, because it has furnished so many fresh insights into forgotten centuries of Jewish life and thought, it still is.

Schechter himself left Cambridge in 1902 to become president of the Jewish Theological Seminary of New York, a post he held until his death in 1915. In the United States, he helped to build the then-struggling

Conservative movement into a major institution of contemporary Judaism. He came to New York hoping to initiate studies in a number of areas suggested by some of the Genizah fragments he had just examined. But the demands of his post soon made this impractical and he began to encourage others at the seminary to undertake such studies.

He did, however, continue to work on two unusual writings he had found in the Cairo Genizah. In 1910 he published the results, a two-volume work entitled *Documents of Jewish Sectaries*. Volume II was called *Fragments of the Book of Commandments by Anan*. Anan is regarded as the eighth-century founder of Karaism, a Jewish schism based on the literal interpretation of Scripture, rejecting the Talmud or Oral Tradition. Karaism still exists and has a small number of followers. Volume I contained Schechter's *Fragments of a Zadokite Work* and was devoted to the now-famous Damascus Document, which would one day be referred to as the first Dead Sea Scroll.

The Damascus Document (CD is its scholarly abbreviation) is a codex—a book. It consists of two partially overlapping and incomplete manuscripts. The first (A) dates to the tenth century, and the second and shorter manuscript (B) dates to the twelfth century. The language of both is biblical Hebrew and reflects none of the later developments in the Hebrew language that took place after Jerusalem fell to the Romans in 70 A.D. From this Schechter correctly concluded that the original text of his two medieval manuscripts must have been written before the Roman destruction of the Temple.

The Damascus Document reveals the history of a Jewish sect that saw itself as the True Israel and was in bitter opposition to the Jewish religious leaders in Jerusalem. The sect's beginnings are traced to an "Age of Wrath," which occurred in about 196 B.C., 390 years after the Babylonian destruction of Jerusalem in 586 B.C. During the Age of Wrath, the document indicates, pious people groped for the way to righteousness. A "Teacher of Righteousness" sent by God arose to guide them. But a powerful enemy arose also, in the person of the "Man of Scoffing." Accordingly, the Teacher and his faithful followers fled from Judea to "the Land of Damascus." There they adopted a "New Covenant," and there, too, the Teacher was "gathered in." He was expected to arise again as a Messiah "in the end of the days."

The second section of the Damascus Document contains the laws of the sect. These reflect a highly structured organization. The sectaries were divided into priests (who were called *"b'nei Zadok"*—the sons of Zadok), Levites, Israelites, and proselytes. The laws also reflect the sect's own interpretation of certain biblical injunctions, and include among other matters strict observance of the Sabbath, strict monogamy without divorce, and rigid rules of cleanliness as a part of religious observance. The sect also followed a heterodox calendar of twelve months of thirty days each, plus four intercalary days.

From the fact that the priests were called the sons of Zadok and other evidence, Schechter advanced the hypothesis that the people of his manuscripts were the same mysterious "Sect of the Zadokites" referred to in the little-known early writings of the Karaites.

Zadok, to whom the Damascus Document makes direct reference, was King David's chief priest and the founder of the line from which the High Priest of the Temple was always chosen until the second century B.C. Then, under the ruling Greeks, the High Priest's office went to the highest bidder, and under the later Maccabees, the Hasmoneans themselves occupied the office. But to the Teacher of Righteousness and his followers, such High Priests were illegitimate. The members of the sect apparently saw themselves as the inheritors of Zadokite tradition and practice and thus the true upholders of Jewish religious belief.

Schechter could only offer a hypothesis about the identity of the sect. But he made a number of observations about their way of life that are startling to read today because his descriptions border, so it seems, on prophecy.

Noting several references to their then-unknown works, he writes: "The Sect must also have been in possession of some Pseudepigrapha now lost." A little later he writes: "This might suggest that the Sect was in possession of some sort of manual containing the tenets of the Sect, and perhaps a regular set of rules of discipline."[9]

Fifty years later, with the discovery of the Dead Sea Scrolls, many of the lost Pseudepigrapha began to make their reappearance. Included was one scroll with "a regular set of rules of discipline" (now known as The Community Rule or Manual of Discipline-1QS).

The publication of the Damascus Document anticipated the discovery of the Dead Sea Scrolls in still another way. Shortly after the scrolls were found, exaggerated claims appeared about their relationship to early Christianity.* Some even identified the Teacher of Righteousness in the scrolls as Jesus. Others saw the Qumran sect as a direct forerunner of Christianity, led possibly by John the Baptist. These same assertions had all been made before, shortly after Schechter published the Damascus

*See Chapter 14.

וְעַתָּה שִׁמְעוּ כָּל יוֹדְעֵי צֶדֶק וּבִינוּ בְּמַעֲשֵׂי

אֵל כִּי רִיב לוֹ עִם כָּל בָּשָׂר וּמִשְׁפָּט יַעֲשֶׂה בְּכָל מְנַאֲצָיו

כִּי בְּמָעֳלָם אֲשֶׁר עֲזָבוּהוּ הִסְתִּיר פָּנָיו מִיִּשְׂרָאֵל וּמִמִּקְדָּשׁוֹ

וַיִּתְּנֵם לֶחָרֶב וּבְזָכְרוֹ בְּרִית רִאשׁוֹנִים הִשְׁאִיר שְׁאֵרִית

לְיִשְׂרָאֵל וְלֹא נְתָנָם לְכָלָה וּבְקֵץ חָרוֹן שְׁנִים שְׁלֹשׁ מֵאוֹת

וְתִשְׁעִים לְתִתּוֹ אוֹתָם בְּיַד נְבוּכַדְנֶאצַּר מֶלֶךְ בָּבֶל

פְּקָדָם וַיַּצְמַח מִיִּשְׂרָאֵל וּמֵאַהֲרֹן שׁוֹרֶשׁ מַטַּעַת לִירוֹשׁ

אֶת אַרְצוֹ וּלְדַשֵּׁן בְּטוּב אַדְמָתוֹ וַיָּבִינוּ בַעֲוֹנָם וַיֵּדְעוּ כִּי

אֲנָשִׁים אֲשֵׁמִים הֵם וַיִּהְיוּ כְעִוְרִים וְכִמְגַשְׁשִׁים דֶּרֶךְ

שָׁנִים עֶשְׂרִים וַיָּבֶן אֵל אֶל מַעֲשֵׂיהֶם כִּי בְּלֵב שָׁלֵם דְּרָשׁוּהוּ

וַיָּקֶם לָהֶם מוֹרֵה צֶדֶק לְהַדְרִיכָם בְּדֶרֶךְ לִבּוֹ וַיּוֹדַע

לְדֹרוֹת אַחֲרוֹנִים אֵת אֲשֶׁר עָשָׂה בְּדוֹר דּוֹר אַחֲרוֹן בַּעֲדַת בֹּגְדִים

הֵם סָרֵי דֶרֶךְ הִיא הָעֵת אֲשֶׁר הָיָה כָתוּב עָלֶיהָ כְּפָרָה סוֹרֵרָה

כֵּן סָרַר יִשְׂרָאֵל בַּעֲמֹד אִישׁ הַלָּצוֹן אֲשֶׁר הִטִּיף לְיִשְׂרָאֵל

מֵימֵי כָזָב וַיַּתְעֵם בְּתֹהוּ לֹא דֶרֶךְ לְהַשַּׁח גַּבְהוּת עוֹלָם וְלָסוּר

מִנְּתִיבוֹת צֶדֶק וְלַסִּיעַ גְּבוּל אֲשֶׁר גָּבְלוּ רִאשֹׁנִים בְּנַחֲלָתָם לְמַעַן

הַדְבֵּק בָּהֶם אֶת אָלוֹת בְּרִיתוֹ לְהַסְגִּירָם לְחֶרֶב נֹקֶמֶת נְקַם

בְּרִית בַּעֲבוּר אֲשֶׁר דָּרְשׁוּ בַּחֲלָקוֹת וַיִּבְחֲרוּ בְּמַהֲתַלּוֹת וַיְצַפּוּ

לְפִרְצוֹת וַיִּבְחֲרוּ בְּטוּב הַצַּוָּאר וַיַּצְדִּיקוּ רָשָׁע וַיַּרְשִׁיעוּ צַדִּיק

וַיַּעַבְרוּ בְרִית וַיָּפֵרוּ חֹק וַיָּגוֹדּוּ עַל נֶפֶשׁ צַדִּיק וְכָל הוֹלְכֵי

תָמִים תִּעֲבָה נַפְשָׁם וַיִּרְדְּפוּם לֶחֶרֶב וַיָּסִיסוּ לְרִיב עָם וַיִּחַר אַף

13. Column from Damascus Document found
in 1897 in Cairo synagogue.

Document. On Christmas Day, 1910, a front-page news story in *The New York Times* carried the following explosive headlines:

JEWISH MANUSCRIPT ANTEDATING GOSPELS

DR. SCHECHTER FINDS A WRITING OF
THE FIRST CENTURY OF THE
CHRISTIAN ERA

REFERS TO ''NEW COVENANT''

DESCRIBES PERSONAGES BELIEVED TO BE
CHRIST, JOHN THE BAPTIST, AND
THE APOSTLE PAUL

One had to read the story very carefully to discover that it was not Schechter who had linked the Damascus Document with the beginnings of Christianity. The headline-catching theory had been advanced by Dr. George Margoliouth, Custodian of Hebrew Manuscripts of the British Museum. Reviewing Schechter's publication, Margoliouth had announced his own conclusions regarding the Damascus Document.

According to Margoliouth, the text originated in a "primitive Judeo-Christian body that . . . strove to combine full observance of Mosaic Law with the principles of the 'New Covenant.' " As Margoliouth read the Damascus Document, the sect had two Messiahs. The first, a priestly Messiah descended from Aaron, was John the Baptist. The other, the "Teacher of Learning" (or Teacher of Righteousness), was surely Jesus! As for the Man of Scoffing, he was none other than Paul, whom the sect abhorred as a Christian Hellenizer.

The *Times* continued to exploit this story of a "Hebrew Gospel earlier than the Gospels of the New Testament" by devoting a full-page feature to it a week later in its Sunday magazine. Schechter himself largely ignored this sensational interpretation, which he had done nothing to encourage. Margoliouth, however, continued to bark his theory at Schechter's heels for several years.

In late 1947 and early 1948, the world had not yet heard of the extraordinary discovery of the Dead Sea Scrolls. But in the tense city of Jerusalem, scholars were examining the first of the newly uncovered scrolls—seven in all. They had been found in a cave near Qumran by Bedouin tribesmen and brought to a dealer in Bethlehem.

The distinguished scholar-archaeologist E. L. Sukenik (father of

Yigael Yadin) immediately saw the connection between the Damascus Document and the Dead Sea Scrolls when he examined the three scrolls he had purchased in late 1947 for the Hebrew University of Jerusalem.

In March 1948, Millar Burrows, director of the American Schools of Oriental Research, independently recognized the relationship. With two young scholars, John C. Trever and William H. Brownlee—both now famous for their Dead Sea Scroll research—Burrows examined the four remaining scrolls, which were then owned by the Metropolitan Samuel, head of the Syrian Orthodox monastery of St. Mark. The Metropolitan had bought them from the same dealer who had sold the first three scrolls to Dr. Sukenik.

The scrolls included both the Habakkuk Commentary (1QpHab) and the Manual of Discipline (or the Community Rule-1QS), the two works most clearly related to Schechter's Damascus Document. Burrows, looking at the Habakkuk Commentary, was struck by the similarity of its details to the strange document that he recalled had been recovered years before in the Cairo Genizah. The three scholars immediately secured Schechter's publication *Fragments of a Zadokite Work* from the school's library.

"The similarity of the contents was unmistakable," Burrows wrote later. "I remember Brownlee's enthusiasm when he found the Teacher of Righteousness and other characters of the Habakkuk Commentary in the Damascus Document."[10] Now it was clear. The sect of the Dead Sea Scrolls and the sect of the Damascus Document were the same.

The relationship between the Qumran sect and the sect described in the Damascus Document was soon to be pinned down beyond any doubt. In September 1952, Bedouin tribesmen discovered what are now known as Qumran Caves 4 and 6. Archaeologists found little in the way of fragments in Cave 6, but that little included small bits of a copy of the Damascus Document! These bits have been dated to about 80–75 B.C.

Qumran Cave 4 contained nearly fifteen thousand scroll fragments representing over five hundred manuscripts. From these, scholars eventually identified fragments of no fewer than seven copies of the Damascus Document!

J. T. Milik, one of the editors of the Dead Sea Scrolls, has studied all of the Damascus Document fragments found at Qumran. He has concluded, as Schechter had earlier, that the Genizah text is incomplete and lacks both its beginning and ending. These lacunae have now been partly restored by the Qumran fragments. The same fragments have supplied additional regulations by which the scroll sect was governed. Milik has also shown that the paging in Manuscript A of the Genizah text is out of order and he has corrected it.

With the fragments from Qumran, scholars have reestablished what the complete Damascus Document said. But the new fragments only supplement, they do not supplant, the manuscripts that Solomon Schechter found in the Genizah. From the Genizah documents, Schechter gave us our first picture of the people of the scrolls—somewhat blurred, but recognizable—well before the scrolls were discovered at Qumran. And from all the rediscovered writings, today's scholars have extracted new insights into who the scroll people really were.

CHAPTER 6

ESSENE ORIGINS—
PALESTINE OR BABYLONIA?

HERSHEL SHANKS

This chapter explains in historical context why the Damascus Document is so important in determining Essene origins. In Chapter 2, Harvard's Frank Cross gave his historical reconstruction of Essene origins in Palestine during the Hasmonean dynasty when the high priesthood was usurped. In this chapter, we consider an alternate theory, propounded by Father Jerome Murphy-O'Connor of the École Biblique in Jerusalem—that Essene origins should be traced to Babylonia during the Judean exile. Murphy-O'Connor's hypothesis is intriguing; it relies heavily on the Damascus Document and the flight to Damascus described there.

This chapter also considers what eventually happened to the Essenes—at least to those who remained in Babylonia. They may have resurfaced hundreds of years later in a sect of Jews known as Karaites, some of whom survive to this day. Hitler wanted to exterminate them; to save their lives, rabbinical authorities ruled that they were not Jews. —ED.

— · —

S cholars have proposed two basic theories concerning the origin of the people who wrote the Dead Sea Scrolls. One theory suggests that the Essenes originated in Palestine, the other in Babylonia. The Damascus Document figures prominently in the formulation of both theories.

In the Palestine-origin theory, the Essene movement was a reaction against the Hellenization of Palestinian Judaism. This process of Hellenization began almost imperceptibly in the third century B.C. In the first part of the second century B.C., however, the forces of Hellenization gained new ground both culturally and politically. Then, in 172 B.C., Onias III, the legitimate High Priest, was murdered in Jerusalem: Onias was a Zadokite, a priest who was descended from Zadok (King David's high priest and originator of the line of High Priests of the Temple in Jerusalem). In Onias' stead, the Syrian overlords appointed Meneleus, a highly Hellenized Jew who was not of the Zadokite line. To many of the faithful, Meneleus could only be a usurper.

Matters were made still worse by the increasingly forced Hellenization and religious oppression of the Syrian overlord, King Antiochus IV. In 165 B.C. Judea finally revolted. Under the brilliant military leadership of Judas Maccabeus, the revolt was successful, and an independent Jewish state was once again established. (This victory is still celebrated by Jews in the festival of Hanukkah.)

Thus began the Hasmonean line of Jewish kings—first Judas himself (165–160 B.C.), then his brother Jonathan (160–143 B.C.), and then, lastly, his brother Simon (143–134 B.C.).

As matters turned out, however, the Hasmoneans brought not a return to orthodoxy but increased Hellenization. Even Judas himself signed a treaty of friendship with the Roman Senate and employed partly Hellenized Jews as his ambassadors. Finally, in 152 B.C., Jonathan had himself appointed High Priest—another usurpation; for many Jews this act was a great provocation and the strongest reason for abhorring the Hasmoneans.

According to the Palestinian theory of Essene origins, it was in this atmosphere that the Essene movement began. Jews, disgusted with what they believed to be the pollution of their ancestral religion and revolted by the usurpation of the High Priesthood by non-Zadokites, rallied behind a man they called Moreh Tzedek, the Teacher of Righteousness. No doubt the Teacher of Righteousness was of the Zadokite line, a legitimate claimant to the title of High Priest. He was opposed, however, by the Wicked Priest who ruled illegitimately in Jerusalem.

The faithful retreated to the desert[1] to live a life of ritual purity, observing the ancient law, following the old calendar that marked the holy times, and awaiting the day when the Teacher of Righteousness would be accepted by all Jews as High Priest and would return once again to Jerusalem. This is the Palestinian theory of Essene origins.

The Babylonian theory of Essene origins traces the beginning of this strange sect to Jews in Babylonia who had been deported there after the destruction of the First Temple in 586 B.C. Many of these Jews, deported from their Judean homeland, perceived the Babylonian Exile as divine punishment. As an appropriately submissive response to this divine judgment, they bound themselves as a group to a perfect observance of the law, determined that history should not repeat itself. Some of this group—whom we may call Essenes—returned to Palestine at what they must have regarded as a propitious moment, the victory of Judas Maccabeus and the renewal of an independent Jewish state. Once there, however, they were bitterly disappointed by the Hellenized forms of Judaism that controlled the state. After an initial attempt to bring their erring brethren to the truth, they retreated to the isolation of Qumran, near the northern end of the Dead Sea. Led by the Teacher of Righteousness, the Essenes believed that adherence to their precepts was the one sure refuge against the coming messianic judgment.

Much of the support for this Babylonian-origin theory comes from the Damascus Document, especially its historical allusions. For example, the Damascus Document alludes to leaving the land of Judah (CD* 4:2; 6:5) and going to the land of the North (CD 7:13) or the land of Damascus (CD 6:5; 20:12). Other passages in the Damascus Document suggest that the Essene movement had been in existence long before the Teacher of Righteousness appeared on the scene.

This earlier origin of the sect is reflected in a story contained in the Damascus Document about the digging of a well of the Law. Some of the diggers of the well do so in response to divine call; others do so on the basis of precepts given to them by the Teacher of Righteousness. The first group is identified as "the returnees of Israel who went out of the land of Judah and were exiled in the land of Damascus." (Qumran, incidentally, is in the land of Judah, so if the passage is to be understood literally, a non-Palestinian journey must be referred to by those who "were exiled in the land of Damascus.")

The Damascus Document contains a historical summary (CD 2:18–

---

*CD is the abbreviation scholars use to designate the Cairo copies of the Damascus Document.

3:12) that culminates with the Babylonian Exile. According to the Damascus Document, among those who survived the Exile, "God established his covenant with Israel forever, revealing to them the hidden things in which all Israel had strayed" (CD 3:13–14). According to Jerome Murphy-O'Connor, the leading proponent of the Babylonian-origin theory, "Israel," in this quotation, refers to the Essenes and "all Israel" refers to the rest of Judaism that strayed. The passage, he says, refers to what the Damascus Document calls the "new covenant in the land of Damascus" (CD 6:19; 19:33–34). "Damascus," according to the Babylonian-origin theory, is a symbolic name for Babylon. This symbolism is made clear in a passage from Amos (5:26–27) that is quoted in the Damascus Document. In this passage from Amos, God speaks of having ordered the exiles from His tent "in Damascus," obviously meaning Babylon.* Similarly, this same passage from Amos is quoted in Acts 7:43, but Babylon is substituted for Damascus.

There are still other indications that the Essenes originated in Babylonia. For example, the great American biblical archaeologist, William F. Albright, pointed out long ago that vocalization of certain Assyro-Babylonian words in the famous Isaiah Scroll from the Dead Sea caves reflects a Babylonian prototype.[2]

Much of the legislation contained in the Damascus Document is designed for a community living in a non-Jewish environment. Many of the regulations govern dealings with Gentiles. Yet Judah can hardly be considered a Gentile environment, despite its profound Hellenization. These regulations, according to the Babylonian-origin theory, were intended for use while the sect was living in Damascus—that is, Babylonia.

The conclusion of the Babylonian-origin theory is that the Damascus Document was originally written by Jews living in the Diaspora, in Babylonian exile. The importance of this document—already ancient when the Jews founded their desert community in Qumran—is reflected in the fact that at least nine copies were kept in the Qumran library. Fragments of these documents were found in the Qumran caves by Bedouin and archaeologists two thousand years later.

Those who maintain the Palestinian-origin of the Essenes contend that the journey to Damascus is simply a symbolic journey, not a real one.

How did this document reflecting Essene origins get to the Cairo Synagogue? The answer may tell us something about the subsequent history of the Qumran sect.

---

*Others read the passage from Amos as ordering the exiles to Damascus. In either case, the symbolism is the same. Damascus is used for Babylon.

According to the Damascus Document, not all those who entered into "the new covenant in the land of Damascus" returned to Palestine. Some remained in Babylonia. What happened to those who remained we do not know.

But over thirteen hundred years after the deportation of Jews to Babylonia following the destruction of Jerusalem in 586 B.C., a new Jewish movement arose in Babylonia. It originated in the eighth century A.D. and was started by a certain Anan ben David who attempted to purify Judaism by a return to the fundamentals of biblical law. This new movement, whose adherents were called Karaites, rejected the Talmud or oral law, which they considered inauthentic accretions to biblical law. The Karaites, like the Essenes, rigorously insisted on exact adherence to a literal interpretation of the written or biblical law.

The remnants of the Essenes or their descendants who remained in Babylonia may have provided some of the inspiration and even some of the core adherents to the Karaites.

No doubt the Essenes represented the ultraconservative branch of Babylonian Jewry. They believed they alone knew, in the words of the Damascus Document, "the exact interpretation of the Law" (CD 4:8; 6:14). Like the Essenes, the Karaites believed that their teaching represented the pure, original Mosaic faith, free of later distortions and corruptions. In this, as well as in other aspects, Karaite doctrine parallels the Essene movement, although this doctrine developed more than a millennium after the Essenes. In two regulations especially—relating to incest and to the Sabbath fire—there is a detailed affinity between the Essenes and the Karaites. According to Jerome Murphy-O'Connor, "A direct relationship [between the Essenes and the Karaites] seems undeniable, and the simplest hypothesis would be that some members of the New Covenant had remained in Babylon and had maintained their identity with the tenacity common to Jewish sects." Eventually, they became Karaites.*

The Karaite movement was a powerful sect within Judaism for many centuries. The Karaites zealously opposed the "rabbanites," that is, those who accepted postbiblical rabbinic regulations and the binding nature of the Talmud or oral law. At its height in the tenth and eleventh centuries,

---

*Even before Solomon Schechter published the Damascus Document, scholars of Karaite history noted the similarities between the Essenes and Karaites. The *Jewish Encyclopedia* of 1902–1905 states that the Karaites "borrowed" from the Essenes. Other scholars reject this contention, however, arguing that "nowhere in early Karaite literature so far known is there mention of the discovery of pre-Karaite documents confirming the righteousness of the Karaite teachings" (*Encyclopedia Judaica,* Vol. 10, p. 762 [1972]).

the Karaite movement had millions of adherents in centers in Egypt, Syria, Palestine, and Persia, as well as in Babylonia. Later, Karaite centers were established in Spain, and in the Ottoman Empire and Eastern Europe. Remnants of the Karaites continued to exist for centuries after the movement ceased to be a significant force in Jewish life, just as, it is conjectured, pockets of Essenes continued to live in Babylonia perhaps even at the time the Karaite movement originated there. At the end of World War II, there were still twelve thousand Karaites in the world.* Even today seven thousand Karaites live in Israel.

Copies of the Damascus Document were probably handed down and recopied by descendants of the Essenes in Babylonia. These copies passed into the hands of the Karaites. Two copies of the Damascus Document, perhaps already containing some Karaite glosses, were then taken to the Egyptian synagogue by Karaites who moved to Cairo.

Solomon Schechter himself detected Karaite elements in the Damascus Document. He found references to a sect of Zadokites in Karaite literature and saw relationships between this literature and references in the Damascus Document. On this basis, he was able to hypothesize that the Damascus Document actually contained "the constitution and teachings of a sect long ago extinct."[3]

The circle became complete when fragments of at least nine copies of the Damascus Document were found among the Dead Sea Scrolls at Qumran.

---

*Nazi authorities were greatly concerned as to whether the Karaites were Jews. They posed this question to three rabbinical authorities who, in order to save the Karaites, all gave the opinion that Karaites were not of Jewish origin. The Karaites were spared by the Nazis.

III

THE TEMPLE SCROLL

CHAPTER 7

THE TEMPLE SCROLL—
THE LONGEST DEAD SEA SCROLL

YIGAEL YADIN

Until his untimely death in 1984, Yigael Yadin was Israel's foremost archaeol-
ogist. His two most famous excavations were Masada, where the Zealots made
their last stand against the Roman conquerors who destroyed Jerusalem in 70
A.D.; and Hazor, which he believed was conquered by Joshua when the
Israelites first entered the Promised Land.

In this chapter, Yadin describes the great Temple Scroll, which he acquired
just after the Six-Day War in 1967. He recounts his earlier aborted effort to
acquire this scroll, its actual recovery, and then the laborious effort to unroll it.
We get a marvelous feel for what it is like working with such a scroll. (Later,
in Chapter 19, we will learn what it is like working with tiny fragments, as
compared to the largely intact Temple Scroll.)

According to Yadin, the Temple Scroll was the Torah of the Essenes. He
describes its contents in some detail and then considers how the Temple Scroll
can help us better understand the doctrines of early Christianity, a topic
discussed in greater detail in Chapter 14. This discussion is an excellent
example of how scholars use the Dead Sea Scrolls to illuminate early Chris-
tianity and rabbinic Judaism.

An appendix to this chapter describes the temple envisioned in the Temple
Scroll. —ED.

—·—

On August 1, 1960, I received a letter from a man who identified himself as a Virginia clergyman. The letter stated that the writer was in a position to negotiate the sale of "important, authentic discoveries of Dead Sea Scrolls."* Obviously, he contacted me because of my intimate involvement in Israel's acquisition of the original Dead Sea Scrolls six years earlier.

In a subsequent letter, Mr. Z, as I shall refer to him, indicated the price for an entire scroll would be around one million dollars, since the Jordanian dealer who possessed the material (and here he named a well-known dealer involved in previous transactions for the purchase of Dead Sea Scrolls, whom I shall call "the dealer" [actually, Kando†]) "knows their true value." I informed Mr. Z of my willingness to negotiate only if the price was reasonable in comparison to the price paid to the Metropolitan Samuel for the original Dead Sea Scrolls.

An exchange of correspondence ensued, and on October 7, I purchased from Mr. Z—or through him—a fragment of the Psalms Scroll from Cave 11 at Qumran. The pieces adjacent to this fragment were in the Rockefeller Museum, and how Mr. Z obtained this fragment— before the other fragments were obtained by the museum, or after—we shall never know. In any event, it was clear he had access to authentic materials from the Dead Sea Scroll caves.

Then on May 29, 1961, Mr. Z wrote that he had for sale not a fragment but an entire scroll. Moreover, the price was realistic: $100,000. On June 1, 1961, I replied that I would try to raise the $100,000 and would be in touch with him soon.

Shortly thereafter, I left for London, where I spent some time on sabbatical. There, by letter of August 9, 1961, Mr. Z informed me that he had clarified all details of the sale with the dealer and that the scroll in question was a large one: "nine inches wide, about fifteen to eighteen feet long." Since, as Mr. Z said in his letter, a purchaser would no doubt be concerned with the authenticity of the scroll, he was enclosing a fragment that had broken off from the scroll.

I examined the envelope and found a fragment of a scroll wrapped in tin foil from a package of cigarettes. The back of the fragment was reinforced with a piece of a British postage stamp. I immediately saw that the fragment was authentic!

*See Chapter 9.
†See Chapter 1.

It did not surprise me that Mr. Z would send me the fragment like this. He had previously sent me the Psalms Scroll fragment in a manila envelope wrapped in a napkin, trusting me to send him the money.

In his letter Mr. Z asked me to make an evaluation of the new fragment and send it back to him by return mail—which is exactly what I did. I advised Mr. Z that the fragment seemed to belong to a genuine scroll of the Dead Sea type and was written by a good scribe.

On August 29, 1961, Mr. Z wrote back that the asking price for the scroll was now $750,000. Angered by this increase in price, I replied that his letter "baffled and infuriated me since it indicates you never took seriously what I told you regarding the price . . . If things remain as you state in your letter, I am afraid you can rule me out as a customer." Soon thereafter I left England for the United States where wearisome and often detailed negotiations continued with Mr. Z.

Finally, a deal was struck. The agreed price was $130,000. An intricate six-page agreement to be signed by the dealer was drafted by a lawyer. The agreement provided that prior to payment we would examine the scroll itself for authenticity and for its correspondence to the fragment. We also agreed on a $10,000 down payment, which I gave to Mr. Z, and he in turn once again gave me the fragment I had returned to him so that I could eventually compare it to the entire scroll. I also gave Mr. Z $1,500 to finance a trip to Bethlehem, then under Jordanian control, which he said was necessary to conclude the agreement with the dealer.

The agreement prepared by the lawyer was never signed by the dealer. On December 1, 1961, I received a letter from Mr. Z saying that difficulties had arisen: The price was now $200,000. Since I had the fragment, he decided to hold the $10,000 "in order to work in good faith on both sides since you have the all-important piece." Further correspondence ensued in January and February 1962, Mr. Z asking for further advances and I trying to get back the $10,000.

The last letter received from Mr. Z was on May 17, 1962. He again made "promises" and again pleaded for more money. That was the last we ever heard from him.*

I consoled myself with the thought that at least I had the fragment. I tried to put the matter out of my mind but obviously could not. In 1963

*I am still keeping his confidence, however, by not revealing his name. I want all these people—whether they are robbers or not (and it is a cloak-and-dagger business)—to know that as far as I am concerned, if they tell me not to reveal their identities, I won't. Otherwise, we have no chance of getting more scrolls. And I believe there still might be another scroll or some fragments here or there. For the same reason, I don't call the dealer by name, even though many know who he is.

I began my excavations at Masada, Herod's desert fortress and the place where the Zealots made their last stand against the Romans. This excavation was a consuming interest, but I nevertheless continued to peruse the scientific archaeological publications concerning the scrolls, wondering whether I would find some reference to a new Dead Sea Scroll. Nothing appeared, however.

— · —

If Masada was not enough to put the matter out of my mind, the Six-Day War in June 1967 was. I was then serving as military advisor to the prime minister. On June 7, the Israel Defense Force captured the Old City of Jerusalem and Bethlehem. Suddenly, I recalled the scroll. The dealer involved had a shop in East Jerusalem and lived in Bethlehem. Both he and his scroll might be within Israeli jurisdiction! I immediately reported this to Prime Minister Levi Eshkol, who put at my disposal a lieutenant colonel from military intelligence.

After I briefed the lieutenant colonel about the supposed scroll and the fragment in my possession, he went to the dealer's shop and informed him of the scroll fragment we had obtained from Mr. Z. After brief negotiations, the dealer agreed to take the officer to his home in Bethlehem. There, the dealer removed from beneath some floor tiles a shoe box containing the scroll. He also produced a cigar box containing fragments that had become detached from the scroll. Later, it was discovered that the dealer had hidden additional fragments behind family pictures, both in his own home and in his brother's home.

The military government confiscated the scroll and fragments in accordance with Jordanian law governing antiquities. Although the dealer had illegally concealed the scroll's existence from the Jordanian authorities and had kept it under dreadful conditions that caused extensive damage, especially to the upper part of the scroll, it was nevertheless decided to pay him for the scroll—for the simple reason that we want to encourage such people to come forward if they have additional scroll materials. The amount finally agreed upon with the dealer, after negotiations lasting almost a year, was $105,000.

Unfortunately, I was given the job of raising the money. This task proved not to be so onerous, however, because of the generosity of Mr. Leonard Wolfson of Great Britain, who contributed $75,000 for this purpose. The balance was paid by the Israeli government. Thus ended the saga of the scroll's acquisition. The saga of its unrolling began.

I first held the scroll in my hands on the evening of Wednesday, June

14. The Temple Scroll as recovered from the home of a Bethlehem antiquities dealer after the Six-Day War.

15. Broken-off fragments of the Temple Scroll kept in a cigar box by Bethlehem antiquities dealer.

16. Interior of Qumran Cave 11, where the
Temple Scroll was recovered by Bedouin.

8, 1967, the day Israeli forces united East and West Jerusalem. On June 11, the war was over, and we started the task of unrolling the scroll shortly thereafter. The work was done under the direction of Joseph "Dodo" Shenhav of the Israel Museum.

The first part of the scroll we unrolled was a separate wad we call Wad Y, which had been wrapped in cellophane inside the shoebox. The fragments in this wad turned out to be the beginning of the extant part of the scroll. Letters and even words had peeled off some of the columns of script and attached themselves, in mirror image, on the backs of preceding columns (the scroll was rolled with the end on the innermost core). The first extant column of Wad Y had the imprint from a preceding but now lost column; unfortunately, the mirror image was so faint I could not decipher the letters. I could conclude only that there must have been at least one earlier column, so I called the first extant column II. Wad Y contained columns II through V.

Next we tried to unroll what we call Wad X, which contained columns VI through XIII. Wad X had been rolled so tightly that at times the entire text was preserved in mirror image on the back of the previous column. Sometimes the text was preserved *only* in this manner.

Other wads were slowly and carefully separated and pieces gradually fitted together and into the main text, based on the contours of the edges. In the end, we were left with a wad consisting of a black macerated mass containing the remnants of two or three columns, but we could neither separate it nor decipher the letters. We photographed the amorphous mass from every angle, with different lightings, with regular, orthochromatic, and infrared film—all with negligible results.

Fortunately, the scroll proper was for the most part easier to unroll than the wads. In general, we used the process developed by H. J. Plenderlieth to open the original Dead Sea Scrolls—softening the outer roll by a process of humidification at 75 to 80 percent. When this process did not work, we used another developed by Plenderlieth—applying nearly 100 percent humidity for several minutes, immediately followed by a few minutes of refrigeration. In some cases, we could not use this process, however, because the adjacent writing was in such fragile condition it would have been damaged by the process. In such cases, we had no choice except to leave the pieces stuck together and try to salvage their contents with photographs from back and front against the light. Occasionally, we were compelled to cut the columns lengthwise, a kind of plastic surgery, and then to rejoin them after their separation.

The animal skin on which the scroll is written is extremely thin, indeed the thinnest I have ever encountered. Nowhere is it more than one-tenth of a millimeter thick. Nevertheless, and despite the use of a sharp instrument, the scribe was able to rule in guidelines (so-called "drylines") without making cuts in the skin. Two different hands, called Scribe A and Scribe B, have been detected in the script.

As I have already indicated, the beginning of the scroll is missing, but we know that we have the end because there is a blank sheet at the end of the scroll, as is customary at the end of all Dead Sea Scrolls.

The scroll contains sixty-six columns of text and is twenty-seven feet long. This makes it the longest of all the Dead Sea Scrolls. Previously, the great Isaiah Scroll—twenty-two feet long—containing the entire text of the book of Isaiah—was the longest of the scrolls, which gives some idea of the length of the Temple Scroll.

On the basis of the script, the scroll can be dated to the Late Herodian period, say mid-first century A.D. or a little earlier. But that is the date of this copy, not necessarily the date of the composition it contains.

I believe the date of the composition of the scroll, however, was much earlier—approximately 150–125 B.C. I have several reasons for this conclusion. One is that we found two unpublished fragments from Qumran Cave 4 in the Rockefeller Museum that came from other, earlier copies of this same composition. The earlier of these fragments was written in a Hasmonean script that can be dated to about the last quarter of the second century B.C. (about 125–100 B.C.), so our scroll could have been composed no later than this. Moreover, I believe I can detect historical allusions in the text that would confirm a dating of 150–125 B.C. This subject is treated at some length in my three-volume edition of the scroll.[1]

A more interesting question is, what *was* this composition? It is my belief that this scroll contains nothing less than the basic torah or law of the Essenes who lived at Qumran on the northwestern shore of the Dead Sea. For them it was a holy book, a part of the canon of what we call the Bible, the Torah of the Lord. Moreover, I believe the scroll was composed by the founder of the sect, the venerated Teacher of Righteousness.

I have several reasons for believing this document was the Essene torah, equal in importance to the traditional Torah, which they naturally also venerated as a holy book. Let me list some of the reasons for believing this scroll was the Essene Torah.

The scroll contains long passages from the Pentateuch,* sometimes whole chapters, but the scroll is frequently written in the first person,

---

*The first five books of the Bible, called in Hebrew translation the Torah of Moses.

17. Unrolling a "wad" from the Temple Scroll.

Courtesy Estate of Yigael Yadin

18. *The Temple Scroll.*

with God himself speaking, instead of Moses referring to God in the third person, as is often the case in the parallel Pentateuchal passages. This change is accomplished by replacing the tetragrammaton* LORD in the Pentateuch by "I" or "me" in the Temple Scroll. Even the supplementary laws in the Temple Scroll, which are not in the Pentateuch, are often written in the first person.

Thus, the text of Numbers 30:3 appears in the Temple Scroll as follows: "When a woman vows a vow *to me . . .* " Obviously, the author wished to present the Law as if handed down by God himself, rather than through the mouth of Moses.†

On the other hand, the tetragrammaton is also used in a number of instances in the Temple Scroll. These passages, however, also contain an important clue regarding the canonical or holy status of the Temple Scroll. To understand this clue, a little background is necessary.

Hebrew was originally written in a script scholars refer to as Old Hebrew, or Palaeo-Hebrew. When the Jews returned from exile in Babylon, they brought with them a square "Aramaic" script that gradually replaced the previously used script. However, the earlier Old Hebrew script continued to be used in certain archaizing contexts. For example, during the First and Second Jewish Revolts against Rome in 66–73 A.D. and 132–135 A.D., the Jews minted coins using the older Hebrew script on them. In the Dead Sea Scrolls, the tetragrammaton is sometimes written in Palaeo-Hebrew in the midst of a text otherwise written in the square Aramaic text that was in common use at the time. In the Dead Sea Scrolls, the archaized, Palaeo-Hebrew tetragrammaton generally occurs in noncanonical, that is, nonbiblical, texts. In the books of the Bible preserved at Qumran, the tetragrammaton is written, by contrast, in the square Aramaic script, just like the rest of the text.

In the Temple Scroll, when the tetragrammaton is used, it is written in the square Aramaic script, as in the biblical books found at Qumran. This is another reason to believe that the Temple Scroll was considered by the Essene community as biblical or canonical.

The subject matter and the fact that such a long scroll—nearly thirty feet—was copied several times at Qumran, as we know from the Rocke-

---

*The tetragrammaton is the ineffable and unpronounced name of God, consisting of the four consonants YHWH, often transcribed in English literature as Yahweh.

†Although Moses is never mentioned by name in the existing columns of the scroll, it is clear that God is speaking to Moses, as we know, for example, by a reference to "Aaron your brother" (column XLIV, line 5).

feller Museum fragments, also indicates that it was probably considered a holy book.

The Temple Scroll probably even contains excerpts from certain lost books referred to in the Bible, according to the Essene tradition, which are otherwise unknown. This again requires some background to understand.

While still in the wilderness, the Israelites were implicitly commanded to build a temple for the Lord once they were established in the Promised Land. For example, in Deuteronomy 12:10–11, we read:

> But when you go over the Jordan, and live in the land which the Lord your God gives you to inherit, and when he gives you rest from all your enemies round about, so that you live in safety; then to the place which the Lord your God will choose, to make his name dwell there, thither you shall bring all that I command you; your burnt offerings and your sacrifices, your tithes and the offering that you present, and all your votive offerings which you vow to the Lord.

The building of the Jerusalem Temple was one of the most important tasks enjoined upon the Israelites in the wilderness. But the Bible contains no laws for the plan of the temple. This is a startling omission. Despite detailed laws and descriptions of the Tabernacle and its utensils, the Torah gives no divine law concerning the plan of the temple!

Later biblical writers noticed this unusual omission. The Chronicler explains:

> Then David gave Solomon his son the plan of the vestibule of the temple, and of its houses, its treasuries, its upper rooms, and its inner chambers, and of the room for the mercy seat; and the plan of all that he had in mind for the courts of the house of the Lord (and the details of all the sacred furniture). . . . All this he made clear *by the writing from the hand* of the Lord concerning it, all the work to be done according to the plan (1 Chronicles 28:11–19).

All this was made clear *in writing* from the Lord? Where was this written in the Torah?

According to the rabbis, a scroll existed in which this Torah was written. They even called it the Temple Scroll *(megillat beth ha-mikdash)*. It was given to David, said the rabbis, through Moses, Joshua and the prophets: "The Temple Scroll which the Holy One blessed Be He committed to Moses . . . , Moses . . . transmitted to Joshua . . . and Joshua to the Elders and the Elders to the Prophets and the Prophets to David and David to Solomon" (Martin Buber, ed., *Midrash Samuel,* xv:3(92)).

The scroll we obtained in 1967 contains elaborate plans for the building of the temple.* Indeed, nearly half of the scroll is taken up with the plans for the temple, sacrifices, and the laws of the city of the temple. That is why I decided to call it the Temple Scroll. I do not claim that this scroll contains the text of the scroll supposedly handed down to David (and definitely not the one the rabbis had in mind). But I do believe that the author of this part of the scroll was writing with knowledge of the existence of a Temple Scroll referred to obliquely in the book of Chronicles. Either believing that he was divinely inspired or basing his descriptions on an older tradition, he considered himself to be preserving this missing part of the Torah, referred to in the biblical book of Chronicles. It is interesting to note that the Temple Scroll concentrates on precisely those elements detailed in the passage from Chronicles in which God's missing laws for the plan of his temple are described—the vestibule, the treasuries, the upper rooms, the inner chambers. In the Temple Scroll, God himself speaks in minute detail concerning His temple to be built by the children of Israel. He is the Master Architect, supplying the plans missing from the Torah. At the end of days, in the New Creation, God himself will build the temple.

Another major portion of the Temple Scroll—nearly four columns—is devoted to what I call the Statutes of the King. This portion of the scroll could also be called the Torah of the King or the Laws of the King or even the Constitution of the King. This portion of the scroll contains laws relating to the marriage of the king, rules for mobilization during war, limited rights of the king to booty in war, provision for an advisory council (consisting of twelve priests, twelve Levites, and twelve lay Israelites), provision for subordinate administrative positions of authority, and other such matters. This too may be related to an otherwise unknown book referred to in the Bible.

While still in the wilderness, the Israelites were commanded to appoint a king after they occupied the Promised Land (Deuteronomy 17:14–15). Yet here too there is a startling omission in the Torah. There is almost a complete absence of laws governing the king. There are a few verses in Deuteronomy 17:15–20 and in 1 Samuel 8:11ff. regarding the rights and duties of the king and "he [Samuel] *wrote down in a book* which he laid before the Lord."

What happened to this book? Jews must have asked themselves. In my

---

*See Chapter 8 for a description of this temple.

view, the author of the Temple Scroll believed he was writing down, in the sections of the Temple Scroll I have labeled Statutes of the King, the contents of this missing book, according to his tradition.

In this connection it is interesting that two of the principal points made in 1 Samuel 8:11–12 are that the king "will appoint for himself commanders of thousands and commanders of fifties" and that the king is entitled to a "tenth of your grain and of your vineyards [and] . . . of your flocks." These two subjects are among the most important dealt with in the Temple Scroll's Statutes of the King.

In Deuteronomy 17:18 we are told, "And when he [the king] sits on the throne of his kingdom, he shall write for himself in a book a copy of this law *(mishneh ha-torah ha-zot),* from that which is in charge of the Levitical priests. . . . " This verse is generally considered by scholars to refer to the whole of Deuteronomy, that is, the second copy of the Law or Torah. The rabbis, or at lest some of them, understood this passage to refer to a copy of the previous verse; there were also other speculations. But the author of the Temple Scroll used this verse from Deuteronomy to introduce the Statues of the King. When he quotes this passage, however, he omits the word *copy,* so instead of its being a *"copy* of this law," it reads in the Temple Scroll as if it were the Law itself: "When he [the king] sits on the throne of his kingdom, they [the priests] shall write for him *this* law in a book from that which is in the charge of the priests." Then, as if to emphasize the point, the Temple Scroll adds: "And this is the Law." The Statutes of the King follow.

For all these reasons, it seems clear to me that the Temple Scroll was, for the Essenes, a holy canonical book on a par, for them, with the other books of the Bible.

In this short chapter, it would be impossible to describe in detail the entire contents of the Temple Scroll. The best I can do here is to provide a summary.

The Temple Scroll is above all a book of the Law, laws for the community both for the present and for the time when the true heirs of the Zadokite priesthood would again reign in Jerusalem. I have referred to the long passages relating to the temple, its plan, its furniture and utensils, its sacrifices, and other cultic laws. I have also referred to the Statutes of the King. Other long sections describe various festivals or holy days, many of which are "additional" holidays not mentioned in the Bible, such as the New Barley festival, the New Wine festival, the New Oil festival (all first-fruits festivals), and the Wood Offering festival. Other more familiar festivals whose observance is described in the Temple Scroll include the Feast of Booths and the Day of Atonement. Sometimes the observances are the same as those described in other sources; sometimes they are different. Other laws relate to such things as idolatry, vows and oaths, pure and impure animals, ritual impurities, and laws of testimony.

I have already mentioned some of the characteristics of the scroll: the frequent use of the first person when God speaks, the tetragrammaton (when it appears) in the square Aramaic script as in other biblical Dead Sea Scrolls, and the Herodian and the Hasmonean letter forms that help to date the scroll. Let me allude to a few other characteristics of the scroll.

The author of the scroll is clearly an expert on the text of the Pentateuch. He often merges passages from different parts of the Bible that deal with the same subject into a single smooth-flowing text. Unlike the Bible, the scroll is arranged according to principal themes—the temple, the festivals, the Statutes of the King—and it brings together disparate Pentateuchal passages bearing on these themes.

More important, the author often harmonizes and unifies duplicate, different, and sometimes even conflicting biblical laws. In case of simple duplication, the scroll will combine the two texts by contractions and deletions. This approach is in contrast with that of the rabbis who taught, "Whenever a scriptural passage is repeated, it is because of some new point contained in it" (Babylonian Talmud *Sota 3a*).

When several biblical passages deal with the same subject but their texts contain different, nonconflicting laws, the scroll will combine them into a single integrated text. For example, in Deuteronomy 12:23–24, the people are commanded to refrain from eating blood; it must be thrown on the ground like water. In Leviticus 17:13, the blood is to be covered with earth. In the Temple Scroll, the two commands are combined: "Blood you shall not eat; you shall pour it on the ground like water; and cover it with earth."

When there are conflicts in biblical passages, the scroll will often harmonize them, sometimes by splitting the difference.

Perhaps the overriding characteristic of the laws in the Temple Scroll is their strictness. I shall discuss here one of the most important applications of this principle of strictness. The principle of strictness, however, permeates the entire scroll.

The Pentateuch describes the rules of ritual cleanliness applicable to the Israelite camp in the wilderness (e.g. Deuteronomy 23:10–14). How are these laws of ritual cleanliness to be applied after the wilderness tabernacle has been replaced by the Jerusalem Temple and the wilderness camp by the city of Jerusalem? In the approach taken by normative Judaism, the rabbis ruled that the Holy City of Jerusalem was to be divided into *three* different camps: the Temple proper (the Divine camp), the area surrounding the Temple (the Levitical camp), and the rest of the city (the Israelite camp). According to rabbinical interpretation, the harshest bans are applicable only to the Temple proper, the less harsh are applicable to the area surrounding the Temple, and the remainder are applicable to the entire city. To achieve this tripartite division, the rabbis gave different interpretations to different occurrences of the word *camp* in the biblical text. But these interpretations were not suggested by the text itself. The rabbis applied them in order to ameliorate the harshness that would result if all the restrictions applicable to the wilderness camp were applied uniformly to the entire city of Jerusalem—indeed to other cities as well. The rabbis who resorted to this tripartite division of restrictions by interpreting *camp* in three different ways were—if you wish—the "Reform Jews" of their day in comparison to the Essenes.

The Essenes, as we learn from the Temple Scroll, would have none of this. For them, the City of the Temple (Jerusalem) was equated with the camp where the tabernacle was kept in the wilderness.* All the laws and bans applicable to the wilderness camp were applicable to the *entire city of Jerusalem*. (In some cases, the camp is equated with *any* city, and the bans are applicable to *all* cities.)

We would consider some of the results quite bizarre. For example, in Deuteronomy 23:12–14, we are told there is to be a place outside the camp in the wilderness for defecation. The Essenes applied this injunction literally to the entire city of Jerusalem. The Temple Scroll forbids the building of toilets in the city. "You shall make a place for the hand (a toilet) outside the city to which they shall go out . . . 3,000 cubits [outside the city] in order that it will not be visible from the city."

A similar rule is found in another Dead Sea Scroll known as the War Scroll. Because three thousand cubits is beyond the limit of permitted walking on the Sabbath, Essenes who lived in Jerusalem could not walk to the latrines on the seventh day—and they therefore refrained from relieving themselves on the Sabbath.

---

*This is apparently spelled out in a still-unpublished letter from Qumran that, according to the editors, was sent by the Teacher of Righteousness himself. The letter is to be published by John Strugnell and Elisha Qimron. See "Jerusalem Rolls Out Red Carpet for Biblical Archaeology Congress," *Biblical Archaeology Review,* July/August 1984, pp. 12–18.

Interestingly enough, Josephus, the first-century Jewish historian who in his youth lived among the Essenes, confirms that they observed these rules—defecating only outside their settlement and refraining from defecation on the Sabbath. Josephus also describes a city gate in Jerusalem, mentioned nowhere else, that he calls the Essene Gate. This may well be the colloquial name for the gate the Essenes used to go out (or rather, to run out) of the city to relieve themselves. Since the Temple Scroll prescribes the building of public toilets "northwest of the city," this reference provides an important clue as to the location of the Essene Gate. Josephus mentions that near the Essene Gate was a place called *Betsoa,* which is obviously *Beth-Soah* in Hebrew, i.e., a lavatory.

The Essenes applied other bans to the entire city of Jerusalem, according to their interpretation of the biblical rules of purity related to the camp. Thus all sexual relations were banned in the city of Jerusalem. (This may perhaps explain the fact that the Essenes were celibate. Moreover, this may be the origin of celibacy as a doctrine.) People afflicted with impurity were forbidden from entering Jerusalem and were confined instead to specially built structures east of the city.

The Dead Sea Scrolls are without doubt one of the most important discoveries, if not *the* most important discovery, for biblical studies ever made in the Holy Land. Their discovery created shock waves among scholars. To change the metaphor, it was as if a powerful telescope with a zoom lens suddenly brought the world of Judaism at the end of the Second Temple period into immediate focus across a barrier of two thousand years. This period was both a tragic turning point in Jewish history—the Romans destroyed the Temple in 70 A.D.—and the cradle in which Christianity was born and began to grow. The Temple Scroll, like the previously discovered Dead Sea Scrolls, will no doubt be scrutinized by generations of scholars in order to illuminate this critical period in the history of Judaism as well as Christianity.

Since we cannot consider here even a fraction of the problems and insights contained in the Temple Scroll (many of which are discussed in my scientific edition of the scroll), what I would like to do is give a few examples of the way scholars might be using the Temple Scroll to broaden and enrich our understanding of the New Testament and early Christianity.*

---

*The literature on the Essene-Christian relationship is vast; some of the very best discussions are contained in K. Stendahl, ed., *The Scrolls and the New Testament* (New York: Harper & Row, 1957).

I have just discussed how strictly the scroll interprets biblical laws. I mentioned the bans on entering the Holy City of Jerusalem, which the Temple Scroll equates with the Tabernacle camp in the wilderness. One of the locations in which the banned were to be isolated may give us a clearer picture of the nature of the place where Jesus stayed, at the house of Simon the Leper, before he entered Jerusalem (Mark 14:3; Matthew 26:6).

The Temple Scroll, of course, bans all lepers from Jerusalem, just as lepers were banned from the Israelite camp in the wilderness. As noted above, we are told (in column XLVI): "And you shall make three places *east* of the city . . . into which shall come the lepers and the people who have a discharge and the men who have had a (nocturnal) emission."

From this and a similar passage, we learn that the lepers must have been confined in a separate place *east* of the city. We know from the Midrash* that at this time it was thought leprosy was carried by the wind. The prevailing wind in Jerusalem is westerly—from west to east. Therefore, the rabbis prohibited walking east of a leper. According to the Temple Scroll, lepers were placed in a colony east of the city to avoid the westerly wind's carrying the disease into the city. In my view, Bethany (east of Jerusalem on the eastern slope of the Mount of Olives) was a village of lepers. Thus, it was not that Jesus just happened to stay in the house of a leper (Simon) before he entered Jerusalem; he deliberately chose a *village* of lepers. This deliberate choice would have compounded the offense—entering Jerusalem after contact with lepers—in the eyes not only of the Essenes but of the Pharisees as well.

From the doctrinal viewpoint, the influence of the Essenes on early Christianity, as has been noted by various scholars, is more complicated. We must distinguish between the various layers, or strata, to use an archaeological term, of early Christianity. The theology, the doctrines, and the practices of Jesus, John the Baptist, and Paul, for example, are not the same. The Dead Sea Scrolls shed new light on these differences.

The similarity between the sectarian doctrines reflected in the Dead Sea Scrolls and in early Christianity were, of course, noted immediately after their discovery. Indeed, one of the chief surprises of the Dead Sea Scrolls for some Christians was that some of what were previously thought to be innovative Christian doctrines and practices were in fact known to the Essenes one hundred or two hundred years before Jesus' time.

*An early collection of Jewish elaborations on scripture.

But these facts must be related to different sources of Christian doctrine. Jesus himself was, in my opinion, quite anti-Essene, as he was anti-Pharisee. Jesus reacted against the strict insistence on ritual purity practiced not only by the Pharisees but even more so by the Essenes.

Indeed, there may well be an anti-Essene reference in the Sermon on the Mount, as was already noted by the Austrian scholar Kurt Schubert. Jesus there says to the multitude, "You have heard it said . . . hate thine enemy. But I say to you, love your enemies" (Matthew 5:43–44). This passage is somewhat of an enigma. Who is it that has said, "Hate your enemy"? We are not told. There is no such doctrine in any Jewish writing. But, as Schubert has shown, in one of the basic texts of the Qumran community called the Manual of Discipline, new members of the sect swear an oath of allegiance to love the Sons of Light (that is, the members of the Essene community) and to hate for all eternity the Sons of Darkness. The reference in the Sermon on the Mount to those who advise hating your enemies may well be to the Essenes and would thus reflect Jesus' own anti-Essene stance.

Another enigmatic passage from the New Testament, Mark 8:14–21, may be clarified by the Temple Scroll itself and, as we shall see, in a manner that reflects Jesus' anti-Essene position. In the pericope from Mark, Jesus is in a boat on the Sea of Galilee, with only a single loaf of bread. He cautions his disciples, "Beware of the leaven of the Pharisees and the leaven of the Herodians." The disciples are concerned at the lack of bread. Jesus berates them: "Having eyes do you not see, and having ears do you not hear? And do you remember?" Jesus recalls for them the miracle of the multiplication of the bread:

"When I broke the five loaves for the 5,000, how many baskets full of broken pieces did you take up?"
They said to him, "Twelve."
"And the seven for the 4,000, how many baskets full of broken pieces did you take up?"
And they said to him, "Seven."
And he said to them, "Do you not yet understand?"

Modern readers have no less difficulty understanding. The passage is full of obscurities. But the Temple Scroll may help us penetrate some of the cruxes: Who were the Herodians and what is the significance of the twelve baskets full of pieces and the seven baskets full of pieces? And why were the disciples supposed to infer that these baskets full of pieces were an allusion to the bread of the Pharisees and the bread of the Herodians?

I previously referred to the many "new" or additional festivals referred to in the Temple Scroll. These were observed by the Essenes but not by normative Jews. One of these additional festivals I did not mention was the annual seven-day celebration known as the Days of the Ordination (or consecration) of the Priests. This celebration is patterned on the seven-day consecration ceremony Moses performed on Aaron and his sons when they became priests of the Lord in the wilderness, as described in Leviticus 8. For normative Judaism, this ordination of the priests was a onetime act. No new consecration or ordination ceremony of this kind was performed on Aaron's descendants. For the Essenes, who ruled by the Temple Scroll, however, this was a yearly ceremony. It was to be performed annually, forever. So the Temple Scroll tells us. The role of Moses was to be taken by the High Priest. When the High Priest himself was to be consecrated, the role of Moses was to be performed by the priestly Elders. The details of the ordination ceremony are spelled out in great detail in the Temple Scroll. They are quite complicated, but here we need focus only on one aspect. Leviticus (8:2) speaks of one basket of bread used for the offering on each of the seven days of the ceremony. In the Temple Scroll, however, there are seven baskets of bread, one for each day. Indeed, it appears from the Temple Scroll that the Essenes had a special ceremony connected with the seven baskets of bread, although they could not then offer the full sacrifice at the Jerusalem Temple because it was not built according to their plan; it was not pure according to their laws, and the priests were not legitimate according to their view.

Now let us return to the passage in Mark. Jesus tells his disciples to beware of the bread of the Pharisees and the Herodians. He then refers to the miracle of the twelve baskets of bread and the seven baskets of bread. The twelve baskets, I think, alludes to the Pharisees who controlled the Jerusalem Temple. Each week the priests ate the twelve loaves of the presence (Leviticus 24:5–9). In effect Jesus is saying, Do not concern yourself with the twelve loaves in the Pharisaic Temple; I created twelve baskets of bread for you.

But what of the seven loaves of the Herodians? What does this allude to? In my view, this refers to the seven loaves the Essenes used in the annual seven-day ceremony of the ordination of the priests. Jesus is telling the disciples not to concern themselves with the Essenes either. Jesus miraculously creates the seven baskets of bread of the Essenes, as well as the twelve baskets of bread of the Pharisees.

But, you may say, the passage from Mark refers to the seven baskets of the Herodians, not the seven baskets of the Essenes. I believe when Jesus refers to the Herodians, he really means the Essenes. I suspect that the Essenes had the nickname "Herodians." Josephus (*Jewish Antiquities* 15:372–379) tells us that Herod was in effect the protector of the Essenes and showed special kindness to them. The suggestion that the Herodians mentioned in Mark, and elsewhere, refer to the Essenes has been made before, but now, from the Temple Scroll, we have considerable evidence for the similarity between Essene beliefs and Herodian beliefs, which strengthens the identification of the Herodians with the Essenes.

Perhaps we can now reply more intelligently to the question Jesus asks: "Do you not yet understand?" Jesus rejects the strict interpretation of the Essenes, as well as the Pharisees. Thus, here again we see Jesus taking an anti-Essene stand.

John the Baptist's relationship to the Essenes is quite different from Jesus'. John may even have been a member of the Essene community. He was active in the area around Qumran; he, like the Essene community at Qumran, was celibate; and he was from a priestly family. Moreover, the type of baptism he was preaching, which gave John his name, was also practiced by the Essenes. We know that the Essenes practiced baptism not only from their literature but also from the baptismal installations found at Qumran.

These baptismal installations are quite different from the ritual baths (*mikvaot*) of the period found, for example, at Masada, in the Jericho area, and in Jerusalem. The normative Judaism ritual baths had to contain "living" water; that is, water either from the rain or from a flowing stream or river. Since this was not available year-round, especially in the desert, ritually pure water was saved and preserved in a reserve pool adjacent to the ritual bath. A channel led from the reserve pool to the bath pool so that a small amount of the living water would be added to each bath to purify it, so to say. The Jewish ritual baths are characterized by these twin pools. At Qumran, however, there is only a single pool (with steps) in which people could be baptized.

Baptism as we know it in early Christianity may have been adopted under Essene influence through John the Baptist.

But the most often noted similarities between Christianity and Essene doctrine came not from John the Baptist, and certainly not from Jesus. The principal similarities are to be found in the Pauline Epistles and in the Johannine literature. How do we explain these similarities—such things as the dualism found both in the New Testament and in the writings of the Dead Sea sect, the contrast between the Sons of Darkness and the Sons of Light (a term often used in the Pauline literature), the spirit and the flesh, good and evil? The communal meal is also something we find in early Christianity and in the Dead Sea sect. It is my belief that these similarities came through Paul.

Paul was himself a Pharisee before his conversion on the road to Damascus, but he surely knew well the doctrines of all the sects he was persecuting, including the Essenes. Paul became the apostle to the Gentiles. He was attempting insofar as possible to avoid the burden of the Mosaic law for those whom he converted and who found the Mosaic law an obstacle to their new allegiance. Paul's problem was how to be a Jew without the restrictions of the Mosaic law. I think he found a ready-made theology in many respects in the doctrines of the Essenes. For the Essenes, like early Christians (but for different reasons), rejected the Jerusalem Temple and its cult: In my view, the striking similarities between early Christianity and the doctrines of the Essenes entered Christianity after Jesus' time via Paul in the period before the Romans destroyed the Jerusalem Temple in 70 A.D. (and Qumran, for that matter).

Yet there is a paradox here: How can it be that a sect (the Essenes) that adhered so tenaciously to the strictest and most legalistic interpretation of all the minutiae of the Law of Moses as prescribed in the Torah could influence—of all sects—the one (Christianity) that in due course essentially rejected this Law, especially those parts of the Law concerned with Temple observance and ritual purity?

The complete answer is no doubt more complicated than the following hesitant outline suggests, but it is in this area that I believe the answer to our paradox is to be found. As I have said, the early Christians came into contact with the Essenes and were influenced by them at a time late in Essene history (first century A.D.). They met Essenes who maintained their own calendar and repudiated the Jerusalem Temple as well as its laws, for reasons mentioned. Thus bereft of a legitimate temple, the Essenes developed a theology and religious practice that enabled them to live without this cultic institution, especially at their own monastic centers such as Qumran in the wilderness. The following paraphrase of Proverbs 15:8 from an Essene document could have appealed to circles of Pauline or Johannine Christianity: "The sacrifice of the wicked is an abomination, but the prayer of the just is an agreeable offering" (Damascus Document 11:20–21).

The Essenes' rejection of the Jerusalem Temple and its cult, like that of the early Christians, permitted the Essenes to influence the early Christians. Without a temple, the Essenes developed a way of life that was a kind of substitute for the temple and the worship in it. It was this way of life and the theology it reflected that appealed to and influenced the early Christians.

For the Essenes, however, the rejection of the Temple was *temporary*. For them, the Jerusalem priests were illegitimate and the Temple polluted because their own rigid legal interpretations of the Law were not applied; even its plan was a wrong one. For the Essenes, the temporary, substitute way of life was applicable only until "the exiles of the Sons of Light return from the Wilderness of the Nations to encamp in the Wilderness of Jerusalem" (War Scroll 3).

What was a temporary substitute for the Essenes, Christianity adopted as a permanent theology, part of their fixed and final canon. In short, what was for the Essenes an ad hoc adaptation to their rejection of the Jerusalem priesthood and Temple, applicable only until the end of days when the Temple would be rebuilt by God according to their own beliefs, became for Christianity a permanent solution. Thus evolved the historical paradox by which the early Christians could be so heavily influenced by a legalistic sect, despite the fact that Christianity itself rejected this legalism.

Let me conclude simply with a few puzzles in the history of Christianity for which the Temple Scroll might provide the hint of a solution.

Of course, even before the acquisition of the Temple Scroll, we knew about the solar calendar used by the Essenes, which contrasted with the lunar calendar practiced by normative Judaism. The Essenes' solar calendar was divided into four sections consisting of three thirty-day months, plus one additional day. Thus, the Essene year contained 364 days, divided into twelve thirty-day months, plus four intercalated days inserted at the end of each three-month group. (In the course of years, this calendar would need additional intercalated days—or leap years—to maintain the same seasons, but we have no information, for the time being, on how the Essenes did this.) Using this calendar, however, results in holidays always falling on the same day of the week.

I have already mentioned the many "new"—or previously unknown—holidays described in the Temple Scroll, including three new (and one well-established) "first fruits" festivals. The Essenes reckoned the date on which each of these festivals began by counting fifty days after a particular Sabbath (counting the day of the preceding festival as the first day of the new counting), with the result that these festivals always began on a Sunday. Sunday thus begins to appear as a most important day.

In the Statutes of the King, the Temple Scroll considers restrictions on the king's marriages. Rabbinic Judaism interpreted Deuteronomy 17:17

to restrict the king to eighteen wives. This was based in part on the fact that King David had eighteen wives.

In contrast, the Temple Scroll provides:

"[The King] shall not take another wife, for she [his first wife] alone shall be with him all the days of her life. But should she die, he may take unto himself another wife." Here we have a clear-cut ruling against bigamy and divorce, the earliest such ruling in any extant Jewish writing. This may well have been a forerunner of Christian doctrine on these subjects.

I have raised more questions than I have answered. But the scholarly riches of the Temple Scroll have just begun to be mined.

APPENDIX

THE PLAN OF THE ESSENE TEMPLE

" . . . I will consecrate my temple by my glory . . . on the day of blessing . . . I will create my temple and establish it for myself for all times . . . " (Column XXIX).

"You shall make a dry moat around the temple, . . . which will separate the holy temple from the city so that they may not come suddenly into my temple and desecrate it. They shall consecrate my temple and fear my people, for I dwell among them" (Column XLVI).

The cardinal prescription of the scroll is that there shall be three square courts around the temple: inner, middle, and outer.* To ensure the purity of the temple and its courts, the scroll ordains two additional precautions: an inner wall (dotted line) to be erected around the temple within the inner court, and, around the outer court, a fosse (moat) is to be made.

The inner court will have four gates, oriented to the four points of the compass. The middle and outer courts each will have twelve gates named after Jacob's twelve sons and assigned in the same order around each court. The outer court will be divided into sixteen chamber areas, eleven allotted to eleven tribes (excluding Levi, from whom the Levites are descended); three to the three sons of Levi—Gershon, Kohath, and Merari (the Levitical families); and two to the sons of Aaron (the priests).

Precise dimensions for the inner court gates are given: the entrances are to be fourteen cubits wide (a cubit is about one and a half feet) and twenty-eight cubits high from threshold to lintel, with another fourteen cubits from lintel to ceiling. Other dimensions given in the scroll are similarly exact.

*See 2 Chronicles 33:5; 1 Kings 6:36, 7:12; 2 Kings 20:4; Ezekiel 40–44.

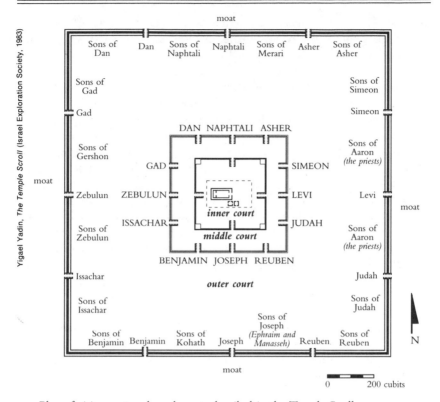

Yigael Yadin, *The Temple Scroll* (Israel Exploration Society, 1983)

19. Plan of visionary temple and courts described in the Temple Scroll.

Lining the inner court stoa, described in column XXXVII of the scroll, are "s[i]tting pl[a]ces for the priests, and tables in front of the sitting places." The scroll author explicitly refers to these tables to emphasize the separation between priests and laity, "so that [there shall be] no mixing of the sacrifices of the peace offerings of the children of Israel with the sacrifices of the priests."

The scroll tells us there are to be "cooking places," kitchens, on either side of each gate. "In the four angles of the court," the scroll continues, there are to be places for stoves "in which they [the priests] shall boil their sacrifices [and] the sin offerings."

The structures to be found within the inner wall of the inner court are described in the scroll in minute detail. They include the temple's furnishings, such as the cherubim, the golden veil, and the lamp stand (menorah).

The staircase, next to the temple, is to be square-shaped, twenty cubits on a side, and located seven cubits from the northwest side of the *heikhal,* or temple building. This would be an extraordinary structure—forty cubits high, ascending to the roof of the temple, and completely plated with gold!

In the house of the laver, the priests would wash themselves and then put on their holy garments, which were to be kept in gold-plated niches in this structure. The house was to be "square on all its sides one and twenty cubits, at a distance of fifty cubits from the altar."

The commands for the house of utensils list the following altar utensils: basin, flagons, firepans, and silver bowls. Even the function of the bowls is defined: "with which one brings up the entrails and the legs on the altar."

The twelve columns with ceiling constituted the Temple's slaughterhouse. Here the sacrificial animal's head would be shackled by a ring embedded in a wooden column. Because of the Hebrew phrase denoting that roofing is used for this structure, we can assume that it would have either low outer walls or none at all.

To the west of the *heikhal,* there is to be made "a stoa of standing columns for the sin offering and the guilt offering." The columns of the stoa are to be "separated from one another: for the sin offering of the priests and for the male goats and for the sin offerings of the people and for their guilt offerings." To make the separation between priests and laity absolutely clear, the scroll author adds, "for their place shall be separated from one another so that the priests may not err with the sin offering of the people."

The altar itself is mentioned several times, but this portion of the scroll is so badly damaged that commands for the altar's construction are fragmentary at best. We can understand, however, that the great altar of burnt offering was to be built of stone, with a ledge, corner, and horns, and that one of its dimensions was to be twenty cubits.

CHAPTER 8

THE GIGANTIC DIMENSIONS
OF THE VISIONARY TEMPLE
IN THE TEMPLE SCROLL

MAGEN BROSHI

Magen Broshi is curator of the Shrine of the Book in Jerusalem where Israel's intact Dead Sea Scrolls are housed. In this short chapter, Broshi calls attention to the enormous size of the temple envisioned in the Temple Scroll, hardly a practical possibility. —ED.

——·——

In the previous chapter Yigael Yadin described the contents of the Temple Scroll. I would like to make one additional point relating to the size of the temple envisioned in it.

Of five major subjects dealt with in the scroll, the foremost is the temple, its design and the ordinances pertaining to it. This subject occupies almost half the length of the scroll; hence the name Yadin gave to the scroll (the original name is unknown).

The temple compound as described in the scroll consists of three concentric square courts—the inner court, the middle court, and the outer court. In the midst of the inner court would stand the temple and the various buildings connected with it.

Clearly, this was not the temple that existed when the scroll was written. Although the date of the scroll's composition is still an open question* it was certainly composed at least a century before Herod the Great began rebuilding the Temple at the end of the first century B.C. The temple described in the Temple Scroll obviously does not refer to the Temple that existed in Herod's time. Nor does it refer to the temple to be built by the Lord at the end of days. Instead, it refers to a man-made edifice, to be constructed on terra firma according to the author's own conception. As would be the case with Herod's temple, the greatest effort was to be expended on the temple courts.

The Temple Scroll Temple and Its Courts

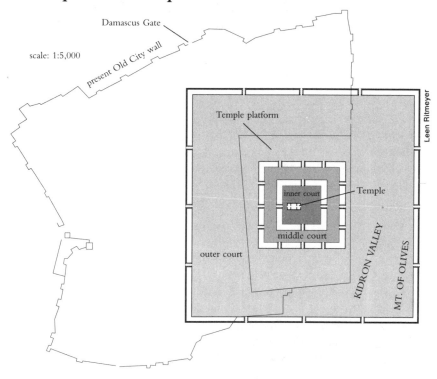

20. *The visionary temple with its courts described in the Temple Scroll is nearly the same size as the walled Old City of Jerusalem.*

*See Chapter 11.

When Herod rebuilt the Second Temple, the temple proper was completed in seventeen months[1] and the porticoes in eight years.[2] The completion of the whole compound, however, lasted, with intervals, for some eighty years. Only under the procurator Albinus (62–64 A.D.) were the "works" of the temple (that is, the gigantic esplanade) finished. At that time, eighteen thousand laborers were laid off.[3] This was only a few years before the Great Revolt, the First Jewish Revolt, against Rome (which broke out in 66 A.D.). The mass unemployment caused by the completion of the temple works may well have caused considerable social unrest, which undoubtedly would have contributed to the outbreak of the revolt.

By comparison with the temple described in the Temple Scroll, the Herodian Temple was a miniature. Let us look at the size of the gigantic temple compound described in the Temple Scroll.

The square outer court would be sixteen hundred cubits on a side. This is about twenty-five hundred feet, or half a mile, on a side.[4] The total area of the temple compound would be 160 acres. In comparison, Herod's Temple compound (which was the largest artificial esplanade in antiquity) was only about a quarter as big. In addition, the temple described in the Temple Scroll would be surrounded by a moat 100 cubits (165 feet) wide. The total area of the temple compound described in the Temple Scroll was, coincidentally, precisely the size of Jerusalem in the second century B.C.[5]

The outer court of the temple would stretch all the way from the present-day Damascus Gate in the west to the slopes of the Mount of Olives in the east.

To build the complex described in the Temple Scroll would require solving serious topographical problems. Creating a level space on which to build this gigantic project would require as much work as the building project itself. Leveling the ground would require filling in the Kidron Valley (to raise it about 250 feet) on the east and quarrying rock on the west. This would have meant removal of millions of tons of soil and rock, all by human muscle. A feasible feat, I suppose, but extremely impractical. But after all, practicality was not the Dead Sea sect's forte.

CHAPTER 9

INTRIGUE AND THE SCROLL

HERSHEL SHANKS

If the first chapter in this book provides the opening drama, this chapter provides the comic relief. It gives a different perspective on Yigael Yadin's acquisition of the Temple Scroll.

In Chapter 7, Yadin describes his dealings with a supposedly disreputable Virginia clergyman who, he claims, snookered him out of $10,000. Yadin identifies the clergyman only as Mr. Z.

When Mr. Z's wife read this article in a Florida church library, she showed it to her husband. He then contacted Biblical Archaeology Review *editor Hershel Shanks and told his side of the story—very different from Yadin's.* —ED.

— · —

Were it not for the efforts of the man who got Jerry Falwell started in television, the famous Dead Sea Scroll known as the Temple Scroll might never have come to light.

At least that is the story according to Reverend Joe Uhrig, now semiretired and living in Florida.

Yigael Yadin, Israel's foremost biblical archaeologist before his death in 1984, tells a somewhat different story. In Chapter 7 (as well as in his magisterial, three-volume edition of *The Temple Scroll*[1]) Yadin describes how he first learned of the Temple Scroll, a scroll that he identifies as the Torah (or Bible) of the Essene community of Jews that lived near the Dead Sea at the time of Jesus.

The existence of the scroll was first brought to Yadin's attention by a man he identifies only as Mr. Z. Mr. Z presented himself to Yadin as a Virginia clergyman. Yadin, however, had his doubts. From Yadin's perspective, Mr. Z did him out of $10,000; Yadin didn't trust Mr. Z or anything he said. Nevertheless, the Israeli archaeologist steadfastly refused to disclose Mr. Z's identity. Yadin explained:

"I am still keeping his confidence, however, by not revealing his name. I want all these people—whether they were robbers or not (and it is a cloak-and-dagger business)—to know that as far as I am concerned, if they tell me not to reveal their identities, I won't. Otherwise, we have no chance of getting more scrolls." Yadin died without ever revealing Mr. Z's identity.

According to Yadin, Mr. Z first wrote him on August 1, 1960, offering to negotiate the sale of "important, authentic discoveries of Dead Sea Scrolls." Mr. Z's source was a well-known Jordanian antiquities dealer.

On October 7, 1960, Yadin purchased from, or through, Mr. Z a small fragment of another Dead Sea Scroll known as the Psalms Scroll. As a result, Yadin knew that Mr. Z had access to authentic scroll materials.

On May 29, 1961, Mr. Z again wrote Yadin, this time saying he had for sale not a fragment, but an entire scroll. In subsequent correspondence, Mr. Z asserted the scroll was between fifteen and eighteen feet long, and he even supplied a small fragment that had broken off from the scroll. Yadin saw immediately that it was authentic.

Frustrating negotiations concerning the price extended over several months. Every time Yadin thought the asking price was within reach, it went wildly up again. At one point, Yadin thought a deal had been struck for $130,000. A $10,000 down payment was given to Mr. Z in New York, plus $1,500 for Mr. Z's transportation to Bethlehem, supposedly necessary to get the Bethlehem dealer's agreement. At that time, Mr. Z once again gave Yadin the fragment from the scroll that Yadin had previously returned.

Mr. Z went to Bethlehem and reported that difficulties had arisen: The price had gone up again. Further correspondence ensued in which Mr. Z pleaded for more money, and Yadin tried to get back his $10,000.

21. Yigael Yadin.

22. Joe Uhrig, aka Mr. Z.

But it was gone for good. "It was plain," Yadin wrote, "that Mr. Z had no intention of returning the advance." Yadin's efforts to get the money back were entirely "futile."

In mid-1962, Yadin heard from Mr. Z for the last time. Mr. Z again made "promises" and again pleaded for more money. Then silence. "Every trace of him has disappeared," Yadin reported.

On June 7, 1967, the Israeli army captured the Old City of Jerusalem and Bethlehem. The next day Yadin arranged for an army officer to go to the Bethlehem dealer's home and claim the scroll he had learned about six years earlier from Mr. Z. That night, the delighted archaeologist held the Temple Scroll in his hands for the first time. It turned out to be the longest relatively intact Dead Sea Scroll ever discovered, nearly twenty-seven feet long.

The scroll contains long passages from the Pentateuch, but with variations in language from the canonical text that has come down to us. According to Yadin, the Temple Scroll also includes excerpts from some books referred to in the Bible, but now lost. The scroll contains detailed plans for the building of the Lord's temple*; hence its name, the Temple Scroll. It also contains many other laws as well as descriptions of religious festivals not mentioned in the Bible or elsewhere. Many scholars consider it the most important Dead Sea Scroll ever discovered, with significant potential for illuminating early Christianity as well as contemporaneous Judaism.

But even according to Yadin's account, if it had not been for Mr. Z, the Temple Scroll might still be deteriorating in a shoe box under the floor tiles of the Bethlehem dealer's home. According to Yadin, the dealer "had kept the scroll under dreadful conditions that caused extensive damage, especially to the upper part of the scroll." We shall never know how much of the scroll became illegible in the period between 1962, when negotiations broke off with Mr. Z, and 1967, when Israel confiscated the scroll. But even more of the scroll would have become illegible if Mr. Z had not alerted Yadin to its existence and it had continued to rot under the Bethlehem dealer's floor.

Yadin published his three-volume Hebrew edition of *The Temple Scroll* in 1977. Six years later, in 1983, the English edition appeared. In connection with the publication of the English edition, Yadin prepared a popular article for *Biblical Archaeology Review*. The article was published in the September/October 1984 issue, two months after Yadin's death.

*See Chapter 7.

In the winter of 1984–1985, Doris Uhrig, the wife of a semiretired minister named Joe Uhrig, was browsing through the library of the Coral Ridge Presbyterian Church in Fort Lauderdale, Florida. There she saw the September/October 1984 BAR, with Yadin's story about the Temple Scroll and an announcement of Yadin's death. She thought her husband might be interested in seeing the magazine, so she brought it home to him. Rev. Uhrig read the article and immediately recognized himself as Mr. Z!

For the first time, Joe Uhrig learned what had happened to the scroll material he had tried to acquire for Israel. For the first time, he also learned of the death of Yigael Yadin.

Yadin's account of his dealings with Mr. Z also made Uhrig realize that the archaeologist had been less than truthful with him about the nature of the scroll material whose sale he was trying to negotiate. But for Yadin's having misled him about the scroll, Uhrig claims he might well have been able to acquire it at a time when additional portions of the scroll were still legible. However, Uhrig holds no animosity toward Yadin.

Uhrig became involved with the Dead Sea Scrolls in a roundabout way, as a result of a trip to the Holy Land. He was one of the first TV evangelists—and one of the most successful. In the 1950s, he had a higher Neilsen rating than *Meet the Press*. He could fill Constitution Hall in Washington, D.C., and was invited to the White House by President Eisenhower. Called *Hand to Heaven,* Uhrig's television program featured such guest celebrities as Roy Rogers and Dale Evans and a choir with nationally famous soloists.

Uhrig felt he really should see the Holy Land. So in 1955, he made the grand tour, starting in Beirut, then going to Jordan, and finally crossing the border to Israel. At the Beirut airport, he was met by Marcos Hazou, a guide his travel agent had arranged. It was a successful trip, partly thanks to the rapport he established with Hazou. The next year, Uhrig received a letter from Hazou asking if Uhrig would sponsor him, his wife, and his two daughters to immigrate to the United States.

Not fully realizing the financial obligation of sponsorship, Uhrig said yes. Hazou and his family arrived on Thanksgiving Day, 1956. Uhrig rented a house for them, bought them food and a houseful of furniture, and employed Hazou in his mail room. In the end, it worked out well all around. Hazou was a faithful employee and later became a travel agent on his own.

In 1960, the grateful Hazou told Uhrig that his brother Aboud, who lived in Bethlehem, had a friend named Khalil Iskander Shahin. They called him Kando. Kando had some ancient manuscripts that came from the Dead Sea Scroll caves. In fact, Kando had served as the intermediary with the Bedouin and had brokered the sale of the famous Dead Sea Scrolls. By trade, Kando was a cobbler with a shop on Manger Square.

According to Uhrig, he told Hazou, "Whatever Kando has belongs to Israel. Maybe something can be worked out to get them into Israel."

Uhrig went to Bethlehem, then under Jordanian control, and stayed with Marcos Hazou's brother, Aboud Hazou, hoping to track down the scrolls. Aboud Hazou and Kando belonged to the same church and on Sunday Kando came to Aboud's house to get acquainted. Later, Kando brought a fragment of a scroll to Aboud's house, a fragment that eventually turned out to belong to the famous Psalm Scroll.

When Uhrig returned to the United States, he telephoned William F. Albright, the prominent biblical archaeologist at the Johns Hopkins University at Baltimore, who had been one of the first scholars to authenticate the original Dead Sea Scrolls. Albright warned the minister against the many fakes that were floating around, but told him his source seemed authentic. Albright suggested that Uhrig should try to contact Yadin.

Uhrig wrote to Yadin and also made many more trips to Bethlehem to try to get the scrolls from Kando, telling Kando frankly that the scrolls should be in Israel with Yadin. Kando replied that he did not want to get into trouble, that he was afraid. Uhrig tried to reassure him. He could be trusted, he told Kando; he would keep it quiet; after all, he had sponsored Aboud's brother to come to the United States. "You believe in Aboud and his brother," he said. "This belongs in Israel. I'm telling you straight out where it's going!"

"What was the use of playing games about it?" Uhrig recounts. "Kando had illusions that there would be some multimillionaire in the United States."

Uhrig agreed to present Kando's million-dollar asking price to Yadin because "I didn't want to get him [Kando] upset and lose him. So that's the way I left him on the million dollars."

When Uhrig wrote Yadin about the million-dollar price, "Yadin wrote back to me and said the demand was crazy. Everyone in our circle, the Hazous and myself, we started calling Kando 'Crazy Kando,' a nickname because of his ridiculous demands."

On one trip, Uhrig purchased the Psalm Scroll fragment Kando had earlier shown him for $2,500. Kando knew the fragment was from the

Book of Psalms; he had been told that by the head of the Jordanian Department of Antiquities. The Virginia clergyman paid Kando his asking price for this piece, without haggling, hoping to gain his confidence and show that he was a serious buyer, so he could get the "main scroll," which he had not yet seen. Uhrig returned home with the fragment, and after a few months, during which he kept the Psalm Scroll fragment in a drawer, he decided to send it to Yadin to demonstrate that the materials he had access to were authentic. So Uhrig simply wrapped the Psalm Scroll fragment in a paper napkin, put it in a brown paper envelope, and mailed it to Yadin in Jerusalem. Uhrig admits this was "a bit unorthodox, but I didn't know just exactly what it was altogether." Uhrig did not ask for any specific amount from Yadin: "He trusted me and I trusted him." A few weeks later, Uhrig got a letter from Yadin and a check for $7,000.

The rest of the extant Psalm Scroll, into which fit the fragment that Uhrig obtained from Kando, had been previously acquired by the Rockefeller Museum in Jerusalem. Yadin speculated as to where Mr. Z had gotten the fragment, before or after the other parts of the Psalm Scroll were obtained by the museum. "We shall never know," Yadin wrote.

Uhrig believes that Kando simply held back this piece when he sold the other pieces of the Psalm Scroll to the Rockefeller. "I believe this to be [the] correct [explanation] because I asked him [Kando] if he had more pieces of this particular scroll, and he said no. He said just this one."

On one trip to Bethlehem—Uhrig is not sure of his dates and has no correspondence to refresh his memory—Kando brought over to Aboud's house, in a shoe box, a tightly wrapped scroll that formed a kind of stick nine inches long. The figures Kando talked about wanting for the scroll were "wild" and gyrated wildly up and down: a million dollars, $750,-000, $250,000, back to a million dollars.

In the meantime, Uhrig was having his own money problems. Already in 1958 he had decided to give up some of the outlying markets for his television program *Hand to Heaven*. One such location was the station in Lynchburg, Virginia. In those days, to broadcast in Lynchburg, you had to rent a coaxial cable to Lynchburg from Washington, D.C., where the show originated. The cost of the Lynchburg cable became too high in face of the falling returns. Instead of closing the show down on Lynchburg Channel 13, Uhrig looked for someone locally to take it over. A twenty-four-year-old minister had come to one of Uhrig's meetings in the Armory in Lynchburg, and Uhrig had asked him to come forward and offer a prayer. According to Uhrig, the young fellow had only a small group of thirty-five people; he didn't even have a church then, but he was impressive and energetic, and Uhrig remembered him. When Uhrig decided to give up the Lynchburg show, he called the young Lynchburg minister to see if he wanted the show. The young minister's name was Jerry Falwell.

At first Falwell said no, because he had never done anything like that and had no experience, but Uhrig persuaded him to try it—and he did. In Uhrig's words, "He was a local guy trying to get started. And did he ever get started!" Falwell has never forgotten Uhrig and even now acknowledges that it was Uhrig who started him in television.

But the Lynchburg program was not Uhrig's only financial drain. He had built a new church that had a mortgage on it. He was hoping that if he could obtain the scroll for Yadin, Yadin would agree to pay him $20,000 that would save his church.

In the continued negotiations, Yadin decided he would offer $130,000 for the scroll he had not yet seen. (Uhrig was hoping that the $20,000 would be in addition to the $130,000). Yadin writes as if Mr. Z assured him that the $130,000 was an agreed price, but according to Uhrig that was simply the price Yadin decided to offer. It was an offer Uhrig hoped he could get Kando to accept—especially because he had spent so much on trips to Bethlehem and badly needed the $20,000 he thought Yadin would give him if he successfully negotiated the purchase of the scroll.

Yadin gave Uhrig $10,000 in cash and a deposit slip showing that $120,000 had been deposited in the Chase Manhattan bank, so Uhrig could assure Kando that $130,000 in cash was available. Thus armed, Uhrig traveled to Bethlehem once more, carrying the $10,000 in cash in his sock.

The negotiations in Bethlehem went badly. Uhrig remembers throwing the $10,000 in cash at Kando's feet. Kando had no idea what the $120,000 bank deposit represented. "He wanted to see the cash. And every time you'd talk to him, he changed his figures," Uhrig remembers. Uhrig tried to persuade Kando to let him take the scroll back with him.

"Now let me take it," he said.

"Oh, no, no, no," Kando replied, according to Uhrig.

"Well, don't you trust me now? We've made a transaction [the Psalm Scroll fragment]. Aboud here you've known all your life. I sponsored his brother to come to America. You've got to believe in me. I've made all these trips. I'm not kidding you."

All to no avail. Uhrig went on: "At that point I was exhausted. The Middle East, as you know in those days, the travel was terrible. And I was exhausted. And I said [to Kando], 'Man, please. You've got it here in a shoe box. You've got to trust me. Aboud here is your friend. You've got to believe it.' But no, he just wouldn't do it."

Frustrated and angry, Uhrig saw that a small piece of the scroll was partially torn. Uhrig finished the job. "I'm the one who tore that piece of the scroll," he confessed. "I saw this piece there and I said, 'Kando, I want to show this to Yadin,' and before he could say anything to me—he got very nervous—I pulled it off. And I said, 'I want to take this with me. This is the only way to prove to Yadin that this is genuine. He's got to know what it is.' "

"In hindsight," Uhrig admitted, "I was a little naïve." Kando let Uhrig take the piece with him. No charge.

On his way back to the United States, Uhrig stopped in London, where Yadin was staying at the time, in order to show the fragment.* Uhrig remembers that he met Yadin in the apartment of someone named Wolfson.† When Uhrig handed the fragment to Yadin, Yadin's "eyes popped." "He looked very calm and relaxed with me, but his eyes just popped. Then he said, 'oh, uh'; he stuttered a little."

Yadin handed the fragment back to Uhrig and told him—falsely—that it was only a deed to property: "He said, 'This is a deed to some property,' and he handed it back to me."

Yadin said it was very good writing, but he wanted to see the rest of the scroll. "But he said, 'Uhrig, I think you've wasted a lot of time.' He seemed to be sympathetic toward me and yet it seemed to me he wanted the rest of the scroll." Uhrig and Yadin agreed that Uhrig would continue the negotiations, in order to see what he could do with Kando.

Uhrig contacted Kando once more through Aboud, but the asking price, Aboud reported, was once again a million dollars. Uhrig responded: "I said, 'He's crazy. Tell him to drop dead. What's the use of me going into the hole further for a deed to some land?' "

Uhrig lost his stomach for the whole affair and decided to discontinue the negotiations:

"Yadin threw me off completely," Uhrig claims. "He told me that it was a deed to some land. I thought Kando had tricked me. I can understand now why Yadin did this, because he didn't want to pay an

---

*Yadin claims he got the fragment in London via a letter from Uhrig. Perhaps Uhrig did not leave the fragment with Yadin then, but later sent it to him.

†Probably Leonard Wolfson, whose Wolfson Foundation supported many of Yadin's projects.

exorbitant price. But I was heartsick. And I lost heart. I thought: What a fool I've been. Kando has fooled me."

Uhrig not only failed to get the scroll, he also lost his church: The mortgage was foreclosed.

"Nobody ever knew that story," he told me, "except the local people. I was heartsick. To think that I was chasing after a deed to property." Not until he read the story in *Biblical Archaeology Review* did Joe Uhrig realize that in fact he had been negotiating for the real thing—the Temple Scroll, the longest of the Dead Sea Scrolls, and, in the opinion of many scholars, the most important.

"If I had known the real truth, I believe I could have delivered the scroll," he said. "I do not hold Yadin responsible in any way. I have no ill feeling about it. I think he was doing what diplomatically he felt he had to do because of Kando's crazy demands. But they really weren't my demands."

Uhrig went on: "Yadin told me, 'One day your name will be in the Shrine of the Book.' I told him I didn't want praise. I just felt the scroll should be in Israel. Through it all, I felt we would come out on top. But not only did I lose my church, there was all the expense for those trips." Uhrig just kept the $10,000—"for a portion of all the expenses of all those trips I was making"—and mailed Yadin back the scroll fragment.

"So the years passed by, and I never contacted him anymore, because I thought: What's the use? Why should I keep pressing this?" Then one day Joe Uhrig's wife decided to visit the library of the Coral Ridge Presbyterian Church in Fort Lauderdale, near where they lived. She picked up the latest issue of BAR. . . .

CHAPTER 10

IS THE TEMPLE SCROLL A SIXTH BOOK OF THE TORAH— LOST FOR 2,500 YEARS?

HARTMUT STEGEMANN

In previous chapters we have considered whether the Qumran Community were Essenes and whether the sectarian documents in the library stored in the caves nearby were Essene literature.

But no scholar contends that all the documents in the library are sectarian documents. For example, the biblical texts cannot be considered sectarian. So even those scholars who accept the view that the sectarian literature of Qumran is Essene must ask themselves whether a particular document is sectarian.

In this chapter, one of Germany's most prominent Dead Sea Scroll scholars, Hartmut Stegemann, faces this question with regard to the famous Temple Scroll. Stegemann assumes the majority view that the Qumran sectarians were Essene. But he questions whether the Temple Scroll is a sectarian—Essene— document. He concludes that it is not. He argues that it is, instead, a document from another, perhaps more mainstream, Jewish group.

And what a document! Stegemann believes it is a lost sixth book of the Torah composed of material rejected when the Pentateuch was canonized, probably under the influence of Ezra in the fifth century B.C.

This chapter thus brings us face to face with the question of how you tell whether or not a Qumran document is sectarian. Stegemann develops several criteria—the number of copies in the library, whether the document is quoted in other Qumran documents, and comparisons in language, style, and content with other concededly sectarian documents from Qumran. Stegemann concludes that the Temple Scroll is not a sectarian document.

If it is not, what is it? Stegemann argues that it is a book of the Torah, intended to be on a par with Genesis, Exodus, Leviticus, Numbers, and Deuteronomy and compiled by priest-editors from additions and expansions Ezra rejected when he effectively canonized the Pentateuch. —ED.

—·—

The Temple Scroll is, in my view, clearly the most important of the preserved Dead Sea Scrolls. It was composed, I believe, as an addition or, still better, a supplement to the Pentateuch, as a sixth book of the Torah, on the same level of authority as Genesis, Exodus, Leviticus, Numbers, and Deuteronomy.

The twenty-seven-foot-long Temple Scroll—the longest of the preserved scrolls—has been brilliantly published with minute commentary in a handsome three-volume set by the late Professor Yigael Yadin of Hebrew University.* His edition of the Temple Scroll is the finest publication of any Dead Sea Scroll that has yet appeared, a masterpiece that will be the basis for all further work on this scroll.†

Yadin almost assumed, however, without seriously discussing the matter, that the Temple Scroll was a sectarian composition belonging to the Jewish group that inhabited the settlement at Qumran near the cave where the scroll was found by Bedouin tribesmen. This group, by extensive scholarly consensus,‡ formed part of the Essenes.

In assuming that the Temple Scroll was an Essene document, Yadin has been followed by nearly all scholars who have considered the Temple Scroll—until very recently.

In my view, the Temple Scroll is not an Essene document. It was composed by other Jews, Jews in the mainstream of Palestinian Judaism in their own time. But it was simply one of the "books," if I may use that term for a scroll, in the Essene library at Qumran, hidden like the others in the caves near their settlement. Its composition had no specific connection whatsoever with the Essene community at Qumran.

*See Chapter 7.

†Yigael Yadin was a good friend of mine and always supported me in my research. I only wish he had lived to criticize the views I express here that diverge from his own.

‡See Chapter 2.

Before explaining the basis for this conclusion, let me set forth several fundamental respects in which I agree with Yadin:

First, the Temple Scroll is, as Yadin emphasized, a *Sefer Torah,* a book of the authoritative religious law, in the strict sense of that term. It is not simply a collection of material pertaining to a particular area of religious life.

Second, like the canonical books of the Torah (Genesis, Exodus, Leviticus, Numbers, and Deuteronomy), this Torah, as Yadin also emphasized, was believed to have been given by God himself on Mt. Sinai.[1]

Third, the text of the Temple Scroll is, in Yadin's words, an "additional" Torah to the Pentateuch, although on the same level as the Torah. It is not a Torah superior to the Pentateuch,[2] nor a substitute for the Pentateuch. The convincing evidence for this is the fact that the Temple Scroll does not cover such subjects as the creation of the world (Genesis), the Decalogue (Exodus 20:1–17; Deuteronomy 5:6–21), the Aharonite Blessing (Numbers 6:22–27), or the Shema (the basic monotheistic affirmation: "Hear, O Israel, the Lord our God is one"—Deuteronomy 6:4–9), which were basic to all of the various Jewish religious orientations of the Second Temple period (515 B.C.–70 A.D.). The Temple Scroll's author only added further materials to the given Pentateuch; he did not render the given Pentateuch itself unnecessary or in some way of inferior quality.

Where I differ with Yadin is in his conclusion that the Temple Scroll was a central Torah of the Essene community. Yadin believed that the Temple Scroll may even have been written by the Essene community's revered founder, the Teacher of Righteousness himself.

If the Temple Scroll was indeed the central Torah of the Essene community at Qumran, we could expect it to have been widely used by this community in all its affairs. But that was not the case.

Only two copies of the Temple Scroll have been found among the approximately eight hundred manuscripts recovered from the eleven Qumran caves. One of these copies is Yadin's Temple Scroll itself, which comes from Cave 11—lying about two kilometers north of the central building at Qumran—and which was written about the turn of the era. The second copy is a mere fragmentary scroll, also from Cave 11, but written about 50 B.C. Not a single copy of the Temple Scroll was found in the main library recovered from Cave 4, which held fragments of about 580 different manuscripts.[3]

The Temple Scroll is a very impressive document by its sheer bulk, and it may seem natural to attribute great significance to it in understanding the Essenes among whom it was found. But we must remember that it was only by sheer chance that the main body of this large scroll survived, while most of the other Qumran scrolls are very fragmentary at best. It may become less impressive within the Essene community when we consider the fact that only two copies of it were found at Qumran, as compared, for example, with twenty-five different copies of Deuteronomy, eighteen of Isaiah, and twenty-seven of the Psalter. Of the nonbiblical manuscripts composed by the Essenes or highly esteemed by them, we have at least eleven copies of the Community Rule, nine of the Songs of the Sabbath Sacrifice, eight of the Thanksgiving Hymns, and seven of the War of the Sons of Light Against the Sons of Darkness.

In light of these numbers, we would hardly expect to find only two copies of the Temple Scroll if it was the central law of the Qumran community. Moreover, there is not a single quotation from the Temple Scroll in all of the specifically Essene documents, such as the Community Rule, the Damascus Documents, or the Thanksgiving Hymns. The Pentateuch is often cited in these writings, from Genesis to Deuteronomy, but not one quotation is from the Temple Scroll. This clearly demonstrates that, regardless of what the members of the Qumran community could learn from copying and reading the Temple Scroll, this text was no legal authority for them, neither a canonical nor an extracanonical one.

When the Essene scrolls quote from the Pentateuch, they often cite the text as coming from the "Book of the Torah" *(Sefer ha-Torah)* or the "Torah of Moses" *(Torath Moshe)*. We may conclude that when the community used these terms they were referring to the Pentateuch as it is known to us, and never to the Temple Scroll.

Another important factor that demonstrates that the Temple Scroll was not part of the authorized law of the Essene community at Qumran is that the religious law *(halakhah)* reflected in the Temple Scroll often differs from the Qumran community's known *halakhah*.

At Qumran, every new interpretation of religious law based on an inquiry into the Torah had to be acknowledged by a central body called "The Council of the Community." Thereafter, all members of the community were obliged to follow the new law. In this way, the uniformity of religious law within the group was guaranteed, and no differences in understanding of the Torah could result.

It is true that some religious laws *(halakhot)* reflected in the Temple Scroll agree with specific religious laws of the Qumran community. But these examples simply demonstrate that some of the *halakhot* of the Qumran community come from the same tradition as represented also in the Temple Scroll. There is no direct dependence, however, and the Temple Scroll's text is never quoted. An example of such a correspondence is the concept that the specific holiness of the Temple includes the whole "Holy City" *('ir ha-qodesh),* that is, the whole city of Jerusalem, an interpretation demanded by the Temple Scroll as well as by the "Laws" of the Damascus Documents.[4]*

But there are also basic halakhic differences between the Temple Scroll and the strictly Essene documents found at Qumran. For example, according to the Temple Scroll, the king is permitted to marry only one wife during her lifetime, but he is allowed a second wife after the death of his first wife. But the "Admonitions" of the Damascus Document in all probability prohibit a second marriage to all Jews "in their own lifetime."

Another example of halakhic differences between the Temple Scroll and Qumran law concerns the death penalty. The Temple Scroll demands the death penalty for a particular crime, even if there are only two witnesses; Essene law (the "Laws" of the Damascus Document), however, requires three witnesses in all cases. Here we have a direct contradiction, as Lawrence Schiffman has noted.[5] It is difficult to imagine a Jewish community or group whose members differ internally on main points of *halakhah;* the *halakhah* is something like God himself. Yet we would have such differences within the Qumran community if we were to conclude that the Temple Scroll was a central Qumranic document. The differences I have cited are, at the very least, difficult to explain if one adheres to the theory that the Temple Scroll played a normative role for the Qumran community.

As other scholars have noted, from a literary and philological perspective, there is a broad range of differences between the Temple Scroll and the specifically Essene texts. For example, the Temple Scroll refers to the high priest by his traditional title *ha-kohen ha-gadol* (the great priest); this title never occurs, however, in other texts from the Qumran caves. There his title is *kohen ha-rosh* (the high priest) or, perhaps, *ha-kohen ha-mashiah* (the anointed priest).[6]

Another example: In the Temple Scroll, Israel is often called *ha-'am* (the people), and sometimes *'am ha-qahal* (the people of the assembly). These expressions never occur in specifically Essene texts, which prefer *'edah* (congregation) or *yahad* (community). The term *'edah* rarely occurs in the Temple Scroll; and the term *yahad* never occurs there.

It would be easy to produce a long list of such examples, the upshot of which would be to show that the language and the style of the Temple

---

*See Chapter 5.

Scroll are much more traditional—that is, nearer to the biblical books—than the equivalents in the specifically Qumranic texts.

The laws prescribing the construction of the temple and its courts consume almost half of the Temple Scroll. The specifically Essene scrolls reflect no interest whatever in this subject. Indeed, these Essene texts contain considerable polemic against some conditions at the Jerusalem Temple. But this entire polemic is aimed against the illegitimate priesthood and the sacrifices they offered there, against people who participate in their cult and against their particular cultic customs. Never are the Temple building or its courts criticized as being at variance with God's commandments. Nor is there any hint in any of the specifically Essene texts of any desire to change the Jerusalem Temple building or its broader architectural features.

In summation: There is not one mention of the Temple Scroll's text in any of the other specifically Essene writings from Qumran. There is not one quotation from the Temple Scroll in the many Qumran scrolls that otherwise, time and time again, cite all the books of the Pentateuch as their unique law. Further, there are clear differences between the Temple Scroll and the specifically Essene texts in matters of religious law, style, terminology, and other linguistic and literary traits. There is also a quite different approach to the Temple buildings in the Temple Scroll, on the one hand, and in the specifically Essene texts on the other. And last but not least, only two copies of the Temple Scroll's text were found in the Qumran caves, both only in Cave 11.

The result is unequivocal in my opinion: Whatever the Temple Scroll was, it was not part of the law of the Qumran community, but only some kind of traditional text copied by them once or twice for reasons unknown to us.

But since, as we noted at the outset and as Yadin also observed, the Temple Scroll was composed as a book of the Torah like the other books of the Pentateuch and was regarded as having been given by God himself on Mt. Sinai, we must conclude that the Temple Scroll was an essential part of the Torah for another group of Jews. But who, where, and when?

The argument that I have already given—that the Temple Scroll was not regarded as part of the Torah by the Essenes at Qumran—has been presented to my colleagues at several scholarly meetings and has met with widespread agreement and approval. The argument I am about to make—as to who, where, and when, and under what circumstances—has not met with such widespread agreement. It is, in fact, a matter of great controversy. What the outcome of this scholarly discussion will be, no one can say for sure—but the discussion will be heated and interesting. Nevertheless, it seems permissible to present my views, controversial though they are, and to observe that, so far, no one has come up with a better suggestion.

I believe that the Temple Scroll is an early expansion of the Torah—a kind of sixth book to be added to the Pentateuch as it has come down to us. Expanded Torah scrolls are nothing new, although it is certainly unusual to find a whole book representing such an expansion. But even before the discoveries at Qumran, we had both the Samaritan Pentateuch,* with its smaller expansions within the text of the traditional five books of the Pentateuch, and the Greek Septuagint,† with its similar expansions.[7] Now we also have expansions of a similar kind in the fragments of Torah scrolls from the Qumran caves.[8]

In my opinion, most of these early expansions to Torah scrolls represent the initiative of priests at the Jerusalem Temple from the period during which the Judean exiles returned from Babylonia and rebuilt the Temple (the Second Temple), from the latter third of the sixth century B.C. onwards. The crucial point is that these expansions developed at the Second Temple before the canonization of the Pentateuch, that is, before an official textual version of the Torah was authorized and finally established there.

According to the Bible, Ezra the Scribe established the canon of the Pentateuch in Jerusalem when he returned from the Babylonian Exile, some fifty to seventy-five years after the Second Temple was built by earlier returnees. The biblical text gives us enough information to fix the precise date for Ezra's return and canonization of the Pentateuch—458 B.C. As we read in the book of Ezra, "During the reign of Artaxerxes [465–424 B.C.] . . . Ezra [whose ancestry is here traced back to Aaron the high priest] came up from Babylon, a scribe expert in the Teaching of Moses" (Ezra 7:1–6). In the next verse, we learn that Ezra arrived with other returnees during the seventh year of Artaxerxes's reign (458 B.C.). According to the letter of authority that Artaxerxes gave to Ezra, "The Law of your God . . . is in your care" (Ezra 7:14). The letter continues: "Ezra, [you are to] appoint magistrates and judges . . . who know the Law of your God . . . to judge and to teach those who do not know. Let anyone who does not obey the Law of your God . . . be punished" (Ezra 7:25–26). That is precisely what Ezra did, establishing the Pentateuch as the central authority in Jerusalem.

*The Samaritan Pentateuch is the Torah in the form canonized by the Samaritans.
†The Septuagint is the Greek version of the Hebrew Bible, as translated by Jews in Alexandria from the third century B.C. onwards.

From form-critical studies of the Pentateuch, we know that when the Pentateuch first took shape, the editors (or redactors, as they are called) used older sources. In the final edition of the Pentateuch, these older sources were combined, augmented, and updated according to the needs and perspectives of a later day. I believe this process occurred in Mesopotamia during the Babylonian Exile. In my opinion, Ezra himself brought this version from Mesopotamia to Jerusalem; he intended it for the future as the only authoritative Torah, proclaiming it the Book of the Torah *(Sefer ha-Torah),* and established it in Jerusalem through the authority of the Persian government. Whether compiled in Jerusalem or Babylonia, however, the consequence of Ezra's actions was necessarily that all other Torah scrolls used at the Temple of Jerusalem up to Ezra's time were no longer in force. Every new scroll with books of the Pentateuch had to conform now to the version Ezra proclaimed as authoritative.

But what of the many expanded and different versions of Torah scrolls that had developed up to that time, Torah scrolls that contained additions such as survived in the Samaritan Pentateuch and the Septuagint? After all, such traditional expansions had been formulated at the Temple by Jerusalem priests based on the authority of God himself. Could they be invalidated by a human decision—that is, by the authority of the pagan king Artaxerxes I, who stood behind the deeds of Ezra the Scribe?

The way out of this dilemma is reflected in the text of the Temple Scroll. Many of the traditional expansions of the hitherto existing Torah scrolls were taken over into this new book, which we now refer to as the Temple Scroll.

At this point, I must explain that the Temple Scroll is itself, like Genesis, for example, a composite document. In a brilliant article by Andrew M. Wilson and Lawrence Wills, with an assist from their mentor, Professor John Strugnell of Harvard,[9] the authors clearly demonstrate that there are at least five different sources in the Temple Scroll. In different parts of the Temple Scroll, for example, God is referred to in the first person and in the third person, the people are addressed in the singular and in the plural, etc. These five distinct sources were not only combined in the Temple Scroll, but were superficially revised by a final editor, or redactor, who added some further material here and there and created the framework of the final text—the same process that is reflected, for example, in Genesis. In my judgment, Wilson and Wills are basically correct about the different strands of texts combined in the Temple Scroll. On only a few minor points would I favor a solution other than the one they have proposed.

When we examine the setting or *Sitz im Leben* of these five sources of the Temple Scroll, we must conclude that they are all shaped by specific priestly interests. Even the final redaction reflects these priestly interests. And there is nothing other than the practice of the priestly cult at the Temple in Jerusalem that is reflected in this setting.

For this reason, it seems clear that the composition of these five sources occurred sometime during the first century of the Second Temple period, and their redaction occurred in reaction to, and not too long after, Ezra's canonization of the Pentateuch in 458 B.C. Once Ezra had established what was essentially a shorter, canonical Pentateuch, in effect outlawing all these former additions and expansions, such additions and expansions were collected and edited to form what we know as the Temple Scroll.

The authority of these old additions and expansions of the Pentateuch was now assumed by the new book as a whole: God himself spoke directly to his people, through this book, as in the Pentateuch, even if all its parts did not conform perfectly to the overall style of direct address. In this way, through the compilation of the Temple Scroll, a sixth book of the Torah was created—the only true Hexateuch that has ever existed historically!

This sixth book of the Torah not only gathered together many of the traditional Torah additions and expansions, but, by the adoption of the five sources, it also brought into the supplemented Torah other materials in which God had spoken to the Fathers in an authoritative way regarding matters of the Temple, its cult, the purity of the participants, and the many revised halakhic laws.

Yadin himself noted the tendency of the Temple Scroll to combine and harmonize divergent commandments found in the Pentateuch and in the books of the prophets. This in effect illustrates the process of collection and combination out of which the Temple Scroll was created. (A similar method, I might add, can be traced through almost all ages of Jewish tradition and is found not only in the Mishnah and in the Talmuds, but even as late as the *Shulhan 'Arukh,* a sixteenth-century collection of laws that remains authoritative to this date for observant Jews.)

My basic thesis depends, I realize, on establishing the date of the sources in the Temple Scroll to the early Second Temple period (from the latter third of the sixth century to the fifth century B.C.), and its redaction to the second half of the fifth century B.C. The most important element in establishing this dating has already been discussed—the priestly *Sitz im Leben* of the sources and the historical context of Ezra's canonization of the Pentateuch. No other set of later historical circumstances fits these aspects of the text of the Temple Scroll and its final editing. Moreover, quite apart from all the other arguments, it is difficult to imagine that a supplementary sixth book of the Torah could have been compiled and acknowledged by at least some Jewish priests much later than the fifth—or the fourth—century B.C.

Nevertheless, this is a somewhat radical redating of the Temple Scroll and will not be easily accepted by a scholarly community already accustomed to arguing about dates for the Temple Scroll ranging between about 200 B.C. and 50 B.C. Possible later historical allusions, philology, grammar, etc., will be adduced by my scholarly colleagues to support a particular dating later than my proposed dating. But I have examined all of the arguments adduced thus far, most of them quite technical, and I can say with some degree of confidence that none presents any particular problem for the dating I have proposed.

True, the extant copies of the Temple Scroll that survived at Qumran are much later, from about 50 B.C. onwards, but this says nothing about the sources' date of composition or about the date of their combination and final redaction.

Let me give an example of the kinds of issues involved in this dating debate. One of the sources of the Temple Scroll consists of a reworking of the laws in Deuteronomy 12–26, arranged in a new way, with many additions and alterations as compared with the biblical text. This source runs from column LI, line 11 of the Temple Scroll to the lost end of the scroll, but is interrupted in columns LVII to LIX by the so-called Statutes of the King. Deuteronomy 21:22–23 requires that a man who has been executed and then publicly exposed by *talah 'al ha-'es*—literally, hanging on a pole, be buried the same day. Otherwise the land will be defiled. In the Temple Scroll, the crimes for which *talah 'al ha-'es* is required is expanded to include, for example, an Israelite who "passes on information about my people and betrays my people to a foreign people." Here the death of the evil-doer will be caused by this "hanging on a pole"— not by killing him before and then "hanging on a pole," as in Deuteronomy. Some scholars have argued that this passage in the Temple Scroll refers specifically to the time of Alexander Jannaeus (first century B.C.), who crucified eight hundred Jews alive, most of them Pharisees. This is reported by Flavius Josephus and is alluded to in the *Pesher Nahum* from Qumran. But there is no reason whatever to connect the discussion of *talah 'al ha-'es* in the Temple Scroll to this historical incident in the first century B.C. Hanging of the people alive by *talah 'al ha-'es* was familiar to the people of Israel, at least as a Gentile punishment, from as early as 701 B.C., when Sennacherib, the king of Assyria, conquered the Israelite town of Lachish. The reliefs portraying this conquest show three nude

Israelites from Lachish being impaled on stakes. This kind of *talah 'al ha-'es* would thus have been usual from as early as the eighth century B.C.

All other indications of a later date for the Temple Scroll can be shown to be inconclusive in this same way, although perhaps less dramatically.

Accordingly, we may conclude that the Temple Scroll was composed from previously existing sources as a sixth book of the Torah. This occurred soon after Ezra's canonization of the "shorter" Pentateuch, the Pentateuch as we know it. If Ezra canonized this "shorter" Pentateuch in 458 B.C., the text of the Temple Scroll would have been redacted some time after this, in the second half of the fifth century B.C.

In the early Second Temple period (beginning in the latter third of the sixth century B.C.), there must have been priestly families, or perhaps priestly "schools," in Jerusalem, that composed the expansions and additions that provided the Temple Scroll with its sources. Ezra's "reform"— his canonization of the Pentateuch—stopped this process of further creating expansions and additions. He established the "original" version of the Pentateuch, known to him, I believe, from Mesopotamia, as the only authorized one in Jerusalem as well.

The Temple Scroll incorporated many of the Palestinian "additions" from expanded Torah scrolls and used them to create a new *Sefer Torah,* a new Book of the Law. The editor of this text represents the end of this kind of creativity in Scripture as far as the Torah is concerned. He used these additions and supplementary sources to compose a sixth book of the Torah. The authority behind this new book, however, was still on the same level as the authority of the Pentateuch itself and of its priestly traditions, that is, God himself. The editor did not have to resort to any other source of authority for his new book. He did not intend to replace the traditional Pentateuch; rather, he intended to complete it.

Somehow, at least two copies of this sixth book of the Torah found their way to the ancient libraries of Qumran. With what authority the Essenes of Qumran regarded it, we do not know. But we have no reason to believe that for them it was a central document of law. But for many mainstream Jews in Jerusalem, it probably was such a document during the mid–Second Temple period (from the end of the fifth century through the fourth, or even third, century B.C.).[10]

The text of the Temple Scroll will now shed new light on that still rather shrouded period of Jewish life in Jerusalem following the return of the first exiles from Babylonia.

IV

THE DEAD SEA
SCROLLS AND
THE BIBLE

CHAPTER 11

THE TEXT BEHIND THE TEXT
OF THE HEBREW BIBLE

FRANK MOORE CROSS

Until the discovery of the Dead Sea Scrolls, the oldest copies of the Rabbinic Recension* of the Bible were from the medieval period. Scholars tried, but were unable to get behind this text to its development in an earlier period. It was assumed—wrongly, as it turned out—that there was a Hebrew veritas, *a single original text that lay behind the Rabbinic Recension. In this chapter, one of the world's greatest text critics of the Bible, Harvard Professor Frank Cross, explains how the approximately two hundred biblical manuscripts among the Dead Sea Scrolls enable us to get behind the Rabbinic Recension and trace its development.*

The term Dead Sea Scrolls *for this purpose includes not only documents from the Wadi Qumran, but also from other sites along the Dead Sea.† These biblical texts can be divided into two groups—an earlier group from Qumran (which predates the Roman destruction of Jerusalem in 70 A.D.) and a later group from sites south of Qumran (which dates to the period between the two Jewish revolts). The latter group are quite uniform, reflecting the fact that a standardized text had already developed. The earlier group (from Qumran),*

---

*A recension is an edition of an ancient text involving a more or less systematic revision of an earlier text form.

†See Introduction, "Of Caves and Scholars: An Overview."

however, shows wide variations, sometimes even different editions of the same book. Cross is able to identify among these different texts three families of texts that appear to have originated in different geographical localities—Palestine, Egypt, and Babylonia. He then describes the process by which these different local texts were chosen for the standardized Rabbinic Recension. He also explains the importance of the great Jewish sage Hillel in this process and the historical turmoil that made a standardized text desirable, if not absolutely necessary. Finally, he relates all this to the process of deciding which books were to be regarded as authoritative—that is, canonical, to be included in the Bible—and which were to be excluded.

All in all, this chapter is a brilliant synthesis of an enormous amount of scholarship. —ED.

— · —

Nearly forty years have passed since that fateful spring day in 1947 when a young Bedouin shepherd threw a stone into a cave in the cliffside on the northwestern shore of the Dead Sea and heard the sound of pottery shattering inside. When he and a companion later gathered nerve to crawl into the cave (now known as Qumran Cave 1), they found seven decaying rolls of leather. These were the original "Dead Sea Scrolls."

William Foxwell Albright, the most distinguished Near Eastern archaeologist and Hebrew epigraphist of his generation, immediately hailed the finds as the greatest manuscript discovery of modern times.

In the years that followed, both archaeologists and Bedouin have explored and dug in hundreds of caves in the great wadis that, like the Wadi Qumran, cut through the towering cliffs that mark the Jordan Rift. In the competition between clandestine Bedouin diggers and archaeologists, it must be confessed that the laurels have gone more frequently to the intrepid and patient shepherds. In any case, eventually ten additional caves with leather and papyrus manuscripts were found in the vicinity of Khirbet Qumran, the ruins of a community of Essenes—Jewish sectaries—to whose library the documents once belonged. So we now have manuscripts from Qumran caves numbered 1 through 11. From Cave 11 came the great Temple Scroll acquired by the late Yigael Yadin in 1967.[1] More manuscripts and papyri were discovered in the large caves in the wadis south of Qumran: the Wadi Murabba'at, the Nahal Hever, and the

Nahal Se'elim. More recently, in 1962, the oldest group of documents from the Jordan Rift was found in the Wadi ed-Daliyeh, north of Jericho. These are the Samaria legal papyri from the fourth century B.C.*

Most recently of all, in 1963–1964, manuscripts were uncovered in Yadin's excavations of the ruins of Herod's fortress, Masada, atop a diamond-shaped mountain overlooking the Dead Sea.

In any other generation each of these finds would have been regarded as nothing short of sensational. Altogether they have been overwhelming—in two senses. First, the magnitude of these discoveries can hardly be comprehended. Second, the labors of piecing together hundreds of thousands of fragments, editing, interpreting, and assimilating these manuscripts have often overwhelmed the scholarly community with a responsibility both glorious and oppressive. Nearly forty years of discovery and research are now past. I suspect that another forty years will pass before the first exploratory investigation of these "treasures of darkness" will be completed. Almost each year a large new volume of previously unpublished material comes into print, and this will be so for many years to come. I am myself in the process of completing three volumes of unpublished manuscripts and papyri. The impact of all these discoveries and of all this research will be enormous.

I should like to explore several important areas of historical study in which new insights and conclusions are emerging.

First, I shall discuss the bearing of new studies upon our understanding of the history of the biblical text. From the Dead Sea Scrolls, we have learned a great deal about the early transmission of biblical books, the fixation of the text of biblical books, and even the procedure by which the canon of the Hebrew Bible came into being. In short, we now know in some detail what the biblical materials were like before they became "biblical," as well as the process by which the texts became fixed and chosen as "biblical."

To replace the new evidence in context, it will be useful to review briefly the status of the study of the history of the text of the Hebrew Bible prior to the discovery of the manuscripts on the shore of the Dead Sea.

The Bible survives in many Hebrew manuscripts and in several ancient versions translated from the Hebrew. In the medieval Hebrew manu-

*See Paul W. Lapp, "Bedouin Find Papyri Three Centuries Older than Dead Sea Scrolls," and Frank Moore Cross, "The Historical Importance of the Samaria Papyri," *Biblical Archaeology Review*, March 1978.

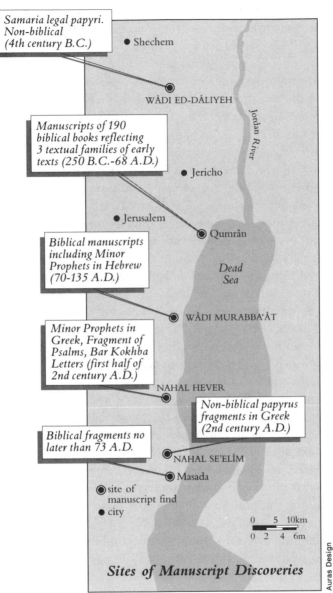

Samaria legal papyri.
Non-biblical
(4th century B.C.)

● Shechem

⦿ WÂDI ED-DÂLIYEH

Manuscripts of 190
biblical books reflecting
3 textual families of early
texts (250 B.C.-68 A.D.)

Jordan River

● Jericho

● Jerusalem

⦿ Qumrân

Dead
Sea

Biblical manuscripts
including Minor
Prophets in Hebrew
(70-135 A.D.)

⦿ WÂDI MURABBA'ÂT

Minor Prophets in
Greek, Fragment of
Psalms, Bar Kokhba
Letters (first half of
2nd century A.D.)

NAHAL HEVER
⦿

Non-biblical papyrus
fragments in Greek
(2nd century A.D.)

Biblical fragments no
later than 73 A.D.

⦿ NAHAL SE'ELÎM

⦿ Masada

⦿ site of
manuscript find
● city

0   5   10km
0   2   4   6m

Auras Design

Sites of Manuscript Discoveries

scripts there are hundreds, even thousands of differences, mostly minor, rarely major. In the old versions, especially in the Old Greek version (which was written beginning in the third century B.C. and is commonly called the Septuagint), there are thousands of variants, many minor, but also many major. Even before the discovery of biblical manuscripts in the caves of Qumran and elsewhere in the Jordan Rift, these manuscripts and versions provided a rich body of resources for the textual critic's attempts to reconstruct the history of the biblical text. At the same time, the history of the text of the Hebrew Bible has been confused and obscured by an assumption, or rather a dogma, on the part of the ancients—rabbis and Church Fathers alike—that the Hebrew text was unchanged and unchanging, unaltered by the usual scribal realities that produce families of texts and different recensions in works that have survived over long periods of transmission.

This dogma of the *Hebraica veritas* may be found as early as the late first century of the Common Era, when Josephus, the Jewish historian, wrote:

> We have given practical proof of our reverence for our scriptures. For, although such long ages have now passed, no one has ventured to add, or to remove, or to alter a syllable; and it is an instinct with every Jew, from the day of his birth, to regard them as decrees of God, to abide by them, and if need be, cheerfully to die for them.[2]

Josephus evidently regarded the Hebrew Bible as having, in theory at least, an immutable text.[3]

Origen, the Church Father, ordinarily used the Old Greek version of the Bible. But he, too, apparently assumed that his Greek Bible was translated from a Hebrew textual base that was the same as the rabbinical Hebrew text in current use in his day. Hence, in his monumental *Hexapla,** he carefully corrected his Greek manuscripts to be the *Hebraica veritas*—incidentally, with catastrophic results for the subsequent transmission of the Greek Bible.

Jerome, writing in the fourth century, applied the principle of "correcting to the Hebrew" to the Latin Bible, displacing earlier Latin trans-

*The *Hexapla* was a six or more columned work in which the first column contained the Hebrew text of the Bible; the second column, a transliteration of the Hebrew text into Greek script; the third, the recension of Aquila; the fourth, the recension of Symmachus; the fifth, Origen's revised text of the Septuagint; and the sixth column, the recension of Theodotion.

lations (based on the Old Greek Bible) with a new Latin translation that has come to be called the Vulgate, a Latin version translated from the standard Rabbinic Recension of the Hebrew Bible in use in Jerome's time.

The search for the early stages in the history of the text of the Hebrew Bible began to be pursued scientifically in the late eighteenth century, but the extant manuscripts were all of medieval date, and the results were disappointing for those who hoped to find traces of archaic forms of the text. The sifting of the medieval manuscripts yielded, in its mass of variant readings, no evidence of alternate textual families or text types. The variants were secondary* and of late date, the slips and errors of medieval scribes. Indeed, it could be argued that the theory of a fixed and unchanging Hebrew text was given added support by the evidence from the collections of medieval manuscripts.

Some of the more astute textual scholars, however, argued that all medieval Hebrew manuscripts derived from a single recension fixed early in the Christian era, and that this recension alone survived in the Jewish communities. Direct access to the early development of the text of the Hebrew Bible (prior to the recensions) was thus effectively blocked.[4] Accordingly, the sea of variants in the great collections of manuscripts was of little or no help in the endeavor to recover ancient readings standing behind corruptions in the *textus receptus*.† It could be, and was, argued that the medieval text stemmed from a single archetype, or from single manuscripts of each biblical work, which already possessed the pattern of errors held in common by the medieval text.[5]

The fact is, however, that in the nineteenth century, there was little hard evidence to determine precisely the procedure by which the Rabbinic Recension, found in all medieval manuscripts, came into being and was promulgated. In the end, the vigorous scholarly debates of the nineteenth century subsided, and while much research and theorizing continued, no major advances were made until the discovery of Hebrew and Greek manuscripts in the Wilderness of Judah—the Dead Sea Scrolls.

The discovery of ancient manuscripts in the eleven caves of Qumran provided the first unambiguous witnesses to an ancient stage of the Hebrew text of the Bible.[6] These caves have yielded some 170 manuscripts of biblical books, most of them in a highly fragmentary state, and their publication is still in progress.[7]

---

*By secondary, I refer to errors creeping into the text after the fixation of the text.
†That is, the received or traditional text.

Although all the evidence is not yet published, we can compare these Qumran manuscripts with a dozen or so biblical manuscripts, again fragmentary and some still unpublished, recovered from the Nahal Hever, the Wadi Murabba'at, and Herod's fortress at Masada. The two groups of manuscripts—the Qumran manuscripts, on the one hand, and the manuscripts found in the southern caves and at Masada—vary in two critical respects. The manuscripts of the Qumran group are earlier (varying in date between about 250 B.C. to 68 A.D.), at which time the Essene community at Qumran was destroyed by the Romans as part of the suppression of the First Jewish Revolt (66–70 A.D.). On palaeographical grounds, we can date most of these biblical manuscripts no later than the first half of the first century of the Common Era, and most are earlier. The second "southern group"—from the caves of the Wadi Murabba'at, from the Nahal Hever, and from Masada—date as a group from a later period. Most important of the manuscripts of the southern group are the great Hebrew Minor Prophets Scroll* from a cave in the Wadi Murabba'at and the Greek Minor Prophets Scroll from the Nahal Hever.

The Minor Prophets Scroll from Murabba'at can be dated palaeographically to the second half of the first century of the Common Era, and the biblical fragments from Masada to no later than 73 A.D., when the Romans stormed the bastion and destroyed its fortifications. A number of the biblical fragments from the southern caves date to the interval between the First and Second Jewish Revolts, that is, between 70 and 135 A.D., and once belonged to followers of Bar Kokhba, the messianic leader of the Second Revolt (132–135 A.D.).

The two groups of biblical manuscripts differ not only in date. The southern (later) group reveals a text that shows no significant deviation from the archetypal Rabbinic Recension—that is, the recension that is ancestral to the Masoretic text,† our traditional Hebrew Bible.[8] This is in marked contrast to the Qumran group of documents, which reveals other text types.

The data drawn from the southern manuscripts enable us to conclude that before the end of the first century of the Common Era, a recension

---

*The Book of the Twelve Minor Prophets included (in traditional order) Hosea, Joel, Amos, Obadiah, Jonah, Micah, Nahum, Habakkuk, Zephaniah, Haggai, Zechariah, and Malachi. The Murabba'at Minor Prophets extends from the middle of Joel to the beginning of Zechariah.

†The term *Masoretic* refers to the schools of Masoretes, Jewish biblical scholars of the late Middle Ages, who handled and standardized traditions of the punctuation (including vocalization), accentuation, divisions, etc. of the consonantal (unpointed) text of the medieval Hebrew Bible.

of the text of the Hebrew Bible had been promulgated that had overwhelming authority, at least in Pharisaic circles, and that came to dominate the Jewish community in the interval between the fall of Jerusalem
to the Romans in 70 A.D., and the Roman suppression of the Second
Jewish Revolt in 135 A.D.

The textual situation at Qumran differed totally. The Qumran manuscripts show no influences that we can detect of the standardization that
marks the Rabbinic Recension. At Qumran we find evidence of discrete
and, indeed, recognizable families of textual tradition, including text types
that are different from the Rabbinic Recension. These variant streams of
tradition have been called "recensions" or "families" or "local texts."[9]

Sometimes one of these text types differs strikingly in detail from the
traditional text that has come down to us. In extreme instances we
discover that a textual tradition is preserved in a manuscript that stems
not merely from textual changes in individual readings; it derives from
an edition of a biblical work different broadly in content and length from
the edition used in the Rabbinic Recension. For example, there are two
editions of Jeremiah represented in manuscripts from Qumran: a long
edition known from our traditional Bible and a short edition that also
differs in the order of the prophetic oracles. There are two editions (or
collections) of the Psalter, one Persian in date, one Hellenistic. There is
a whole Daniel literature, of which the book of Daniel is only a single
part. Instances of different editions of biblical books, however, are relatively rare. For the most part the textual families reflected in extant
biblical manuscripts are marked by variants in individual readings; grammatical changes, alternate vocabulary, omissions or additions of words,
phrases, and even, on occasion, paragraphs.

The different text types of most biblical books appear to be the
product of natural growth, or of local development, in the process of
scribal transmission, not of a controlled or systematic recension, revision,
or collation at a given place or time. At the same time, the different texts
possess traits, some more or less systematic, that permit them to be
classified in different families. The common traits of a textual family
include, for example, their "bad genes," an inherited group of mistakes
or secondary readings perpetuated by copyists generation after generation. Other distinguishing traits may be a particular orthographic (spelling) style, the type of script utilized, the repeated appearance of a peculiar
chronology or numeral calculation (arising often in attempts to resolve
apparent or real errors in traditional numbers), the systematic introduction into the text of parallel readings (especially in legal sections with

parallel sections in other books), and repeated use of archaizing or "modernized" grammatical and lexical features.

The Qumran manuscripts not only provide evidence of early textual traditions; perhaps even more important, the data drawn from the Qumran discoveries enable us to identify and delineate other textual traditions that survive from times before the Common Era—including the Hebrew textual base of the Old Greek translation, the textual background of the Samaritan Recension of the Pentateuch, and the text type that was utilized in the Rabbinic Recension. In this great complex of textual materials, as many as three textual families have been identified in certain biblical books (the Pentateuchal books and the books of Samuel), two textual families in other books, notably in Jeremiah and Job, and in many books only one textual tradition is reflected in extant data (for example, Isaiah and Ezekiel). The textual critic is thus confronted with the task of organizing this evidence: the existence of a plurality of textual types in the early era, the limited number of distinct textual families, and the relative homogeneity of the variant textual traditions over several centuries of time.

I have proposed a theory of "local texts" to satisfy the requirements of this data. As applied to those books where three textual families exist, namely in the Pentateuch and Samuel, this theory may be sketched as follows: Three forms of the text appear to have developed slowly between the fifth century B.C. and the first century B.C., in the Jewish communities in Palestine, in Egypt, and in Babylon, respectively. The Palestinian text is the dominant family in the Qumran manuscripts. Its earliest witness is found in the Chronicler's citations of the Pentateuch and Samuel. This Palestinian text was also used in the Samaritan Recension of the Pentateuch. At least in its late form, the Palestinian text can be characterized as expansionistic, a full text marked frequently by conflation,* glosses,†
synoptic additions (that is, the insertion of readings from parallel passages in other sources), and other evidence of intense scribal activity. Omissions owing to scribal lapses are relatively infrequent. To this family belong the Pentateuchal manuscripts inscribed in the Palaeo-Hebrew script, a derivative of the old national script of pre-Exilic Israel.‡

---

*Conflation is the technical term used when two variant readings are combined into one reading in the course of scribal transmission. The scribe thus conflates the manuscripts available to him.

†A gloss is a brief explanatory note or reading either in the margin or between the lines of a manuscript. Often glosses were introduced into the text itself by a scribe who supposed the gloss a correction of the manuscripts.

‡The Palaeo-Hebrew script survives to the present day in manuscripts of the Samaritan Pentateuch. The Jewish character of the Hellenistic and Roman periods, the ancestor of

Local Texts Theory: History of the Text of Exodus

6th century B.C.	4th century B.C.	3rd century B.C.		1st century A.D.	10th century A.D.
ARCHETYPE OF THE BOOK OF EXODUS	BABYLONIAN TEXTUAL FAMILY		PROTO-RABBINIC TEXT	RABBINIC RECENSION	MASORETIC TEXT
	OLD PALESTINIAN TEXTUAL FAMILY	4 Q EXODUS[J]	LATE PALES-TINIAN TEXTS	SAMARITAN RECENSION	
		EGYPTIAN TEXTUAL FAMILY	OLD GREEK TRANSLATION *(SEPTUAGINT)*		

Auras Design

The second textual family, which we label Egyptian, is found in the Old Greek (Septuagint) translation of the Pentateuch and Reigns (the Greek version of Samuel and Kings), and in the short edition of Jeremiah found in one Hebrew manuscript at Qumran. In some respects the Egyptian family resembles the Palestinian text, especially the earliest of the Palestinian witnesses, and may be regarded as a branch of the Old Palestinian family.

The third family we designate "Babylonian," although we are, in fact, uncertain of the locale of its origin. As we shall see, the intellectual influence of the powerful Babylonian community was to exercise a decisive role in the emergence of the authoritative Rabbinic Recension. This third text type, known thus far only in the Pentateuch and Samuel, forms the base of the Rabbinic Recension. In the Pentateuch, it is a conservative, often pristine text, which shows little expansion and relatively few traces of revision and modernizing.

Thus at Qumran, and in traditions of the biblical text that broke off from the main Jewish stream before the turn of the Common Era, we find several textual families. None, including the text type ancestral to the Rabbinic Recension, shows evidence of a systematic recension or stabilization.

In the southern caves and at Masada, however, we find only a single text type, one that shows every evidence of the external controls that fixed the text we call the Rabbinic Recension. The southern group of manuscripts stands very close to the archetype of this recension. We are

---

the modern Hebrew bookhand, is a derivative of the Aramaic script of the Persian chancelleries.

led, therefore, to the conclusion that the Rabbinic Recension of the Hebrew Bible—what we may also call the authoritative Pharisaic text— was fixed by the time of the Roman destruction of Jerusalem in 70 A.D. This recension became regnant only in the interval between the two Jewish Revolts, when the Pharisaic party came wholly to dominate the surviving Jewish community and rival parties diminished and disappeared. Sects like the Christians and Samaritans continued to exist but only as separate communities, isolated from Pharisaic influence. Rabbinic Judaism survived and with it the Rabbinic Recension.

The Rabbinic Recension was promulgated as a response and solution to a textual crisis that developed in late Hellenistic and early Roman times. The Maccabean Revolt, initiated in 167 B.C., ultimately reestablished an independent Jewish state, which had not existed since the time the Babylonians destroyed Jerusalem and the First Temple in 587 B.C. In the wake of Maccabean victories that led eventually to the full independence of Judea under the rule of Simon the Maccabee (140–134 B.C.), a Zionist revival was fueled, augmented by Parthian expulsions of the Jews. A flood of Jews returned to Jerusalem from Babylon, Syria, and Egypt.[10] By the first century before and the first century after the Common Era, competing local texts and editions had found their way to Judah, causing considerable confusion, as reflected in the library at Qumran. Moreover, the uncontrolled development of the text of individual textual families became intolerable and precipitated a textual crisis when the urgent need for precise doctrinal and legal (halakhic) exegesis arose in Hellenistic Judaism. Party strife began in earnest in the mid-second century B.C. with the emergence of the Sadducean, Pharisaic, and Essene parties, and the subsequent religious disputes between the parties increased the need for a fixed, authoritative text. By the beginning of the first century of the Common Era, there was further splintering into sectarian groups, and there is evidence of intense intraparty and sectarian dispute and contention.

These data provide the general time and historical context for the creation of the Rabbinic Recension. Other hints, limiting the time frame in which we must place the promulgation of the Rabbinic Recension, are found in the history of the Greek recensions.[11] The Rabbinic Recension was promulgated in the first half of the first century of the present era. In these same days we witness also the fixing of hermeneutical rules,* as well as read reports of Pharisaic discussions of the schools of Hillel and

*Hermeneutical rules are the logical principles that may be used to interpret a text— guides to exegesis.

Shammai, which presume a more or less fixed text. I think it is not too much to go even further and to attribute the initiation of the recensional labors that fixed the text of the Pharisaic Bible to the great sage Hillel himself (early first century A.D.)—or at least to the school of rabbinic scholars he inspired.

Hillel, it should be remembered, came to Palestine from Babylon and became the dominant and most creative spirit of his day; he was a giant whose impress on Pharisaism cannot be exaggerated, and his direct descendants were the principal leaders in the normative Jewish community for many generations.

The fact that Hillel (and his circle) were responsible for the selection of the protorabbinic manuscripts that stood behind the Rabbinic Recension would explain a number of its peculiarities. For example, the texts of the Pentateuch and Samuel that were chosen for the Rabbinic Recension appear to be of Babylonian origin rather than the prevailing late Palestinian texts that were available.[12] In their recensional activities, the rabbis also rejected the Palaeo-Hebrew script and its orthographic style, which was used in the most elegant Pentateuchal manuscripts inscribed in Palestine, choosing instead the common Jewish script in broad use in Palestine and throughout the Diaspora Jewish communities. The choice of the common Jewish script is particularly striking in view of the official use of the old national script by the ruling high priests for temple inscriptions and for their coinage.

The fixation of the text by Pharisaic scholars followed a pattern unusual in the textual history of ancient literary documents. The Pharisaic scholars did not produce an eclectic text by choosing preferred readings and rejecting obvious glosses or additions. This was the procedure followed by Greek scholars in Alexandria in establishing a short, if artificial, recension of the text of Homer. Nor did the rabbis combine variant readings from different textual traditions, a recensional technique that produced conflate recensions of the Septuagint and the New Testament. Instead, the rabbis selected a single textual tradition, which I term the protorabbinic text, a text that had been in existence in individual manuscripts for some time.[13] In a given biblical book of the Hebrew Bible the rabbis chose exemplars of one textual family or even a single manuscript as a base. They did not collate all the wide variety of text types available; on the contrary, they firmly rejected in some instances a dominant late Palestinian text. It should be noted, however, that they did not select, in the case of every book, texts having a common origin or local background. In the Pentateuch they chose a short, relatively uncon-

flated text—a superb text from the point of view of the modern critic—
which we believe derived from a conservative Babylonian textual tradition. In the Major Prophets, on the other hand, they chose the relatively
late and full Palestinian text of Isaiah, Ezekiel, and Jeremiah. In Jeremiah,
in fact, they selected the long edition of Jeremiah in preference to the
shorter, and in some ways, superior edition.

The choice of a non-Palestinian text of the Pentateuch is of particular
interest. The books of the Torah (the Pentateuch) held central authority
for all the Jewish parties. Indeed, the Sadducees and the Zadokite priest
of the separatist Samaritan community regarded the Pentateuch alone as
the basis of religious doctrine and practice. The Samaritans, in contrast
to the rabbis, chose for their sectarian recension of the Pentateuch a late
Palestinian text inscribed in Palaeo-Hebrew, also known from the finds
at Qumran.

We may speculate that Hillel's personal preference was responsible for
the surprising choice of the Babylonian textual base for the Pharisaic
Pentateuch. In this case, the conservative Torah scrolls that he knew and
to which he was accustomed became, under his urging, the basis of the
new Rabbinic Recension. It is quite possible that an old saying embedded in the Babylonian Talmud preserves a memory of Hillel's role in the
events, leading to the fixation of the Hebrew text and canon: "When
Israel forgot the Torah, Ezra came up from Babylon and reestablished it;
and when Israel once again forgot the Torah, Hillel the Babylonian came
up and reestablished it . . ."[14]

This much is certain. The vigorous religious community in Babylon
repeatedly in Jewish history developed spiritual and intellectual leaders
who reshaped the direction of Palestinian Judaism and defined its norms.
Such was the case in the restoration after the Exile, again in the person
of Hillel, and finally in the rise of the Babylonian Talmud.

In the lines above, I have written almost exclusively about the fixation
of the text as opposed to the stabilization of the canon. In the remarks
that follow I shall focus on the latter, and specifically on the fixation of
the Pharisaic canon on the Hebrew Bible. I shall use the term *canon* in
its strict sense: a fixed list of books of scripture that was deemed unvaria-
ble, not to be added to or subtracted from. In origin, the term *canon*
meant a rule, and concretely in the usage of the Church Fathers, a closed
list of books defined as authoritative for religious faith and practice.

The earliest clear definition of the "closed" Hebrew canon is found
in Josephus in his apologetic work, *Contra Apionem,* written in Rome in
the last decade of the first century of the Common Era. He asserted that

there was a fixed and immutable number of "justly accredited" books, twenty-two in number.* Their authority was founded on their derivation from a period of uncontested prophetic inspiration beginning with Moses and ending in the era of Nehemiah.

> [W]e do not possess myriads of inconsistent books, conflicting with each other. Our books, those which are justly accredited, are but two and twenty, and contain the record of all time. Of these, five are the books of Moses, comprising the laws, and the traditional history from the birth of man down to the death of the lawgiver. . . . From the death of Moses until Artaxerxes, who succeeded Xerxes as king of Persia, the prophets subsequent to Moses wrote the history of the events of their own times in thirteen books. The remaining four books contain hymns to God and precepts for the conduct of human life. From Artaxerxes to our own time the complete history has been written, but has not been deemed worthy of equal credit with the earlier records, because of the failure in the exact succession of prophets.[15]

Josephus' canon specifically excludes works of Hellenistic date, and by implication works attributed to pre-Mosaic patriarchs. In the paragraph subsequent to the one cited, he adds that the precise text of the twenty-two books was fixed to the syllable.

Where are we to seek the origin of Josephus' doctrine of a fixed text and a fixed canon? Josephus was a Pharisee, and I believe that he is here drawing upon his Pharisaic tradition and ultimately the work and teachings of Hillel.

There is no evidence in non-Pharisaic Jewish circles before 70 A.D. of either a fixed canon or text. The Essenes at Qumran exhibit no knowledge of this fixed text or canon. The same is true in the Hellenistic Jewish community in Alexandria, and in the early Christian communities. Until recently there has been a scholarly consensus that the acts of inclusion and exclusion that fixed the canon were completed only at the "Council of Jamnia (Yabneh)"† meeting about the end of the first century of the Common Era. However, recent sifting of the rabbinic evidence makes

---

*Josephus' canon of twenty-two books no doubt was the same as the traditional Hebrew canon that has been transmitted to us. For the reckoning, see endnote 17.

†The "Council of Jamnia" is a common and somewhat misleading designation of a particular session of the rabbinic academy (or court) at Yabneh at which it was asserted that Ecclesiastes and Song of Songs "defile the hands," i.e., are holy scripture. The session in question was held about 90 A.D., although even this date is far from certain. The academy was founded by Yohanan ben Zakkai, a disciple of Hillel. It was presided over

The Canon of the Hebrew Bible and the Excluded Books

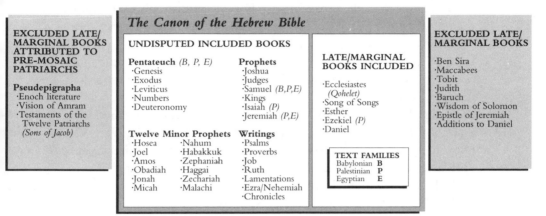

EXCLUDED LATE/ MARGINAL BOOKS ATTRIBUTED TO PRE-MOSAIC PATRIARCHS	The Canon of the Hebrew Bible			EXCLUDED LATE/ MARGINAL BOOKS
	UNDISPUTED INCLUDED BOOKS		**LATE/MARGINAL BOOKS INCLUDED**	·Ben Sira ·Maccabees
Pseudepigrapha ·Enoch literature ·Vision of Amram ·Testaments of the Twelve Patriarchs *(Sons of Jacob)*	**Pentateuch** *(B, P, E)* ·Genesis ·Exodus ·Leviticus ·Numbers ·Deuteronomy	**Prophets** ·Joshua ·Judges ·Samuel *(B,P,E)* ·Kings ·Isaiah *(P)* ·Jeremiah *(P,E)*	·Ecclesiastes (Qohelet) ·Song of Songs ·Esther ·Ezekiel *(P)* ·Daniel	·Tobit ·Judith ·Baruch ·Wisdom of Solomon ·Epistle of Jeremiah ·Additions to Daniel
	Twelve Minor Prophets ·Hosea ·Nahum ·Joel ·Habakkuk ·Amos ·Zephaniah ·Obadiah ·Haggai ·Jonah ·Zechariah ·Micah ·Malachi	**Writings** ·Psalms ·Proverbs ·Job ·Ruth ·Lamentations ·Ezra/Nehemiah ·Chronicles	**TEXT FAMILIES** Babylonian **B** Palestinian **P** Egyptian **E**	

The tentative identification of the textual families (B.P.E.) by Frank Moore Cross is based on all of the data, old and new, including Qumran fragments, the Masoretic text and the Old Greek versions. Usually the Qumran material is Palestinian (P). In the case of Jeremiah both the Palestinian and the Egyptian families are represented by manuscripts from Qumran.

Auras Design

clear that in the proceedings of the academy of Yabneh the Rabbis did *not* fix the canon, but at most discussed marginal books, notably Ecclesiastes (Qohelet) and the Song of Songs. The rabbis asserted that both Ecclesiastes and the Song of Songs "defile the hands," i.e., are holy books. They should thus be included in the canon. This decision thereby ratified the dicta of the house of Hillel in the case of Ecclesiastes and probably in the case of the Song of Songs as well.[16] Moreover, it must be insisted that the proceedings at Yabneh were not a "council," certainly not in the late ecclesiastical sense. Whatever decisions were taken at Yabneh, they were based on earlier opinions, and they failed to halt continued disputes concerning marginal books: Song of Songs, Ecclesiastes, and Esther of the "included" books, Ben Sira among the "excluded" or apocryphal. In any case, it is clear that Josephus in Rome did not take his clue from contemporary or later proceedings or Yabneh, nor did he manufacture a theory of canon from whole cloth. Thinly concealed behind Josephus' Greek apologetics is a clear and coherent theological

by Gamaliel II, a descendant of Hillel, during much of the era between the two Jewish Revolts against Rome. The academy, in effect, resurrected the institution of the Sanhedrin, which exercised religious authority over the Jewish community before the Roman destruction of Jerusalem in 70 A.D.

doctrine of canon that must stem, we believe, from the canonical doctrine of Hillel and his school.[17]

We cannot press the date of the fixation of the Pharisaic canon earlier than the time of Hillel, as an occasional scholar has attempted to do. Our evidence comes from the so-called Kaige Recension referred to in endnote 11. The Kaige Recension, at the end of the first century B.C., revised the Greek Bible to accord with the protorabbinic text, not with the later fixed Rabbinic Recension. Similarly, the revision embodied in the Kaige Recension extended to the book of Baruch and the longer edition of Daniel, works excluded from the Rabbinic Recension. This effort to update Baruch and the longer edition of Daniel would be most difficult to explain if at the time of the preparation of the Kaige Recension, the book of Baruch and the additions to Daniel had already been excluded from the Pharisaic canon. Since the recensional labors in the Kaige Recension can be dated to about the turn of the Common Era, and its Pharisaic bias is clear, it follows that as late as the end of the first century B.C., an authoritative, canonical list had not yet emerged, at least in its final form, even in Pharisaic circles.

I am persuaded by the accumulation of evidence that the same circumstances that brought on the textual crisis that led to the fixation of the Hebrew text—varied texts and editions, party strife and sectarian division, the systematization of hermeneutic principles and halakhic dialectic*—were the occasion as well for a canonical crisis, requiring the fixation of a Pharisaic canon, and further, that Hillel was the central figure in sharpening the crisis and responding to it. The fixation of the text and the fixation of the canon were thus two aspects of a single if complex endeavor. Both were essential to erect "Hillelite" protection against rival doctrines of cult and calendar, alternate legal dicta and theological doctrines, and indeed against the speculative systems and mythological excesses of certain apocalyptic schools and proto-Gnostic sects. To promulgate a textual recension, moreover, one must set some sort of limit on the books whose text is to be fixed. In electing the text of one edition of a book over the text of an alternate edition—in the case of Jeremiah or Chronicles or Daniel—one makes decisions that are at once textual and canonical. Ultimately, the strategies that initiate the fixation of the biblical text lead to the de facto, if not de jure, fixation of a canon.

*By halakhic dialectic I mean the mode of legal reasoning by which religious law was derived from Scripture.

The principles guiding the exclusion of works from the Pharisaic canon reflected in Josephus' notices no doubt also operated in eliminating works offensive to Hillel and the house of Hillel. The host of pseudepigraphical works written in the name of Enoch, Melchizedek, the sons of Jacob, Amram, and the like, which became popular in Hellenistic times, and which fill the library of Qumran, were excluded from the canon. The prophetic sequence began with Moses. There can be little doubt, moreover, that the rabbis recognized the recent date of certain apocryphal and pseudepigraphic works since such cycles as Enoch and the Testaments of the Patriarchs were still in their creative, fluid phase of composition, unfixed as literary works, in the Roman period. The principle of excluding works of "post-Prophetic" authorship permitted also the suppression of the propagandistic book of Maccabees, certain of the Hellenistic novellas, and Ben Sira, although the case of pseudepigraphs written in the name of the "Prophets," especially the Jeremianic apocrypha, Baruch, and the Letter of Jeremiah must have caused difficulty and dispute. Ezekiel, Song of Songs, and Ecclesiastes were controversial works, in all probability, because of their content, but were sufficiently old and recognized to prevent their being excluded from the canon.[18] Most mysterious is the selection for inclusion of an edition of Daniel not earlier than the Maccabean age, although it contains earlier material, and of Esther. It must be said, however, that in general, the rabbis chose for inclusion in their canon works or editions that in fact reached their final literary form (that is, when compositional activity ceased) by the end of the Persian period (late fourth century B.C.).

If I am correct in perceiving the hand of Hillel in the promulgation of a Pharisaic text and canon, and in recognizing a reference to this achievement in the rabbinic saying, "When Israel once again forgot [the Torah], Hillel the Babylonian came up and reestablished it," I must nevertheless acknowledge that this canon and text did not immediately supplant other traditions or receive uniform acceptance even in Pharisaic circles. The ascendancy of the Hillelite text and canon came with the victory of the Pharisaic party and the Hillelite house in the interval between the two Jewish Revolts against Rome. After that, the text and the canon of the Hebrew Bible—despite rabbinical queries about marginal books from time to time—remained fixed and guarded down to our own day.

CHAPTER 12

LIGHT ON THE BIBLE
FROM THE DEAD SEA CAVES

FRANK MOORE CROSS

In this short chapter, Professor Cross provides two examples of how the Dead Sea Scrolls enable us to understand the biblical text better. In the first example, a paragraph missing from the Rabbinic Recension of the book of Samuel, but present in a fragmentary copy of this book from Qumran, helps to explain an otherwise difficult-to-understand passage in the Hebrew Bible as it has come down to us.

In the second, very different example, Cross demonstrates how the scrolls help us to appreciate the development of late biblical religion. After the period of classical prophecy, an apocalyptic element entered the Jewish religion in a way that was to affect both rabbinic Judaism and Christianity. Until now, this apocalyptic element in biblical religion has been largely ignored by scholars. —ED.

——·——

The manuscripts from Qumran that differ from the received texts not only provide data for the history of the biblical text, as I described in Chapter 11, on occasion we find in these manuscripts readings of exceptional interest for the reconstruction of the original text of the Bible.

Let me give a single example of such a reading. In the received text of Samuel, we read about a critical confrontation between Saul and Nahash, king of the Ammonites. Saul is victorious and as a result he is confirmed as Israel's first king.

In the biblical account as it has come down to us in 1 Samuel 11, Nahash besieged the Israelite city of Jabesh-Gilead. The men of Jabesh-Gilead asked Nahash for surrender terms. Nahash's terms were harsh: In addition to the Israelites becoming servants to the Ammonites, the Israelite men's right eyes would be gouged out. The men of the town asked for a week's respite before agreeing to the terms to see if their fellow Israelites would come to their aid. Saul, hearing of their plight, rallied the militia of Israel, crossed the Jordan, and met Nahash and the Ammonites in battle. Saul was overwhelmingly victorious and delivered Jabesh-Gilead, thereby demonstrating his leadership. He was promptly confirmed as king.

Why did Nahash suddenly attack Jabesh-Gilead, an Israelite city allied with the house of Saul? We are not told. The question is especially puzzling because Jabesh-Gilead lay far north of the boundary claimed by the Ammonites. And the question is particularly interesting because by his attack Nahash not only brought defeat on his own head, but more serious for Ammon's future, the attack proved to be the catalyst that united Israel and initiated forces that led to the rise of the Israelite empire under Saul's successor David. Ammon then became subject to this empire. Nahash's attack on Jabesh-Gilead was a pivotal event both in Israelite and in Ammonite history.

A first-century B.C. manuscript of the books of Samuel found in Qumran Cave 4 contains a long passage, not found in our Bible, introducing chapter 11 of 1 Samuel. This manuscript (designated 4QSam^a in the technical literature) is the best preserved of the biblical manuscripts from Cave 4. When fully published, it will consist of more than twenty-five printed plates of fragments. The manuscript belongs to a Palestinian textual tradition at variance with the text type used in the Rabbinic Recension.* The received text of Samuel is, in fact, notorious for its scribal lapses, especially omissions. The present example is only one of a number of instances (though perhaps the most dramatic) where 4QSam^a preserves lost bits of the text of Samuel.

*See Chapter 11.

The full text of 1 Samuel 11 (New Jewish Publication Society translation): Nahash the Ammonite marched up and besieged Jabesh-gilead. All the men of Jabesh-gilead said to Nahash, "Make a pact with us, and we will serve you." But Nahash the Ammonite answered them. "I will make a pact with you on this condition, that everyone's right eye be gouged out; I will make this a humiliation for all Israel." The elders of Jabesh said to him, "Give us seven days' respite, so that we may send messengers throughout the territory of Israel; if no one comes to our aid, we will surrender to you." When the messengers came to Gibeah of Saul and gave this report in the hearing of the people, all the people broke into weeping.

Saul was just coming from the field driving the cattle; and Saul asked, "Why are the people crying?" And they told him about the situation of the men of Jabesh. When he heard these things, the spirit of God gripped Saul and his anger blazed up. He took a yoke of oxen and cut them into pieces, which he sent by messengers throughout the territory of Israel, with the warning, "Thus shall be done to the cattle of anyone who does not follow Saul and Samuel into battle!" Terror from the Lord fell upon the people, and they came out as one man. [Saul] mustered them in Bezek, and the Israelites numbered 300,000, the men of Judah 30,000. The messengers who had come were told, "Thus shall you speak to the men of Jabesh-gilead: Tomorrow, when the sun grows hot, you shall be saved." When the messengers came and told this to the men of Jabesh-gilead, they rejoiced. The men of Jabesh then told [the Ammonites], "Tomorrow we will surrender to you, and you can do to us whatever you please."

The next day, Saul divided the troops into three columns; at the morning watch they entered the camp and struck down the Ammonites until the day grew hot. The survivors scattered; no two were left together.

The people then said to Samuel, "Who was it said, 'Shall Saul be king over us?' Hand the men over and we will put them to death!" But Saul replied, "No man shall be put to death this day! For this day the Lord has brought victory to Israel."

Samuel said to the people, "Come, let us go to Gilgal and there inaugurate the monarchy." So all the people went to Gilgal, and there at Gilgal they declared Saul king before the Lord. They offered sacrifices of well-being there before the Lord; and Saul and all the men of Israel held a great celebration there.

This lost-and-now-recovered passage gives the background for Nahash's attack on Jabesh-Gilead: Nahash,* leading a resurgent Ammonite

---

*The name of Nahash has often been taken as meaning "snake," a not inappropriate appellation. In fact, it is a shortened term (nickname) of *Nahash-tob,* meaning "good luck"—*mazzal tob* in modern Hebrew.

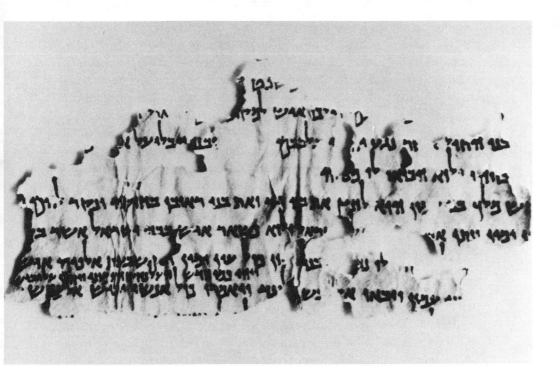

26. A fragment of the book of Samuel from Qumran that contains a passage apparently inadvertently omitted from the Hebrew Bible in the course of transmission.

nation, had earlier reconquered land long claimed both by Ammon and by the Israelite tribes of Reuben and Gad east of the Jordan River. Nahash, in his own view, had resubjugated people occupying his own domain. Nahash therefore punished his old Israelite enemies (and sometime subjects) with a systematic policy of mutilation—gouging out the right eyes of all able-bodied men. In ancient times mutilation was the standard treatment for rebels, enemies of long standing and treaty violators. Examples of rebels or arch foes being blinded include the putting out of the eyes of Samson by the Philistines (Judges 16:21) and of Zedekiah by the Babylonians (2 Kings 25:7; Jeremiah 39:7, 52:11). Blinding as a punishment for rebels is also documented in the Assyrian annals. Mutilation or dismemberment for violation of treaty is also well documented in biblical and extrabiblical sources.[1]

Mutilation by blinding was not, however, the treatment due newly conquered subjects in a city lying outside the conqueror's domain, like Jabesh-Gilead. The mutilation as recounted in the received text of Samuel has always been a puzzle for this reason. It is unmotivated.

From the now-recovered passage we learn that Israelite warriors of Reuben and Gad who survived defeat at the hands of Nahash's forces, some seven thousand in number, fled and found refuge north of the traditional border of Ammon (at the Jabbok River), in the Gileadite city of Jabesh. A month or so after their escape, Nahash determined to subjugate Jabesh-Gilead for sheltering his escaped "subjects." This was Nahash's motivation, or excuse, for striking at Jabesh-Gilead far north of his claimed borders, at a Gileadite city allied with Benjamin and Saul.

Now we know not only why Nahash attacked Jabesh-Gilead, but also why he insisted on mutilation as a term of surrender. He insisted on the same harsh punishment that he had inflicted on the Israelites of Gad and Reuben, the gouging out of right eyes. Those who harbored enemies merited punishment equal to that inflicted on the enemy. But Nahash thereby sealed his own fate. Saul of Benjamin, enraged by news of the affair, and "seized by the spirit," rallied elements of the western tribes, crossed the Jordan with an Israelite militia, and "slaughtered the Ammonites until the heat of day." Saul's great victory over Nahash at Jabesh-Gilead consolidated recognition of Saul's kingship over all Israel and in the end sealed the Ammonites' fate as well.

Here is the account of the episode, with the additional passage retrieved from Qumran indicated in italics.* The reader might try reading

---

*Brackets record lacunae in the manuscript, reconstructed by the writer.

the unitalicized portion first, then the italicized portion, to appreciate how the newly found text illuminates the background of the received text.[2]

[Na]hash, king of the children of Ammon, sorely oppressed the children of Gad and the children of Reuben, and he gouged out a[ll] their right eyes and struck ter[ror and dread] in Israel. There was not left one among the children of Israel bey[ond the Jordan who]se right eye was no[t put o]ut by Naha[sh king] of the children of Ammon; except that seven thousand men [fled from] the children of [A]mmon and entered [J]abesh-Gilead. About a month later Nahash the Ammonite went up and besieged Jabesh-Gilead. All the men of Jabesh-Gilead said to Nahash, "Make a treaty with us and we shall become your subjects." Nahash the Ammonite replied to them, "On this condition I shall make a treaty with you, that all your right eyes be gouged out, so that I may bring humiliation on all Israel." The elders at Jabesh said to him, "Give us seven days to send messengers throughout the territory of Israel. If no one rescues us, we shall surrender to you."

The missing paragraph was lost probably as a result of a scribal lapse—the scribe's eye jumped from one line break to the other, both beginning with Nahash as subject.

It has been suggested that the extra paragraph in this manuscript of Samuel is not part of the original composition but a late addition, a haggadic* expansion.[3] I see no evidence whatever for this. The added text gives rather flat historical "facts." There is no edifying element, no theological bias, no theory the addition is trying to prove, no hortatory motif, in short no haggadic element that I can perceive.

On the contrary, there are a number of telltale signs that the additional passage was in the original. For example, consider the following: In the received text of Samuel, the king of the Ammonites is introduced in his first appearance simply as "Nahash the Ammonite." This is most extraordinary. In the books of Samuel and Kings there is otherwise an invariable pattern; when a reigning king of a foreign nation is introduced for the first time, his full or official title is given, "So-and-so, king of So-and-so." There are some twenty examples of this. The received text's omission of Nahash's full title is the sole exception to the practice. Indeed, the pattern obtains for the whole of the Deuteronomistic history (Deuteronomy, Joshua, Judges, Samuel, and Kings) and is violated in the received

---

*The term *haggadah* is used by the rabbis for those materials containing the interpretation of Scripture, ordinarily exclusive of legal exposition.

text only here. However, if the paragraph from 4QSam³ is original, Nahash is introduced first as "king of the children of Ammon," his full title, precisely in accord with the Deuteronomistic historian's unvarying practice. This is a very strong argument for the originality of the passage in Samuel and its subsequent loss by simple scribal error.

Incidentally, the Ammonite king's official title as given in the newly found passage, "king of the children of Ammon," appears on a recently discovered Ammonite inscription from Tell Siran.⁴

Now that we have this additional paragraph in our text of Samuel, we can recognize that Josephus had this paragraph in his Bible. In his *Antiquities of the Jews* (6. 68–70), Josephus vividly describes the background of the attack on Jabesh-Gilead, a description that he must have based on a passage in his Bible identical with the passage from Samuel that has now been recovered from Qumran Cave 4:

> However, a month later, he [Saul] began to win the esteem of all by the war with Naas [Nahash], king of the Ammonites. For this monarch had done much harm to the Jews who had settled beyond the river Jordan, having invaded their territory with a large and warlike army. Reducing their cities to servitude, he not only by force and violence secured their subjection in the present, but by cunning and ingenuity weakened them in order that they might never again be able to revolt and escape from servitude to him; for he cut out the right eyes of all who either surrendered to him under oath or were captured by right of war . . . Having then so dealt with the people beyond Jordan, the king of the Ammonites carried his arms against those called Galadenians [Gileadites]. Pitching his camp near the capital of his enemies, to wit Jabis [Jabesh], he sent envoys to them, bidding them instantly to surrender on the understanding that their right eyes would be put out: if not, he threatened to besiege and over-throw their cities: it was for them to choose, whether they preferred the cutting out of a small portion of the body, or to perish utterly.

Obviously, Josephus is here paraphrasing the lost passage from Samuel.

In such ways do the Dead Sea Scrolls help us to restore a more original stage of the biblical text.

Another major area of study that will be greatly affected by the manu-script discoveries in the Jordan Rift is the history of biblical religion—or perhaps we should say the *development* of biblical religion.

For example, we are now in a better position to compare the psalms of the canonical Psalter with the corpus of later Hellenistic hymns found at Qumran, especially in the collection of psalms from Cave 11; or we can describe the development of slave law in Persian Palestine on the basis of Samaria papyri.

The impact of the discovery of the Qumran manuscripts has nowhere been greater than on our emerging view of the apocalyptic movement and its place in the history of late biblical religion.

The term *apocalyptic* usually conjures up the book of Daniel, a late, full-blown exemplar of the apocalyptic literature. The Bible also contains a much earlier apocalypse in the book of Isaiah (chapters 24–27), the date of which has been debated by several generations of biblical scholars. From Qumran, we now have an immense apocalyptic literature and works colored by apocalyptic eschatology.*

As reflected in the Qumran literature, these apocalyptists saw world history in terms of warring forces, God and Satan, the spirits of truth and error, light and darkness. The struggle of God with man and the struggle of man with sin, evil, and death were objectified into a cosmic struggle. Dualistic themes from archaic myths were transformed into historical myths. The world, captive to evil powers and principalities that had been given authority in the era of divine wrath, could be freed only by the Divine Might. The apocalyptist saw—or believed he saw—the dawning of the day of God's salvation and judgment. The old age had come to the end of its allotted time, and the age of consummation was at hand, the age when the world would be redeemed and the elect vindicated. The apocalyptist saw the signals of the approaching end of days. For him, the final war, Armageddon, had begun. The Messiah was about to appear "bringing the sword." The Satanic forces, brought to bay, had already lashed out in a final defiant convulsion, manifested in the persecution, temptations, and tribulations of the faithful. In short, the apocalyptist lived in a world in which the sovereignty of God was the sole hope of salvation; in the earnestness of his faith and the vividness of his hope, he was certain that God was about to act.

Apocalypticism has generally been regarded as a late, short-lived phenomenon in Judaism. This view is changing, however, in the light of massive new data and careful research utilizing old and new data. The earliest parts of the Enoch literature, for example, dated a generation ago

---

*The term *apocalyptic* in its strict sense means "pertaining to an apocalypse," a salient genre of the literature of the religious movement described below. Apocalypse means "revelation" in Greek and came to apply to the revelation of last things (eschatological events) to a seer, e.g., the apocalypse of John, commonly called the Revelation of John. We shall use the term *apocalyptic* in a wider sense, to designate a religious movement marked by an eschatological viewpoint found inter alia in the apocalypses.

to the Roman period (after 64 B.C.), or at the earliest to the late Hellenistic period (second or early first centuries B.C.), must now be pushed back in date to the late Persian period (fourth century B.C.). We actually have an Enoch manuscript—certainly not an autograph of the original—from about 200 B.C. Studies of early biblical apocalyptic (or protoapocalyptic) literature, notably the Isaianic apocalypse (Isaiah 24–27) have shown that it should be dated to the sixth century B.C. Indeed, the first strains of apocalyptic dualism and eschatology arise, I should argue, with the decline of classical prophecy in the sixth and fifth centuries B.C. And we must now recognize that protoapocalyptic works, together with later apocalyptic works, reflect a religious development spanning more than half a millennium in duration.

In the nineteenth and early twentieth centuries, apocalypticism figured little or not at all in scholars' descriptions of the history of Israelite religion. Apocalypticism was treated as an idiosyncratic product of a few Jewish seers, a fringe phenomenon.

For Christian scholars of the older view (which largely disregarded apocalypticism), biblical religion developed according to a dialectic in which the "free, ethical, and historical spirit" of prophetic religion was frozen in legalism whose "enslaving and static modes" marked post-Exilic religion. According to this view, the free and gracious spirit of prophecy reemerged *only* in New Testament Christianity. Hence, Christian scholars were inclined to bypass apocalyptic works in an attempt to trace continuities between prophecy and primitive Christianity. Older Jewish scholars shared the prevailing distaste for apocalyptic literature, viewing it as sectarian, even though a bit of it had slipped into the Hebrew canon. Influenced by the antiapocalyptic and anti-Gnostic reaction of rabbinic Judaism, Jewish scholars read back into Hellenistic- and even Persian-era Judaism the prevailing ethos of later rabbinic Judaism. As late as 1929, George Foote Moore wrote in his influential study of Judaism: " . . . inasmuch as these writings [the apocalypses] have never been recognized by Judaism, it is a fallacy of method for the historian to make them a primary source for the eschatology of Judaism, much more, to contaminate its theology with them."[5]

Thus, all joined hands in a conspiracy of silence on the subject of apocalypticism.

In the last generation, apocalypticism was rediscovered, so to speak, in its special import for the study of Christian origins. The rich resources from Qumran confirm and reinforce these new insights. Indeed, the study of Christian origins has been transformed by new data from the

Qumran library. The pace of this new research will increase as new manuscripts are published.

The movements of John the Baptist and of Jesus of Nazareth must now be redefined as apocalyptic rather than prophetic in their essential character. Gershom Scholem shocked my generation by his demonstration of the survivals of apocalyptic mysticism in the era of Rabbi Akiba (late first and second centuries of the Common Era). In the younger generation of scholars, I venture to say, these insights into the importance of apocalypticism for both early Judaism and primitive Christianity will be confirmed and extended.[6]

The apocalyptic communities of the last centuries B.C. were a major force in the complex matrix in which both Christianity and rabbinic Judaism were born. We are now beginning to recognize the enormous distance through which Judaism evolved, from the origins of the Pharisees in the multihued religious milieu of the Hellenistic era, down to the oral codification of the Mishnah (about 200 A.D.). This should not be surprising if we remember that in an even shorter period the Christian community moved from its Jewish sectarian origins in Jerusalem to Nicene orthodoxy in Constantine's Byzantium.

In my judgment, in the years ahead the apocalyptic movement will become recognized as a major phase in the evolution of biblical religion, flourishing between the death of prophecy in its institutionalized form in the sixth century B.C. and the rise of rabbinic Judaism, gentile Christianity, and Gnosticism in the first and second centuries of the Common Era. In this interval of more than five hundred years, Jewish apocalypticism was a mainstream of religious life as well as speculation. Nonapocalyptic strains existed alongside apocalypticism, of course. But there can be no question that the apocalyptic movement was one of the ancestors of both Pharisaic Judaism and Jewish Christianity, as well as of the Gnostic syncretism that characterized both movements in the first centuries of the Common Era.

I venture to predict that the descriptions of the Jewish parties of the Hellenistic and Roman periods to be written for our histories and handbooks will become far more complex and nuanced, replacing the simple, neat images of the past. The Sadducees whom we have pictured as religious conservatives and worldly bureaucrats now prove to have spawned a radical apocalyptic wing at Qumran.* The Pharisees also appear to have been variegated within their communes (*haburot* in He-

*See Chapter 3.

brew), accepting in their canon such apocalyptic works as Deutero-Zechariah and Daniel, though rejecting such others as Enoch and the Testaments of the Twelve Patriarchs. By and large, the Pharisees appear to have been dominated by moderates. Their radical elements broke off to join in the Zealot movement. Their conservative members were overcome by the school of Hillel.

The discoveries in the Jordan Rift, especially at Qumran, have initiated a new era in the study of the history of late biblical religion and of Jewish sectarianism. The assimilation of the new data will be slow. Older scholars will prefer to ignore the new materials: The ferment they produce is too strong for their stomachs. I listened to the late Yigael Yadin read diatribes against his colleagues accusing them of ignoring the Temple Scroll he published. Of course, it is uncomfortable to be told that here is a new scroll—go rewrite all your books. Or, "Here is a new Jewish library of the third to first centuries B.C.; examine all your old presuppositions, retool, and start afresh." New directions in research will rest largely on a young generation of scholars. I envy those who will live to read the new syntheses the future will bring.

CHAPTER 13

WHEN THE SONS OF GOD
CAVORTED WITH
THE DAUGHTERS OF MEN

RONALD S. HENDEL

This chapter illustrates how the Dead Sea Scrolls are used tangentially, as part of the solution to a biblical crux. The subject is not the Dead Sea Scrolls, but a strange story in Genesis in which the "Sons of God" come down and have sexual relations with beautiful earth-bound women. We are treated to a brilliant, wide-ranging exegesis of the puzzling story by a rising star among biblical scholars, Ronald S. Hendel of Southern Methodist University.

The first question Hendel considers is what is meant by the term Sons of God. To understand it, Hendel turns to other biblical passages, including one which, in the Hebrew Bible, refers to the "sons of Israel" (Deuteronomy 32:8). But in the Hebrew text of Deuteronomy 32:8 found at Qumran, this passage reads not "sons of Israel," but "Sons of God," the same phrase that appears in the Genesis story. This makes the passage in Deuteronomy relevant to Hendel's interpretation of the story of the "Sons of God" who came down and slept with earthly women. —ED.

—·—

I f someone asked you to name the origin of a story about gods who take human wives and then give birth to a race of semidivine heroes, you might answer: It's a Greek myth, or perhaps a Norse legend, or maybe a folktale from Africa or India. Surely this story couldn't come from the sacred scriptures of Judaism and Christianity. Or could it?

In fact, it is one of the seldom-told stories in the Hebrew Bible. The passage from Genesis 6:1–4 is short enough to quote in full:

> When mankind began to multiply on the face of the earth, and daughters were born to them, the Sons of God* saw that the daughters of men were beautiful, and they took wives of them, from any whom they chose. And Yahweh said, "My spirit will not be strong[1] in man forever, for indeed he is but flesh. His lifetime will be 120 years." The Nephilim were on the earth in those days, and also afterwards, when the Sons of God mated with the daughters of men and they bore children for them: these were the heroes of old, the men of renown.

For thousands of years this story has scandalized readers of the Bible, and for good reason. The story appears to go against the grain of our traditional understanding of biblical religion.

But the story is there, and since it is, perhaps our traditional understanding is what's wrong. Perhaps, to paraphrase Hamlet, there are more things in the Bible than are dreamt of in our philosophy. Let us look more closely.[2]

In the past, many scholars have simply dismissed the story as a kind of biblical aberration. The reaction of the great nineteenth-century scholar Julius Wellhausen is typical; he characterized the story as "a cracked erratic boulder."[3] Like a cracked boulder, it might best be just hauled away.

*The Hebrew word for "God" is *'Elohim*. In other Semitic languages, and occasionally in Hebrew, this word means "gods" in the plural. The general usage in Hebrew is in the singular, referring to Yahweh, the God of Israel. The singular usage is clear in these contexts, since *'Elohim* takes a singular verb, as in this passage. Why the plural form was originally used to signify the single god, Yahweh, is unclear. Probably the shift in religious belief from the worship of a pantheon of gods to the worship of a single god is involved. In a sense we might say that, for the Israelites, Yahweh takes over the functions of the whole pantheon. Here we have the transition from "gods" to "god." The "Sons of God" still exist in Israelite mythology, but they are no longer the object of worship and of the cult.

Early Jewish and Christian commentators were also perplexed by the story. Since it was already anchored in the holy text, the only way to avoid the unpleasant implications of gods and humans marrying and having offspring was to provide an interpretation that would render it more palatable. The early rabbis therefore understood the phrase *bene ha'elohim* to refer not to "the Sons of God," but to righteous men. The Church Fathers, on the other hand, interpreted the phrase as a reference to the descendants of Seth, who was born of Adam and Eve after Cain killed Abel ("Adam knew his wife again, and she bore a son and named him 'Seth' meaning 'God has provided me with another offspring in place of Abel' " Genesis 4:25). In this way both the early Jewish and the early Christian interpreters avoided the problem of the polytheistic implications suggested by the "Sons of God." Neither of these early interpretations is supported by the evidence. They simply illustrate how early interpreters tried to tame this troublesome text.

How are *we* to understand the story? Amorous gods, beautiful women, sex, curses, and fame—it has all the elements of a successful soap opera, with mythic motifs thrown in for good measure. Is there enough here to understand—or is the story too cryptic, too broken?

I believe the text can be understood, but only by following a trail of clues that will lead us to other texts in the Hebrew Bible and other ancient mythologies.

The first stop in our investigative trail is to ascertain the identity of "the Sons of God." This is relatively easy. The Sons of God (Hebrew, *bene ha'elohim*) are known from several texts in the Hebrew Bible. In Job 1:6 and 2:1, the Sons of God present themselves to Yahweh in the heavenly divine assembly. Later, in Job 38:7, we learn that the Sons of God have been with Yahweh at the creation of the world; when they see what God has wrought "The Sons of God shout[ed] for joy." The Sons of God (Hebrew, *bene 'elim**) again appear at Yahweh's divine assembly in Psalm 89:7, where Yahweh's incomparability among the gods is proclaimed. A similar scene is found in Psalm 29:1, where the Sons of God (Hebrew, *bene 'elim*) sing praises to Yahweh.[4]

Perhaps the most intriguing reference to the Sons of God is in the famous Song of Moses in Deuteronomy 32, just before Moses ascends Mt. Nebo to die without entering the Promised Land. Deuteronomy

---

*The Hebrew form *'elim* is a variant form of *'elohim,* "God." The —*oh*— in *'elohim* is a particle that originally added an emphatic or particularizing quality to the plural form *'elim.*

32:8 contains what is apparently an old mythological reference to the early history of humanity. The traditional Hebrew text reads: "When the Most High apportioned the nations, when he divided the sons of man, he established the borders of the peoples according to the number of *the sons of Israel.*"

The sense of this passage is fairly clear until one comes to the last phrase. How can the borders of the peoples (including non-Israelite nations) be established according to the number of the *sons of Israel?* Has Israel already been established? Not yet, according to the sense of the text. There is something wrong in this passage: The end contradicts the beginning.

The contradiction does not appear in all Bibles, however. Look at the Revised Standard Versions (RSV), for example. There we read in Deuteronomy 32:8 that the borders of the peoples (or nations) are fixed, not according to the number of the sons of Israel, but "according to the number of the Sons of God." This reading is based on the Greek Septuagint, a Bible translation made in the third century B.C. for Jews living in Alexandria who could not read Hebrew. The modern RSV translators decided that in this case the Septuagint, rather than the received Hebrew text (the Masoretic text), has preserved the original reading.[5] Bible translations that adhere to the received Hebrew text, however, read "sons of Israel" instead of "Sons of God."

Recently a fragmentary text from among the Dead Sea Scrolls was found to contain Deuteronomy 32:8. Written in late Herodian script (late first century B.C. to early first century A.D.), this fragment is now our earliest Hebrew text of Deuteronomy 32:8; the last phrase in the verse in this fragment clearly reads "the Sons of God," not "the sons of Israel." This reading, preserved in Greek in the Septuagint but not in the received Hebrew text, seems rather clearly to be the authentic original reading.

Apparently, somewhere along the line in the transmission of the standard rabbinic Bible someone felt the need to clean up the text by literally rewriting it and substituting "sons of Israel" for the original "Sons of God" in Deuteronomy 32:8.

Now that we have established the correct text of Deuteronomy 32:8, we can use it to complete our portrait of the Sons of God. According to this passage in Deuteronomy, the Sons of God were not only present at the beginning of the world, but also figure importantly in the division of the nations. According to the following verse, Yahweh chose Israel as his own portion, implying that each of the other deities, the Sons of God,

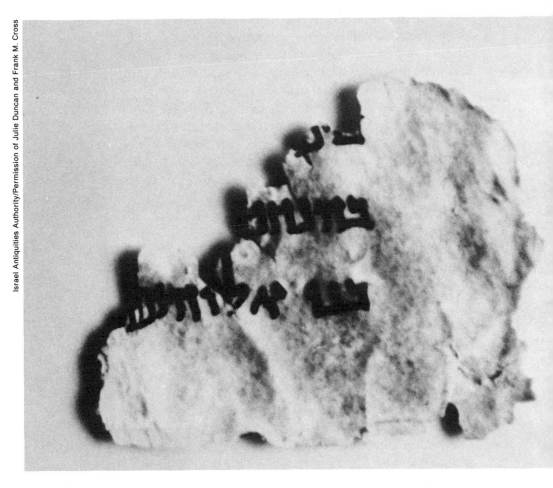

27. Hebrew fragment of Deuteronomy 32:8 containing the term "Sons of God."

also received a nation to rule over. This would make sense of the division of the nations according to the number of the Sons of God. We can see in this passage an indication that the Sons of God at one time played a far more important role in the early history of humanity than is generally remembered in the biblical traditions.

For even earlier history of the Sons of God, we have to look outside the Hebrew Bible. As with many other elements of Israel's religious traditions, the ancestry of the concept of the Sons of God can be traced to pre-Israelite Canaanite traditions. Especially valuable in this regard are the fourteenth-century B.C. Canaanite texts written in cuneiform on clay tablets. Discovered in 1928 at the ancient city of Ugarit on the Syrian coast,* these texts provide a wealth of information about the society, religion, and narrative traditions of Canaan in the period before the emergence of Israel.

In the myths, epics, and ritual texts from Ugarit, the phrase *the Sons of God (banu ili* or *banu ili-mi)* occurs frequently. In the Canaanite pantheon, the chief god is El, whose name literally means "God." He and his wife Asherah are the father and mother of the gods. The phrase *the Sons of God* can be translated literally as "the Sons (or children) of El."

The *bene 'elim* are found not only in Ugaritic texts, but also in Phoenician inscriptions of the eighth to seventh centuries B.C.[6] and in an Ammonite inscription of the ninth century recently found in Amman, Jordan.[7] So the concept of the Sons of God pervades Canaanite lore over an extended period of time.

The Canaanite roots of the Sons of God allow us a glimpse into the antiquity of these figures and make it clear that these are indeed divine beings. The Israelite use of the term derives from the body of traditional lore inherited from the Canaanites. The concept of the Sons of God as well as the stories about them doubtless goes back to Canaanite time.

In Israelite tradition the Sons of God are the lesser deities who accompany Yahweh in his heavenly assembly.[8] Their sphere of activity is restricted in comparison to that of their Canaanite forebears; this, of course, is due to the fact that in Israelite worship Yahweh had subsumed the essential functions of the other gods. Only in a few passages are the activities of the Sons of God prominent. These passages, especially Genesis 6:1–4 and Deuteronomy 32:8, reflect traditions that are quite early.

---

*See "An Appreciation of Claude Frederic-Armand Schaeffer-Forrer (1898–1982)," by James M. Robinson, and "The Last Days of Ugarit," by Claude F. A. Schaeffer, *Biblical Archaeology Review*, September/October 1983. See also the review of *Ugarit and the Old Testament* by Peter C. Craigie in the same issue.

Indeed, these two passages would be quite at home among the Ugaritic mythological texts, except that the chief god is Yahweh rather than El!

Let us turn now from the Sons of God to the offspring produced when they united with the daughters of men, as described in Genesis 6:1–4. Although the language of the text is a bit choppy, it nevertheless seems clear that the offspring are referred to as the Nephilim. These Nephilim are described as the "heroes of old, the men of renown." Who are the Nephilim?

Nephilim literally means "the fallen ones." In Hebrew the word is a common euphemism for "the dead." (For example, Jeremiah 6:15 tell us, "They will fall among the fallen [Hebrew, *nopelim*].")

In Ezekiel 32:27, we read of the Nephilim as warriors who have fallen.[9]

> They lie with the warriors,
> The Nephilim of old,
> who descended to Sheol
> with their weapons of war.

Elsewhere in biblical tradition the Nephilim are described as the giants who were native inhabitants of Canaan. In the report Moses' advance scouts give of their foray into Canaan (Numbers 13:33), they advise Moses: "All the people whom we saw in its midst were people of great size; there we saw the Nephilim—the Anaqim are part of the Nephilim—and we seemed in our own eyes like grasshoppers, and so we must have seemed in their eyes."

In Deuteronomy 2:11 the giant Anaqim—part of the Nephilim—are also called Rephaim, a more general term for the giant native inhabitants of Canaan. Two of the most famous of the Rephaim are King Og of Bashan, whose huge iron bed could still be seen on display in Rabbah of Ammon (Deuteronomy 3:11), and the giant warrior Goliath, who is described as descended from the Raphah in Gath (2 Samuel 21:19ff).[10]

The Nephilim thus appear to be a race of heroes who lived both before the Flood and in Canaan before the Israelites conquered the Promised Land. In these eras, the Nephilim end up, as their name suggests, as "the dead ones." The Rephaim and Anaqim are said to have been wiped out by Joshua, Moses, and Caleb,[11] though some stragglers remained to be slain by David and his men.[12] In Joshua 11:22, we are told that "No Anaqim remained in the land of Israel, but some remained in Gaza, Gath, and Ashdod."

The function of the Nephilim-Rephaim-Anaqim, the giant demigods—half god, half human—is constant in all these traditions. They exist in order to be wiped out: by the Flood, by Moses, by David and others.[13] The function of the Nephilim in Israelite tradition is to die.[14] As we have already noted, Nephilim actually means "the fallen ones." The connection between death and the Nephilim appears to be basic to the several forms of the tradition.

I believe that in the original version of the mating story in Genesis 6:1–4, the Nephilim were destroyed by the Flood; indeed they were the cause of the Flood. To understand this argument, however, we must explore the Mesopotamian flood story, which is obviously related in some way to the flood story preserved in the Bible.

In the Mesopotamian flood story, the gods' motive for the flood, as we now know from the Old Babylonian myth of Atrahasis, is a cosmic imbalance between the human world and the divine world; the human world is overpopulated with humans, and the gods cannot sleep because of the noise.[15]

> . . . the people multiplied,
> the land was bellowing like a bull.
> At their uproar the god became angry;
> Enlil heard their noise.
> He addressed the great gods,
> "The noise of mankind has become oppressive to me.
> Because of their uproar I am deprived of sleep."

In this primeval era, according to Babylonian understanding, humans live forever; this is what has created the overpopulation. People can still die from violence or starvation, but natural death has not yet been instituted. After other efforts at population control fail, Enlil decrees the flood, which will kill all humans and take care of the noise problem—Enlil's final solution.

However, Enlil's wily adversary, the god Enki, attempts to thwart Enlil's plan. Enki advises an "exceedingly wise" man named Atrahasis to build an ark for himself and his family, together with a menagerie of animals, in order to survive the flood. When the flood recedes, and Atrahasis and his family have survived, the gods Enlil and Enki have a showdown. Finally, they agree on an acceptable compromise, suggested by Enki, to control the size of human population: People will henceforth die natural deaths.*

Natural death becomes the fate of humanity. This is the solution to the cosmic imbalance that brought on the flood in the Babylonian account of the flood.

In the story in Genesis 6:1–4, the divine response to the cosmic imbalance represented by the Sons of God mating with the daughters of men is likewise to limit human lifespan: "My spirit will not be strong in man forever [says Yahweh in Genesis 6:3], for indeed, he is but flesh. His lifetime will be 120 years."

The punishment, a decree of a limited lifespan, is directed at humans, however, not at the Nephilim.

I believe that originally, in early Israelite tradition, the motive for the Flood was the destruction of the Nephilim. The sexual mingling of the Sons of God and the daughters of men created a cosmic imbalance and a confusion in the cosmic order. The birth of the demigods threatened the fabric of the cosmos. The natural response in myth, as exemplified by the Babylonian flood tradition, was to suppress the imbalance by destroying its cause. In the Atrahasis myth, humanity is destroyed so that its noise would be eliminated. The natural conclusion of Genesis 6:1–4, according to the logic of the myth, is the deluge—the destruction of humanity, and the concomitant annihilation of the disorder. The cosmic imbalance is resolved by a great destruction out of which a new order arises.

In Genesis 6:1–4 as it has come down to us, however, the conclusion of the old myth has been transformed. The Flood is no longer the result of the Sons of God mating with the daughters of men. The conclusion of the myth has been detached from the Flood narrative (though it still immediately follows it, beginning in Genesis 6:5), and a new motive

---

*The crucial passage has recently been restored:

> Enki opened his mouth
> and addressed Nintu, the birth-goddess,
> "[You], birth-goddess, creatress of destinies,
> [create death] for the peoples."

[For the restorations in this text, see W. G. Lambert, "The Theology of Death" in *Death in Mesopotamia,* B. Alster, ed. (Copenhagen: Akademisk, 1980), pp. 54–58. The restorations are based on the Gilgamesh Epic, tablet 10, column 6, lines 28–32, where the gods' decree of human mortality after the flood is recalled.]

has been supplied in the biblical account. The motive in Genesis 6:5–8 is the increase of mankind's evil on the earth, not the increase of population (as in the Babylonian myth), nor the mixing of gods and mortals (as was originally the case in the myth partially preserved in Genesis 6:1–4).

Note the parallel use of the word *multiply* at the beginning of the mating myth (Genesis 6:1–4) and the beginning of the Flood story that follows, beginning in Genesis 6:5. The story of the mating of the Sons of God with the daughters of men begins: "When mankind began to multiply on the face of the earth" (Genesis 6:1). The Flood story begins: "Yahweh saw that the evil of mankind multiplied on earth."[16] In Genesis 6:1–4, the problem is the mating between gods and humans. In the Flood story it is human evil. The parallel use of "multiply on earth" suggests a parallel construction introducing cosmic imbalance. In Genesis 6:1–4, it is the mating of gods and humans; in the Genesis Flood story, it is human evil. In the Babylonian flood story, it is overpopulation.

The ethical nature of the biblical Flood story is highlighted by this change in motive—in the Bible, the flood is brought on not by the cosmic imbalance caused by human overpopulation, but by the evil engaged in by humankind. The new motive for the Flood is found in Genesis 6:5–7:

> Yahweh saw that the evil of mankind had multiplied on the earth, and that all the thoughts of his heart were only evil continually. And Yahweh repented that he had created mankind, and he was grieved in his heart. Yahweh said, "I will wipe out mankind, whom I created, from the face of the earth . . ."

By truncating the original ending of the story in Genesis 6:1–4 from its logical sequel—the flood that would eliminate the cosmic imbalance of gods mating with humans—the story of the Sons of God taking wives of the daughters of men becomes simply one example of man's evil inclination. Similar stories in the Primeval Cycle precede the Flood story in Genesis. Thus, a new motive for the great destruction of the Flood is presented; the story of the Sons of God and the daughters of men has been rearranged and no longer serves as the primary motive for the great destruction.

While the Nephilim appear to die in the Flood, they are still around later; they die in another great destruction, the Israelite conquest of the Promised Land. These great destructions bring to an end a "primeval" era: before the Flood and before Israel. In both of these primeval eras, the Nephilim are doomed to die.*

The story of the Sons of God mating with the daughters of men is thus understandable on its own, transposed as it is, and is also understandable as a part of a carefully crafted larger whole—the cycle of stories leading up to the Flood. This cycle itself feeds into the stories of the patriarchs and the narration of the covenant between Yahweh and Israel.

The Primeval Cycle in Genesis is characterized by a series of mythological transgressions of boundaries that result in a range of divine responses. Slowly these responses build up to a new ordering of the cosmos. The mixing of gods and mortals in Genesis 6:1–4 is mirrored by the mixing of the divine and the human in the Garden of Eden story, in which humans desire to "be as gods, knowing good and evil" (Genesis 3:5,22), another cosmic imbalance. As a result, Adam and Eve are expelled from the Garden. Similarly, in the Tower of Babel story, where humans want to build "a tower with its top in heaven" (Genesis 11:4), they are divinely punished by a confusion of tongues. In Genesis 6:1–4 the bounds between divine and human are also breached, and the result is the decree of the limit of man's lifespan to one hundred and twenty years. The basic pattern persists.

The stories proceed in a dialectical fashion, generating oppositions and resolving them, all the while sketching a transition from a mythical "nature" to human "culture," from an era when humans are naked and immortal to an era of clothing, mortality, hard labor, and nations—the era of the present world. Genesis 6:1–4 fits snugly into this context—the repetition of mythological transgressions of boundaries and the slow building up of the limitation of the human world.

---

*This double dimension of the Nephilim need not disturb us once we understand the essential fluidity of mythological traditions. Just as Goliath can be killed by Elhanan (2 Samuel 21:19) or by David (1 Samuel 17) in different stories, so the Nephilim can be destroyed by the Flood or by the conquest. In either case, the semidivine Nephilim are no longer here in the present world. They are "the fallen ones."

V

THE DEAD SEA
SCROLLS AND
CHRISTIANITY

CHAPTER 14

THE DEAD SEA SCROLLS
AND CHRISTIANITY

JAMES C. VANDERKAM

This chapter is a masterful survey of the relationship between the Dead Sea Scrolls and early Christianity by James VanderKam.

VanderKam first considers some of the more extreme claims that place Jesus' brother James at Qumran, or that identify Paul and even Jesus as the Wicked Priest of the Qumran texts, or that argue that books of the New Testament have been found at Qumran.

VanderKam then discusses some of the many similarities between the Qumran covenanters and the early Christians, for example, in their rituals and community practices. In this connection he asks whether there is any relationship between the community meals at Qumran and the Last Supper.

VanderKam also looks at the similarities in texts—for example, between the Sermon on the Mount and Qumran documents—and treats doctrinal similarities between the Qumran covenanters and early Christians.

His conclusion: We now better understand the Jewish soil out of which the early Church emerged. Moreover, we now understand that many of the beliefs and practices of the early Church that were once thought to be unique were in many cases prefigured at Qumran.   —ED.

— · —

Almost from the moment the first Dead Sea Scrolls came under scholarly scrutiny, the question of their relation to early Christianity became a key issue.

The early days of Qumran research produced some spectacular theories regarding the relationship among Jesus, the first Christians, and the Qumran community. In 1950 the French scholar Andre Dupont-Sommer argued that the Teacher of Righteousness—the founder and first leader of the Qumran group according to the scrolls—had a career that prefigured and paralleled that of Jesus:

> The Galilean Master, as He is presented to us in the writings of the New Testament, appears in many respects as an astonishing reincarnation of the Master of Justice [that is, the Teacher of Righteousness, as the title came to be translated]. Like the latter He preached penitence, poverty, humility, love of one's neighbour, chastity. Like him, He prescribed the observance of the Law of Moses, the whole Law, but the Law finished and perfected, thanks to His own revelations. Like him He was the Elect and Messiah of God, the Messiah redeemer of the world. Like him He was the object of the hostility of the priests, the party of the Sadducees. Like him He was condemned and put to death. Like him He pronounced judgement on Jerusalem, which was taken and destroyed by the Romans for having put Him to death. Like him, at the end of time, He will be the supreme judge. Like him He founded a Church whose adherents fervently awaited His glorious return.[1]

Dupont-Sommer's speculations strongly influenced Edmund Wilson, the literary critic who wrote the famous *New Yorker* article (later published as a best-selling book) "The Scrolls from the Dead Sea," which stimulated great popular interest in and controversy about the scrolls.[2] Wilson argued that the relation of the covenanters of Qumran to Jesus and the first Christians could be seen as "the successive phases of a movement"[3]:

> The monastery, this structure of stone that endures, between the bitter waters and precipitous cliffs, with its oven and its inkwells, its mill and its cesspool, its constellation of sacred fonts and the unadorned graves of its dead, is perhaps, more than Bethlehem or Nazareth, the cradle of Christianity.[4]

According to Wilson, Jewish and Christian scholars were reluctant to admit the implications of the scrolls because of their religious biases.

Jewish scholars were supposedly anxious lest the authority of the Masoretic text (the traditional Jewish text of the Hebrew Bible) be shaken, especially by the variant readings in the biblical texts found at Qumran. Jews would also be uncomfortable, he suggested, if Christianity were seen, as the scrolls indicated, as a natural development from a particular brand of Judaism. Christianity too was supposedly threatened by the content of the scrolls: The uniqueness of Christ was imperiled. In an oft-quoted passage the iconoclastic Wilson concluded:

> [I]t would seem an immense advantage for cultural and social inter-course—that is, for civilization—that the rise of Christianity should, at last, be generally understood as simply an episode of human history rather than propagated as dogma and divine revelation. The study of the Dead Sea Scrolls—with the direction it is now taking—cannot fail, one would think, to conduce this.[5]

At the same time other scholars were going about the patient labor of establishing just where the points of contact and difference were. Millar Burrows of Yale, for example, embraced a minimalist thesis in his widely used *The Dead Sea Scrolls*.[6] Against those who claimed the scrolls would revolutionize New Testament study, he wrote: "There is no danger, however, that our understanding of the New Testament will be so revolutionized by the Dead Sea Scrolls as to require a revision of any basic article of Christian faith. All scholars who have worked on the texts will agree that this has not happened and will not happen."[7]

In a less pastoral vein, Burrows stated his view of the relationship between the Qumran sect and early Christians in these words:

> Direct influence of the Qumran sect on the early church may turn out to be less probable than parallel developments in the same general situation. The question here is the same one encountered when we attempt to explain similarities between Judaism and Zoroastrianism, or between Christianity and the pagan mystery cults.[8]

As matters developed, this viewpoint has largely set the general framework within which the relationship between Qumran and Christianity is still understood today. Many Qumran scholars would agree with Burrows's conclusion: "[A]fter studying the Dead Sea Scrolls for seven years, I do not find my understanding of the New Testament substantially affected. Its Jewish background is clearer and better understood, but its meaning has neither been changed nor significantly clarified."[9]

Under the title *The Scrolls and the New Testament,* Krister Stendahl of Harvard collected thirteen detailed studies of the sect by eleven different scholars (one man wrote three) examining the major similarities between the Qumran sect and early Christianity.[10] None of Dupont-Sommer's writings was selected for inclusion. In his perceptive introductory essay, Stendahl concluded: "It is true to say that the Scrolls add to the background of Christianity, but they add so much that we arrive at a point where the significance of similarities definitely rescues Christianity from false claims of originality in the popular sense and leads us back to a new grasp of its true foundation in the person and the events of its Messiah,"[11] a conclusion with which I agree.

One of the most influential books about Qumran was written by Frank M. Cross, also of Harvard. In *The Ancient Library of Qumran and Modern Biblical Studies,* Cross lays special stress on the Essenes (a Jewish movement of which the Qumran group was a part) as bearers and producers of the Jewish apocalyptic tradition and on the importance of this tradition for early Christianity:

> The background of the institutions and patterns typical of the communal life of the earliest Church in an earlier apocalyptic milieu can now be investigated seriously for the first time. The Essene literature [from Qumran] enables us to discover the concrete Jewish setting in which an apocalyptic understanding of history was living and integral to communal existence. Like the primitive Church, the Essene community was distinguished from Pharisaic associations and other movements within Judaism precisely in its consciousness "of being already the called and chosen Congregation of the end of days."[12] Contrary to the tendency of New Testament theologians to assume that the "eschatological existence" of the early Church, that is, its community life lived in anticipation of the Kingdom of God, together with the forms shaped by this life, was a uniquely Christian phenomenon, we must now affirm that in the Essene communities we discover antecedents of Christian forms and concepts.[13]

Within this general framework Cross then considers parallels in three areas: in theological language (especially in John), in eschatological motifs (especially in the way Scripture was interpreted to refer to their own time, but also in their understanding of themselves as people of the new covenant and their messianic outlook) and in their order and liturgical institutions (baptism, liturgical meals, community of goods, leadership). In each case, the Qumran covenanters and early Christians shared essential viewpoints.

In 1966 a German scholar, Herbert Braun, published a two-volume work entitled *Qumran und das Neue Testament* containing a chainlike treatment of all New Testament passages, from Matthew through Revelation, for which a Qumran parallel arguably exists.[14] The book totals 326 pages of rather small print. Naturally these parallels vary in quality and importance, but, whatever the limits of the collection, the sheer quantity is certainly impressive.

In sum, as Qumran research has matured, it has been widely recognized that, although there were major differences between the Qumran literature and early Christian literature and between the Qumran community and the early Christian community, nevertheless, they were also remarkably similar in theological vocabulary, in some major doctrinal tenets, and in several organizational and ritual practices. Yet, most scholars were reluctant to explain early Christian teachings as *direct* borrowings from Qumran Essenism. The better view is that the two are offspring of a common tradition in Judaism, with perhaps some points of direct borrowing (especially organizational ones).[15] As more of the scrolls have been published, this general conclusion has been substantially sustained.

True, even today a scholar here and there departs from this mainline view. For example, Robert Eisenman of California State University at Long Beach has posited a Zadokite movement, of which the Qumran community was a part, that supposedly existed for centuries and included Ezra, Judas Maccabee, John the Baptist, Jesus, and his brother James[16]; only in the first century A.D. did this movement become a separate group and compose the sectarian documents of Qumran. Barbara Thiering of the University of Sydney in Australia has identified John the Baptist as the Teacher of Righteousness and Jesus as the Wicked Priest of the Qumran texts.[17] J. L. Teicher of Cambridge University argues, on the other hand, that the apostle Paul is the Wicked Priest.[18] Few, if any, scholars have been convinced by the arguments adduced by Eisenman, Thiering, or Teicher, but the popular press has sometimes given their sensational views widespread coverage.[19]

Let's look more closely at some of the significant similarities between the New Testament and the Qumran literature and assess them. But before doing so, two thoughts should be expressed:

First, we must appreciate the insights provided by the Qumran literature in light of the paucity of any other Hebrew or Aramaic literature contemporary with the beginnings of Christianity. The books of the Hebrew Bible are, in almost all cases, considerably earlier. The vast corpus of rabbinic texts was written centuries later. Before the Qumran discoveries, most of the first-century comparative material for studying early Christianity came from Greek and Latin sources. The sudden availability of an entire library of Hebrew and Aramaic texts dating from approximately the time of the New Testament events has naturally, and rightfully, captured the attention of New Testament scholars.

Second, proving direct dependence of something in the New Testament on an item in the scrolls is no simple task. Even now we know very little about the various groups of Jews in the last centuries of the Second Temple period. (The Second Temple was destroyed by the Romans in 70 A.D.) Even if we show that the only places where a particular item or concept is found are the New Testament and the Qumran texts, this would not prove either a direct borrowing or that the feature was unique to these two groups. The feature may have been shared more widely, with most of its attestation now lost. Given these limitations, we can, at most, do little more than isolate areas where Christians and Essenes agreed and all other known groups seem to have disagreed.

One of the clearest examples of the insights the Qumran literature can provide for New Testament literature relates to language and verbal formulas. The New Testament is written in Greek. Jesus, however, spoke Aramaic, and all of the first disciples were Semitic-speaking Jews of Galilee or Judea. The Qumran texts now supply us, for the first time, with the original Hebrew (and sometimes Aramaic) of a number of New Testament words and phrases.

Take the Greek expression *tōn pleionōn,* which is usually translated "many" or "majority." This is a very general term that became, in several New Testament passages, a designation for entire groups of Jesus' followers (Matthew 26:28; see also Mark 14:24; [cf. Luke 22:20]; Acts 6:2,5, 15:12,30; 2 Corinthians 2:5–6). For example, Paul writes to the Corinthians: "But if anyone has caused pain, he has caused it not to me, but in some measure—not to put it too severely—to you all. For such a one as this punishment by the majority [*tōn pleionōn*] is enough" (2 Corinthians 2:5–6). The Qumran scroll known as the Manual of Discipline (1QS) contains rules regarding who may speak and when during general meetings of the group: "And in an Assembly of the Congregation no man shall speak without the consent of the Congregation, nor indeed of the Guardian of the Congregation" (Manual of Discipline 6:11–12).[20] The Hebrew word translated "congregation" in this passage is *hrbym* (vocalized, with vowels, as *harabbim*), which literally means "the many." In short, *hrbym* is the Hebrew word that lies behind the New Testament Greek *tōn pleionōn.*

There may be another example in this same passage. The Hebrew word rendered "guardian" *(hmbqr)* in this passage (and others where it refers to a man who has a supervisory role in the Qumran community[21]) may be the equivalent of *episkopos* (bishop/overseer), which is used several times in the New Testament (Philippians 1:1; 1 Timothy 3:1–7; Titus 1:7), where it also refers to a man with a similar role.

With the help of the scrolls we can uncover the Hebrew or Aramaic originals of several other expressions in the New Testament, not only in the Gospels, but in the Pauline corpus as well. Joseph Fitzmyer, of Catholic University of America in Washington, D.C., has identified the Semitic original of a number of Pauline expressions of this kind: The righteousness of God *(dikaiosyne theou = sidqat 'el),* works of the Law *(erga nomou = ma'aseh torah),* the church of God *(he ekklesia tou theou = gehal 'el),* and Sons of Light *(huloi photos = bene 'or).*[22]

Can we go further? Is it possible that a fragment of a gospel has been found at Qumran? The Qumran settlement was destroyed by the Romans in 68 A.D. Many believe that by this date Mark, the earliest of the canonical Gospels, had been composed. So it is not beyond the realm of possibility that a gospel text would turn up at Qumran. Indeed, one scholar has claimed to have identified several scraps from Qumran Cave 7, where Greek fragments were found, as containing not only parts of the text of Mark, but also Acts, Romans, 1 Timothy, James, and 2 Peter.[23] Jose O'Callaghan, a Spanish Jesuit scholar, created a worldwide sensation in the 1970s when he made this proposal, but today his thesis has generally been abandoned. The scraps on which O'Callaghan relied are tiny, nearly illegible texts that seem not to agree entirely with the relevant texts even for the few letters that can be read. Naturally, if O'Callaghan's identification were correct, it would require major changes in the generally accepted theories about who the residents of Qumran were, at least in the later phases of the settlement.

Although no actual copies of New Testament books have been found at Qumran, parts of some New Testament books may have been drawn from Qumran or Essene sources and then revised and edited into their present contexts. Consider 2 Corinthians 6:14–15: "Do not be unequally yoked together with unbelievers. For what fellowship has righteousness with lawlessness? And what communion has light with darkness? And what accord has Christ with Belial? Or what part has a believer with an unbeliever?"

The entire passage sounds very much like what we find at Qumran— the light/darkness contrast and the strong consciousness of an exclusive group. The name Belial (or Beliar) occurs only here in the whole New Testament, but it occurs several times at Qumran—in the Hymns Scroll and in the unpublished halakhic letter known as 4QMMT, as well as elsewhere. We cannot prove that this passage from 2 Corinthians is a revised Essene text, but Paul uses language here that is known only from Qumran texts.[24]

A similar claim can be made about the Sermon on the Mount in Matthew 5–7. It, too, includes a number of expressions that are attested at Qumran but nowhere else. For example, the "poor in spirit" (Matthew 5:3) is found in the War of the Sons of Light Against the Sons of Darkness (14:7) but in no other ancient text. Likewise, the sermon's teaching that oaths should be avoided as unnecessary since one's word should suffice (Matthew 5:33–37) echoes the great emphasis on truth in the scrolls (for example, Manual of Discipline 2:24,26 calls the group "the community of truth") and perhaps explains Josephus' statement that the Essenes were excused from taking the oath of loyalty to Herod.[25] The duty to turn the other cheek (Matthew 5:38–39) is found at Qumran in the Manual of Discipline (10:17–18),[26] but not elsewhere. Finally, the antitheses in the Sermon on the Mount ("You have heard that it was said . . . , but I say unto you . . . ") are reminiscent of the way in which the still-unpublished halakhic letter (4QMMT)[27] introduces disagreements between the sect and its opponents: "You know . . . We think/say . . ."

Not surprisingly, the question has arisen as to whether some New Testament characters can be placed at Qumran. As we have seen, Dupont-Sommer long ago argued that the Teacher of Righteousness, who figures so prominently in the Qumran documents, prefigured Jesus. But even he does not equate the two. I have also mentioned the widely rejected view that Jesus' brother James the Just (proposed by Robert Eisenman) and the apostle Paul (proposed by Teicher) appear in the scrolls.

The most likely candidate to have had contact with the Qumran community, however, is John the Baptist. From the beginning, scholars have been intrigued by the similarities between John and his teachings, on the one hand, and Qumran and its doctrines, on the other. The Baptist is therefore the prime candidate for contact with Qumran. The contention is not without some force:

John the Baptist came from a priestly family (Luke 1:5). At his birth his father said of him:

And you, child, will be called the prophet of the Most High; for you will go before the Lord to prepare his ways, to give knowledge of salvation to his people in the forgiveness of sins, through the tender mercy of our God, when the day shall dawn upon us from on high (Luke 1:76–78).

Luke then adds: "And the child grew and became strong in spirit, and he was in the wilderness till the day of his manifestation to Israel" (Luke 1:80).

This particular wilderness is the Wilderness of Judea near the Jordan River, which flows into the Dead Sea very near Qumran (Luke 3:3; see also Matthew 3:1,5–6; Mark 1:4–5).

Accordingly, John lived in the Wilderness of Judea before his ministry began, and it was there that the word of God came to him in the fifteenth year of the emperor Tiberius (Luke 3:1–2). All three Synoptic Gospels introduce John's public ministry in similar fashion by noting that his was a preaching of repentance (Matthew 3:2; Mark 1:4; Luke 3:3). In the passage in Luke, he is described as "preaching a baptism of repentance for the forgiveness of sins" (Luke 3:3). We are told that his preaching had a larger purpose in the divine plan for the latter days, since it fulfilled the words of Isaiah: John is "[t]he voice of one crying in the wilderness: 'Prepare the way of the Lord, make his paths straight. Every valley shall be filled, and every mountain and hill shall be brought low, and the crooked shall be made straight, and the rough places shall be made smooth; and all flesh shall see the salvation of God.' " Luke (3:3–6) is here quoting Isaiah 40:3–4. Matthew 3:3 and Mark 1:2–3 also quote this passage, although not at such length. John's preaching is characterized by an eschatological urgency, by the need for repentance before the great day dawns and the Lord comes.

Both Matthew and Mark append a description of John's unusual clothing and diet: he wears a camel's hair vestment with a leather belt and eats locusts and wild honey (Matthew 3:4; Mark 1:6). All three Synoptic Gospels specify that John's baptizing took place in the Jordan River (Matthew 3:5–6; Mark 1:5; Luke 3:3). His imperative message stirred the people, as John forthrightly brought people's sins to their attention (Matthew 3:7–10; Luke 3:7–14). Luke reports that John himself became the object of his audience's interest: "As the people were in expectation, and all men questioned in their hearts concerning John, whether perhaps he were the Christ [that is, the messiah]" (Luke 3:15). At this point he proclaims the coming of a greater one who would baptize, not with water as John did, but with the Holy Spirit and with fire, one who would come for judgment (Luke 3:16–18; see also Matthew 3:11–12; Mark 1:7–8; John 1:19–28). John later baptized Jesus (Matthew 3:13–15; Mark 1:8; Luke 3:21) and was eventually imprisoned and executed (Matthew 14:1–12).

A great deal of this picture is reminiscent of the Qumran community. John's geographical location seems to have been very close to Qumran. The Gospel of John locates his baptizing ministry "in Bethany beyond the Jordan" (John 1:28) and "at Aenon near Salim, because there was plenty of water" (John 3:23). Neither of these sites is known with certainty, but they seem to have lain somewhat north of Qumran. Yet the fact that he worked in the wilderness near the Jordan could well have brought him to the vicinity of, or even to, Qumran. The baptism of repentance that John administered parallels the Qumran teaching about washing in water for cleansing and sanctification (Manual of Discipline, 3:4–5,9). According to another passage in the same Qumran text (5:13–14): "They shall not enter the water to partake of the pure Meal of the saints, for they shall not be cleansed, unless they turn from their wickedness: for all who transgress His word are unclean."

The Qumran settlement includes a number of cisterns, some of which were used for the frequent ritual baths of those who belonged to the community. There were probably differences between the baptism of John and the Qumran rituals (John's baptism may have occurred just once for each penitent; the Qumran ablutions seem to have been more frequent), but both were connected with repentance and, unlike proselyte baptism, were meant for Jews. It should also be recalled that both the Qumran community and John the Baptist have their missions explained in our records by the same scriptural citation—Isaiah 40:3. The Manual of Discipline (8:12–15) quotes this same verse to indicate that the group believed it was fulfilling the prophet's words by going literally into the wilderness, there to prepare the way of the Lord through study of Moses' Torah. The various similarities between the Qumran sect and John add up to something less than an identification of John as an Essene, but they are certainly suggestive and have led some to make such claims about this New Testament forerunner.[28] On the other hand, if John was a member of the Qumran community, he must have later separated from it to pursue his independent, solitary ministry.*

Another New Testament personality on whom several Qumran texts in fact cast a new light is Melchizedek. He appears a number of times in

*See Chapter 16.

*28. A water installation at the
Qumran settlement that may have been
used for ritual purification.*

the New Testament book referred to as the Letter to the Hebrews as a priest to whose order Jesus belonged. The Gospel genealogies, however, show that Jesus was *not* a member of the tribe of Levi from which the priests came. In these genealogies, Jesus is descended from David (Matthew 1:1–17; Luke 3:23–38). In his attempt to portray the Davidic Jesus as a priest, the author of Hebrews elaborates traditions about the mysterious priest-king Melchizedek of Salem who appears in Genesis. There Melchizedek meets Abram and blesses the patriarch (Genesis 14:18–20). In the following quotation from Hebrews, the first sentence accurately describes what happened in Genesis; the remainder elaborates this text and joins it with a sentence in Psalm 110:4:

> For this Melchizedek, king of Salem, priest of the Most High God, met Abraham returning from the slaughter of the kings and blessed him; and to him Abraham apportioned a tenth part of everything [of the booty]. He is first, by translation of his name, king of righteousness, and then he is also king of Salem, that is, king of peace. He is without father or mother or genealogy, and has neither beginning of days nor end of life, but resembling the Son of God he continues a priest forever (Hebrews 7:1–3).

The author of Hebrews fashions an extraordinary portrait of Melchizedek, based on inferences (for example, his eternity, his superiority to Levi) from a combination of Genesis 14:18–20 and Psalm 110:4 (which he quotes at Hebrews 7:17).

A text from Qumran, appropriately labeled 11QMelchizedek, now provides at least something of a parallel to the exalted status and characteristics of Melchizedek in Hebrews. In the Qumran text Melchizedek is presented as an angelic being who raises up God's holy ones for deeds of judgment and who takes divine vengeance on evil. Here Melchizedek has superhuman status, which clearly involves living eternally,[29] just as he has in Hebrews.

More recently, another Qumran text was published that appears to mention Melchizedek—the Songs of the Sabbath Sacrifice.[30] Although the relevant fragments are poorly preserved, here Melchizedek seems to officiate as the heavenly high priest, just as Jesus does in Hebrews.

We have surveyed the theories of scholars—some bold and some cautious—about the relationship between Jesus, the New Testament, and the Qumran texts. We have looked at the Qumran texts for what they can teach us about New Testament language, for their striking parallels with New Testament passages, and to ask whether some of the same characters may walk on both stages. We will consider the ritual and community practices common to Qumran covenanters and New Testament Christians and compare the messianic views that both groups held along with their confident expectations that the end of days would soon come.

Many of the ritual and community practices of the Qumran covenanters, who lived near the Dead Sea and who produced what we call the Dead Sea Scrolls, have impressive parallels among New Testament Christians. Here are just a few:

Acts describes the events of the first Pentecost after Jesus' crucifixion. It then describes the property the community holds in common: "And all who believed were together and had all things in common; and they sold their possessions and goods and distributed them to all, as any had need" (Acts 2:44–45; see also Acts 4:32).

Later, in Acts 5:1–11, Luke narrates the celebrated case of Ananias and Sapphira who sold some land but presented to the community only a part of the proceeds. Peter accuses them of withholding, and they both fall down dead. Here Acts is reflecting the situation in the early Christian community in Jerusalem. Paul, on the other hand, writes as if members of the churches that he founded had private means with which to contribute to the needs of others (1 Corinthians 16:2). Moreover, even in Jerusalem, contribution to the community may have been voluntary. (Acts 5:4 states: "After [the property] was sold, were not the proceeds at your disposal?" If so, the sin of Ananias and Sapphira was not withholding, but making a partial donation of the proceeds while giving the impression that it was the whole.)

The Manual of Discipline from Qumran makes several allusions to the merging of members' private property with the possessions of the group. This theme is especially prominent in the section that describes initiatory procedures for potential members. At first, the novice is not allowed to share the pure meal of the congregation, "nor shall he have any share of the property of the Congregation" (6:17). Once he has completed a full year within the group and it is determined that he may remain, "his property and earnings shall be handed over to the Bursar of the Congregation who shall register it to his account [but] shall not spend it for the Congregation" (6:19–20). Only after an additional, successful year of probation is it stipulated that "his property shall be merged" with the community's possessions (6:22). The practice is compulsory at Qumran and follows full admission to the congregation.[31]

A sacred meal with eschatological significance also seems to be something the Qumran covenanters and the early Christians shared. The Last Supper, which Jesus shared with his immediate followers, is presented in two ways in the Gospels: For Matthew, Mark, and Luke, it is a Passover meal complete with bread and wine; for John, it was eaten the night before Passover and neither bread nor wine is mentioned. In the Passover version of the Last Supper, bread and wine play prominent roles; indeed, they attain a sacramental significance:

> Now as they were eating, Jesus took the bread, and blessed, and broke it, and gave it to the disciples and said, "Take, eat; this is my body." And he took a cup, and when he had given thanks he gave it to them, saying, "Drink of it, all of you; for this is my blood of the covenant, which is poured out for many for the forgiveness of sins. I tell you I shall not drink again of this fruit of the vine until that day when I drink it new with you in my Father's kingdom" (Matthew 26:26–29; see also Mark 14:22–25; Luke 22:17–20).

These words give special meaning to the physical elements of the meal and place the ceremony within a context of expectation for "that day when I drink it new with you in my Father's kingdom."

The Qumran texts, too, describe a special meal that involved the basic elements of bread and wine. The Manual of Discipline refers to the meals of the group: "And when the table has been prepared for eating, and the new wine for drinking, the Priest shall be the first to stretch out his hand to bless the first-fruits of the bread and new wine" (6:4–6).[32] This text also mentions a "pure meal" that only those who have passed through a year-long probationary period were permitted to eat (6:16–17); they were not allowed to partake of the "drink of the congregation" until a second such year had passed (6:20–21). Those who were guilty of slandering another member of the community were excluded from this meal for one year (7:16).

The clearest statement about a special meal at Qumran comes from the Rule of the Congregation (1QSa) (which was originally part of the Manual of Discipline):

> [The ses]sion of the men of renown, [invited to] the feast for the council of the community when [at the end] (of days) the messiah [shall assemble] with them. [The priest] shall enter [at] the head of all the congregation of Israel, and [all his brethren the sons of] Aaron, the priests, [who are invited] to the feast, the men of renown, and they shall sit be[fore him, each] according to his importance. Afterwards, [the messiah] of Israel [shall enter] and the heads of the [thousands of Israel] shall sit before him [ea]ch

according to his importance, according to [his station] in their encampments and their journeys. And all of the heads of the [households of the congrega]tion, [their] sag[es and wise men,] shall sit before them, each according to his importance. [When they] mee[t at the] communal [tab]le, [to set out bread and wi]ne, and the communal table is arranged [to eat and] to dri[nk] wine, [no] one [shall extend] his hand to the first (portion) of the bread and [the wine] before the priest. Fo[r he shall] bless the first (portion) of the bread and the wi[ne and shall extend] his hand to the bread first. Afterwa[rds,] the messiah of Israel [shall exten]d his hands to the bread. [Afterwards,] all of the congregation of the community [shall ble]ss, ea[ch according to] his importance. [They] shall act according to this statute whenever (the meal) is ar[ranged] when as many as ten [meet] together" (Rule of the Congregation 2:11–22).[33]

This meal, eaten in the presence of the two messiahs postulated at Qumran, was only for those who were ritually pure (compare 1 Corinthians 11:27–29).

Lawrence Schiffman, of New York University, argues that the Qumran meals were nonsacral or cultic in nature; rather, "[t]hese meals, conducted regularly as part of the present-age way of life of the sect, were preenactments of the final messianic banquet which the sectarians expected in the soon-to-come end of days. Again, the life of the sect in this world mirrored its dreams for the age to come."[34] But however the meal of the Qumran covenanters is interpreted, its messianic character, the prominence of bread and wine, the fact that it was repeated regularly, and the explicit eschatological associations do in fact remind one of elements found in the New Testament words about the Lord's Last Supper.[35]

According to at least one scholar, the Qumran texts may provide a solution to an old calendrical problem in Gospel studies.[36] The Synoptic Gospels (Matthew, Mark, and Luke), on the one hand, and John, on the other, place the Last Supper on different dates. The synoptics place the Last Supper on a Friday and treat it as a Passover meal; John, however, puts it on a Thursday, the day before Passover, and dates Jesus' death to the next day—at a time when the Passover lambs were being slaughtered. The official Hebrew calendar used in the Jerusalem Temple was a lunar calendar with some solar adjustments. At Qumran, the covenanters used a 364-day solar calendar. A French scholar, Annie Jaubert, has proposed that, since two calendars were used in Judaism at this time, it is possible that the synoptic writers followed one calendar (the solar calendar) and that John followed the official lunar calendar.[37]

Some have found this solution attractive, but there is no evidence that the writers of the Gospels followed different calendar systems. Moreover, it is evident that John had a larger purpose in mind in arranging events in the passion week as he did. John does not emphasize the bread and wine at Jesus' meal; they are not even mentioned. Instead, foot washing and mutual love are highlighted. By dying when he did in John's chronology, Jesus is presented as the Passover lamb of his people, slaughtered the following day.

There is no doubt that the Qumran covenanters and the early Christians shared a similar eschatological outlook. Both must be regarded as eschatological communities in the sense that both had a lively expectation that the end of days would come soon and ordered their communal beliefs and practices according to this article of faith. Under this broad heading, several points may be distinguished.

Although both groups had messianic expectations, they are different in some respects. The faith of Qumran was that the last days would bring two messiahs: "They shall depart from none of the counsels of the Law to walk in the stubbornness of their hearts, but shall be ruled by the primitive precepts in which the men of the Community were first instructed until there shall come the Prophet and the Messiahs of Aaron and Israel" (Manual of Discipline 9:9–11, see also the Rule of the Congregation). The more prominent messiah is the priestly one—the messiah of Aaron. The second and apparently lower-ranking messiah is the lay one—the messiah of Israel. Precisely what the messiahs would do, other than officiate at the messianic banquet, is not clear; no text says either that they would save others or that they would atone for others' sins, as in the case of the Christian messiah.

The New Testament picture of Jesus is familiar: the Gospel genealogies trace his ancestry through David's line. Jesus, however, is not only the messiah as descendant of David, but also as the son of God and savior.

Perhaps the Qumran messiah of Israel is also Davidic. But there is no second messiah in the New Testament, as there was at Qumran. While the New Testament has only one messiah, however, it assigns to him the offices filled by the two Qumran messiahs. The New Testament also speaks of Jesus as a priestly messiah: In the Letter to the Hebrews, as we have seen, Jesus is regarded as a priest after the order of Melchizedek; Jesus as high priest presides over a heavenly sanctuary.

One of the messianic titles given to Jesus in the New Testament is now attested at Qumran—for the first time in its Semitic form. In Luke 1:32–33 the angel who appears to Mary to announce that she would conceive a wondrous child, describes him this way: " 'He will be great and will be called the Son of the Most High; and the Lord God will give to him the throne of his father David, and he will reign over the house of Jacob forever; and of his kingdom there will be no end.' " The child will also be called " 'holy, the Son of God' " (Luke 1:35).

An intriguing and still only partially published parallel to some of these titles comes from a Qumran document. The relevant portion reads: "[He] shall be great upon the earth, [O King! All shall] make [peace], and all shall serve [him. He shall be called the son of] the [G]reat [God], and by his name shall he be named. He shall be hailed the Son of God, and they shall call him Son of the Most High . . . , and his kingdom will be a kingdom forever."[38]

This is not simply a matter of one title found in two texts; it is an entire context that has striking similarities: The individual in question will be great, son of God (a title found in the Hebrew Bible), son of the Most High (a new title), and his kingdom will be eternal. It is a pity that the referent of these titles in the Qumran text remains unknown; that part of the text has not been preserved.

Joseph Fitzmyer has also drawn attention to some interesting parallels between the infancy stories of Jesus in Matthew and Luke and of Noah as preserved in the Qumran text known as the Genesis Apocryphon (1QapGen) (and 1 Enoch 106–107). For example, in the latter texts, it is suspected that Noah does not have a natural father. In Matthew and Luke, Mary's conception is through the overshadowing of the Holy Spirit (Matthew 1:18; Luke 1:35). In Noah's case, his father Lamech suspects that his mother Batenosh has had an extramarital affair with an angel.[39]

Another shared perspective by both Qumran covenanters and early Christians was the way that they interpreted biblical texts—with a strong eschatological consciousness that the end of days was near.

Among the earliest of the scrolls to be discovered and published was the commentary (or *pesher*) on the Book of Habakkuk. Karl Elliger published a book about this commentary as early as 1953. He summarized the assumptions underlying this and similar Qumran commentaries *(pesharim)* on biblical books: The biblical writers are speaking about the last days, and the last days are now.[40] Based on these presuppositions, the Qumran sectarians interpreted the biblical texts as referring to themselves and their leaders; the events of their community's history were being foretold in the biblical texts.

For example, Habakkuk 2:1–2 states:

> I will take my stand to watch, and station myself on the tower, and look forth to see what he will say to me, and what I will answer concerning my

complaint. And the Lord answered me: "Write the vision; make it plain upon tablets, so he may run who reads it."

The Habakkuk Commentary (1QpHab) from Qumran explains the passage this way: "God told Habakkuk to write down that which would happen to the final generation, but He did not make known to him when time would come to an end. And as for that which He said, *'That he who reads may read it speedily'* ["so he may run who reads it" in Habakkuk 2:2], interpreted, this concerns the Teacher of Righteousness, to whom God made known all the mysteries of the words of His servants the Prophets" (Habakkuk Commentary 7:1–5).

Many New Testament passages evidence the same eschatological reading of biblical texts, interpreting them as if they foretold and applied directly to contemporary events. Take the story of Pentecost in Acts 2. The apostolic band had been speaking in tongues by virtue of the Holy Spirit that had been poured over them. The local population is perplexed and mocks them. Peter defends those who were speaking in tongues, citing Scripture in support of the linguistic miracle that has just occurred:

> For these men are not drunk, as you suppose, since it is only the third hour of the day; but this is what was spoken by the prophet Joel: "And in the last days [Joel does not actually say "in the last days"; he says only "afterward"[41]] it shall be, God declares, that I will pour out my Spirit upon all flesh, and your sons and your daughters shall prophesy, and your young men shall see visions, and your old men shall dream dreams. . . ." (Acts 2:15–17)

Thus, according to Acts, the prophet Joel proclaimed that the divine Spirit would be poured out in the last days, and that eschatological event actually occurred at the first Christian celebration of Pentecost. This way of interpreting Scripture (Joel in Acts and Habakkuk in the Habakkuk Commentary from Qumran) is identical.

At times the authors of the New Testament and of the Qumran texts rely on the same biblical text, interpreting it in the same way. We have already seen this in the case of Isaiah 40:3 ("A voice cries out: 'In the wilderness prepare the way of the Lord, make straight in the desert a highway for our God' "). John the Baptist, for the Gospel writers, and the Qumran community, for the Qumran covenanters, are both said to be preparing the Lord's way in the wilderness.

Another instance of this is Habakkuk 2:4b: "The righteous live by their faith," one of Paul's favorite proof texts. He uses it in Galatians 3:11 to support his argument that faith, not works, is the way to become right with God: "Now it is evident that no man is justified before God by the law; for 'He who through faith is righteous shall live' " (see also Romans 1:17).

The Habakkuk Commentary from Qumran offers another angle on Habakkuk 2:4b: "Interpreted, this concerns those who observe the Law in the House of Judah, whom God will deliver from the House of Judgment because of their suffering and because of their faith in [or: fidelity to] the Teacher of Righteousness" (Habakkuk Commentary 8:1–3). Interestingly, the same passage that for Paul dealt with a way of righteousness other than the path of the Law was at Qumran a verse that encouraged faithfulness to that Law and fidelity to the Teacher who expounded it correctly. Yet both use the same text and the same method of interpretation.

The eschatological nature of these two communities can also be seen in some of the major doctrines they embraced. For example, both employ dualistic language to describe the options in the universe: There are just two positions, with no mediating ground between. Since both communities are still Jewish at this time, the dualism is ethical; the two opposing camps (or principles) are light and darkness. One of the best-known passages in the scrolls says:

He [God] has created man to govern the world, and has appointed for him two spirits in which to walk until the time of His visitation: the spirits of truth and falsehood. Those born of truth spring from a fountain of light, but those born of falsehood spring from a source of darkness. All the children of righteousness are ruled by the Prince of Light and walk in the ways of light, but all the children of falsehood are ruled by the Angel of Darkness and walk in the ways of darkness (Manual of Discipline 3:18–21).

Perpetual conflict marks the relation between the two camps:

For God has established the spirits in equal measure until the final age, and has set everlasting hatred between their divisions. Truth abhors the works of falsehood, and falsehood hates all the ways of truth. And their struggle is fierce in all their arguments for they do not walk together (Manual of Discipline 4:16–18).

However, God has "ordained an end for falsehood, and at the time of the visitation He will destroy it for ever" (Manual of Discipline 4:18–19).

Another Qumran text, The Scroll of the War of the Sons of Light Against the Sons of Darkness, contains an elaborate description of the final battles between the Sons of Light and the Sons of Darkness. Though powerful angels will fight on both sides, God will, in his good time, decide the issue in favor of the light.

This language is hardly strange to readers of the New Testament. Similar rhetoric appears in the writings of both Paul (in 2 Corinthians 6:14–7:1) and John.

In John 8:12, the author quotes Jesus as saying: "I am the light of the world; he who follows me will not walk in darkness, but will have the light of life."

As at Qumran, John uses the light/darkness contrast, not in its literal, but in an ethical, sense. As at Qumran, so in John the realms of light and darkness are in conflict: "The light shines in the darkness, and the darkness has not overcome it" (John 1:5). In John 12:35–36, the evangelist tells us: "The light is with you a little longer. Walk while you have the light, lest the darkness overtake you; he who walks in darkness does not know where he goes. While you have the light, believe in the light, that you may be sons of the light" (see also John 3:19–20; 1 John 1:6, 2:9–10). Thus, the followers of Jesus, like the Qumran covenanters, styled themselves "the sons of the light."

The Christian belief about the end is clear: A number of passages speak of Christ's return, the resurrection of the good and the evil and the ultimate victory of the former under Christ's banner (for example, 1 Corinthians 15:20–28, 51–57). The resurrection of Jesus is a guarantee that those who belong to him will also rise in physical form.

Whether the Qumran covenanters believed in a bodily resurrection is not entirely clear, but they certainly believed in the immortality of the soul. The first-century Jewish historian Josephus tells of Essenes who under torture "cheerfully resigned their souls, confident that they would receive them back again. For it is a fixed belief of theirs that the body is corruptible and its constituent matter impermanent, but that the soul is immortal and imperishable."[42] The implication from this passage seems to be that, while the Essenes believe in the immortality of the soul, they do not believe in the resurrection of the body, as did the early Christians. The Qumran texts too mention "life without end" (Manual of Discipline 4:7; The Damascus Rule [CD] 3:20, etc.). But they may also mention a resurrection of bodies, although this is not absolutely clear. The difficulty arises because the best available evidence from the published Qumran texts is a poetic passage, and thus its reference to the author's being raised from *sheol* (the realm of the dead) to an eternal height may be figurative language for God's delivering him from dire straits to a renewed life, rather than a literal bodily resurrection (see the Hymn Scroll 3:19–22). However, Hippolytus, an early Christian writer (c. 170–236) who, like Josephus, describes Essene beliefs, claims that the Essenes did accept the doctrine of the resurrection of bodies.[43] An as-yet-unpublished Qumran text may now confirm Hippolytus' statement.[44] Émile Puech of the École Biblique in Jerusalem is editing a Hebrew text, inherited from the late Jean Starcky, that Puech dates to the first half of the first century B.C. It reads in part: "And they [those who curse] will be for death [while] the One who gives life will [rai]se to life the dead of his people."[45] So the Qumran covenanters may well have believed, as did the early Christians, in a bodily resurrection.

What can we conclude from all this? Clearly, the Qumran literature and the New Testament are similar to one another in numerous and diverse ways. From the similarities, two conclusions can be drawn: (1) The early Church grew upon Jewish soil to a far greater extent than previously supposed; and (2) a larger number of the early Church's beliefs and practices than previously suspected were not unique to it.

On the other hand, the Qumran scrolls also help to highlight Christianity's uniqueness: This lies not so much in its communal practices and eschatological expectations but in its confession that the son of a carpenter from Nazareth in Galilee was indeed the Messiah and son of God who taught, healed, suffered, died, rose, ascended, and promised to return some day in glory to judge the living and the dead.

By confessing that their Messiah had come, the Christians also placed themselves further along on the eschatological timetable than the Qumran covenanters who were still awaiting the arrival of their two messiahs.

As more of the Qumran library is published, I strongly suspect we will also find that the centrality of Torah, its proper interpretation, and obedience to it figured more prominently in Essene doctrine.* This, too, stands in stark contrast with at least the Pauline form of Christianity, in which the Mosaic Torah was not to be imposed upon Gentile Christians and justification was obtained through faith, quite apart from observance of the Law.

One final note: In light of the significant parallels—and major differences—between the Qumran texts and the New Testament, it is puzzling that the Essenes are never mentioned by name in the New

---

*See Chapters 3 and 4.

Testament. Some have suggested that they are mentioned but by a different designation (for example, the Herodians[46]). Others have tried to explain their absence on the grounds that the groups who are mentioned—the Pharisees and Sadducees—tend to figure in polemical contexts, while the Essenes, with whom Jesus and the first Christians had more in common, do not appear precisely because there were fewer controversies with them or because the Essenes did not debate with outsiders.[47] A fully satisfying answer escapes us—perhaps because we do not actually know the Semitic term that lies behind the Greek name "Essenes." As this statement implies, the Essenes are not mentioned by that name in rabbinic literature either.[48] Nor, for that matter, does the name Essene appear in the Qumran literature. So we are still left with a few puzzles to figure out.

CHAPTER 15

AN UNPUBLISHED DEAD SEA
SCROLL TEXT PARALLELS
LUKE'S INFANCY NARRATIVE

HERSHEL SHANKS

One of the major conclusions of the last chapter was that the Qumran literature helps us to understand better the Jewish soil out of which Christianity grew. For example, many facets of early Christian concepts that were once thought to have entered Christianity at a later time via Hellenistic culture can now be traced to first-century Jewish Palestine.

This short notice illustrates this point—on the basis of a leaked, still-unpublished Qumran text that may be fully available by the time this appears in print. The unpublished text uses terms like Son of the Most High, which was once thought to originate in Hellenistic circles outside Palestine. This text also illustrates the kinds of insights we may expect from the unpublished corpus after scholars have had an opportunity to read and digest it.

The unpublished text discussed here has striking parallels to a passage in the Gospel of Luke. It contains the phrase Son of God, the first time this phrase has been found in a text outside the Bible. —ED.

—·—

A still-unpublished Dead Sea Scroll fragment, whose siglum is 4Q246, bears striking similarities to a passage from the annunciation scene in Luke's Gospel. In the Gospel, God sends the angel Gabriel to announce to Mary, a virgin betrothed to Joseph, that she will conceive a son whom she is to call Jesus. In making the announcement, Gabriel says to her: "He will be great, and will be called the Son of the Most High. . . . The power of the Most High will overshadow you; therefore the child to be born will be called holy, the Son of God" (Luke 1:32,35).

In the fragment from Qumran, we do not know who is speaking or who is being spoken of, but this is what the fragment says: "[X] shall be great upon the earth. [O king, all (people) shall] make [peace], and all shall serve [him. He shall be called the son of] the [G]reat [God], and by his name shall he be hailed (as) the Son of God, and they shall call him Son of the Most High."

In both passages, we are told that he will be "great"; that he will be "called" "Son of the Most High" and "Son of God." This is the first time that the term *Son of God* has been found in a Palestinian text outside the Bible.

Obviously this text is of extraordinary importance to all New Testament scholars who want to understand the background of this passage from Luke's Gospel and the usage of terms like *Most High* (found elsewhere in Luke) and *Son of God* (found throughout the New Testament). Previously some scholars have insisted that the origins of terms like *Most High* and *Son of the Most High* were to be found in Hellenistic usage outside Palestine and that therefore they relate to later development of Christian doctrine. Now we know that these terms were part of Christianity's original Jewish heritage. This unpublished Dead Sea Scroll fragment is especially important because Luke's Gospel, like all the Gospels, has been preserved only in Greek, a language that Jesus probably did not speak. The fragment from the Dead Sea caves, however, is in Aramaic, the language that Jesus almost certainly did speak.

This particular fragment was acquired in 1958 through Kando, the Bethlehem and East Jerusalem antiquities dealer who had served as middleman for the purchase of most of the Dead Sea Scrolls from the Bedouin shepherds. The fragment was given for publication to J. T. Milik, a Polish scholar now living in Paris. More than thirty years later, it has still not been published.

CHAPTER 16

WAS JOHN THE BAPTIST
AN ESSENE?

OTTO BETZ

In Chapter 14 James VanderKam referred to the possibility that John the Baptist might have lived at Qumran. In this chapter, the distinguished German scholar Otto Betz explores this possibility in some depth, in the course of which we learn a great deal about Qumran doctrine.

Betz first considers the similarities between John the Baptist's life and teaching, on one hand, and the life and teaching at Qumran, on the other. But Betz also examines the differences. At the end of his career, the Baptist's mission included a call to action that seems far removed from the withdrawn, largely passive community of Qumran. Betz concludes that John the Baptist was probably raised at the Qumran settlement and lived there during his early years, but then left to preach his message to the Jewish masses. Betz calls our attention to the fact that our sources tell not only of isolated Essenes, as at Qumran, but also of fiery Essene prophets who called for repentance. John may have regarded himself as one of them. —ED.

—·—

The Dead Sea Scrolls provide us with a picture of a first-century Jewish community that could well have been the home of John the Baptist. At the very least, the possibility is worth exploring. The question is not answered easily, nor is it without difficulty. My own view is that the Baptist was raised in this community by the Dead Sea and was strongly influenced by it, but later left it to preach directly to a wider community of Jews.

Paradoxically, our sources in some ways portray John the Baptist more clearly than Jesus. It is certainly easier to place John in relationship to the contemporaneous Jewish community. Moreover, for John, we have an additional, nonbiblical witness—the first-century Jewish historian Josephus who refers to Jesus but tells little about him. Even among hypercritical exegetes, there is little doubt about who John was and what he stood for.

The Dead Sea Scrolls give us an extraordinary contemporary picture of a Jewish sect, living in the wilderness, with an outlook, customs, and laws that seem to be very much like John's.

Most scholars, including myself, identify the Dead Sea Scroll community as Essene—a separatist Jewish sect or philosophy described, along with the Pharisees and Sadducees, by Josephus.

Recently some few scholars have questioned whether the Dead Sea Scroll community was Essene.* They contend that the library of scrolls found in the Dead Sea caves represents broader Jewish thought. However this may be, it is clear that the library's core documents—to which I shall refer—are, at the least, Essenic, and represent the commitment of a Jewish community quite distinct from—even opposed to—the Jerusalem authorities.

Moreover, in the Judean wilderness, archaeologists have identified and excavated a settlement near where the scrolls were found. According to Pliny the Elder, in *Historia Naturelis,* the Essenes lived in just this location. Indeed, of the eleven caves with inscriptional material, the one with the greatest number of documents—Cave 4—could be entered from the adjacent settlement. It is difficult for me to understand the contention, recently put forward by Norman Golb of the University of Chicago, that the settlement is unrelated to the library.

*See Chapters 3 and 4.

In any event, we shall assume that this settlement, which overlooks the Wadi Qumran, was Essene and that the sectarian documents found in the Qumran caves are also Essene.

As portrayed in the Gospels, John the Baptist stands at the threshold of the Kingdom. He marks the transition from Judaism to Christianity.

Not only is the Gospel picture generally consistent with Josephus, but the four canonical Gospels are themselves in general agreement. In the case of John, there is little room for historical skepticism.

The Gospels portray John as a prophet who came out of the Judean wilderness to proclaim the Kingdom of God and to call for repentance. It seems clear that he had a successful ministry of his own, baptizing with water those who repented.

After Herod the Great died in 4 B.C., his son Herod Antipas became tetrarch of Galilee. John denounced Antipas' marriage to Herodias, his half-niece, who had abandoned her previous husband. Antipas threw John into prison for his criticism. Antipas' new wife Herodias, however, was to go one step further. At Antipas' birthday party, Salome, Herodias's daughter by her previous marriage and now Antipas' step-daughter,* danced for Antipas, who was so delighted with her performance that he promised on oath to give Salome whatever she desired. Induced by her mother Herodias, Salome asked for the head of John the Baptist on a platter. Antipas was unhappy at the request but was bound by his oath. He had John beheaded in prison, which Josephus locates at the fortress of Machaerus, east of the Jordan,[1] and his head was duly delivered to Salome on a platter (Matthew 14:3–12; Mark 6:17–29).

John's stature is reflected in the fact that when Antipas is informed of Jesus' ministry and wondrous deeds, his first thought is that John had been resurrected and had come back to life (Matthew 14:1–2; Mark 6:14–16; Luke 9:7–9).

The Gospels portray John as the forerunner of Jesus. Jesus himself proclaims John's stature: "Truly, I say to you, among those born of women there has risen no one greater than John the Baptist" (Matthew 11:11; compare Luke 7:28). John, Jesus tells the crowd, is "more than a prophet" (Matthew 11:9; Luke 5:26). Indeed, "he is Elijah to come" (Matthew 11:14), the traditional precursor of the Messiah. Jesus himself was baptized by John (Matthew 3:13–17; Mark 1:9–11; Luke 3:21–22). It is clear that the populace considered John a true prophet (Matthew

---

*In the Gospels, Salome is identified only as the daughter of Herodias (Mark 6:2; Matthew 14:6).

21:26; Mark 11:32; Luke 20:6). According to Josephus, John "was a good man and had commanded the Jews to lead a virtuous life."[2]

Years after Jesus' death, Paul encountered a man in faraway Ephesus (in Asia Minor) who "knew only the baptism of John" (Acts 18:25). John's movement apparently endured (see Acts 19:3).

According to the third- and fourth-century pseudo-Clementines (*Recognitiones* 1. 60), John's disciples claimed that their master had been greater than Jesus and that John was the true messiah.

John the Baptist has been immortalized through innumerable works of art—novels, operas, movies, and especially paintings—showing the prophet preaching in the desert, baptizing in the Jordan River, or pointing to the lamb of God. We see him as a prisoner in a dark cell, or sometimes only his bloody head on a platter being delivered to the beautiful Salome. The Baptist was also a favorite of icon painters. As the *prodromos,* the precursor of Christ, he stands at the left hand of the Judge of the World.

More than twenty years ago, when I was teaching at the University of Chicago, one of my black students said to me, "I want to be like John: a voice in the desert, crying for the outcasts, unmasking the hypocrites, showing the sinners the way to righteousness!" A year later the wave of student revolts had reached my own university at Tübingen, where I had returned. I recall a good Christian student who suddenly declared: "Please, not Jesus! John the Baptist is my man!" And he gave up his theological studies.

It is not surprising that the discovery and partial publication of the Dead Sea Scrolls has led to speculation that John the Baptist was an Essene who lived at Qumran. The Essenes flourished at Qumran at the same time John was preaching and baptizing people in the nearby Jordan River. The Qumran settlement was destroyed by the Romans in about 68 A.D. as part of their effort to suppress the First Jewish Revolt against Rome (66 to 70 A.D.), which culminated in the destruction of Jerusalem.

The Dead Sea Scroll known as the Manual of Discipline, also called the Rule of the Community (designated by the scholarly siglum IQS, which stands for "Qumran Cave 1, *Serekh ha-yahad,*" the Hebrew name of the text), appears to be the main organizational document of the Qumran community. There we read that the people of the community must separate themselves

> . . . from the dwelling-place of the men of perversion [the Jerusalem authorities] in order to go to the wilderness to prepare the way of HIM, as it is written [quoting Isaiah 40:3]: "In the wilderness prepare the way of

. . . . [the divine name is marked in this scroll by four dots], make straight in the desert a road for our God!"—this [way] is the search of the Law (Manual of Discipline 8:13–15).

The Essenes were thus led to the wilderness by the same scriptural directions that motivated the life and ministry of John. The early Christians understood John as " 'the voice of one crying in the wilderness: Prepare the way of the Lord, make his paths straight' " (Mark 1:3). This passage from Mark quotes the same words from Isaiah 40:3 that are quoted in the Qumran Manual of Discipline.

The Qumran settlement and the adjacent caves where the scrolls were found are located in the vicinity of the traditional place of John's activity near Jericho. Luke's account of John's birth ends with the astonishing remark: "And the child grew and became strong in spirit, and he was in the wilderness till the day of his manifestation to Israel" (Luke 1:80). How could this little child, the only son of aged parents, grow up in the wilderness? Well, the Essenes lived there, leading a kind of monastic life. According to Josephus they would receive the children of other people when they were "still young and capable of instruction" and would care for them as their own and raise them according to their way of life.[3] It would seem that John the Baptist was raised at Qumran—or at a place very much like it—until he became the voice of one crying in the wilderness, calling for repentance.

Correspondences between the life and teachings of the Qumran community and the life and teachings of John are often extraordinary. John's baptism, as we learn from the Gospels, is but the outward sign of the reality of repentance and the assurance of God's forgiveness (Mark 1:4). After the penitent people had confessed their sins, John baptized them. This probably consisted of immersion in the waters of the Jordan River. However, without the "fruit worthy of repentance" (Matthew 3:8), this rite of purification was useless; as Josephus puts it: "The soul must be already thoroughly cleansed by righteousness."[4] In the Manual of Discipline (3:3–8) we read that cleansing of the body must be accompanied by purification of the soul. Someone who is still guided by the stubbornness of his heart, who does not want to be disciplined in the community of God, cannot become holy, but instead remains unclean, even if he should wash himself in the sea or in rivers; for he must be cleansed by the holy spirit and by the truth of God.

According to the Gospels, John the Baptist announced the coming of a "Stronger One" who would baptize with the Holy Spirit and with fire (Mark 1:7–8). The Qumran community had a similar expectation: They anticipated that their ritual washings would be superseded with a purification by the Holy Spirit at the end of time; then God himself will pour his spirit like water from heaven and remove the spirit of perversion from the hearts of his chosen people. Then they would receive the "knowledge of the Most High and all the glory of Adam" (Manual of Discipline 4:20–22).

In Matthew 21:32, we read that Jesus himself said that "John came to you in the way of righteousness, and you did not believe him . . . [E]ven when you saw it, you did not afterwards repent and believe him." Similarly with the high priests and elders in Jerusalem who did not accept John (Matthew 21:23–27). John may be compared with the most influential man in the Qumran movement, the Teacher of Righteousness. This great anonymous figure announced the events that would come upon the last generation, but the people who "do violence to the covenant" did "not believe" his words (Commentary on Habakkuk 2:2–9).

The Teacher of Righteousness was the priest ordained by God to lead the repentant to the way of His heart (Commentary of Habakkuk 2:8; Cairo Damascus Document 1:11). His teaching was like that of a prophet, inspired by the holy spirit. John too was a priest, the son of the priest Zacharias (Luke 1:5). Like the Qumran Teacher of Righteousness, John separated himself from the priesthood in Jerusalem and from the service in the Temple. And, like the Teacher of Righteousness, he was also a prophet.

Both the Teacher of Righteousness and John the Baptist nevertheless remained faithful to the laws of purity; they both practiced them in a radical, even ascetic, way. Both the Teacher of Righteousness and John the Baptist believed that the messianic age and the final judgment were soon to come. That is why they both practiced the purification of body and soul in such a strict way. The prophetic call for repentance and the apocalyptic expectation of the end of history led to the radicalization and generalization of the priestly laws of purity.

We are told that John the Baptist "did not eat nor drink" (Matthew 11:18), which means that he lived an ascetic life, eating locusts and wild honey (Mark 1:6), foods found in the desert. John wanted to be independent, unpolluted by civilization, which he considered unclean. In this he was not unlike the Essenes living at Qumran. John's cloak was made of camel's hair and the girdle around his waist was leather, well suited to his aim of strict purity.

In ancient Israel the spirit of prophecy often opposed the theology of the priests (see, for example Amos 5:22; Isaiah 1:11–13; and Jeremiah 7:21–26). The prophets warned the people not to rely too heavily on the Temple and on the atoning effect of sacrifice. Both the Essenes and John the Baptist, however, succeeded in combining the prophetic and the priestly ideals in a holy life, ritually pure, but characterized by repentance and the expectancy of the final judgment. John's disciples were known to fast (Mark 2:18) and to recite their special prayers (Luke 11:1). These two acts of piety also appear in the Qumran texts. Infraction of even minor rules was punished by a reduction in the food ration, which meant severe fasting (Manual of Discipline 7:2–15). And there are several special prayers in the Dead Sea Scrolls. Among them are the beautiful Thanksgiving Hymns from the scroll found in Cave 1. Cave 11 also produced a scroll of psalms in which new prayers were inserted into a series of Psalms of David.

The Qumran Essenes separated themselves from the Jerusalem Temple and its sacrificial cult. The Temple's offerings of animals were replaced by the "offerings of the lips" (that is, prayers) and by works of the law. Man must render himself to God as a pleasing sacrifice; he must bring his spirit and body, his mental and physical capacities, together with his material goods and property, into the community of God. In this community all these gifts will be cleansed of the pollution of selfish ambition through humble obedience to the commandments of God (Manual of Discipline 1:11–13).

The Qumran community was intended to be a living sanctuary. They believed this living temple, consisting of people, rendered a better service to God than the Jerusalem sanctuary made of stones. The chosen "stones" of the community were witnesses to the truth of God and made atonement for the land (Manual of Discipline 8:6–10); in this way, the community protects the land and its people from the consuming wrath of God and the catastrophe of his judgment. The Jerusalem Temple could not do this as long as disobedient priests served in it.

John the Baptist, the son of a priest, also had a conflict with the Jerusalem hierarchy, similar to the conflict of the Essenes with the Jerusalem hierarchy. He must have shared the Essenes' belief in the superior quality of the spiritual temple of God. He warned the people not to rely on the fact that Abraham was their father, for "God is able from these stones to raise up children to Abraham [That is, a truly repentant community]" (Matthew 3:9). This famous saying contains a marvelous play on words in Hebrew. "Children" is *banim;* stones is *abanim.* The saying thus presupposes the idea of a living temple "of men." John is saying that God can create genuine *children* of Abraham "from these *stones"* and build them into the sanctuary of His community.

In the Temple Scroll from Qumran, God promises that he will "create" a sanctuary at the beginning of the new age; this he will do according to the covenant made with Jacob at Bethel (Temple Scroll 29:7–10). At Bethel, Jacob had declared: "This stone [the pillar that Jacob had erected] shall become the house of God" (Genesis 28:22). Both the Qumran community and John the Baptist believed in the creative power of God that will manifest itself at the end of time, as it did in the beginning. Then God will establish the true sanctuary and the ideal worship, which are anticipated both in the life of the Qumran community and in the life that John preached.

John's preaching had several characteristics that can also be found at Qumran. For example, John used prophetic forms of rebuke and threat (Matthew 3:7–10). The hypocrites who came to him for baptism without repenting he called "a brood of vipers" (Matthews 3:7). I believe this strange term is the Hebrew equivalent of *ma'ase 'eph'eh* or "creatures of the Snake"—that is, Sons of the Devil. This same phrase occurs in the Thanksgiving Hymns from Qumran (1QH 3:17). In short, the prophetic language of John the Baptist was enriched by the polemics of the Qumran community of Essenes.

While there are thus many reasons to suppose that John the Baptist was an Essene who may have lived at Qumran, there are also impediments to this conclusion that must be as assiduously pursued as the correspondences. First, John is never mentioned in the Dead Sea Scrolls that have been published so far.

Perhaps more telling is the fact that John is never called an Essene in either the New Testament or in Josephus. The absence of such a reference is especially significant in Josephus, because in both *Antiquities of the Jews* and *The Jewish War,* Josephus discusses the Essene sect several times as a Jewish "philosophy," on a par with the Sadduccees and the Pharisees. In *The Jewish War* (2:567), Josephus even mentions another John, whom he identifies as "John, the Essene," who served as a Jewish general in the First Jewish Revolt against Rome. Josephus also identifies three prophetic figures as Essenes (although he does not call them prophets). All of this indicates that Josephus would have identified John the Baptist as an Essene if he knew him to be a member of that group.

Even more significantly, John the Baptist was outspokenly critical of the civil government, which would be uncharacteristic of an Essene. The Baptist went so far as to criticize the tetrarch Antipas himself for marrying his "brother's wife" (Mark 6:18). With his preaching, John created such excitement among the crowds that Herod became afraid that this might lead to a revolt.[5] John's outspokenness seems unlike an Essene.

A similar objection can be raised regarding John's courageous concern for the salvation of his Jewish countrymen. This too seems unlike the Essenes. Indeed, after some serious but unsuccessful criticism of the religious and political leaders in the second century B.C., the Essenes seem to have withdrawn from public life in order to work out their own salvation. They never developed missionary activity, but preferred simply to wait for those whom God chose to join their community of salvation.

John the Baptist, on the other hand, dared to address all the people. He became the incarnation of the divine voice, calling from the desert into the inhabited world: "I am the voice of one calling in the wilderness" (John 1:23). John did not relegate people to a sacred place in the desert, nor did he incorporate them into a holy community with monastic rules. Rather, after they had confessed their sins, he baptized them once and for all. Then he sent them back to their profane world—to their work and their families. There they were to enjoy the "true fruits of repentance" in a life of righteousness. This does not sound at all like an Essene.

For these reasons, we could easily conclude that John the Baptist was not an Essene. The Essene community, on the one hand, and John, on the other, seem to have lived in two different worlds: the one a closed community of saints whose sole concern was for their own salvation; the other, a lonely prophet who is concerned for all his people and their salvation.

But this is not the end of the discussion. There is a way to reconcile both the pros and cons. As Josephus reminds us, not all Essenes led a monastic life in the wilderness of Judah. Indeed some sound almost like John the Baptist. Josephus even speaks of Essene prophets. Nor were these pseudoprophets, impostors and deceivers, of whom Josephus has much to say, but men who foresaw and told the truth, much like the classic prophets of ancient Israel. These Essene seers appeared suddenly, standing up to kings, criticizing their conduct or foretelling their downfall. Josephus does not describe their teaching and way of life; he simply characterizes them as Essenes.[6]

In short, there is no clear-cut conflict between the priestly way of life (Essene) and the prophetic. Both biblical traditions—the priestly and the prophetic one—influenced the Essenes just as they did John the Baptist.

I believe that John grew up as an Essene, probably in the desert settlement at Qumran. Then he heard a special call of God; he became independent of the community—perhaps even more than the Essene prophets described by Josephus. With his baptism of repentance, John addressed all Israel directly; he wanted to serve his people and to save as many of them as possible.

The Essenes of Qumran no doubt prepared the way for this prophetic voice in the wilderness. They succeeded in combining Israel's priestly and prophetic heritage in a kind of eschatological existence. The Essenes radicalized and democratized the concept of priestly purity; they wanted a true theocracy and they sought to turn the people of God into a "kingdom of priests" (Exodus 19:5–6).

A particular motif for their peculiar piety was the eschatological hope. In the age to come, they believed, there would be only one congregation of the holy ones in heaven and on earth; then angels and men would worship together. Therefore, the liturgy and the sacred calendar used in heaven for the time of prayer and the celebration of the feasts served as a model for Essene worship even in the present. In heaven, animals are not sacrificed and offered to God; the angels use incense and sing hymns of praise. Therefore, on earth they had no need of the Jerusalem Temple. The Essenes believed that a living sanctuary of holy men could render a more efficient ministry of atonement than animal sacrifices, offered by an unclean priesthood (Manual of Discipline 8:6–10, 9:4–5).

But the Essenes also incorporated the traditions of the prophets into their beliefs. The prophet had little if anything to do with Temple and sacrifice; the prophet tried to accomplish atonement through his personal commitment and the effort to change the hearts of his audience. Because the Essenes were a movement of repentance, they adopted the prophetic tradition, despite their leadership of priests. Their Teacher of Righteousness was a priest who acted in a prophetic way.

This was true as well for John the Baptist. He was the son of a priest and practiced the laws of priestly purity in a radical way. But in his ministry for Israel he acted as a prophet, as the *Elijah redivivus** to announce the coming of the Messiah. In his baptism, both traditions were combined, just as they were in the Essene philosophy: The priestly laws of ritual purity were combined with the prophetic concern for repenting, returning to God, and offering oneself to Him. Accordingly, it is reasonable to conclude that John the Baptist was raised in the tradition of the Essenes and may well have lived at Qumran before taking his message to a wider public.

---

*Literally, "Elijah will come to life again." This refers to God's promise that he will "send Elijah the prophet before the great and terrible day of the Lord comes." (Malachi 4:5)

VI

THE DEAD SEA SCROLLS AND RABBINIC JUDAISM

CHAPTER 17

NEW LIGHT ON THE PHARISEES

LAWRENCE H. SCHIFFMAN

Until recently, many scholars rejected as historically unreliable the descriptions of the Pharisees and their laws contained in rabbinic literature compiled hundreds of years after the Roman destruction of the Temple in 70 A.D. Now, according to Lawrence Schiffman of New York University, the Dead Sea Scrolls are changing this view. Sensitively read, the Dead Sea Scrolls tell us a great deal about the Pharisees during the period before 70 A.D. The postdestruction rabbinic descriptions of the Pharisees and their religious practices are turning out to be remarkably accurate. The continuities between the laws and practices of predestruction Pharisees and postdestruction rabbinic Judaism are far greater than had previously been supposed. —ED.

———·———

In my judgment, the texts from Qumran will lead to a new understanding of the history of Judaism in the Second Temple period. Initial research on the scrolls naturally concentrated on the Dead Sea Scroll sect. But the full corpus will teach us a tremendous amount about other Jewish groups as well.[1]

Judaism in all its modern manifestations ultimately derives from rabbinic Judaism, the religious system of the rabbis of the Mishnah (compiled in about 200 C.E.) and the Talmud (compiled between about 400 and 600 C.E.). First codified in the Mishnah, rabbinic tradition claims to be the continuation of the teachings of the Pharisees, a group of lay teachers of the Torah who arose in the years following the Maccabean uprising (168–164 B.C.E.) and who continued teaching up to the time of the Roman destruction of the Temple in 70 C.E. The Pharisees were succeeded, in a sense, by the *tannaim,* the teachers of the Mishnah.[2] (The texts from the period of the Mishnah are known as tannaitic literature.)

Modern critical scholarship has challenged much of what talmudic sources (including the Mishnah) say about the Pharisees in the predestruction period on the grounds that the scant evidence preserved in these texts actually comes from the post-70 period. Many scholars have simply rejected out of hand the claims made in postdestruction rabbinic literature that the Pharisees were the dominant religious group in the affairs of the Temple as early as the Maccabean period and during the reign of the Hasmonean dynasty which succeeded the Maccabean uprising.[3] Yet ultimately, rabbinic Judaism's claim to authority rests on the continuity of the Pharisaic-rabbinic tradition from predestruction to postdestruction times. For the rabbis, the traditions of the Pharisees had been transmitted orally to the tannaitic masters of the Mishnah and in this way had formed the basis for postdestruction tannaitic Judaism. But to the modern critical historian the evidence was sparse.

Accordingly, any light that might be cast on the history of the Pharisees and their teachings in the predestruction period would be critically important. With new evidence from the Dead Sea Scrolls it is now possible to demonstrate that for much of the Hasmonean period Pharisaic views were indeed dominant in the Jerusalem Temple. In short, the reports of the religious laws, or *halakhah,** attributed to the Pharisees in later talmudic texts are basically accurate. Moreover, we can now prove that some of the teaching attributed to rabbinic sages who lived after the Roman destruction of the Temple actually goes back to earlier predestruction, Pharisaic traditions.

Most of the Qumran material that sheds light on the Pharisees is in the form of polemics against their views. The Qumran sect virulently dis-

---

*Halakhah (plural: *halakhot*) is the obligatory, legal side of Judaism, including Jewish practices and observances, covering daily life, festivals, dietary laws, purity rituals, civil and criminal law.

agreed with Pharisaic teachings on a wide variety of theological and halakhic matters. When we evaluate this material carefully, however, and then compare it to later statements of rabbinic tradition, we can reconstruct a great deal about the predestruction Pharisees.

Let us begin by looking at the so-called Damascus Document (see Chapter 5), two copies of which were found nearly a century ago in a Cairo synagogue. (At that time they were called the Zadokite Fragments.) Fragments of at least eight other copies of the Damascus Document were found a half century later in the caves of Qumran.

The first part of the text as preserved in Cairo manuscripts (designated by the siglum CD) is known as the Admonition, and among other things includes a list of legal transgressions. These transgressions were committed by "the builders of the wall who followed [literally, walked after] the 'commander.' The 'commander' is the preacher about whom He [either God or the prophet] said, 'They shall surely preach' " (CD 4:19–20).

Who are the builders of the wall? Who is the commander or preacher? For the sect, they are the villains; that is for sure. Buried in the text are two scriptural allusions that make this clear. One is Hosea 5:10–11:

> The commanders of Judah have acted
> Like shifters of field boundaries.
> On them I will pour out
> My wrath like water.
> Ephraim is defrauded
> Robbed of redress.

The other allusion is to a passage in Micah 2:6:

> "Stop preaching" they preach.
> "That's no way to preach."

The key to the identity of these villains is the content of the laws that the Damascus Document condemns. In a series of laws listed there, the views of the preacher (the "commander") and of the builders of the wall turn out to be laws known from tannaitic sources as being associated with the Pharisees. With these laws the Qumran sectarians violently disagreed.

The designation "builders of the wall" is apparently an adaptation of the concept, known from the Mishnah (Avot 1:1), which teaches, "build a fence around the Torah."[4] According to this rabbinic maxim, laws not found in the Bible may be created in order to make certain that those laws which are in the Torah are not transgressed. That is the "fence" around the Torah. Tannaitic sources consider this "fence" *(siyyag)* a positive feature of rabbinic *halakhah;* the authors of the Damascus Document, on the other hand, opposed this approach—apparently not only because they disagreed with these nonbiblical laws but also because they rejected the idea of expanding the biblical commandments in this way. In short, they objected to such laws because, in their view, these laws had no biblical basis.

That this difference of views between the Qumran sect and the Pharisees went to the heart of many *halakhot* is clear from another passage from the Damascus Document:

> They [whom we have now identified as the Pharisees] even rendered impure their holy spirit and in revelous terms opened (their) mouth against the laws of the covenant of God, saying, "They are not correct" (CD 5:11–13).

Later in the Damascus Document, the Pharisees are again called "the builders of the wall" who lack understanding:

> All these things the builders of the wall and the plasterers of nothingness did not understand. For one who takes wind and preaches falsehood preached to them, for which reason God became angry with his entire congregation (CD 8:12–13) . . . Since He hated the builders of the wall He became angry (CD 8:18).

Because the Qumran sectarians objected to Pharisaic *halakhah* not based directly on Scripture, the Pharisees are referred to in the scrolls as *dorshe halaqot,* literally "seekers after smooth things." The phrase draws on the biblical usage of *halaqot* as lies or falsehoods (cf. Isaiah 30:10; Psalms 12:3, 12:4, 73:18; and Daniel 11:32). But *halaqot* is also a pun on *halakhot,* the plural of *halakhah* and the term for religious laws known to us from later rabbinic usage. This pun indicates that *halakhah* as a term for religious laws was already in common Pharisaic usage as early as the Hasmonean period. Indeed, a study of the rabbinic sources regarding this term shows that the word's original reference was to a law that did not have a direct basis in Scripture—for example, a law based on the "tradition of the fathers" or "the elders."

The Damascus Document clearly refers to the Pharisees when it speaks of those who "interpreted false laws" *(darshu be-halaqot)* and choose falsehoods, seek out breaches (opportunities to violate the law), choose luxury, declare innocent the guilty, and declare guilty the innocent. They violate the covenant and annul the law, and band together to do away with the righteous (CD 1:18–20).

The entire corpus of the Pharisaic laws thus constitutes, in the view of the sectarians, "annulment" of the Torah, because it replaces biblical laws with the Pharisees' own rulings.

A passage in the Thanksgiving *(Hodayot)* Scroll from Cave 1 may also refer to the Pharisees:

> They planned evil [literally, Belial] against me
> to replace your Torah which you taught in my heart
> with smooth things [that is, false laws which they taught]
> to Your people (1QH 4:10–11).

The Qumran sectarians object to the Pharisaic laws because they regard these Pharisaic *halakhot* as replacements for the biblical laws given by God Himself. The very notion of laws to be added to those of the Bible was anathema to the Qumran sectarians. They countenanced only laws derived directly from the Torah by what they regarded as inspired biblical exegesis.[5]

The *Pesher Nahum*—that is, a sectarian commentary on the book of the prophet Nahum—from Cave 4 states:

> [Its] interpretation [that is, Nahum 3:4] [con]cerns those
> who lead Ephraim astray, whose falseness is in their
> teaching [*talmud*], and whose lying tongue and dishonest
> lip(s) lead many astray (4QpNah 3–4 II, 8).

Ephraim is a code word for the Pharisees. This designation results from the similar sound of Ephraim and the Hebrew word *Perushim,* Pharisees. Manasseh, on the other hand, designates the Sadducees.[6] The author of the commentary clearly intended to refer to the Pharisaic leaders and teachers—that is, those who lead Ephraim (the Pharisees). It is these people that the text likens to those who commit the harlotry mentioned in Nahum 3:4.

Note that the word used for teaching is the Hebrew word *talmud,* the same word used to designate the massive commentaries on the Mishnah—the Babylonian and Palestinian Talmuds.

The presence of the word *talmud* in this text was, in the early years of scrolls research, used to argue for a medieval dating of the scrolls.[7] The scholars who made this argument mistakenly took the word *talmud* as a reference to the rabbinic text by that name. The matter is much more complex, however. In early tannaitic literature, *talmud* already refers to a method of study—namely, the Pharisaic-rabbinic tradition that permits laws to be deduced logically from the biblical text. This method is what the Qumran sectarians are excoriating. The text proves, however, that this method of legal argument was already being used in the later half of the Hasmonean period.[8]

From the Pharisaic viewpoint, this method was intended to derive laws from the Torah. Why, then, was this considered illegitimate by the Qumran sectarians since they too practiced legal exegesis? The method used by the Pharisees, designated here as *talmud,* made no claim to divine inspiration. For the Qumran sectarians, it was therefore illegitimate—a falsehood.

What do we know of the content of these supposedly false, illegitimate Pharisaic laws? A number of Pharisaic rulings are alluded to in polemical parts of the Damascus Document—for example, Pharisaic rulings permitting remarriage after divorce (CD 4:20–5:1) and marriage to one's niece (CD 5:7–11).

Recently, our knowledge of these laws has been greatly increased as a result of the accessability of the widely discussed, but still unpublished, text known as MMT (4Q Miqsat Ma'aseh ha-Torah) (see Chapter 3). In MMT's diatribe against the views of their opponents, the Qumran sectarians often describe the views of the Pharisees. From this it is possible to reconstruct specific halakhic material that can be reliably dated to the early Hasmonean period.

MMT contains twenty-two laws the authors claim were the cause of the schism that led to the founding of the Qumran sect. I believe the sect was formed when a group of Sadducean priests left the Temple service in the aftermath of the Hasmonean takeover of the Temple soon after the Maccabean Revolt, probably by about 152 B.C.E.[9] In any event, the laws espoused by the Qumran sectarians in MMT are phrased so as to stress the views of the authors and present approaches drawn from Sadducean tradition.[10] In Chapter 3, I explore in greater detail the Sadducean background of these laws. Here we are concerned with what we can learn from MMT about the Pharisees.[11]

The text of MMT—and also the Temple Scroll—on several occasions opposes a principle known in tannaitic *halakhah* as *tevul yom,* which literally means "one immersed on that day." According to the concept of *tevul yom,* if a person completes all the purificatory rites—including immersion in a ritual bath *(mikveh)*—but still awaits the setting of the sun on the last day of his purificatory period, he is considered pure for purposes of coming into contact with pure food. The authors of both MMT and the Temple Scroll oppose this view, however. We are specifically told that their opponents—those who follow the Pharisaic approach—accept the concept of *tevul yom* and consider such people ritually pure even though the sun has not set on the last day of their purificatory period.

MMT specifically requires the priests who slaughter, and who gather and burn the ashes of the red heifer, to be completely pure—that is, they must have completed the entire purification period and the sun must have set on the day that concludes that period.

According to the Mishnah (*Parah* 3:7), compiled in about 200 C.E., this same issue was the subject of controversy between the Sadducees and the "elders of Israel," apparently the Pharisees. The Pharisees would purposely defile the priest so as to make him perform the ritual involved in a state of *tevul yom,* in order to contest the Saducean view that prohibited such a priest from officiating because of his impurity.

MMT demonstrates that this was an issue hundreds of years earlier at the time of the founding of the Qumran sect. The Pharisaic sages, therefore, took this position early in the Hasmonean period. Examples like this could be multiplied. In each case a Pharisaic view known from later rabbinic sources can be shown to have existed at a much earlier period.

A number of other laws referred to in MMT do not explicitly match disputes between the Pharisees and Sadducees as recorded in later rabbinic literature, but the view opposed by the Qumran sect is attributed in rabbinic literature to the tannaitic (Mishnaic) period. MMT thus proves that in some of these cases the tannaitic views are in fact those of Hasmonean period Pharisees that continued into the tannaitic period.

MMT is a foundation text of the Qumran sect. It was written in the early Hasmonean period when the Temple was managed and its rituals conducted in accord with Pharisaic views. The Hasmoneans made common cause with the Pharisees in order to cleanse the Temple of the excessive Hellenization that they blamed to a great extent on the Saducean priests who had become, in their view, too Hellenized.[12]

Various elements in MMT and in the Temple Scroll represent the polemic of those who continued piously to hold fast to Saducean views against the Hasmoneans and their Pharisaic allies. In this way, we learn that predestruction Pharisaic views are indeed to be found in later tannaitic sources, both in passages specifically labeled as Pharisaic and elsewhere tannaitic laws are discussed.

Thus, evidence of the ideological underpinnings of Pharisaism and its *halakhic* principles can be found in the Qumran corpus. Sensitively read, the Qumran corpus reveals the role of the Pharisees as allies of the Hasmoneans in the early Hasmonean period.[13] More important, it can no longer be claimed that there is no evidence for the Pharisees earlier than the tannaitic materials and Josephus, who wrote after the Roman destruction of Jerusalem. In fact, the scrolls provide extensive and wide ranging testimony about the predestruction history of the Pharisees and their ideology.

MMT and the Temple Scroll provide evidence of Pharisaic dominance over the Temple ritual in the early days of the Hasmonean period. These Pharisees held views similar to those claimed for them in rabbinic literature. Moreover, they also expressed many positions—substantive and theological—later found among the *tannaim* of the Mishnah.

In sum, the broad outlines of the Pharisees that emerge from the Dead Sea Scrolls are much closer to those described in later rabbinic literature than many of us would have thought possible a few years ago. It is now clear that we cannot look at rabbinic Judaism as a post-70 invention, a consensus brought about by the vicissitudes of the Temple's destruction. Rather, rabbinic Judaism must be seen as a continuation of the predestruction Pharisaic tradition. Much more of the rabbinic tradition has its roots in Pharisaic teachings than had been thought by some. Indeed, the testimony of the rabbis about the Pharisees turns out to have been accurate in most details. Many specific laws and teachings first attested in the tannaitic (Mishnaic) period can be traced back at least to the Hasmonean age. In these years Pharisaic views dominated Temple procedure most of the time. It was only natural that the successors of the Pharisees would assume the mantle of national leadership after the devastation of 70 C.E. In short, we must now abandon the model of discontinuity between predestruction and postdestruction Judaism and return to a model that takes account of the continuities we have observed.

From this perspective, we are now on the verge of a new era in research on Pharisaic-rabbinic Judaism. The Dead Sea Scrolls will allow us to uncover much of the early history of this approach to Judaism which attained—already in the days of the Temple—the dominant position in the Jewish community of the land of Israel. The Qumran corpus thus provides a background against which to understand many aspects of rabbinic Judaism.

VII

THE COPPER SCROLL

CHAPTER 18

THE MYSTERY OF THE
COPPER SCROLL

P. KYLE MCCARTER, JR.

Just when you think you have measured the true dimensions of the Dead Sea Scroll archive, along comes the Copper Scroll—from out in left field. It's totally different. What, if anything, does it have to do with the rest of the scrolls? Can it be used to interpret the corpus as a whole or the nature of the sectarian texts? Or is it simply the odd scroll out?

It's different. No question about that. Written on copper foil, it is a description of sixty-four locations containing hidden treasure. Imaginary or real? And, if real, are we talking about the Temple treasure itself?

The author of this chapter, P. Kyle McCarter, is the William F. Albright Professor of Biblical and Ancient Near Eastern Studies at the Johns Hopkins University. He is preparing a new edition of the Copper Scroll, using some extraordinary new pictures taken by the world's leading photographers of ancient inscriptions, Bruce and Kenneth Zuckerman. No one is in a better position to guide us through the mysteries of the Copper Scroll than Professor McCarter. —ED.

—·—

The Copper Scroll (known to scholars by the siglum 3Q15 or 3QTreasure [3Q stands for Qumran Cave 3]) is an anomaly in the inventory of Qumran scrolls. It does not fit readily into any of the categories customarily included when the scrolls are discussed. It is not biblical, it is not literary, and it does not contain sectarian doctrine. Written in a language—a form of Hebrew—different from the language of any of the other scrolls, and in a script that is not quite like any of the others, it is even made of a different material. Most of the scrolls are leather, and a few are papyrus, but 3Q15 is a sheet of copper. And its content has no true parallel at Qumran or anywhere else. It is unique.

The Copper Scroll was found in 1952. Though the first discoveries at Qumran were made in 1947, the process of exploration was interrupted by the war that followed the United Nations resolution creating the nation of Israel. Because of this interruption, only two caves were known to the scholarly community in the early 1950s. By that time, however, fragments of leather with writing on them were showing up regularly in Jerusalem's antiquities market, and it was clear that other caves had been found by the Bedouin. Early in 1952, a major archaeological expedition was mounted under the aegis of Jordan's Department of Antiquities. It was a joint project involving a number of the international research institutions working in Jerusalem at the time, including principally the École Biblique and the American School of Oriental Research. A survey of caves was begun in a kind of loose cooperation with the Ta'amireh Bedouin, who knew the area best. This survey began the process that led, over a period of a few years, to the discovery of the rest of the eleven caves.

In Cave 3, the first discovered in the 1952 survey, the Copper Scroll was found. Other, more conventional leather scrolls were also found in Cave 3, but in the back of the cave, off by themselves, were two rolls of copper. It later became clear that these were two pieces of one scroll, and that was the discovery of 3Q15.

The scholars who found the Copper Scroll could see that there was writing on the inside, because the letters that were punched into the thin sheet of metal had embossed the back of the surface with their outlines. K. G. Kuhn, a German scholar visiting Jerusalem, noticed that the writing seemed to describe the hiding places of treasures of silver and gold! He hypothesized that the scroll was an inventory of the hidden treasures of the Essene community.[1] There was general excitement and

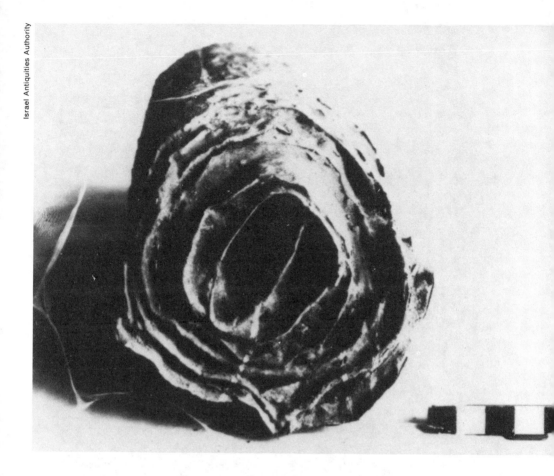

29. One of the two copper rolls before it was cut open.

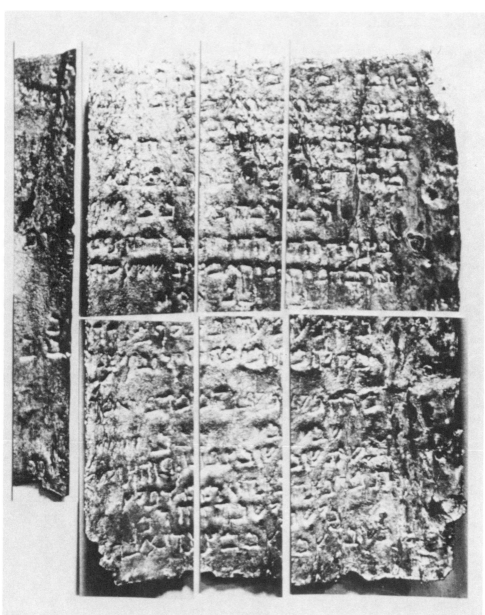

Israel Antiquities Authority

*30. An early picture of the Copper Scroll
after being cut apart.*

a great eagerness to unroll the copper so that the scroll could reveal its secrets. Unfortunately, the oxidized metal was extremely brittle. The scroll would crumble into pieces if anyone tried to unroll it, and the techniques being developed at that time for working with leather materials did not apply to copper.

After a great deal of discussion, the Copper Scroll was taken to the Manchester College of Technology in England and opened by being cut into sections with a saw. Soon afterwards, photographs of the several sections, now laid out side by side, were taken. These were not good-quality photographs even for the mid-1950s, and when the Copper Scroll was published, they were reproduced on a grainy surface. It is frustrating to go to the publication volume and try to use the photographs to reconstruct the text. As a result people have been largely dependent over the years on the official edition made by J. T. Milik, the scholar who published the text.[2] His drawing is what most people use when they read the Copper Scroll.

Milik's edition was published in 1962 amid controversy. Although formal publication rights had been assigned to Milik, another member of the official publication team, John Allegro, was very excited by the prospect of a treasure hunt and did not want to wait. An Englishman, Allegro went along to Manchester to be present at the opening. Two years before Milik's official edition came out, Allegro published his own edition,[3] and then went to the West Bank to start looking for the treasure. It was an embarrassing episode that caused great consternation.[4] Nevertheless, as idiosyncratic and uncollegial as he was, Allegro was a good scholar, and his edition contains much that is still useful.

A few years ago I was asked to prepare a new edition of the Copper Scroll to be published under the general editorship of Professor James Charlesworth of Princeton Theological Seminary. At the time I assumed, quite mistakenly, that I would have to work from the existing photographs, because copper and bronze artifacts are subject to bronze disease, a particularly destructive form of oxidation. Most bronze artifacts that have been out of the ground for very long have deteriorated badly. I had faced this problem before, working with texts of a quite different type. After making inquiries, however, I was delighted to find out that is not the case with the Copper Scroll.

The Copper Scroll is unusually pure copper—with only about 1 percent tin—and that seems to have protected it from severe oxidation. There has been some deterioration; it is not in the same condition as it was in 1952, or even in 1956 when it was opened. But in general, we still have the Copper Scroll. It is in the Archaeological Museum of Jordan in Amman. (This, by the way, is another way in which the Copper Scroll is anomalous: It is not in the Rockefeller Museum in Jerusalem or in the Shrine of the Book. The vicissitudes of history were such that it wound up in Amman. The Jordanians prize the scroll greatly, and have it on display in a special case of wood and velvet that was built for it in the 1950s.)

After I learned these things, it became clear to me that what I needed first was new photographs. I could go look at the Copper Scroll (and I did that), but I knew I could not work from the scroll itself. Because the fragile copper cannot tolerate the kind of handling and manipulation that would be necessary to work directly from it, most would have to be done from photographs. My hope, therefore, was that we could get new ones using the best modern techniques and the highest-quality film available.

It was possible to obtain new photographs only because of a collaborative international effort involving the American Center for Oriental Research (ACOR), the West Semitic Research Project, and Department of Antiquities of Jordan. ACOR, the American archaeological center in Amman, facilitates scientific projects in Jordan. The staff of ACOR has a close working relationship with antiquities officials in Jordan. The director at this time was Professor Bert DeVries, a scholar and an archaeologist. He was the key to the success of the project to rephotograph the Copper Scroll.

The director of the West Semitic Research Project is Professor Bruce Zuckerman of the University of Southern California, a preeminent photographer of inscriptions and ancient manuscripts, which is the principal work of the project. He and his brother Ken Zuckerman have developed techniques for photographing many kinds of materials, and were excited by the challenge of photographing a copper document.

The director of the Department of Antiquities of Jordan, Dr. Ghazi Bisheh, was very supportive of the plan to produce a new edition of the Copper Scroll and of the proposed photography project. His only requirement was that we should also develop a conservation plan. Not only would we rephotograph the Copper Scroll, but we would also try to conserve it.

The agreement was that the photographs would be taken in December 1988. The photographs would be published first in the *Annual of the Department of Antiquities of Jordan* and then as a separate volume, which would include the text I would establish on the basis of the photographs—that is, a new edition of the scroll—and my English translation.

A Jordanian scholar, Professor Fawzi Zayadine, would prepare an Arabic translation so that both English and Arabic translations could be included.

The museum where the Copper Scroll is kept is on the Amman Citadel, the ancient capital that rises as a sharp hill in the middle of the modern city. Appropriately enough, the Jordanian Archaeological Museum stands near the summit of the citadel. The Copper Scroll is in a glass case along with a couple of fragments of leather scrolls. The individual pieces (sections) of the Copper Scroll itself are laid down on velvet-lined trays in the wooden box that was built for them.

The first step in the process was to remove the individual trays from the case. The director of the museum supervised their move into a photography lab that the Zuckerman brothers had set up in the museum. They took a series of very high resolution photographs of each section with both top and bottom lighting. At the same time, they took 35mm shots to keep a record of the project, and a large number of Polaroid shots as a preliminary check to be sure that the expected results would be achieved. When the Zuckermans returned to California, they developed the film both as color prints and as transparencies to be studied with back illumination. The results are spectacular. The new photographs are vastly superior to the black and whites taken in the 1950s.

Before turning to an analysis of the contents of this unusual document, let me comment on its conservation needs. The Copper Scroll is in jeopardy. The places touched by the saw in England exhibit an oxidation pattern. Centuries in the caves did minimal harm, but somehow the insult of the modern tool has started a process of deterioration along the cuts. By comparing the new photographs with those taken in 1950s, one can see that a fair amount of material has been lost—in some sample locations a full centimeter—on both sides of each saw cut. The Copper Scroll, in other words, is slowly disappearing. There is a substantial amount of crumbling along the top and bottom edges, and a number of small pieces have fallen down into the case. We have approached conservation experts about this project, and they have shown a keen interest in our project.

What will conservation of the Copper Scroll mean? First of all, an expert in copper and bronze conservation must go to Jordan and try to find some kind of treatment that will stop the oxidation process. Second, a new case must be made with special equipment to regulate the climate inside. Finally, if the surface of the copper can tolerate it, latex casts should be made from which copies of the Copper Scroll can be made for distribution to scholars.

31. The Copper Scroll as displayed in a museum case in Amman. Each section retains the curve of the formerly intact, rolled scroll.

32. One of the new photographs of a section of the Copper Scroll by Bruce and Kenneth Zuckerman.

Now let me list the peculiarities and problems in working with this text. It is written in a form of Hebrew that has a lot in common with Mishnaic Hebrew, but is not identical to it.[5] In fact, it is not identical to any Hebrew that we know, and is probably a village dialect of Hebrew. Although at this time Aramaic was the primary language, Hebrew was still spoken in villages, so that we may assume that the scribe who produced the Copper Scroll, whoever he might have been, was writing in his own dialect with all of its idiosyncracies.

To continue, the spelling of individual words is often peculiar. We know a variety of spelling systems—a variety of kinds of orthography, as it is called—from the various Qumran scrolls and from other manuscripts; but no orthographic system quite matches the one used in the Copper Scroll. Sometimes this seems to be because mistakes are being made. At others, it may be that it is not a spelling peculiarity but a grammatical peculiarity with which we are not familiar.

Next, the script itself is unusual. Anyone who takes a sheet of copper and attempts to write on it with a stylus or some other sharp object would probably produce something quite different from his or her normal handwriting. Someone who, like our scribe, was accustomed to writing with brush and ink on a piece of leather, would find that his handwriting, when transferred to a metal surface, would be considerably distorted. In part, therefore, the handwriting is peculiar because the scribe is working on an unfamiliar material. In addition, however, it seems likely that this is not the hand of an expert scribe such as those who wrote most of the leather manuscripts in the Qumran archive.

In content, the Copper Scroll is a list of sixty-four locations of hidden treasures. It has no introduction and no embellishment. It simply lists one place after another, usually beginning with a prepositional phrase ("In such and such a place . . .") followed by one of the locations; then a quantity of valuables is given. Most of the hidden material is silver or gold. Some of it seems to consist of items related to certain religious practices, but most of it is silver and gold. The quantities are extremely large, perhaps even unreasonably large, and they are measured primarily in terms of talents. By Milik's count,[6] approximately 4,630 talents of silver and gold are listed in 3Q15. There has been a lot of discussion about the exact size of a talent at that time, and there is more than one possibility, ranging from about twenty-five to fifty or even seventy-five pounds. A rough calculation suggests that the total treasure consisted of something between 58 and 174 tons of precious metal! Many scholars have found these statistics incredible. In any case, they raise a series of questions that must be addressed. Was this a real treasure? If so, whose treasure was it? If not, why did someone go to the trouble of making the list?

Before addressing these questions, let me offer some sample locations. The first location is "In the ruin that is in the Valley of Achor." Although the biblical Valley of Achor lay south of Jericho, Jewish and Christian sources contemporary with the Copper Scroll place it northeast of Jericho, probably the Wadi Nuwei'imeh.[7] We have no way of knowing what ruin *(hrybh)* is referred to; perhaps it was the name of a village ("Heribah"). The text continues "beneath the steps that enter to the east, forty cubits west: a chest of silver and its articles. Weight: 17 talents." The second location, apparently also associated with the ruin of the first location, is "In the funerary shrine, in the third course of stones: 100 gold ingots." The third location reads, "In the large cistern that is within the Court of the Peristylion, in a recess of its bottom, sealed in the entrenchment opposite the upper door: nine hundred talents." A peristylion is a small peristyle, that is, a small court surrounded by a colonnade. Unless there was such a structure in the ruin where the first two caches were hidden, the third location must be in Jerusalem, somewhere in the Temple Court.

The list goes on in this fashion for sixty-four locations. Many times the locations are in or near known cities or villages, but often they are in villages unknown to us. A few of the locations lie fairly far afield from Qumran. Some are to the north, at Shechem and beyond, almost into the Galilee. A few seem to be on the east bank of the Jordan. Most, however, are either in Jerusalem itself or down the main wadi system that goes from Jerusalem toward Jericho and, on one of its branches, toward the Wadi Qumran.

Of the many peculiarities of the Copper Scroll, perhaps the strangest of all is the existence of groups of two or three *Greek* letters that follow seven of the locations. These groups of letters—ΚεΝ, ΧΑΓ, ΗΝ, Θε, ΔΙ, ΤΡ and ΣΚ—are not words or known abbreviations. Various attempts have been made to explain their significance. One scholar tried to interpret them as numerical signs related to the quantities of treasure in the corresponding locations,[8] but this and other efforts to make sense of them have failed to be convincing.

Many scholars believe that the groups of Greek letters are part of some kind of code that helped preserve the secrecy of the hiding places, and there are other reasons to believe that the text of the Copper Scroll is partly encoded or at least not entirely straightforward. The sixty-fourth and last location, for example, is not said to contain more treasure but "a duplicate of this document and an explanation and their measurements and a precise reckoning of everything, one by one." This gives the impression that the second copy contained more complete information than our scroll and perhaps instructions for interpreting its cryptic prepositional phrases and gargantuan numbers. It might well be that neither 3Q15 nor the duplicate hidden at location 64 was sufficient by itself to locate the hiding places, so that both documents were necessary to the successful recovery of the treasure.

The total amount of gold and silver is so large that the question arises whether the treasure was imaginary. Milik believed so and compared it to ancient documents from Jewish folklore purporting to describe the concealment of the treasure and sacred vessels from the First Temple. Documents of that kind, however, are very different in character from the Copper Scroll. Typically, they refer to Moses and the holy objects whose construction he supervised, such as the Ark, the incense altar, the lamp stand (menorah), etc. They often credit Jeremiah or some other famous figure of the past with concealing the sacred treasures. There is nothing of this kind in the Copper Scroll. It is plodding and businesslike. Neither Moses nor Jeremiah is there, nor is any famous relic—neither the Ark nor the ashes of the red heifer. In fact, it is extremely difficult to imagine that anyone would have gone to the trouble to prepare a costly sheet of pure copper and imprint it with such an extensive and sober list of locations unless he had been entrusted with hiding a real and immensely valuable treasure and wanted to make a record of his work that could withstand the ravages of time.

But could the Qumran community have possessed such a treasure? We know that the members of the community gave up their property to live a communal life, but even so it is difficult to believe that the value of their shared property could have amounted to even a fraction of the riches recorded in the Copper Scroll. So how are we to solve this conundrum?

Scholars have taken at least three approaches. Some follow Milik in supposing the treasure to be imaginary. Others use the Copper Scroll as evidence that the material found in the eleven caves did not come from the site of Khirbet Qumran but from Jerusalem.[9] A third approach, which I prefer, is to argue that the Copper Scroll was placed in Cave 3 independently and had nothing to do with the rest of the Qumran library. At first glance, this idea may seem difficult to accept. It assumes that an extraordinary coincidence took place with two caches of roughly contemporary documents being hidden in a single cave by independent parties. On the other hand, there are a number of things about the Copper Scroll that favor the assumption. We have already noted that the Copper Scroll is unique at Qumran. Many of its characteristics—the material from which it was made, its content, even its language—have no parallel in any of the hundreds of other scrolls from the eleven caves. It was found in an isolated part of Cave 3, lying apart from the jars and broken pottery where the other scrolls were found. There were no scraps of leather or papyrus near the two rolls of copper. Roland de Vaux, the chief excavator of Qumran and its caves, seriously entertained the possibility that the Copper Scroll was deposited independently of the other artifacts in Cave 3.

Thus far we have concluded that the treasure of the Copper Scroll was probably a real treasure and that it probably was not a treasure that belonged to the Qumran community. We must now attempt to discover its origin. It is natural to turn our attention first to the Temple in Jerusalem. Probably no other institution in the region at the time had the capacity to accumulate a fortune of the magnitude indicated in the scroll. Moreover, apart from the gold and silver, most of the hidden things listed in the text have associations with the Temple and its priesthood, as explained below. For these reasons, most of those scholars who study the Copper Scroll think that the treasure belonged to the Temple. Many think that the treasure is imaginary, as we have noted, but most of those who think so think it the imaginary treasure of the Temple.

Moreover, a specific reference, in location 32, links the Copper Scroll to the Temple treasury. Unfortunately, the text describing location 32 occurs on a damaged edge of cut 13, and it is not as well preserved as other parts of the text. Nevertheless, we can read this much:

> In the cave that is next to the *founta*[in]
> belonging to the House of Hakkoz, dig six cubits.
> (There are) six bars of gold.

It is interesting to find treasure hidden on the property of the House of Hakkoz *(bet haqqos)*. Hakkoz was the name of a priestly family that traced its ancestry to the time of David (1 Chronicles 24:10). The family was prominent at the time of the return of the Jews from exile in Babylon. Moreover, it remained important in the Hasmonean period: In 1 Maccabees 8:17, we are told that Judas Maccabeus appointed Eupolemus son of John son of Hakkoz *(tou Akkos)* ambassador to Rome.

The Hakkoz estate was in the Jordan Valley not far from Jericho. This is shown by the lists of peoples involved in the restoration of the walls and gates of Jerusalem under Nehemiah, where one contingent of the Hakkoz family (Nehemiah 3:4) works near the men of Jericho (Nehemiah 3:2) and immediately alongside the family of Hassenaah, whose estate was located a few miles north of Jericho, and the other contingent of the Hakkoz family (Nehemiah 3:21) works alongside "the men of the Kikkar," that is, "the men of the district of the Jordan *(kikkar hayyarden),*" the southern part of the Jordan Valley (Nehemiah 3:22). So the Hakkoz estate was located in the center of the region where most of the Copper Scroll hiding places are located.

Ezra 2:59–63 and Nehemiah 7:61–65 show that the members of the House of Hakkoz were unable to substantiate their genealogy after their return from exile, so that they were disqualified from priestly duties. We should expect that under such circumstances they would have been assigned some other task that supported the Temple operation but did not require the highest degree of genealogical purity. In Nehemiah 3:4 we learn that the leader of the family at the time of Nehemiah's reconstruction of the walls of Jerusalem was "Meremoth son of Uriah son of Hakkoz," and in Ezra 8:33 we are told that the Temple treasure, when it was brought back from Babylon, was entrusted to "the priest Meremoth son of Uriah." In short, the Hakkoz family were the treasurers of the Temple!

It seems very likely, then, that the Copper Scroll treasure was wealth associated somehow with the Temple in Jerusalem. It may be possible to explain this association more precisely by examining some of the technical religious terminology found in the text. We can do this by moving on to the fourth location, which is "On the mound of Kochlit," a prominent place in the Copper Scroll, though its location is disputed. This time the treasure is not gold or silver but "vessels of contribution with a lagin and ephods." The term translated "contribution" is *demaᶜ,* which refers to the portion of agricultural produce that was contributed to the Temple for the support of the priesthood. It is a synonym for the so-called "heave offering" *(teruma),* and it occurs many times in the Copper Scroll. Other terms also have sacerdotal connections. A lagin was a type of vessel, sometimes used to hold grain from the priests' share of the produce.[10] Ephods were priestly garments.

Our text goes on to explain that "All of the contribution and the accumulation of the seventh (year) is second tithe." The "accumulation of the seventh year" is the seventh-year produce, probably redeemed as money, which was collected and delivered to the central treasury in

Jerusalem.[11] The second tithe was either eaten by the tither in Jerusalem or converted into money and then brought to Jerusalem (cf. Deuteronomy 14:22–26).

These technical terms—*contribution, accumulation of the seventh year,* and *second tithe*—provide the clue to solving the riddle of the Copper Scroll. They all refer to tithes and other priestly contributions that were required by law to be set aside, collected, and taken to Jerusalem for the support of the Temple and the priesthood. Twenty-five years ago, Manfred Lehmann followed these clues to their logical conclusion. He noted that if for some reason it was not possible to take the wealth accumulated from tithes and contributions to Jerusalem, it had to be hidden or buried.[12] He believed that the Copper Scroll treasure was accumulated when the Temple lay in ruins during the period between the First and Second Revolts, that is, between 70 and 130 A.D. The basis of the treasure was "taxes, gifts, tithes and consecrations." As Lehmann explained:

> . . . the Scroll reflects a period when various types of such items had been redeemed for money or precious metals and had been centrally gathered and accumulated for the purpose of delivery to Jerusalem and/or the Temple, but for political or Halakhic reasons [reasons of religious law] could not be taken to their legal destination. Because of the prolonged inaccessibility of Jerusalem and/or the Temple, these objects had to be, temporarily or permanently, committed to Genizah [a storage place for sacred objects] according to legal requirements.[13]

Although Lehmann's argument has been given little scholarly attention, I believe that it advances our understanding of the Copper Scroll immensely. It takes seriously the technical meaning of 3Q15's religious terminology, which most other studies have failed to understand.[14] It also makes sense of the enormous quantities of gold and silver listed in the scroll; they could easily have accumulated during the period between the two revolts. Nevertheless, one serious problem stands in the way of Lehmann's hypothesis. The script of the Copper Scroll belongs to the latter part of the Herodian period, roughly 25–75 A.D.[15] In all probability the Copper Scroll, like the rest of the Qumran library, was deposited in Cave 3 before or very soon after the destruction of the Temple in 70 A.D.

It seems likely, then, that the Copper Scroll treasure consisted of tithes and contributions gathered in the final, turbulent years before the destruction of the Temple. It is possible that the treasure arrived at the Temple shortly before the war began, then was removed from the city in secret and hidden when the Roman army appeared in the Galilee. It seems more likely, however, that much of the treasure never reached the Temple. In view of the steadily growing chaos in the last years before the arrival of Vespasian's army, the Jews who had the responsibility for gathering tithes and contributions may have felt it unwise to deposit them in the public treasury. Instead they elected to divide up the treasure and hide it in a large number of different locations east of the city.

VIII

RECONSTRUCTING THE SCROLLS

CHAPTER 19

HOW TO CONNECT DEAD SEA SCROLL FRAGMENTS

HARTMUT STEGEMANN

This chapter describes how scholars attempt to solve the various types of jigsaw puzzles that the fragmentary scrolls present. The large intact scrolls, mostly from Cave 1, are easy. There is not much to put together; it's almost all there.

The fragmentary scrolls present a more difficult problem. Numerous clues enable scholars to segregate fragments of a particular scroll—the nature of the material on which it is written, various physical characteristics of the scroll and the writing on it, the literary characteristics of the text, and the handwriting of the scribe.

The next task is arranging the fragments in some kind of order. When the complete text is known from later exemplars—as in the case of books of the Bible, apocrypha and pseudepigrapha—the known text provides a guide just as a picture on the box of a jigsaw puzzle does.

The really hard cases are unknown documents without joins. The author of this chapter, Hartmut Stegemann, has devised an imaginative and creative way of arranging these fragments in a meaningful order based on the pattern of damage—damage caused by rodents, insects, and humidity each eating through a rolled-up scroll. The results of the author's new method are nothing short of astounding. —ED.

— · —

Whuen the first Dead Sea Scrolls came to light, putting their pieces together wasn't really a problem. Indeed, one scroll from Qumran Cave 1 is almost complete. There was nothing to put together. That was the famous Isaiah Scroll, known to scholars as 1QIs^a. The siglum stands for Qumran Cave 1, Isaiah Scroll; the superscript "a" distinguishes this Isaiah scroll from another one found in the same cave, known as 1QIs^b.

Other scrolls from Cave 1—as much as survived—are mainly in one large piece, so there is little to put together. That is true of such scrolls as the Habakkuk Commentary, the scroll of the War of the Sons of Light and Sons of Darkness, and the Manual of Discipline. Only two of the seven intact scrolls from Cave 1 were partly broken into pieces and had to be restored, although, in addition to these intact scrolls, many fragments were also found in Qumran's Cave 1. Approximately seventy-five fragmentary scrolls have now been identified from Cave 1.

Gradually, as a result of searches by both professional archaeologists and Bedouin tribesmen, scrolls and fragments of scrolls have also been found in ten other Qumran caves, designated 2Q through 11Q. In addition, scroll materials were found in excavations and in caves in other wadis leading down to the Dead Sea—Masada, Nahal Hever, Wadi Murabba'at, Nahal Se'elem and Wadi Daliyeh.*

In all, fragments from about eight hundred different scrolls have been recovered from the eleven Qumran caves alone. Their fragments vary in size from large panels containing several columns to thumbnail pieces containing only a single letter. One composition, found in 3Q and known appropriately enough as the Copper Scroll, is written on copper sheets. In addition, a few ostraca (inscriptions on pieces of pottery) have been found. But the balance are all written on leather (parchment) or papyrus.

The quantity of fragments varies, of course, from cave to cave. The biggest cache came from 4Q, which contained more different documents than all the other caves combined—about 580 different manuscripts. The number of fragments into which these 580 manuscripts were broken has never been determined with any accuracy. Estimates vary between tens of thousands to hundreds of thousands. About 75 percent of these manuscripts from 4Q still remain unpublished and are therefore not yet available to most scholars.

*See Introduction, "Of Caves and Scholars: An Overview."

The first task in reconstituting any fragmentary Dead Sea document is to isolate and collect the pieces that come from the same scroll. Sometimes it's easy to identify such fragments because they are stuck together. But more often they are scattered all over the place.

Three basic clues enable the scholar to gather together the fragments from a single scroll. The first clue comes from the material on which it is written. Obviously, a fragment on leather parchment is not part of the same scroll as a fragment on papyrus. But beyond this, parchment itself varies and so does papyrus. Some scrolls are written on thick material, others on thin. The color may also vary from brown to yellow or reddish, and it may be bright, or dark, or in between.

Another clue comes from the fact that ancient scribes prepared their scrolls for inscribing by scoring the scroll at regular intervals with fine lines to guide their hand. The space between these lines varies and, after inscribing the text, the space between the lines of text varies. The text is sometimes written hanging on the lines, sometimes between them; this, too, helps identify the fragments from the same sample. The size of the spaces between the lines is another important clue as to which fragments come from the same document. Finally, the number of lines in each column of a given scroll is somewhat regular, as is the width of the columns. Observation of these similarities also helps in correlating fragments coming from the same scroll.

Third, the handwriting of the different scribes varies. Scholars who work with these scrolls regularly are able to distinguish between these different hands. Usually, although not always, a single scribe worked on each scroll. By identifying his handwriting, a modern scholar can tell whether or not a particular fragment belongs to a scroll written by that scribe.

In this way, the pieces of a single scroll are assembled. The result is often a box of scraps that resembles a jigsaw puzzle. There is a difference, however. Many, often most, of the pieces of this jigsaw puzzle remain missing. How then do we reconstruct the scroll itself? How do we tell the way in which the pieces related to one another in the original manuscript?

In the case of biblical manuscripts, this is not too difficult. The biblical text itself, like the picture on the box of a jigsaw puzzle, provides the grid, or pattern, on which each of the surviving pieces of the ancient manuscript can be located. The complete biblical text, as it has come down to us, serves as a kind of mirror of the ancient text, onto which surviving pieces of the ancient text can be placed. We can place these pieces on the mirror even if we have very few pieces. This process becomes somewhat, but not much, more complicated because there are variations, usually minor, even in biblical texts.

This same method of reconstruction is used for nonbiblical manuscripts of which we have other, complete copies of ancient versions. Fragments of apocryphal books such as Tobit and Ben Sira are among the Dead Sea fragments that can be reconstructed by using a modern edition of these well-known books. Other Dead Sea fragments come from still other manuscripts of which we have later documents—such as the so-called Damascus Document* or fragments of the books of Enoch.

Finally, sometimes more than one copy of a text has been found at Qumran itself. Fragments from eight or nine copies of the Songs of the Sabbath Sacrifice were recovered there. In addition to the large Temple Scroll—which is nearly twenty-six and a half feet long—fragments from another copy survived. Occasionally, as in these cases, one copy can serve as a grid for the reconstruction of another copy.

Nearly 40 percent of the Dead Sea Scrolls can be reconstructed totally, or at least partly, in this way. About 20 percent of the documents are biblical documents—approximately 170 manuscripts. Fragments from every book of the Hebrew Bible, except Esther, have shown up at Qumran. Another 20 percent of the documents are from texts otherwise known, either from modern copies of ancient versions or from ancient copies. In addition, some fragments, while not strictly biblical, quote biblical passages or paraphrase biblical texts, so the Bible provides help in the reconstruction of the original order of the surviving fragments.

But this leaves more than 50 percent of the Dead Sea Scroll manuscripts—formerly unknown texts—with no grid to use for reconstructing the fragments, for placing the pieces in relationship to one another. Most of these previously unknown texts found in the Dead Sea caves have survived in very fragmentary pieces that are in a poor state of preservation.

The first Dead Sea Scroll publication of previously unknown texts that survived partly in fragments made no effort to place them in any order, let alone to reconstruct the text. In 1954 (two years after the death of the senior editor, E. L. Sukenik), Nahman Avigad published the fragments from the famous Thanksgiving Hymns scroll from Cave 1. He divided the dislocated pieces according to the different scribal hands that had copied the hymns, presented the large fragments first, and concluded with the smaller ones, a total of sixty-six dislocated fragments from this

*See Chapter 5.

scroll. This pattern has generally been followed by later editors. Usually the editors of such manuscripts arrange the fragments of their scrolls according to size, from the larger ones to the smaller ones, without any attempt at reconstructing the original state of the scroll. Indeed, very few attempts have been made in the Qumran editions—most of which have been published by J. T. Milik—toward any kind of reconstruction of the original scrolls. The main problem is the total lack of any well-established method for reconstructing fragmentary scrolls without the help of parallel texts.

The principal means for reconstructing such texts is that employed in jigsaw puzzles—finding pieces that join. They have complementary borders. The join has to be sufficient and sufficiently distinct to assure that in fact the two pieces do connect. In addition to the physical shape of the pieces, joins are often indicated because the two pieces divide a word or even a letter. These kinds of connecting joins are called "material joins" because they are based on the physical characteristics, rather than on the thematic content, of the pieces.

Incidentally, material joins are also useful in connection with manuscripts for which we have modern texts to use as a grid. The material join is often even more reliable than the grid of a parallel text, for the particular text may vary from the text in the grid. Even in the case of biblical manuscripts, few of them are word-for-word identical.

In addition to material joins, some reconstruction can be accomplished on the basis of thematic context. Even though the fragments themselves do not connect with one another, they can be arranged in relation to one another.[1] These are called "distant joins." Obviously, such joins are often rather speculative.

Recently, however, I have developed a method of identifying distant joins—placing nonconnecting fragments in relation to one another—that has produced some remarkable results. The key element in this new method is the relationship of fragments containing similarly shaped, damaged areas.

By definition, scroll fragments are damaged. That is why they are fragments instead of complete scrolls. But studying how they were damaged, we can learn how—at least in part—they can be put together again.

Almost all of these Qumranic fragments come from scrolls (as opposed to separate sheets[2]) that had been rolled up and then damaged in the Dead Sea caves while still rolled up.

Those who are familiar with modern Torah scrolls used in synagogues know that these scrolls, containing the five books of Moses, have posts or rolling sticks at both ends of the scroll to facilitate rolling from one end to the other. But that was not true of ancient scrolls such as the Qumran scrolls.[3] They were simply rolled up, forming a hollow tube or shaft in the center of the rolled-up scroll. At both the beginning and end of the ancient scroll were blank sheets that the reader could hold to roll the scroll backward or forward without having to place his hands on the inscribed parchment or papyrus. These blank sheets at the beginning and end of the scroll are called "handle sheets."

Some of the scrolls found in the Dead Sea caves were stored there in jars, but most were simply laid, stacked or leaned against one another, otherwise unprotected. Over the millennia, many of the scrolls were very extensively damaged. The two principal agents of damage were humidity and animals (rodents and insects). The damage thus produced, however, was patterned and repeated. When the bottom part of the scroll touched a wet place, the last lines of all the columns often disappeared. When the scroll stood on its head, it was the tops of all the columns that vanished in the course of the centuries. The edges thus damaged follow a repeated pattern. Other than at the edges, humidity might attack a scroll from the outer layer or from the inner layer (via the hollow shaft at the center of the rolled-up scroll). Sometimes the damage would eat all the way through, but occasionally the innermost layers would remain undamaged, protected by the sheer bulk of the scroll. Damage by rodents and insects, who enjoyed eating the scrolls, occurred in much the same patterned way.

The result is that the holes and breaks in a scroll have similar or even identical shapes through the several damaged layers. This pattern is also found in the fragments that originated from these holes and breaks.

If one tries to reconstruct the *text* of a scroll (what is *written* on it), all the holes and breaks are annoying and only sources of trouble, repeatedly interrupting the text. But if one tries to reconstruct the *scroll itself,* the patterned shapes of these holes and breaks are a reliable aid in arriving at the original order of what remains of the scroll fragments.

What can we learn from these patterned shapes of damage? First, fragments showing *corresponding shapes of damage* must be positioned along the same horizontal axis as measured from the top or the bottom of the original scroll.

Second, the distance between the repeated patterns can often enable us to place the fragments in a particular order. This is because the distance between corresponding damage *increases* as one moves from the inner layers of the scroll outward, and *decreases* as one moves inward from the

33. Whatever agent of destruction ate into this scroll (the War Scroll from Cave 1) penetrated several layers, leaving corresponding shapes as indicated by the arrows. When unrolled these corresponding shapes form a pattern that can guide reconstruction.

34. The Psalm Scroll from Cave 11. The arrows identify corresponding points of damage inflicted when the scroll was rolled up. The distance between the points of damage (greater on the outer layers) tells the restorer where to place fragments.

35. *The Temple Scroll. Left arrow points to the sewing margin, which has left an impression at right arrow. A mirror-image text has been picked up on the back of the scroll, as seen on the roll at right. These provide valuable clues for reconstructing the text.*

exterior layers. The rate of this increase or decrease can actually be mathematically calculated, based on the thickness of the leather or papyrus, and the tightness with which the scroll was rolled or wrapped.

Other clues are also helpful. Was the beginning of the scroll in the outer layer or the inner layer? Generally, the larger scrolls—those with fifty or more columns, often exceeding twenty feet in length—were rolled with the end on the inside. These scrolls were also tightly rolled, so the increase in distance between corresponding points of damage is quite short—from about one twenty-fifth to one-fifth of an inch. Shorter scrolls—a class generally between five and six feet long and containing between twelve and twenty columns—were more loosely rolled. The increase in distance between corresponding points of damage in these scrolls is mostly about one-fifth of an inch. Finally, a third class of scrolls begins the text on the innermost layer, instead of on the outermost layer. Such scrolls are almost always loosely rolled, regardless of their length. In these, the increase in distance between corresponding points of damage is relatively large.

Accordingly, once we identify corresponding points of damage, we measure the thickness of the leather, or papyrus, and attempt to determine the tightness of the wrap, the original length of the scroll, and whether it began on the innermost or outermost layer. It is also helpful to know the width of the columns; strangely enough, there was no standard column width at Qumran. We also like to know the number of columns on a sheet; remember that all scrolls are ultimately made up of sheets that were sewn or pasted together. Lastly, it helps to know the number of lines in a column, which varies from about seven to about fifty in a given scroll, but is relatively constant through all its columns.

Unfortunately, there is no comprehensive, up-to-date survey of the physical characteristics of the Dead Sea Scrolls. Most of the published editions of the Dead Sea Scrolls present very little information of this kind and often totally lack it. An exception is Yigael Yadin's edition of the Temple Scroll: What he presents is excellent, but unfortunately relates only to that scroll.

A survey of the scrolls' physical characteristics would be of enormous assistance in reconstructing both published and unpublished scrolls. With this information, we could in many cases establish the position of scattered fragments in the original scrolls and thus make evident the structure and content of many ancient texts. This is true even with regard to scroll fragments that have long been published.

One example from my own work will suffice. In 1982, 215 fragments

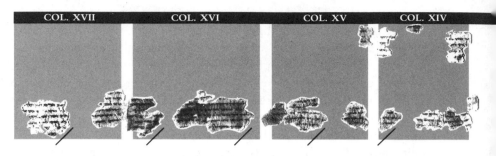

of a scroll from Cave 4 were published by Maurice Baillet.[4] One fragment of twelve lines (4Q511, fragment no. 10) was clearly from the beginning of the text. Another fragment from another scroll (4Q510) was a parallel text; so on this basis, the first column of this scroll, with eighteen lines of the text, could be reliably reconstructed without any technical support. The distance between corresponding points of damage on this first fragment is about 4.7 inches. Another long strip from the top of the scroll represents the last two columns of the text. On this strip the distance between points of damage is only about 1.9 inches at the left end. Other fragments reveal a distance between corresponding points of damage of 2.75 inches and 3.5 inches. These fragments can thus be arranged according to their original positions in the scroll. The final result is a continuous sequence of all twelve columns of the original scroll, representing about 80 percent of the original text. This scroll is called Sons of the Sage. Instead of the 215 scattered fragments in the published edition,[5] we now have a nice, well-established sequence of several songs. One can study their contents and style of composition, relate them to other poetical texts of their time, etc. True, it takes several weeks to complete such a reconstruction. But the reward is, instead of a list of hypothetical suggestions, an accurate, methodically well-established, new edition of a text formerly unknown to the scholarly world. We should hardly be surprised that the fragments as published give only a very poor notion of their true importance.

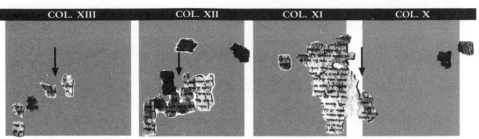

Israel Antiquities Authority/Courtesy Carol Newsom

36. The unjoined fragments from the scroll known as the Songs of the Sabbath Sacrifice were placed in relation to one another by identifying corresponding points of damage (marked by lines and arrows).

IX

CONTROVERSY
AND THE
SCROLLS

CHAPTER 20

INTERVIEW WITH CHIEF SCROLL EDITOR JOHN STRUGNELL

AVI KATZMAN

Anti-Semitism (and anti-Israeli sentiments) have always been in the back-ground of what has become known as the Dead Sea Scroll scandal—starting with the fact that Jews were excluded from the team of editors assembled to edit this library of Jewish religious treasures.

In late 1990 anti-Semitism took center stage when chief scroll editor John Strugnell expressed virulently anti-Jewish (and anti-Israeli) views in an inter-view with an Israeli reporter that was published first in the Tel Aviv daily newspaper Ha-Aretz *and then in the* Biblical Archaeology Review.

Shortly after the interview, his fellow editors voted to relieve Strugnell of his position as chief editor for "health" reasons (they did not take away from him his hoard of unpublished scroll assignments, however).

This chapter contains the interview that led to Strugnell's dismissal. In this interview, Strugnell claims to know of four other Dead Sea Scrolls. These have not yet come to light. From time to time rumors of more scrolls have surfaced, but nothing more concrete has ensued. —ED.

— . —

John Strugnell, chief editor of the Dead Sea Scrolls, agreed to an interview provided I report it not only in the Hebrew paper for which I write, *Ha-Aretz,* but also in an English-language publication. This fulfills my obligation to report the interview in English. The interview took place on October 28, 1990, in Professor Strugnell's small room at the "French School," the École Biblique et Archéologique Française in East Jerusalem.

It was he who first brought up the subject of his anti-Semitism. When I asked him whether he was anti-Israel, he replied, "That's a sneaky way of coming at the anti-Semitic question, isn't it?"

Later in the interview, I asked him directly whether he was an anti-Semite. He rejected this term: "I can't allow the word anti-Semitism to be used. I think it's a sort of mixed-up, messed-up term that was introduced in Germany, a country of muddle-headed philosophers. It's a cover word for: Are you against Jews? Are you against Israelis? Are you against the state of Israel? Are you against Zionism? [It has] nothing to do with being against Semites. I'm not an anti-Semite. I've spent my life studying various Semites from Ethiopia to Baghdad. I don't know anyone in the world who's an anti-Semite."

He was, he said, an "anti-Judaist." "Judaism," he said, "is originally racist . . . it's a folk religion; it's not a higher religion. An anti-Judaist, that's what I am. There, I plead guilty. I plead guilty in the way the Church has pleaded guilty all along, because we're not guilty; we're right. Christianity presents itself as a religion which replaces the Jewish religion. The correct answer of Jews to Christianity is to become Christian. I agree that there have been monstrosities in the past—the Inquisition, things like that. We should certainly behave ourselves like Christian gentlemen. But the basic judgment on the Jewish religion is, for me, a negative one."

Strugnell denied that his attitude toward Judaism affected his work. "Unless someone talks to me about the subject [of Judaism], I don't, when I'm working on a Qumran text, think how stupid and wrong the Jews were. I'm concerned with trying to find out what a document is saying in its context."

I asked him what annoyed him about Judaism. He replied, "The fact that it has survived when it should have disappeared. Christianity now uses much more irenic language for all this. These are brutal terms; I'm putting it in harsh terms. For me the answer [to the Jewish problem] is mass conversion."

"But what annoys you about it?" I asked.

"It's the subsistence of the group, of Jews, of the Jewish religion. It's a horrible religion. It's a Christian heresy, and we deal with our heretics in different ways. You are a phenomenon that we haven't managed to convert—and we should have managed.

"I believe that the answer for Islam, and Buddhism, and all other religions is to become Christian. Judaism disturbs me in a different sense, because, whereas the others became Christians when we worked hard on them, the Jews stuck to an anti-Christian position."

Strugnell also expressed himself regarding the state of Israel. His "first love," he said, "was Jordan":

"That's where the scrolls were found; the Jordanian government collected the scrolls. I worked with the Jordanians and I got to know and like them. I dislike Israel as an occupier of part of Jordan. And it's quite obvious that this was part of Jordan."

Despite his views about Israel and Judaism, Strugnell says some of his friends are Israelis:

"You know what the anti-Semites say: 'Some of my best friends are Jews.' Well, some of my friends are Israelis. But the occupation of Jerusalem—and maybe of the whole state—is founded on a lie, or at least on a premise that cannot be sustained. That's putting it as crudely as I can. The occupation of Jerusalem cannot be sustained."

"Just look at the Crusades," he continued. "We couldn't maintain it. We—the English and the French—couldn't maintain the Crusades even though we had immense military superiority at the start and we did great things in the country. One of the great building periods was the Crusades; but, basically, they were unsustainable. That's me on Israel."

Although he found Israel's position untenable, he was not ready to recommend dismantling the Jewish state:

"The question whether I'm against the state of Israel is a political question, just like whether I'm against Kuwait or Iraq. I think I answered that. At the moment I find your position untenable, but I don't think that the maintenance of an Israeli state or a Zionist state is impossible. In the future. It will require certain negotiation, but I see no reason why it . . ."

"But you're not in favor of it?"

"Well, it's a fact. You've got four million people here, even though the Zionists based themselves on a lie. But they're here now; you're not going to move populations of four million. Not even the Nazis managed that.

"I disapprove of the present state of Israel but I'm not opposed to a

262 · *Understanding the Dead Sea Scrolls*

'Jewish national home,' in the old language [of the Balfour Declaration], which could well be a state, or which could well be a canton or federation.

"Am I opposed to Zionism? I think we've had enough of it, but you can't say it's not there. It would've been nice if it hadn't existed, but it has, so it's covered by a sort of grandfather clause."

Regarding the scrolls, Strugnell claims at least four other scrolls have been found that have not yet come to light: "I've seen, with my own eyes, two." One of the two is a complete copy of the book of Enoch. According to Strugnell, Israeli archaeologist Yigael Yadin is the reason these scrolls have still not come into scholarly hands. After the Six-Day War, Yadin confiscated the famous Temple Scroll* from a Bethlehem antiquities dealer known as Kando. Yadin paid Kando $250,000, according to Strugnell (according to Yadin, the sum was $105,000), to encourage anyone else with scroll materials to come forward. But this was not enough, says Strugnell: "Yadin gave Kando two hundred fifty thousand dollars where we'd offered Kando one million five weeks earlier. When the owners of the manuscripts heard that, they just crossed the Jordan River." These scrolls, like the Temple Scroll, came from Cave 11 at Qumran, according to Strugnell. The manuscripts are now "somewhere in Jordan. Various people own them. Several of them have been sold to big bankers. They're investments for these people. There's no point in forcing a sale. If they really need cash—as one seems to now—I have the money."

As for the other two scrolls—the ones Strugnell has not seen— "[Lankester] Harding [the director of Jordan's Department of Antiquities] on his death bed told me he'd seen three, only one of which I've seen—so that makes four."

Strugnell is not concerned that the scrolls may deteriorate before scholars can look at them: "They're all being kept very carefully; no one need worry about them. They're a better investment than anything on the Israeli or the New York stock exchanges," he added.

Strugnell blames Israel's Antiquities Authority for the loss of a quarter million dollars in research funds by delaying the confirmation of his appointment as chief editor of the scrolls following the death of the former chief editor in 1987, Père Pierre Benoit:

"The Israeli Department of Antiquities took such a long time about it [confirming Strugnell as chief editor] that we lost quite a large amount

*See Chapter 7.

of money. People who were wanting to give us money wanted to make sure that I was in charge, so we lost one very handsome gift of some two hundred fifty thousand dollars."

Strugnell came across quite humanly. He even told me about the humor he enjoyed:

"Racial stereotypes are one of the greatest things in our humor—where would we be without Armenian jokes, Polish jokes, Jewish jokes? This may be taken to mean that I detest a whole class of people, but that's not true."

Strugnell claims that many Jews were able to see the Dead Sea Scrolls even when they were in Jordanian hands:

"Although tourists had to get a certificate of baptism [to enter Jordan], I saw the most Jewish-looking people come into the museum [in Amman] with [these certificates]."

Although Strugnell reads Hebrew, he does not speak it:

"I read [it], but speaking it requires people to speak to. In my work, people speak much better English."

Nor is Strugnell much interested in Jewish law. He leaves this aspect of his work to Jewish colleagues. I asked Strugnell if he had studied the Talmud:

"I studied it at university, though to me it's not existentially interesting. St. Paul said Christ set us free from the Law. I'm glad my Jewish colleagues handle this aspect [of his work]."

"The fact that you're not interested in Jewish law doesn't prevent you from appreciating the importance of some of this material?" I asked.

"I know enough to know who to go to. The text I'm working on now [MMT] is of course full of law. And the thing that really delayed me from finishing that work was knowing that I was incompetent to deal with that side of things."

CHAPTER 21

SILENCE, ANTI-SEMITISM, AND THE SCROLLS

HERSHEL SHANKS

The interview published in the previous chapter led not only to John Strug-
nell's dismissal as chief editor, but also to a discussion of anti-Semitism as it
related to the scroll publication process. Eighty-six of Strugnell's colleagues and
former students signed a letter expressing their gratitude to Strugnell as "a man
who has contributed so much to the study of ancient Judaism." While
indicating their "dismay" at the "grossly insensitive and reprehensible state-
ments about Jews and Judaism," the signatories suggested that these state-
ments might have been the result of illness. At least, the signatories said, they
had "never read or heard any evidence of anti-Judaism in [Strugnell's]
scholarship or teaching."

Biblical Archaeology Review decided to publish a full-blown treatment
of the issue of anti-Semitism in relation to the scrolls. This forms the following
chapter. —ED.

— . —

For years the issue of anti-Semitism has lurked beneath the surface of
the scrolls. Everyone hoped it wouldn't surface. To introduce the
issue into the scrolls controversy would do no one any good, it was
universally conceded. So silence about anti-Semitism has a long and
honorable tradition in Dead Sea Scroll history.

No one has been happy that, with the Strugnell interview, anti-Semitism has now raised its ugly head. Everyone thought the issue was finally dead and buried, since scroll research had been opened to Jewish scholars (including Israelis).

On October 27, 1990, just one day before Strugnell gave his interview to the *Ha-Aretz* correspondent, I myself tried to lay the issue to rest at an all-day public forum sponsored by the Smithsonian Institution in Washington, D.C. In my opening remarks, I went out of my way to emphasize that the current members of the publication team were "certainly without prejudice." In the question period, someone asked me about the fact that the original eight-man scroll publication team, appointed in 1953 under Jordanian auspices, was *Judenrein* (Jewish-free). I explained that the "bias [of the Jordanians] did not extend to the scholars themselves" and that today Jews are on the publication team. "That bias," I said, "plays no part today." I even cited John Strugnell as an example: "He has enlisted several prominent Israeli scholars [on the project]."

In retrospect, one wonders whether it was right to remain silent in 1953 when, under Jordanian auspices, a "Jew-free" team was appointed to publish the scrolls. The Dead Sea Scrolls are, after all, a library of ancient Jewish religious texts. If anyone protested at the time the team was appointed, there is no record of it. Presumably—if anyone thought of it—it was considered wiser to accede to Jordanian sensitivities than to jeopardize the project. Perhaps so. But what would have happened if some Jews had been added to the team along the way? In any event, until the Six-Day War in 1967, Jewish scholars were completely cut out of the work on the scrolls under the editing team's authority.

In the Six-Day War, however, the unpublished scrolls, which were housed in the Palestine Archaeological Museum in East Jerusalem, fell into Israeli hands. The Israelis were now in control of the scrolls. Yet a funny thing happened. Not a single voice was raised to correct the situation. No one said now that the Jordanian government is no longer in control, we can appoint some Jewish scholars, maybe even some Israeli scholars, to the team.

On the contrary, timid Israelis affirmed the "publication rights" of the "Jew-free" team, provided only that the scholars on the team publish the scrolls quickly.* The rest of the community of scholars remained silent.

---

*Of course, this restriction did not apply to scrolls that early on came into Israeli hands and were promptly published by Israeli and American scholars. The latest was Yigael Yadin, *The Temple Scroll: The Hidden Law of the Dead Sea Sect* (London: Weidenfeld and Nicolson, 1985), p. 45.

One factor that further complicated the matter was that several members of the original editing team were openly and vehemently anti-Israel. Harvard's Frank Cross was a notable and distinguished exception to the anti-Israel bias of the team of editors. In contrast, another surviving member of the original team has to this day never set foot in Israel. For years after 1967, team scholars working in East Jerusalem refused to cross the old border between East and West Jerusalem, thus, in their own way, denying Israel's existence. A latter-day vestige of this attitude was John Strugnell's refusal in late 1990 to be treated in a Jewish hospital in West Jerusalem despite a serious medical problem and despite the inferior facilities in the Arab hospital to which he was admitted. Even the sheikhs of Saudi Arabia don't go that far in their animosity toward the state of Israel. Strugnell's refusal to go to an Israeli hospital is consistent with the statements in his interview that "it would've been nice if it [Zionism] never existed" and that the whole state of Israel is "founded on a lie."

When a young graduate student named Michael Klein, now dean of the Jerusalem campus of Hebrew Union College, wrote to Monsignor Patrick Skehan of Catholic University for permission to see a Targum fragment from Qumran that Klein mistakenly thought was assigned to Skehan, Skehan replied that the fragment was in fact assigned to Milik (who does not answer correspondence), so Klein never got to see the fragment. But in his reply to Klein, Skehan stated as follows:

> Since I note that your letter included a carbon copy to Dr. Magen Broshi, I feel obliged to tell you in addition, that I should not under any circumstance grant through any Israeli functionary, any permission to dispense, for any purpose, or to any extent, of anything whatsoever that is lawfully housed in the Palestine Archaeological Museum.

This attitude was shared by some other members of the editing team.

For about fifteen years after the scrolls in the Rockefeller Museum (as the Palestine Archaeological Museum is now called) fell into Israeli hands, no Jew worked on the texts. Finally, in the mid-1980s, John Strugnell broke the barrier and enlisted the aid of Israeli scholar Elisha Qimron to work with him on the important unpublished text known as MMT. In another project, Strugnell worked with Devorah Dimant of Haifa University. Emanuel Tov of Hebrew University was assigned a biblical scroll to publish. When, under Strugnell's tenure as chief editor, J. T. Milik was persuaded to release some of his hoard of unpublished texts, assignments from Milik's hoard were given to Joseph Baumgarten of Baltimore Hebrew University and Jonas Greenfield of Hebrew University. Strugnell also brought in talmudic scholar Jacob Sussman to interpret Jewish religious laws *(halakhah)* contained in MMT, and Shemaryahu Talmon to interpret the calendar provisions in the same text. The "No Jews Allowed" sign was effectively removed from the Dead Sea Scroll publication project, largely as a result of assignments made by John Strugnell.

Everyone was relieved that anti-Semitism was now no longer even a potential issue. Then came the Strugnell interview.

The reaction in the United States to the Strugnell interview has been very different from the reaction in Israel. The initial reaction in the United States was a kind of denial: "This is not the John Strugnell I knew." Close associates lined up to proclaim that in ten or twenty or thirty years they had never heard Strugnell talk like this. "After all, didn't he bring Jewish scholars into the project?"

Everything Strugnell said in the interview was the result of his mental condition, I was repeatedly told. In the words of a graduate student quoted in the *Harvard Crimson,* "I'm sure it's his illness that's speaking."

There is no question that John Strugnell is a very sick man, physically and mentally. Now it can be talked about. For one thing, it is inextricably involved in the question of his anti-Semitism. For another, it has already been in the newspapers, so we cannot be considered guilty of impropriety. Perhaps most importantly, nothing we discuss can erase—or add to—the humiliation of, and embarrassment to, John Strugnell or the painful personal tragedy that this reflects.

For years Strugnell has been an alcoholic, a disease that has seriously affected his ability to do his work. Everyone knew about this. But no one mentioned it publicly. There was a kind of gentlemen's agreement, somewhat like the press used to observe with respect to the drinking habits of members of Congress. The closest reference in print to Strugnell's alcoholism was in a *Boston Herald* article in 1989 that described his "dilapidated side room of a Jerusalem convent" as "adorned with American and Israeli beer bottles . . . Empty cardboard beer cases are promptly converted into file cabinets still bearing names like Budweiser and Maccabi, a local beer."

Despite the fact that his drinking was seriously impeding his work, no effort was made to remove Strugnell from his position either by his fellow team members or by the Israeli Antiquities Authority. In addition, John Strugnell is said by his colleagues to be a manic-depressive. These facts obviously complicate the question of whether John Strugnell is an anti-Semite.

As noted, one theory is that the views he expressed in his interview are solely the product of his disturbed mind. According to this theory, the interview does not reflect what the man actually thinks: He simply made it up as a result of his mental condition.

The opposing theory is that his mental condition simply loosened his tongue. *In vino veritas,* so to speak. Perhaps he expressed himself more extremely than he would otherwise have done, but his core attitudes and beliefs are accurately reflected in the interview, according to this view.

The first theory is espoused by many of his students and colleagues. They are naturally and understandably pained at the public humiliation and disgrace that has fallen on their mentor and friend. In a letter signed by his colleagues and students, they suggest this possibility, without necessarily embracing it ("We cannot know how much his illness influenced what he said").

If we could conclude that Strugnell's statements were simply the product of a disturbed mind and that they had no relation to his real attitudes toward Jews and Judaism, we could avoid the questions that arise when an anti-Semite is discovered holding the position of chief editor of the Dead Sea Scrolls. To decide whether his anti-Semitic statements in the interview were due to the effects of his present mental illness, we can look at Strugnell's views prior to this interview. Some of this evidence has come out in press reports only since the publication of the interview: The fact is John Strugnell was and is an anti-Semite and rabidly anti-Israel.

According to Magen Broshi, curator of Jerusalem's Shrine of the Book, where most of the original intact Dead Sea Scrolls are housed, "We've known for twenty years that he [Strugnell] is an anti-Semite" (quoted in a British newspaper, *The Independent,* December 14, 1990). In a *Jerusalem Report* article, Broshi is quoted as referring to Strugnell's "rabid anti-Semitism."

Broshi was not the only one who knew of Strugnell's anti-Semitism. According to the *Boston Jewish Advocate* (January 10, 1991), "The anti-Judaic attitudes of [Strugnell] were known for a long time by many of his colleagues." Nahum Sarna, emeritus professor of biblical studies at Brandeis University, is quoted as saying, "Strugnell was known by several people to be anti-Semitic from the first days he came to Harvard. He did not hide his anti-Semitic views. Some of his students say they never heard an anti-Semitic remark from him, but some faculty members did."

The same article quotes Cyrus Gordon, emeritus professor at both Brandeis and New York University: "His [Strugnell's] habits and remarks had gotten around and were well known. But it's like having a bad boy—he's still your child and you don't like to talk about it to colleagues, friends, and neighbors."

According to *Time* magazine (European and Mid-East edition, December 24, 1990), "Scholars have long gossiped about Strugnell's offensive ideas." On one occasion several years ago, reported *Time,* "Strugnell ˌɔasted Austrian President Kurt Waldheim, whose Nazi unit committed atrocities during World War II, as the greatest man of the half-century."

Newsweek reported his "adamant dislike for the state of Israel." While criticism of Israel is not necessarily anti-Semitism, at a certain point the line between anti-Zionism and anti-Semitism becomes blurred. Strugnell's anti-Zionism approached that line if it did not cross it.

According to an article in the *Baltimore Sun* (December 23, 1990), "Several [students and colleagues] say he [Strugnell] demonstrated an upper-class British hauteur to Jews and Judaism," adding that to individual Jews he was often "warm, generous and supportive."

One former student who is Jewish (incidentally, a signatory to the letter) is quoted as saying, "He has said derogatory things to me before, and I called him on it. He would laugh and back down." According to a Jewish Telegraphic Agency report, a senior member of the editing team, Eugene Ulrich, "acknowledged that Strugnell had long had a reputation for making inappropriate remarks." Ulrich referred to them as "slurs."

A scholar who was being interviewed for a faculty position recalls Strugnell's making anti-Semitic remarks to him. Another former student who is Jewish told me that he worked closely with Strugnell on theological matters and knew him to be a very "conservative" Christian theologian who believes in a "supersessionist" theology according to which Christianity has "superseded" Judaism as the "true Israel." Jews are therefore the false Israel. Judaism is therefore no longer valid; the covenant recorded in the Old Testament has been broken. As quoted in *The Jerusalem Report* (December 20, 1990) in a later discussion after he had returned to the United States, Strugnell stated, "It's the old Christian response to the Jewish problem."

As noted above, the colleagues and students who signed the letter of support carefully refrain from considering the indelicate question of whether John Strugnell is an anti-Semite. Several of the signatories admitted to me that they don't really know whether John Strugnell is anti-Semitic. Moreover, they concede that it is quite possible for a person to be an excellent scholar—as John Strugnell surely is—to produce unbiased work and to teach in an unbiased manner—and yet still be an anti-Semite.

The point they make in their letter is simply that in his professional work, his anti-Semitism, if he is anti-Semitic, did not have any effect. We have no evidence that his anti-Semitism did affect his work, although some scholars contend that it did. We are in no position to judge this matter. His students and colleagues may well be right.

But, unlike them, we must go further. Simply because his anti-Semitism may not have affected his work, we cannot finesse the question of whether he is anti-Semitic. We must also explore the nature of his anti-Semitism; we must also ask whether an anti-Semite should be working on these Jewish religious treasures even if he is otherwise competent to do so.

On the evidence already presented, we conclude that John Strugnell is an anti-Semite. That needs to be said. That does not mean we should go looking for anti-Semitism under every green leaf. We are not advocating an academic witch-hunt. But when it manifests itself—in whatever unfortunate way—we should not avert our eyes. As we should not go searching for it, we should not avoid the issue when it arises. That there are dangers on either side must be conceded.

It is especially important that we look at the nature of John Strugnell's anti-Semitism because it comes not from a street fighter like Louis Farrakhan, but from an erudite professor of Christian origins at Harvard Divinity School. His interview was laced with crude vitriol: "a horrible religion," "originally racist," "it never should have survived"—this, less than fifty years since the ovens of Auschwitz were put out (some might fear, banked). He even referred to Hitler's inability to "move" four million Jews (the customary estimate of Jews killed in the Holocaust is, of course, six million, a figure disputed by those who deny the Holocaust). It is easy to condemn this form of anti-Semitism—as, of course, everyone has done.

Certainly but for his illness, Strugnell would not have expressed himself in these crude terms publicly. But beneath this name-calling lies a far more sophisticated, intellectual, carefully developed form of anti-Jewish polemic. It is the repudiated doctrine of a past age. It is the view that Judaism is not a valid religion, the view that Christianity is the true Israel and the Jews the false Israel, the view that the Jews are "stubborn" because they have not accepted Christ, the view that the New Testament has invalidated the covenant reflected in the Old Testament, the view that Christianity has "superseded" Judaism and that Judaism should disappear. This position is summed up in academic jargon by the term *supersessionism*. This is the position that underlies Strugnell's name-calling. This is the position, we are told by one of his former students who knows him well, that John Strugnell espouses—espoused long before his illness affected his mind. One doesn't come up with a theory like this because one is mentally ill. This well-developed theory has long been part of John Strugnell's philosophy of Christianity. Although the British-born Strugnell is a converted Roman Catholic, supersessionism is no part of the Church's teaching today.

What follows from this? First, what does *not* follow: We certainly do not deny John Strugnell or any other anti-Semite the right to express his or her views. Anti-Semites are free to state their views in as crudely, or in as sophisticated, a way as they like. But we—Christian and Jew alike—are free and morally obliged to condemn it when it surfaces. This is as true when the anti-Semite is a great scholar and teacher as it is when the anti-Semite is a popular pop singer.

In their carefully crafted letter, Strugnell's students and colleagues not only avoid the question of whether their teacher and friend is an anti-Semite, they also affirm that his anti-Semitism, if he is indeed anti-Semitic, did not affect his work: "We have never read or heard any evidence of anti-Judaism *in his scholarship or teaching*" (italics supplied). The italicized qualification is important. *Outside his scholarship and teaching,* the man has expressed anti-Semitic views, as some of the signatories recognize, yet they do not say this in their letter.

Assuming that his anti-Semitic views do not affect his scholarship, is he nevertheless unfit, by virtue of his personal anti-Semitism, to head the scroll publication team and to be honored by being given exclusive control of these Jewish cultural treasures? John Strugnell is—and should be—as free as any other scholar to study and interpret the Dead Sea Scrolls. But a known anti-Semite who has espoused his views publicly should not be on a publication team that has exclusive control of unpublished Jewish religious texts.

Our position was stated in an editorial that accompanied the Strugnell interview:

"It is clear that Strugnell cannot be permitted to function any longer as chief editor of the Dead Sea Scrolls. When a person with John Strugnell's views handles these documents, he can only stain them. We say this despite his brilliance and competence as a scholar."

So far, the team of editors has avoided all these questions.

In the official letter from the editing team announcing Strugnell's removal, the team (F. M. Cross, J. T. Milik, Émile Puech, Emanuel Tov, and Eugene Ulrich) cited only "his health and various complications," adding, "We will remain grateful to Professor Strugnell for his many years of devoted service and his wide-ranging and unique positive contributions." No mention of the anti-Semitic interview. As *The New York Times* reported: "In announcing the decision [to remove Strugnell] on Monday, they gave only his health and recent hospitalization as the reason for the action." Yet, as came out in personal interviews with the various actors in this charade, Strugnell's anti-Semitic statements, in the words of *The New York Times,* concededly "forced the issue."

If Strugnell's health had been the real reason for sacking him, there would have been no need for such undue haste. Indeed, it would be unseemly to remove him just when he entered the hospital. Shouldn't he have been given some time to recover? (Co–chief editor Tov, who would be replacing Strugnell, was away on a sabbatical in Holland and would not be back in Jerusalem until August 1991 anyway.) The fact that Strugnell was in a hospital meant that he would now face his problems. He would be "dried out" and his mental problem could likely be controlled by drugs. If it was "only" his health that was a concern, as the *Times* said, why did they not at least wait to see the effect of his stay in the hospital?

Perhaps sensing that the "health" explanation did not really hold water and not wanting to face the anti-Semitism issue, some team members put forward another reason for removing Strugnell—a reason that is as unfair as it is untrue: He didn't push the team hard enough to get the scrolls published. According to an Associated Press story, one editing team member called Strugnell ineffective as chief editor "because he has not pushed researchers to work faster." Ironically, as the butt of this charge, Strugnell was being made a scapegoat. The tardy scholars themselves sacked him—supposedly for not pushing *them* hard enough to complete *their* work. In fact, it was Strugnell who played the major role in developing a "Suggested Timetable" for publication and who persuaded Milik to divest himself of nearly a third of his hoard and to assign it to other scholars. The same scholars who fired Strugnell, supposedly for not pressing hard enough, were the very people who defended his policies regarding publication—and continue to defend them—provided only that *they,* rather than Strugnell, are at the helm. Prior to Strugnell's anti-Semitic interview, no one on the team of editors criticized Strugnell's policies or his failure to pressure others to complete their work.

The team obviously fired Strugnell—or recommended to the Israel Antiquities Authority that he be fired (it is not clear where this authority lies)—because of the anti-Semitic interview, but they gave other reasons—his health and his inefficiency—that avoided all the thorny questions involved in the anti-Semitic issue.

The reaction in Israel to the Strugnell interview is as puzzling as the reaction in the rest of the world is disturbing.

Shortly after the Strugnell interview appeared in *Ha-Aretz,* I called Magen Broshi, curator of Israel's Shrine of the Book and a member of the Israeli oversight committee, to get his reaction to the story. He seemed unconcerned. "Don't waste your time on it," he told me.

I then called Hebrew University professor Shemaryahu Talmon, another member of the Israeli oversight committee. "We are not perturbed," he said.

Later, Broshi told the press that Strugnell's anti-Semitism—which he said he knew about for twenty years—was "entirely irrelevant"! For Broshi, the only question was whether Strugnell was competent to do the job. This attitude was echoed by Amir Drori, director of the Israel Antiquities Authority, who told a *Ha-Aretz* reporter that "the only [!] consideration facing the Antiquities Authority [in deciding whether to remove Strugnell] is the quality of [Strugnell's] work on the details of the scrolls." (When the Antiquities Authority announced his removal, it was only because of "his physical and mental condition.")

I cannot explain or understand this attitude. I don't know what to call it—timidity, diffidence, restraint? There is an old Yiddish proverb that goes something like this: "When someone spits on him, he says it's raining." Some have suggested that Israelis are so accustomed to bias against them that they simply expect it and learn to overlook it.

As we have seen, the rest of the scholars who have a hand in the scroll-pot managed largely to avoid the question by attributing Strugnell's anti-Semitic remarks to his mental illness. No doubt they were motivated by a desire to spare Strugnell from what they considered additional humiliation. To be hospitalized for a psychiatric condition, to be an alcoholic, to have these matters discussed publicly, to be removed as chief editor—all these represent a terrible personal tragedy that is inevitably painful to all concerned, especially to Strugnell himself. It was only natural that his students and colleagues wished to spare him, as one of the signatories to the letter told me, the additional burden of being branded an anti-Semite. He has already had to bear more pain than should be asked of anyone.

In retrospect, however, the issue was too obvious, too insistent, too important to be avoided. The personal dimensions of the tragedy cannot be gainsaid. May John Strugnell recover fully and speedily. Let him be honored as a brilliant scholar, as a wonderful teacher, as a warm, generous, and caring mentor and colleague. But for his anti-Semitism, he must also bear the shame.

CHAPTER 22

IS THE VATICAN SUPPRESSING
THE DEAD SEA SCROLLS?

HERSHEL SHANKS

The obsessive secrecy with which the scroll editing team members have pursued their labors has spawned numerous conspiracy theories that the scrolls were being kept from public scrutiny because their contents would somehow undermine fundamental tenets of Christianity or Judaism. Fuel was added to the fire by the fact that the official editing team included no Jews until the late 1980s and indeed for decades consisted mainly of Roman Catholic clerics.

Both the team editors and their principal critics, such as the editor of Biblical Archaeology Review, *denied that there was any conspiracy to suppress the scrolls or that there were any bombshells in the unpublished texts that would embarrass Judaism or Christianity. On the other hand, it was difficult effectively to refute the conspiracy theories while the texts remained inaccessible to all but the privileged few.*

The conspiracy theory flowered in 1991 in a book that charged the Vatican with attempting to suppress the scrolls and any interpretation of them that deviated from the party line. In this chapter the editor of Biblical Archaeology Review *discusses the evidence and concludes that the charge is hogwash. More importantly, he explains why nothing that is likely to be found in the unpublished scrolls will undermine the faith of either Christians or Jews. Evolution didn't do it. Neither did the archaeologists' conclusion that there was no city at Jericho when Joshua was supposed to have conquered it. Nor did the fact that the author of the biblical flood story copied part of it from a Mesopotamian myth.* —ED.

— · —

A book that will soon be available in the United States was recently published in England under the title *The Dead Sea Scroll Deception* by Michael Baigent and Richard Leigh.[1] The book's thesis is that the Vatican is suppressing the Dead Sea Scrolls because they will undermine vital Christian doctrine.

The authors' first bit of evidence is the unconscionable publication delays: Of over five hundred texts found in Qumran Cave 4 beginning in 1952, only approximately one hundred have been published after nearly forty years. (The three hundred texts from other caves have almost all been published.) Even more sinister is the fact that the small coterie of editors who control access to the four hundred unpublished texts from Cave 4 won't let other scholars see their secret hoard.

The team of Cave 4 editors are largely Catholic clerics, centered at the Dominican-sponsored École Biblique et Archéologique Française in what was until 1967 Jordanian-controlled East Jerusalem. The editorial team was assembled beginning in 1953 by Père Roland de Vaux, who, according to Baigent and Leigh, exercised "virtually supreme authority" over the scrolls until his death in 1971. The team de Vaux assembled included Monsignor Patrick Skehan from the United States; Abbé Jean Starcky from France; Father Jozef Milik, a Polish priest who has since left the priesthood and resettled in France; a German scholar who was soon replaced by another French priest, Father Maurice Baillet; and John Strugnell, who subsequently converted to Catholicism. The sole Protestant on the team was Frank Cross, then of McCormick Theological Seminary and now at Harvard. Rounding out the team was an Englishman and an agnostic, John Allegro. Naturally no Jews were included on the team.

When de Vaux died in 1971, he was replaced as editor in chief by Father Pierre Benoit, another Dominican priest from the École Biblique. When Benoit died in 1987, he was succeeded by the now–Catholic John Strugnell, who served until 1991 when he was dismissed by his colleagues following the publication of some rabidly anti-Semitic remarks he made

37. Father Jean Starcky conducting mass in the 1950s at the excavation of the Qumran settlement.

38. *The scroll team relaxes.*
Père de Vaux is fifth from
left in white cassock.

39. *J. T. Milik in the 1950s.*

to an Israeli journalist.* Upon Starcky's death, his hoard was bequeathed to Father Émile Puech, also of the École Biblique. When Skehan died, his hoard was bequeathed to Eugene Ulrich of Notre Dame University.

Baigent and Leigh do not stop here, however. They explore at some length where final authority actually lies: "To whom, ultimately, were the international team accountable? In theory they should have been accountable to their peers, to other scholars. . . . In reality, the international team seemed to recognize no accountability whatever, except to the École Biblique. And to whom was the École Biblique accountable?"

From their own detailed investigation Baigent and Leigh uncovered what they describe as "a major revelation, not just to us, but to other independent researchers in the field as well." The École Biblique had direct lines to the Pope himself.

The École Biblique has from its earliest days been "close(ly) affiliat-[ed]" with the Pontifical Biblical Commission. The authors describe the École Biblique as "an adjunct of the [Pontifical Biblical] Commission's propaganda machine—an instrument for promulgating Catholic doctrine under the guise of historical and archaeological research." De Vaux himself was made a consultant to the commission; on his death Benoit was made a consultant to the commission. On Benoit's death, his successor as head of the École Biblique was made a consultant to the commission.

The head of the commission is Cardinal Joseph Ratzinger. Ratzinger is also head of another Catholic institution, the Congregation for the Doctrine of the Faith. The Congregation has what the authors call a "long-established pedigree": "In 1542, it had become known officially as the Holy Office. Prior to that it was called the Holy Inquisition."

While Ratzinger is the executive head of the congregation, the official head is always the reigning pope. Today Ratzinger, as executive head, is called its secretary; "in earlier times [the executive head] was known as the Grand Inquisitor."

The authors continue: "Of all the departments of the Curia, that of the Congregation for the Doctrine of the Faith is the most powerful. Ratzinger is perhaps the closest to the Pope of all the Curia cardinals."

"Through the Congregation for the Doctrine of the Faith, Ratzinger's attitudes determine the attitudes of the Pontifical Biblical Commission, of which he is also head, and filter down from there into the École Biblique." Ratzinger is described as "a deeply pessimistic man" who feels

*See Chapter 20.

that "only the suppression of all dissent can assure [the Church's] survival as a unified faith. He regards those who do not share his pessimism as 'blind or deluded.' " "The Church's high-level involvement in Dead Sea Scrolls scholarship," as thus demonstrated, the authors conclude, "must inevitably foster a grave element of suspicion."

This suspicion is buttressed by attitudes expressed by members of the Dead Sea Scroll editorial team like Monsignor Skehan, who is quoted as expressing the view that "ultimately, the biblical scholar's work should be guided and determined by Church doctrine and [now quoting Skehan] 'be subject always to the sovereign right of Holy Mother Church to witness definitively what is in fact concordant with the teaching she has received from Christ.' "

"What if something comes to light which can't be made thus to conform?" the authors ask. "From Father Skehan's statements, the answer to that question would seem clear. Anything that can't be subordinated or accommodated to existing Church doctrine *must,* of necessity, be suppressed."

Father Skehan's position, we are told, "was effectively echoed by Pope Pius XII himself, who maintained 'that the biblical exegete has a function and a responsibility to perform in matters of importance to the church.' "

With this background, it is easy to understand why "De Vaux wanted, so far as it was possible, to avoid embarrassing the Christian establishment," the authors state. "Some of the Qumran material was clearly deemed capable of doing precisely that." In order to avoid this "embarrassment," the de Vaux–led team devised and "imposed . . . a rigid orthodoxy of interpretation" of the scrolls.

"Any deviation [from this interpretation] was tantamount to heresy . . . [Any scholar] who presumed to challenge [the team's interpretation] did so at severe risk to his credibility . . . This orthodoxy of interpretation [has grown] progressively more dogmatic over the years."

The authors imply that de Vaux and his colleagues might even destroy—have destroyed—some incriminating documents. "What exactly would the École Biblique do if, among the unpublished or perhaps as yet undiscovered Qumran material, something inimical to Church doctrine turned up?" And again: "Even if the Israeli government clamped down and ordered the immediate release of all Qumran material, how could we be sure that items potentially compromising to the Church would ever see the light of day?"

Straying scholars could be kept in line by means less drastic, however, than destroying documents. Take the case of John Allegro, not only the only agnostic on the team but the only member to publish all the scrolls assigned to him. Strugnell then wrote "a long [113-page] and hostile critique" which Robert Eisenman, chair of the Religious Studies Department at California State University in Long Beach, has called a "hatchet-job." Early on, Allegro "grew exasperated with [the team's] strained attempt to distance Christianity from the scrolls and the Qumran community" and was soon estranged from the rest of the team, especially after their efforts to prevent his airing views they objected to. Other critics of the team's views were likewise silenced.

The chief tenet of the orthodox interpretation of the scroll relates to their date. "The key factor in determining the significance of the scrolls, and their relation, or lack of it, to Christianity, consisted, of course, in their dating." Therefore, in the "consensus view," as the team's views are called, "the Qumran texts were seen as dating from long prior to the Christian era." Anything that "would upset the 'safe' dating and chronology which the international team had established for the entire corpus of scrolls" was squelched. Once "set safely back in pre-Christian times, [the scrolls became] disarmed of any possible challenge to New Testament teaching and tradition." In this way the team "effectively defused the Dead Sea Scrolls of whatever explosive potential they might have." "When expediency and the stability of Christian theology so dictated, contrary evidence was 'ignored.'"

Another tenet of orthodox interpretation was that "the scrolls and their authors had to be kept as dissociated as possible from 'early Christianity'—as depicted in the New Testament." Thus, in the orthodox consensus, "The beliefs of the Qumran community were presented as entirely different from Christianity."

To anyone unfamiliar with the Byzantine complexity of the high-stakes struggle for control of the Dead Sea Scrolls, Baigent and Leigh make an appealing—perhaps even convincing—case that the Vatican—or at least Catholic clerics—are suppressing the scrolls for doctrinal reasons. In fact, however, the charge is hogwash.

I confess it seems ungracious of me to say so because Baigent and Leigh make some highly flattering remarks about *Biblical Archaeology Review*'s six-year campaign to obtain release of the still-secret scrolls. The authors call us "influential"; they quote us at length approvingly; they say our "contribution has been immense." But, still, their central thesis is so badly flawed as to be ludicrous.

Let us begin with a general statement: Catholic scholars are today in the forefront of modern critical biblical scholarship.[2] The *Catholic Biblical*

40. John Allegro in the 1950s.

Quarterly is among the most highly respected journals of biblical scholarship in the world. It ranks right up there with the *Journal of Biblical Literature,* published by the Society of Biblical Literature. Neither Protestants nor Jews have a journal devoted to biblical studies comparable to *CBQ.* The *Revue Biblique,* published by the École Biblique, is also a highly respected journal that publishes articles by Jewish and Protestant, as well as Catholic, scholars.

This is not to say that Catholic scholars are never biased. They sometimes are—and in subtle ways. But—let's confess it—so are we all, including agnostics and nonbelievers. All we can do is conscientiously become aware of our predilections, maintaining continual vigilance to prevent their affecting our scholarship. Each case of alleged bias must be decided on its own merits. There is today simply no basis for a wholesale condemnation of Catholic biblical scholarship as biased.

Let's look at a few more specific facts. As Baigent and Leigh recount, a number of scholars have contested the consensus view. Among these scholars is Robert North, whose position goes to the very heart of the consensus view by questioning the team's dating of the scrolls. The consensus, North says, is "disquieting . . . It is important to emphasize the frailty of the evidences." North calls attention to four cases in which de Vaux had been forced to retract his dating. In Baigent and Leigh's words, "North also found it distressing that, even on so crucial a matter, specialists 'independently of de Vaux's influence' were not asked to contribute to their conclusion."

Baigent and Leigh recognize, however, that North is in fact a Jesuit priest. But it's worse than that. North is not simply a Catholic priest somewhere out in the boonies who failed to get the word from on high. North is the editor of the *Elenchus of Biblica,* an annual index of all articles published the previous year that in any way relate to the Bible, and a professor of archaeology at the Pontifical Biblical Institute. As such, he works in the shadow of the Vatican itself. If anyone should have gotten the word—if there was a word to be gotten—it should be North.

Or take the case of Father Joseph Fitzmyer, a distinguished emeritus professor at Catholic University of America in Washington, D.C., who has been among the most vocal critics of the team for failing to publish their texts,[3] who has unsuccessfully pleaded with Milik to release some of the latter's texts so that Fitzmyer himself could publish them[4]—how come Joe Fitzmyer never got the word?

But that is by no means the weakest element of the authors' position. Their entire structure is based on the foolish supposition that independent scholars in this day and age can be cowed into suppressing their views. Baigent and Leigh cite what happened to John Allegro; his publication of the texts assigned to him was savagely reviewed by Strugnell, who spent over one hundred pages correcting Allegro's errors. But this could only be done because Allegro's reading of the text was so bad; it was not done because Allegro's interpretations were contrary to the team's. No doubt Strugnell took a certain glee in correcting Allegro's errors, but no one I know has provided a substantive defense of Allegro's work as against Strugnell's criticisms. Fitzmyer, himself an outsider, has said that Allegro's work must be used only with "extreme caution." Moreover, as Baigent and Leigh recognize, Allegro went on to self-destruct by publishing a book entitled *The Sacred Mushroom and the Cross*[5] in which he contended that Jesus had never existed in historical reality, but was only an image evoked in the psyche under the influence of a hallucinating drug, psilocybin, the active ingredient in hallucinogenic mushrooms. Fourteen prominent British scholars repudiated the book in a letter to the *London Times*. The publisher apologized for issuing the book.

Allegro's views failed to gain acceptance, but he was not cowed or suppressed. Many other scholars have dissented from the reigning team's views. Barbara Thiering of the University of Sydney in Australia contends that the Teacher of Righteousness, who figures prominently in Qumran texts, is John the Baptist and Jesus is the Wicked Priest. J. L. Teicher of Cambridge University contends that Paul is the Wicked Priest. Otto Betz of the University of Tübingen suggests that John the Baptist lived at Qumran.* Norman Golb of the University of Chicago argues that the Qumran library really came from Jerusalem and represents the views of mainline Judaism. Lawrence Schiffman of New York University contends that the underlying doctrines of the Qumran sect are not Essenic, but Sadducean.†

Jose O'Callaghan contends that fragments of the Gospel of Mark, as well as Acts and Paul's letter to the Romans, have been found among the texts recovered from one of the Dead Sea Scroll caves. Who is this independent voice challenging the authority of the Vatican's representatives by suggesting that such late Christian documents have been found at Qumran? He is a Spanish Jesuit! These Catholics—like North, Fitzmyer, and O'Callaghan—ought to get their act together if they're going

*See Chapter 16.
†See Chapter 3.

to suppress unorthodox ideas, especially ideas that relate the Qumran documents to the New Testament. To add insult to injury, O'Callaghan publishes his ideas in Catholic journals like *Biblica* and *Civita cattolica*.

No one can deny all these dissenting scholars a voice. They may be denied a forum at conclaves that the editorial team controls. But their views are made widely known in alternative publications. Whether their arguments will prevail will be determined by their acceptance or rejection by their peers, not by the coercive efforts of the editorial team.

Indeed Baigent and Leigh themselves adopt the views of an independent scholar who vigorously disagrees with the views of the editorial team, Robert Eisenman. According to Eisenman—and Baigent and Leigh—the Qumran leader known as the Teacher of Righteousness is actually James the Righteous, who is referred to in the New Testament as the brother of Jesus. According to Eisenman, James was the leader of the Zealots, a militant Jewish sect that was in the forefront of the First Jewish Revolt against Rome (66–70 A.D.) that effectively ended with the burning of Jerusalem and the destruction of the Temple. Eisenman contends that the Qumran community were Zealots, not Essenes. As such, they were heirs to a long line of Jewish Zadokites—from Ezra, to Judas Maccabeus, to John the Baptist, to Jesus, and finally to Jesus' brother James. Paul, in this scenario, was James' archopponent. It was Paul who turned Jesus into a God. According to Eisenman, Paul is "the Liar" of the Qumran texts, the adversary of the Teacher of Righteousness. Paul, according to Eisenman, spent three years at Qumran. The second adversary of the Teacher of Righteousness, the Wicked Priest is, according to this theory, Ananas, the high priest in Jerusalem. Ananas contrived to have James put to death, an event recorded in the New Testament where, again according to Eisenman, Stephen has been substituted for James. At this point, according to Eisenman, Judea rose in revolt. This was the beginning of the First Jewish Revolt against Rome. The Romans dispatched an expeditionary force under Vespasian and Jerusalem was destroyed. Paul prevailed by creating Christianity. The story of James (and the real, the militant Jesus) was suppressed, until resurrected in Eisenman's interpretation of the Dead Sea Scrolls.

If Père de Vaux is the Wicked Priest according to the gospel of Baigent and Leigh, Robert Eisenman is the Teacher of Righteousness. Aware that my summary of Eisenman's view is grossly inadequate, I may well be cast in the role of the Liar.

Truth to tell, no short summary of Eisenman's views would be adequate. (I have omitted Eisenman's suggestion that Paul may actually have been a secret Roman agent.) As Baigent and Leigh themselves state toward the end of a 266-page book in large part devoted to Eisenman's ideas, "In our own pages, it would be impossible to do adequate justice to the weight of evidence Eisenman amasses." (A few pages later, on the other hand, they say, "Eisenman's research has revealed the underlying *simplicity* of what had previously seemed a dauntingly complicated situation.")

Eisenman's views may yet prevail (although Baigent and Leigh are badly mistaken when they state that "an ever-increasing phalanx of supporters is gathering around Robert Eisenman, and his cause is being espoused by more and more scholars of influence and prominence." I do not know of a single scholar who has expressed agreement in print with Eisenman's scenario.)

But whether Eisenman's views will ultimately prevail is not the point. What is important is that they are free to make their way in the marketplace of ideas. They have been presented to the public and to his fellow scholars. The first book in which he makes his case *(Maccabees, Zadokites, Christians and Qumran)* was published by the prestigious scholarly publishing house of E. J. Brill of Leiden in 1983. The second of his books *(James the Just in the Habakkuk Pesher)* was published in 1985 by—now hold on to your seats, as my grandfather used to say—by one of the Vatican's own presses, *Tipographia Gregoriana!* (It was later revised and brought out by Brill.) Like Father North, Father Fitzmyer, and Father O'Callaghan, the Vatican press apparently failed to get the word as to what was doctrinally kosher and what was not. Otherwise, what was a Vatican press doing publishing Eisenman?

In short, in this day and age, it is difficult to suppress ideas. Moreover, the team certainly chose a strange tenet to enforce doctrinal purity—an early dating for the scrolls. The team dates the scrolls between about 250 B.C. and 68 A.D. when, according to de Vaux's interpretation of the archaeological evidence, the Qumran settlement was destroyed by the Roman forces. This early date, according to the accusation against the team editors, distances the scrolls from Christianity. Really? It coincides with Jesus's life on this earth. If, for example, a virgin birth was attested in a Qumran text dating from the first or second century B.C. instead of the first or second century A.D., would this really matter much in terms of its destructive potential for Christian doctrine?

This leads us to an even more deeply flawed element in Baigent and Leigh's contention. They assume that something in these arcane ancient scrolls could seriously undermine Christian doctrine or faith. It is hard to imagine what that would be. And Baigent and Leigh do not even hint at its content. Suppose a text recounted a virgin birth that prefigured the virgin birth of Jesus. So what? We already know that virgin birth stories were in the air at the time. Both Judaism and Christianity have survived the discovery of evolution, as well as the discovery of a Mesopotamian flood story that was used by the biblical writer when he composed the story about Noah. Nor has Jewish or Christian faith been undermined by the fact that archaeologists tell us there was no city at Jericho when Joshua was supposed to have marched around it seven times before the walls came tumbling down.

Allegro once wrote Strugnell: "By the time I've finished there won't be any Church left for you to join." Clearly, Allegro underestimated the strength of the Church's theological foundations. And so have Baigent and Leigh.

The supreme irony, however, is that the very threat that Baigent and Leigh postulate that the Church fears has in fact already occurred—and without the slightest shake of or shock to the Church's foundation. Moreover, it has occurred with a strong assist from Catholic scholars. Baigent and Leigh suggest that the scrolls might contain "something compromising, something challenging, possibly [something that] even refutes, established traditions." They picture de Vaux and his colleagues as fearful that something in the scrolls "might just conceivably demolish the entire edifice of Christian teaching and belief." This is because, according to our authors, "It had hitherto been believed that Jesus' teachings were unique."

Well, yes and no. Modern scholarship has emphasized the connections of Jesus' teaching with other social and ideological movements of the time. On the other hand, the particular combination of ideas was and is unique.

All scholars are agreed that the Qumran documents are highly significant to our understanding of early Christianity. These documents have added a new dimension to our understanding of Christian origins: Dozens of books and hundreds of articles have been written about the relationship of the Qumran texts to the New Testament. One of the principal conclusions of all this research is that early Christian doctrine and belief systems were *not* unique. In Chapter 14 James VanderKam draws two principal conclusions from decades of studying the effect of the Qumran texts on our understanding of early Christianity: "(1) the early Church grew upon Jewish soil to a far greater extent than previously supposed; and (2) a larger number of the early Church's beliefs and practices than previously suspected were not unique to it."

There has been no resistance, either generally or in Catholic circles,

41. *John Strugnell in the 1950s.*

to these conclusions or to the publication of the evidence for it. Yet this is supposed to be the destructive conclusion the Vatican conspiracy is designed to prevent—or at least to prevent reaching the light of day.

Baigent and Leigh cite a passage from a still-unpublished Qumran text that refers to someone who will be called "Son of the Most High" and "Son of God," echoing names that in Luke 1:32–35 are attributed to Jesus. This is "an extraordinary discovery," they say. We agree. But we are happy to reveal that this material was provided to *Biblical Archaeology Review* by a prominent Catholic scholar—and the doctrinal supports of the Church have not fallen as a result of its publication.*

Even more recently, an article has appeared revealing that a Qumran text contained beatitudes that in many respects prefigured the beatitudes in the Sermon on the Mount. The author? Father Émile Puech of the École Biblique.[6]

Baigent and Leigh accuse the team of editors of "painstakingly conceal[ing]" links between Qumran texts and New Testament events. On the contrary, the implications of the Qumran texts for New Testament studies have been widely and openly debated with the result that concepts and doctrines once regarded as uniquely Christian are no longer so understood.

Yet there remains a puzzle: Why have the scholars who control the scrolls insisted on keeping so many of them secret? The answer, I am afraid, is not nearly so dramatic as Baigent and Leigh would have us believe. The explanation, alas, is quite pedestrian.

Originally, in my judgment, they kept their goodies secret because of what motivates all monopolists: power. They were exclusive members of what one outsider called a "charmed circle." They controlled an entire discipline. It was they who were the experts. It was their names that would go down in history as authors of the first editions. It was they who could entice graduate students with an unpublished Dead Sea Scroll to edit as a doctoral dissertation.

More recently, something else has been at work: sheer obstinacy. The scroll editors answer to no one. They are a law unto themselves. They deeply resent the pressure that has been brought on them by outsiders. And not simply by outside scholars, but by untutored nonscholars like the editor of *Biblical Archaeology Review* and the general press. The reaction of the editors has been to dig in their heels. In their own terms, they will not be pushed around.

*See Chapter 15.

That this, rather than a Vatican-directed conspiracy, lies behind the refusal to grant open access to the unpublished scrolls is demonstrated by the fact that the Israelis who have recently asserted their control of the scrolls concur in the monopoly exercised by the scroll editors—provided the team is expanded, as it has been, to include Israelis. Surely the Israelis would not be a part of a Vatican-directed conspiracy. Yet prominent Israeli scholars are part of the consensus view. Baigent and Leigh do not explain how the Israelis were enticed to join a conspiracy whose purpose is to preserve the purity of Church doctrine.

Notes

OF CAVES AND SCHOLARS: AN OVERVIEW

1. Ben Zion Wacholder, *The Dawn of Qumran* (Cincinnati: Hebrew Union College Press, 1983).
2. *The New York Times,* September 7, 1991.
3. Edmund Wilson, *The Scrolls from the Dead Sea* (London: Collins, 1955).

CHAPTER 1.
DISCOVERING THE SCROLLS

1. *The Shrine of the Book and Its Scrolls* (a pamphlet published by the Shrine of the Book Museum, Jerusalem), p. 5.

CHAPTER 2.
THE HISTORICAL CONTEXT OF THE SCROLLS

1. As claimed by G. R. Driver, for example, in his erratic and arbitrary study, *The Judean Scrolls* (Oxford: Blackwell, 1965).
2. See W. F. Albright, "A Biblical Fragment from the Maccabean Age: The Nash Papyrus," *Journal of Biblical Literature,* Vol. 56 (1937), pp. 145–176.
3. See F. M. Cross, "The Development of Jewish Scripts," in G. Ernest Wright, ed., *The Bible and the Ancient Near East (New York: Doubleday, 1961),* pp. 133–202.

CHAPTER 3.

THE SADDUCEAN ORIGINS OF THE

DEAD SEA SCROLL SECT

1. See Louis Ginzberg, "Eine unbekannte jüdische Sekte," originally published in *Monatsschrift für die Geschichte und Wissenschaft des Judentums* 55–58 [1911–1914], and later privately published as a book in 1922. Ginzberg expected to publish additional material, but when World War II came he forswore publishing in German. As a result, only with the appearance of the English edition, *An Unknown Jewish Sect* (New York: Jewish Theological Seminary, 1976) was his full study published.

2. *Megillat Ha-Miqdash,* 3 vols. (Jerusalem: Israel Exploration Society, 1977); *The Temple Scroll,* 3 vols. (Jerusalem: Israel Exploration Society, 1983); and the more popularly written *The Temple Scroll, The Hidden Law of the Dead Sea Sect* (New York: Random House, 1985). See also Yigael Yadin, "The Temple Scroll—The Longest and Most Recently Discovered Dead Sea Scroll" and Jacob Milgrom's review of *The Temple Scroll,* both in *Biblical Archaeology Review,* September/October 1984. See also Lawrence Schiffman, review of Yadin's *The Temple Scroll: The Hidden Law of the Dead Sea Sect, Biblical Archaeology Review,* July/August 1985.

3. J. T. Milik, *The Books of Enoch, Aramaic Fragments from Qumran Cave* (Oxford: Clarendon Press, 1976).

4. Maurice Baillet, *Qumran grotte 4, III (4Q482–4Q520),* Discoveries in the Judaean Desert VII (Oxford: Clarendon Press, 1982).

5. Solomon Zeitlin, *The Zadokite Fragments,* Jewish Quarterly Review Monograph series (Philadelphia: Dropsie College, 1952).

6. G. Bonani, M. Broshi, I. Carmi, S. Ivy, J. Strugnell, W. Wolfli, "Radiocarbon Dating of the Dead Sea Scrolls," *'Atiqot* 20 (1991), pp. 27–32.

7. E. L. Sukenik, *Megillot Genuzot, Seqirah Rishonah* (Jerusalem: Mossad Bialik, 1948).

8. Frank M. Cross, *The Ancient Library of Qumran and Modern Biblical Studies* (Garden City, NY: Doubleday, 1958); Millar Burrows, *The Dead Sea Scrolls* (New York: Viking, 1956), and *More Light on the Dead Sea Scrolls* (London: Secker and Warburg, 1958); and Andre Dupont-Sommer, *Les écrits esséniens découverts près de la Mer Morte* (Paris: Payot, 1959).

9. The site was excavated in 1953–1956. Preliminary reports appeared in *Revue Biblique* 61–63 (1954–1956). The survey volume was first published in French in 1961 and then revised as Roland de Vaux, *Archaeology and the Dead Sea Scrolls* (London: Oxford University Press, 1973).

10. Under the sponsorship of the Hagop Kevorkian Center for Near Eastern Studies. The conference volume was published under the title *Archaeology and History in the Dead Sea Scrolls,* Lawrence H. Schiffman, ed., Journal for the Study of the Old Testament Supplement Series 8 and JSOT/ASOR Monographs 2 (Sheffield, UK: Sheffield Academic Press, 1990). Subsequent

conferences were held at London and Manchester (England), Mogilany (Poland), Jerusalem (Israel), Groningen (Netherlands), again at Mogilany, and Madrid, all of which have generated volumes of the papers presented.

11. Elisha Qimron and John Strugnell, "An Unpublished Halakhic Letter from Qumran," in *Biblical Archaeology Today,* Janet Amitai, ed. (Jerusalem: Israel Exploration Society, 1985), pp. 400–407; and a different article by the same name, *Israel Museum Journal* 4 (1985), pp. 9–12.

12. See Schiffman, "The Temple Scroll and the Systems of Jewish Law in the Second Temple Period," in *Temple Scroll Studies,* George J. Brooke, ed. (Sheffield, UK: Journal for the Study of the Old Testament Press, 1989), pp. 239–255; *"Miqsat Ma'aseh Ha-Torah* and the *Temple Scroll,"* *Revue de Qumran* 14 (1990), pp. 435–457; "The Prohibition of the Skins of Animals in the Temple Scroll and *Miqsat Ma'aseh Ha-Torah,"* *Proceedings of the Tenth World Congress of Jewish Studies,* Division A (Jerusalem: World Union of Jewish Studies, 1990), pp. 191–198; "The New Halakhic Letter (4QMMT) and the Origins of the Dead Sea Sect," *Biblical Archaeologist* 53, no. 2 (June 1990), pp. 64–73; and the extremely important study of Y. Sussmann, "History of *Halakha* and the Dead Sea Scrolls—Preliminary Observations on *Miqsat Ma'aseh ha-Torah* (4QMMT)" (Hebrew), *Tarbiz* 59 (1989–1990), pp. 11–76.

13. *Pesher Nahum* 3–4 i 12; ii 2,8; iii 5; *Pesher Psalms (A)* 1–2 ii 17.

14. Damascus Document 4:19, 8:12, 19:25,31.

15. *Hodayot* 2:15,32; *Pesher Nahum* 3–4 i 2,7; ii 2,4; iii 3,7; Damascus Document 1:18.

16. Jacob Neusner, *The Rabbinic Traditions about the Pharisees before 70,* 3 vols. (Leiden, Netherlands: E. J. Brill, 1971).

17. *Pesher Nahum* 3–4 iii 9; iv 1,3,6; *Pesher Psalms (A)* 1–2 ii 17.

18. Norman Golb, "The Dead Sea Scrolls, A New Perspective," *The American Scholar* (Spring 1989), pp. 177–207.

19. A complete and methodical refutation of the Golb hypothesis is included in Florentino García-Martínez, "A 'Groningen' Hypothesis of Qumran Origins and Early History," to appear in the volume of *Revue de Qumran* devoted to the Groningen conference proceedings. The "Groningen" hypothesis, however, will also have to be seriously modified after the publication of MMT.

20. See García-Martínez, "Significado de los Manuscritos de Qumran para el Conocimiento de Jesucristo y del Cristianismo," *Communio* 22 (1989), pp. 338–342.

21. See Shemaryahu Talmon, *The World of Qumran from Within* (Jerusalem and Leiden, Netherlands: Magnes Press and E. J. Brill, 1989), pp. 71–141.

22. William F. Albright, "New Light on Early Recensions of the Hebrew Bible," *Bulletin of American Schools of Oriental Research* 140 (1955), pp. 27–33.

23. Cross, "The History of the Biblical Text in Light of Discoveries in the

Judaean Desert," *Harvard Theological Review* 57 (1964), pp. 281–299; *Ancient Library*, pp. 120–145.

24. See Emanuel Tov, "A Modern Textual Outlook Based on the Qumran Scrolls," *Hebrew Union College Annual* 53 (1982), pp. 11–27; "Hebrew Biblical Manuscripts from the Judaean Desert: Their Contribution to Textual Criticism," *Journal of Jewish Studies* 39 (1988), pp. 5–37.

CHAPTER 4.

THE PEOPLE OF THE DEAD SEA SCROLLS:

ESSENES OR SADDUCEES?

1. Josephus, *Jewish Antiquities* 13.5, 9, 171–172. Ralph Marcus, transl. Loeb Classical Library (London: Heinemann/Cambridge, MA: Harvard University Press, 1966).

2. Pliny, *Natural History* 2, 5.15, 73, H. Rackham, transl. Loeb Classical Library (London: Heinemann/Cambridge, MA: Harvard University Press, 1969).

3. Pliny, *Natural History* 1 [1938], Preface, p. viii.

4. Pliny, *Natural History* 1, p. ix. A possible source for the passage under discussion is Marcus Agrippa, who wrote before 12 B.C.; he is the first authority whom Pliny lists for the information in Book 5 (the lengthy catalogue of sources constitutes the first book of Pliny's composition). See the comments of J. J. Tierney, "The Map of Agrippa," *Proceedings of the Royal Irish Academy*, vol. 63, section C, no. 4 (Dublin: Hodges, Figgis, 1963), p. 155. I thank my colleague Stephen Goranson for this reference.

5. *The Dead Sea Scrolls of St. Mark's Monastery*, vol. II, fasc. 2: *Plates and Transcription of the Manual of Discipline*, ed. Millar Burrows (New Haven, CT: American Schools of Oriental Research, 1951).

6. Josephus, *Antiquities* 13.5, 9, 171–173.

7. All translations from Qumran texts are those from Geza Vermes, *The Dead Sea Scrolls in English* (Sheffield, UK: Journal for the Study of the Old Testament Press, 3rd ed., 1987); Vermes refers to the Manual of Discipline (IQS) as the Community Rule, 3.15–16.

8. Vermes, *The Dead Sea Scrolls*, 3.21–23.

9. Josephus, *The Jewish War* 2.8, 3, 122. H. St. J. Thackeray, transl. Loeb Classical Library (London: Heinemann/Cambridge, MA: Harvard University Press, 1976).

10. Vermes, *The Dead Sea Scrolls*, 6.17–22.

11. Josephus, *The Jewish War* 2.8, 9, 147.

12. Vermes, *The Dead Sea Scrolls*, 7.13.

13. Todd Beall, *Josephus' Description of the Essenes Illustrated by the Dead Sea Scrolls*, Society for New Testament Studies Monograph Series 58 (Cambridge, UK: Cambridge University Press, 1988).

14. Vermes, *The Dead Sea Scrolls,* 14.12–13, cf. 9,10–16.

15. See the valuable recent study of Carol Newsom, " 'Sexually Explicit' Literature from Qumran," in *The Hebrew Bible and Its Interpreters,* William H. Propp, Baruch Halpern, and David Noel Freedman, eds. Biblical and Judaic Studies 1 (Winona Lake, IN: Eisenbrauns, 1990), pp. 167–187.

16. Frank Moore Cross, "The Early History of the Qumran Community," in *New Directions in Biblical Archaeology,* David Noel Freedman and Jonas C. Greenfield, eds. (Garden City, NY: Doubleday, 1971), pp. 77.

17. See Elisha Qimron and John Strugnell, "An Unpublished Halakhic Letter from Qumran," in *Biblical Archaeology Today,* Janet Amitai, ed. (Jerusalem: Israel Exploration Society, 1985), pp. 400–407.

18. Schiffman deals with this subject in Chapter 3. For a fuller elaboration, see his "The Temple Scroll and Systems of Jewish Law of the Second Temple Period," in *Temple Scroll Studies,* George J. Brooke, ed. Journal for the Study of the Pseudepigrapha Supplement Series 7 (Sheffield, UK: Sheffield Academic Press, 1989), pp. 245–251.

19. Emil Schürer, *The History of the Jewish People in the Age of Jesus Christ,* revised and edited by Vermes, Fergus Millar, and Matthew Black (Edinburgh: T. & T. Clark, 1979), p. 410, n. 31. MMT shows that the authors did in fact embrace one position—regarding the liquid stream discussed in the chapter appendix—that Schürer thought was a joke.

20. David Daube, in "On Acts 23: Sadducees and Angels," *Journal of Biblical Literature* 109 (1990), pp. 493–497, has recently made the interesting suggestion that Acts 23:8—the only ancient passage that says the Sadducees denied there were angels and spirits—means that the Sadducees rejected the notion of an angelic- or spirit-like interim phase for the departed prior to the general resurrection (which they also rejected). I am not convinced that he is correct and that his theory explains the Pharisaic jibe in Acts 23:9, but it would have been strange for the Sadducees to deny there were angels when their Bibles were full of them. It has been suggested that Acts 23:8 means only that they denied there were vast armies of angels while accepting the existence of a smaller number.

APPENDIX TO CHAPTER 4.
TRACKING THE LAW IN THE MISHNAH
AND IN A QUMRAN TEXT

1. *The Mishnah,* Herbert Danby, transl. (Oxford: Oxford University Press, 1933), with revisions.

2. The meaning of this obscure term has been debated at length. Philip Blackman (*Mishnayoth,* vol. 6: *Order Taharoth* [Gateshead, UK: Judaica Press, 2nd ed. 1977], p. 771) lists the following suggested interpretations:

Jesus ben Sira, ben Laanah, the author of the Book of Tagla, Homer, or the apostate, heretic.

3. See MMT, lines B18–23.
4. See Joseph M. Baumgarten, "The Pharisaic-Sadducean Controversies about Purity and Qumran Texts," *Journal of Jewish Studies* 31 (1980), pp. 161–163.
5. Baumgarten first called attention to this agreement in "The Pharisaic-Sadducean Controversies," pp. 163–164.

CHAPTER 5.

"FIRST DEAD SEA SCROLL" FOUND IN EGYPT
FIFTY YEARS BEFORE QUMRAN DISCOVERIES

1. Solomon Schechter, *Documents of Jewish Sectaries: Fragments of a Zadokite Work* (Cambridge: Cambridge University Press, 1910), Introduction, p. xviii.
2. Ibid., p. xiii.
3. A. Whigham Price, *The Ladies of Castlebrae* (Durham, UK: University of Durham Press, 1964), p. 1.
4. Norman Bentwich, *Solomon Schechter, A Biography* (Philadelphia: The Jewish Publication Society of America, 1938), p. 130.
5. Solomon Schechter, *Studies in Judaism Second Series* (Philadelphia: The Jewish Publication Society of America, 1908), p. 6.
6. Ibid., p. 6.
7. Ibid., p. 8.
8. Ibid., p. 10.
9. Solomon Schechter, *Documents of Jewish Sectaries,* pp. xv, xvi.
10. Millar Burrows, *The Dead Sea Scrolls* (New York: Viking, 1955), p. 1887.

CHAPTER 6.

ESSENE ORIGINS—PALESTINE OR BABYLONIA?

1. Consistent with this theory, there may well have been other centers of Essenes in Palestine. Some scholars contend they have found archaeological evidence of Essene occupation on Mount Zion (see Bargil Pixner, "An Essene Quarter on Mt. Zion?" *Studia Hierosolymitana in onore di P. Bellarmino Bagatti, Studium Biblicum Franciscanum Collectio Maior. N. 22–23 Vol. I Studi Archeologici* (Jerusalem: Franciscan Printing, 1979), pp. 245–284; and at Haifa (see Stephen Goranson, "On the Hypothesis That Essenes Lived on Mt. Carmel," *Revue de Qumran,* Vol. 9, No. 4, 1978, pp. 563–567). Josephus notes that the Essenes "occupy no one city, but settle in large numbers in every town" (*The Jewish War 2,* 122–128 [4].)

2. See William F. Albright, *From the Stone Age to Christianity* (Garden City, NJ: Doubleday, 1957), p. 376.
3. Solomon Schechter, *Documents of Jewish Sectaries: Fragments of a Zadokite Work* (Cambridge: Cambridge University Press, 1910).

CHAPTER 7.
THE TEMPLE SCROLL—THE LONGEST
DEAD SEA SCROLL

1. Yigael Yadin, ed., *The Temple Scroll* (Jerusalem: Israel Exploration Society, The Institute of Archaeology of the Hebrew University of Jerusalem, The Shrine of the Book, 1977), 3 volumes.

CHAPTER 8.
THE GIGANTIC DIMENSIONS OF THE
VISIONARY TEMPLE IN THE TEMPLE SCROLL

1. Josephus, *Antiquities of the Jews,* 15.421.
2. Ibid., 15.420.
3. Ibid., 20.219.
4. The exact size of the cubit referred to in the scroll is, unfortunately, unknown to us. I have assumed, somewhat arbitrarily, that the cubit is 0.5 meter or 19.7 inches long, which is 10 to 15 percent longer or shorter than the length of the cubit according to various scholars.
5. See Magen Broshi, "Estimating the Population of Jerusalem," *Biblical Archaeology Review,* March 1978.

CHAPTER 9.
INTRIGUE AND THE SCROLL

1. Yigael Yadin, ed., *The Temple Scroll,* 3 vols. (Jerusalem: Israel Exploration Society, 1983).

CHAPTER 10.
IS THE TEMPLE SCROLL A SIXTH BOOK
OF THE TORAH—LOST FOR 2,500 YEARS?

1. The question of Mosaic authority in the Temple Scroll is still much debated. Indeed, the name of Moses does not appear in the extant text of the Temple Scroll. Compare this with Deuteronomy 12–26. For this reason, Baruch

Levine ("The Temple Scroll: Aspects of its Historical Provenance and Literary Character," *Bulletin of the American Schools of Oriental Research* 232 (1978), pp. 5–23, especially pp. 17–21) denies any Mosaic authority for the Temple Scroll. His conclusion was challenged by Yadin ("Is the Temple Scroll a Sectarian Document?" in Gene M. Tucker and Douglas A. Knight, eds., *Humanizing America's Iconic Book: SBL Centennial Addresses 1980* (Chico, CA: Scholars Press, 1982), pp. 153–169), who relies on Temple Scroll 44:5 and 51:5–7, where Moses is indeed indirectly addressed. But Levine correctly demonstrates the tendency of the Temple Scroll to replace the traditional authority of Moses with God himself. Probably, this is to be interpreted as polemical—against any human authority in Jewish legal matters.

2. In this Ben Zion Wachholder is wrong. See his book *The Dawn of Qumran* (Cincinnati, OH: Hebrew Union College Press, 1983), where he claims that the Temple Scroll "may have been intended to supersede not only the canonical Pentateuch but the other books of the Hebrew Scriptures as well" (p. 30).

3. See Lawrence H. Schiffman, *Sectarian Law in the Dead Sea Scrolls: Courts, Testimony and the Penal Code* (Chico, CA: Scholars Press, 1983), p. 77.

4. The so-called Damascus Documents includes two different sections, the "Admonitions" represented by columns I–VIII and XIX–XX, and the "Laws" represented by columns XV–XVI and IX–XIV. Both sections were composed evidently by the Essenes, and fragments of both of them were also found in the Qumran caves.

5. See Schiffman, op. cit., *Scrolls: Courts*, p. 77.

6. Yadin recognized this problem and tried to resolve it with the suggestion that in other scrolls from Qumran we are always dealing with high priests who are mentioned in contexts relating to the End of Days with specific titles for them. But this is, at least, disputable: In those scrolls, the high priest at the end of days is called *ha-kohen ha'-aharon* or sometimes *meshia'Aharon,* while *kohen ha-rosh* seems to be the more usual title used by the Qumran community, but strange to the Temple Scroll.

7. The Cambridge edition of the Septuagint by Allen E. Brooke and Norman McLean, *The Old Testament in Greek According to the Text of Codex Vaticanus* (Cambridge, UK: Cambridge University Press, 1906–1911), vol. I, Part I–III.

8. Yadin mistakenly thought these were references to other copies of the Temple Scroll. They were not that, but were simply fragments of scrolls of the same genre, or expansions within the Pentateuchal books themselves. Unfortunately, some of these are still unpublished, so they cannot be treated very thoroughly, even by scholars.

9. "Literary Sources of the Temple Scroll," *Harvard Theological Review,* vol. 75 (1982), pp. 275–288.

10. Dating the composition of the Temple Scroll to the second half of the fifth century B.C. results in some provocative suggestions for further research:

First, the Pentateuch as we know it from our Bible must have been finally redacted at least a century before the composition of the Temple Scroll; at least a century would be needed to develop all the additions and alterations of the text used in the Temple Scroll.

Second, some scholars already noticed that specific aspects of the Temple Scroll are closely related to the biblical books of Chronicles—for example, the status of the Levites. The state of development of the Hebrew language is similar in both Chronicles and in the Temple Scroll. These relationships and similarities are much easier to explain if both Chronicles and the Temple Scroll are contemporaneous compositions, but they would be puzzling if the Temple Scroll was composed about three centuries later, as supposed by Yadin and those who agree with him.

Third, over the centuries, even Palestinian Jews no longer continued to regard the Temple Scroll as a canonical book, as the sixth book of the Torah, as it was in the mind of its author. Nevertheless, the preserved text of Yadin's Temple Scroll demonstrates the way in which some priestly families at the Jerusalem Temple interpreted, augmented, and used the canonical Pentateuch during the first century of the Second Temple period. This insight will enable us to understand much better the way priestly teaching developed at the Jerusalem Temple before Ezra returned there.

CHAPTER 11.
THE TEXT BEHIND THE TEXT
OF THE HEBREW BIBLE

1. The English edition was published shortly before Yadin's death: *The Temple Scroll* (Israel Exploration Society: Jerusalem, 1983), 3 volumes.
2. Josephus, *Contra Apionem 1.42* (ed. Loeb, trans. H. St. John Thackeray).
3. To be sure, it must be recognized that Josephus was writing a polemical work addressed to a Greek-speaking audience and does not hesitate on occasion to overstate or exaggerate.
4. For a contemporary evaluation of the medieval variants in manuscripts of the Hebrew Bible and rabbinical literature, see M. H. Goshen-Gottstein, "Hebrew Biblical Manuscripts, Their History and Their Place in the HUBP Edition," *Biblica 48* (1967), pp. 243–290; and F. M. Cross, "The History of the Biblical Text in the Light of Discoveries in the Judean Desert," *Harvard Theological Review* 57 (1964), pp. 281–299, esp. 287–292. Both papers are republished in Cross and S. Talmon, *Qumran and the History of the Biblical Text* (Cambridge: Harvard University Press, 1975), pp. 42–89 (Goshen-Gottstein) and 177–195.

5. The history of the textual scholarship of this era, the emergence of the "one-recension" theory, the "archetype" theory, and the confusion of the two in subsequent scholarly discussion, is given definitive treatment by Goshen-Gottstein in the article listed above (note 4).

6. In fact, the Nash Papyrus had already given a glimpse of an earlier stage of the Pentateuchal text before the fixing of the Rabbinic Recension, but its witness was largely ignored. See W. F. Albright, "A Biblical Fragment from the Maccabean Age: The Nash Papyrus," *Journal of Biblical Literature* 56 (1937), pp. 145–176.

7. A review of the biblical texts from Qumran and publication data on those that have been edited may be found in P. W. Skehan, "Qumran Literature," *Supplement on Dictionnaire de la Bible IX,* cols. 805–828. Cf. F. M. Cross, *The Ancient Library of Qumran,* rev. ed. (Grand Rapids, MI: Baker Book House, 1980), pp. xi–xxi [Preface to German edition, supplementing 1961 English edition].

8. See P. Benoit, J. T. Milik, and R. de Vaux, *Le grottes de Murabba'at DJDII* (Oxford: Clarendon Press, 1961), pp. 75–85 (Plates XIX–XXIV), and 181–205 (Plates LVI–LXXIII).

9. See Cross, "The Contribution of the Qumran Discoveries to the Study of the Biblical Text," *Israel Exploration Journal* 16 (1966), pp. 81–95, and esp. 282, n. 21.

10. 1 Maccabees 1:56–58 contains an interesting reference to massive destruction of books in the Antiochan conflict and their replacement by Judah.

11. The first evidence of the protorabbinic text in Samuel is found in the recension of the Theodotionic School, the so-called Kaige Recension. This systematic Greek recension from the end of the first century B.C. is inspired by principles similar to those that emerged in the era of Hillel and, no doubt, may be assigned to scholars of the same party that published the Rabbinic Recension. The Hebrew text used as the base of this revision is protorabbinic, to be sure, not identical with the fully fixed Pharisaic Bible at all points. Only the revision of the Kaige Recension by Aquila brought the Greek text fully in line with the Rabbinic Recension.

12. See Cross, "The History of the Biblical Text in the Light of Discoveries in the Judean Desert," see note 4, p. 291. D. Barthelemy notes Josephus' reference to increased contacts between the Palestinian Jewish community and the Babylonian Jewish community during the reign of Herod (*Antiquities* 17.24–27); see his *Études d'histoire du texte de l'Ancien Testament* (Fribourg: Editions Universitaires, 1978), pp. 241f.

13. This textual tradition has also been called "proto-Masoretic," a designation that perhaps should be reserved for early exemplars of the Rabbinic Recension.

14. *Sukkah* 20a. Hillel's "establishment of the Torah" has, of course, been taken heretofore more generally to apply to his role in the interpretation of oral

and written law, or even figuratively to his exemplary "living the Torah."
Cf. E. E. Urbach, *The Sages, Their Concepts and Beliefs* (Jerusalem: Magnes,
1975), p. 588 and n. 91 (p. 955).

15. Josephus, *Contra Apionem*, op. cit., 1.37–41.

16. See S. Leiman, *The Canonization of the Hebrew Scripture: The Talmudic and
Midrashic Evidence*, Transactions of the Connecticut Academy of Arts and
Sciences (Hamden, CT: Archon Books, 1976), esp. pp. 72–120.

17. Josephus is not alone in his testimony. We are now able to reconstruct an
old canonical list, the common source of the so-called Bryennios List and
the canon of Epiphanius, which must be dated to the end of the first century
or the beginning of the second century of the Common Era. It is a list of
biblical works "according to the Hebrews," and reflects the same twenty-
two-book canon we find in Josephus, echoed in the independent canonical
lists of Origen and Jerome. The twenty-four-book canon mentioned in
Fourth Ezra (c. 100 A.D.) and in the rabbinic sources is doubtless identical
in content but reckons Ruth and Lamentations separately. The writing of
Ruth with Judges, Lamentations with Jeremiah is quite old, to judge from
its survival in the Septuagint, and the explicit testimony of Origen to the
Hebrew ordering.

18. In the case of Ecclesiastes, it is not without interest that the book has proven
to be much earlier than scholars generally have thought. A copy of the work
from about 200 B.C. is known from Qumran, and a date for its composition
as early as the Persian period is not excluded.

CHAPTER 12.
LIGHT ON THE BIBLE
FROM THE DEAD SEA CAVES

1. See F. M. Cross, *Canaanite Myth and Hebrew Epic* (Cambridge, MA: Harvard
University Press, 1976), p. 266 and references.

2. For a detailed discussion (and photograph) of the fragment of Samuel, see
Cross, "The Ammonite Oppression of the Tribes of Gad and Reuben:
Missing Verses from 1 Samuel 11 Found in 4QSamuel[a]," in *History, Histori-
ography, and Interpretation,* H. Tadmor and M. Weinfeld, eds. (Jerusalem:
Magnes Press, 1983), pp. 148–158.

3. See Alexander Rofe's comments, *Israel Exploration Journal* 32 (1982), pp.
129–133. I have anticipated such views in the paper cited in note 2.

4. See Cross, "Notes on the Ammonite Inscription from Tell Siran," *Bulletin
of the American Schools of Oriental Research* 212 (1973), esp. p. 15, where the
title on the Tell Siran bottle and the Amman citadel inscription are discussed.

5. George Foote Moore, *Judaism in the First Centuries of the Christian Era: The*

Age of the Tannaim, Vol. I (Cambridge: Harvard University Press, 1962), p. 127

6. The treatment of Jewish mysticism has undergone a similar transformation in contemporary scholarship; it is now regarded as a major component of Jewish history owing largely to the researches of Gershom Scholem and his students.

CHAPTER 13.

WHEN THE SONS OF GOD CAVORTED
WITH THE DAUGHTERS OF MEN

1. Most modern English versions translate this troublesome verb as "abide" or "remain." This is simply a guess from the context. I read the verb (Hebrew *yadon*) as a perfectly normal formation from the root *dnn,* "to be strong." This same root appears in the name of an Israelite village in the Judean hill country, Dannah (Joshua 15:49). The name of this village means "stronghold." The root *dnn* is therefore attested in biblical Hebrew, both in the placename and in Genesis 6:3.

2. For a more detailed discussion of what follows, with complete references, see Ronald S. Hendel, "Of Demigods and the Deluge: Toward an Interpretation of Genesis 6:1–4," *Journal of Biblical Literature,* 106 (1987), pp. 13–26.

3. Julius Wellhausen, *Prolegomena to the History of Israel,* J. S. Black and A. Menzies, transl. (Edinburgh: Adam and Charles Black, 1885), p. 317.

4. See also Psalm 82:6 *(bene elyon)* and Daniel 3:25 *(bar elahin).*

5. The Septuagint reads literally "the angels of God" *(aggelon theou);* this, however, is the usual and normal Septuagint translation of the Hebrew "Sons of God."

6. Arslan Tash (KAI 27.11) and Karatepe (KAI 26.A.III.19). Translations of the Karatepe inscription and one of the inscriptions from Arslan Tash may be found in *Ancient Near Eastern Texts Related to the Old Testament,* James B. Pritchard, ed. (Princeton: Princeton University Press, 3rd ed., 1969), p. 654 (Karatepe), and p. 658 (Arslan Tash).

7. Siegfried H. Horn, "The Amman Citadel Inscription," *BASOR* 193 (1969), pp. 2–13.

8. For other descriptions of Yahweh's divine assembly, see 1 Kings 22:19, Isaiah 6, Psalm 82, and, from a later era, Daniel 7:9–10. References or allusions to the divine assembly are found in many texts, including Jeremiah 23:18 and the plural addresses ("let us . . ." or "like one of us . . .") in Genesis 1:26, 3:22, and 11:7. For more discussion, see E. Theodore Mullen, Jr., *The Assembly of the Gods,* Harvard Semitic Monographs 24 (Chico, CA: Scholars Press, 1980).

9. Some of my readings in this passage diverge from the traditional translations

for textual and linguistic reasons. For a discussion of this passage, see Walther Zimmerli, *Ezekiel 2*, Hermeneia (Philadelphia: Fortress Press, 1983), pp. 168, 176.

10. In 2 Samuel 21 it is a warrior named Elhanan who defeats Goliath. This story is more familiar to us in 1 Samuel 17, where David is Goliath's opponent. This is an example of a story that "floats" in oral tradition from a lesser hero to a greater hero.

11. Moses: Joshua 12:4–6, 13:12; Joshua: Joshua 11:21–22; Caleb: Joshua 15:14, Judges 1:20.

12. 2 Samuel 21:18–22; 1 Chronicles 20:4–8.

13. Note that the giant aboriginal inhabitants of Seir, Ammon, and Gaza are also utterly annihilated, generally by Yahweh (Deuteronomy 2:12, 20–23). See also Deuteronomy 9:1–3; Amos 2–9.

14. Compare Mario Liverani's remarks on the function of the Amorites in Israelite tradition, *The Amorites in Peoples of Old Testament Times,* D. J. Wiseman, ed. (Oxford: Clarendon Press, 1973).

15. W. G. Lambert and Alan R. Millard, *Atrahasis: the Babylonian Story of the Flood* (Oxford: Clarendon Press, 1969), pp. 66–67, 72–73.

16. Several scholars have suggested that the increase of population referred to in Genesis 6:1 is a vestige of the theme in Atrahasis of human overpopulation. See Alexander Heidel, *The Gilagamesh Epic and Old Testament Parallels* (Chicago: University of Chicago, 1949), pp. 225–226; Alan R. Millard, "A New Babylonian 'Genesis' Story," *Tyndale Bulletin* 18 (1967), pp. 11–12; Claus Westermann, Genesis 1/1, BKAT (Neukirchen-Vluyn: Neukirchener, 1974), pp. 500–501; see also H. Schwarzbaum, "The Overcrowded Earth," *Numen* 4 (1957), pp. 59–74. The connection seems rather forced, however, since an increase of population is to be expected in myths of primeval humanity. The distinctive features of the Atrahasis myth—excess of population and its accompanying noise—are both absent in the Israelite tradition. For a nuanced view of the contrast between the Israelite and Mesopotamian traditions, see William L. Moran, "Atrahasis: The Babylonian Story of the Flood," *Biblica* 52 (1971), p. 61.

CHAPTER 14.
THE DEAD SEA SCROLLS AND CHRISTIANITY

1. Andre Dupont-Sommer, *The Dead Sea Scrolls: A Preliminary Survey* (Oxford: Basil Blackwell, 1952), p. 99 (the author's preface is dated July 14, 1950). He felt the need to defend these striking formulations in a later book; see his *The Jewish Sect of Qumran and the Essenes: New Studies on the Dead Sea Scrolls* (New York: Macmillan, 1955 [transl. from French 1953 edition]), pp. 160–162. Note, "I drew attention to these comparisons in the *Dead Sea*

Scrolls. In my desire to draw attention to this unexpected fact, which the new texts seemed to disclose, I sketched out a rapid parallel which was intended to stimulate the curiosity of the reader, without pretending to solve a most complex problem at the price of oversimplification" (p. 160). As he said in this later publication, the resemblance between Jesus and the Teacher ". . . is far from being complete" (p. 161).

2. Edmund Wilson, "The Scrolls from the Dead Sea," *The New Yorker* (May, 1955), pp. 45–131. The book was published under the same title in the same year (London: Collins). It remained on best-seller lists for some time. In fairness, it should be said that Wilson was critical of Dupont-Sommer's use of some passages from the Habakkuk Commentary on the grounds that they referred to the Wicked Priest, the archenemy of the Teacher, not to the Teacher himself (e.g., *The Scrolls from the Dead Sea*, pp. 92–93). But he does add unusually strong words of praise for the scholar of the Sorbonne (*New Yorker*, pp. 106–108).

3. Wilson, *The Scrolls from the Dead Sea*, p. 102.

4. Ibid., p. 104.

5. Ibid., p. 114.

6. Millar Burrows, *The Dead Sea Scrolls* (New York: Viking, 1955).

7. Ibid., p. 327.

8. Ibid., p. 328.

9. Ibid., p. 343. In the same context he claims one need not think that any of the New Testament writers had ever heard of the Qumran group (pp. 342–343).

10. Krister Stendahl, ed., *The Scrolls and the New Testament,* (New York: Harper & Row, 1957). All of the papers except two (and Stendahl's introduction) had already been published between 1950 and 1955. Actually, two of the essays are not centrally about Qumran and the New Testament: Joseph Fitzmyer's on the Ebionites (though he was responding to J. L. Teicher's claim that the Qumran sect was Ebionite—a Jewish Christian group) and Nahum Glatzer's on Hillel the Elder.

11. Stendahl, "An Introduction and a Perspective," in *The Scrolls and the New Testament,* pp. 16–17.

12. The quotation is from Rudolf Bultmann, *Theology of the New Testament,* 2 vols. (New York: Charles Scribner's Sons, 1951–1955), vol. 1, p. 42.

13. Frank M. Cross, *The Ancient Library of Qumran and Modern Biblical Studies* (Grand Rapids, MI: Baker Book House, reprint, 1980), pp. 203–204. A revised edition was issued in 1961; a German translation in 1967; and a reprint in 1980. References to the book are to this latest version.

   Mention should also be made of the very brief statement that J. T. Milik devotes to the subject in his *Ten Years of Discovery in the Wilderness of Judaea,* Studies in Biblical Theology 26 (London: SCM Press, 1959 [French edition, 1957]). He notes literary, institutional, and doctrinal parallels and argues that

Essene influence on the early Church increased after the time of Jesus and the first disciples, especially in Jewish Christianity: "Slightly later we find in one part of the Church Essene influence almost taking over and submerging the authentically Christian doctrinal element; indeed, it may be considered responsible for the break between the Judaeo-Christians and the Great Church" (pp. 142–143).

14. Herbert Braun, *Qumran und das Neue Testament* (Tübingen: J.C.B. Mohr [Paul Siebeck], 1966).

15. See, for example, Geza Vermes, *The Dead Sea Scrolls: Qumran in Perspective* (Philadelphia: Fortress, 1977), pp. 211–221.

16. See, for example, Robert H. Eisenman, *Maccabees, Zadokites, Christians and Qumran: A New Hypothesis of Qumran Origins,* Studie Post-Biblica 34 (Leiden, Netherlands: E. J. Brill, 1983).

17. Barbara Thiering, *Redating the Teacher of Righteousness,* Australian and New Zealand Studies in Theology and Religion (Sydney: Theological Explorations, 1979); and *The Gospels and Qumran: A New Hypothesis,* Australian and New Zealand Studies in Theology and Religion (Sydney: Theological Explorations, 1981).

18. J. L. Teicher, "The Dead Sea Scrolls—Documents of the Jewish-Christian Sect of Ebionites," *Journal of Jewish Studies* 3 (1951), pp. 67–99.

19. Regarding Eisenman, see Michael Baigent and Richard Leigh, *The Dead Sea Scrolls Deception* (London: Jonathan Cape, 1991). Also see Chapter 22.

20. Translation of Vermes, *The Dead Sea Scrolls in English* (Harmondsworth, UK: Penguin Books, 1962), as are all other quotations from the scrolls, unless otherwise indicated.

21. Cross (*The Ancient Library of Qumran,* p. 233) notes that the *hmbqr* and the *pgyd* (usually translated as *episkopos* in the Greek version of the Hebrew Bible) appear to be the same individual.

22. Joseph Fitzmyer, "The Qumran Scrolls and the New Testament after Forty Years," *Revue de Qumran* 13 (1988), pp. 613–615.

23. Jose O'Callaghan, "Papiros neotestamentarios en la cueva 7 de Qumran?" *Biblica* 53 (1972), pp. 91–100. The scroll 7Q5, supposedly the best example, is said to offer letters from Mark 6:52–53—twenty legible letters in all. The texts are, however, extremely difficult to read, and other identifications have been proposed for them. For the texts and other bibliography, see Florentino García-Martínez, "Lista de MSS procedentes de Qumran," *Henoch* 11 (1989), p. 223.

24. For bibliography and discussion of this point, see Braun, *Qumran und das Neue Testament,* vol. 1, pp. 201–204. As Fitzmyer has pointed out, 2 Corinthians 6:18 cites 2 Samuel 7:14, a passage that is also quoted in 4QFlorilegium ("4Q Testimonia and the New Testament," *Theological Studies* 18 [1957], pp. 534–535).

25. Josephus, *Antiquities of the Jews* 15.10,4; sec. 371. Translation of H. St. J.

Thackeray, Loeb Classical Library (Cambridge, MA: Harvard University Press/London: William Heinemann, 1978).

26. See Kurt Schubert, "The Sermon on the Mount and the Qumran Texts" in Stendahl, ed., *The Scrolls and the New Testament,* pp. 118–128.

27. The letters MMT stand for the Hebrew words *miqsat ma'aseh ha-Torah* (some of the deeds of the Torah), a phrase found toward the end of the work.

28. William H. Brownlee ("John the Baptist in the New Light of Ancient Scrolls" in Stendahl, ed., *The Scrolls and the New Testament,* pp. 33–53) discussed these issues at length and proposed that John may have been raised by the Essenes, who, according to Josephus, adopted the children of others and taught them their principles while they were still young (*The Jewish War* 2.8,2 [sec. 120]).

29. For the text and extensive discussion and comparison of it with New Testament passages, see P. J. Kobelski, *Melchizedek and Melchiresaᶜ,* The Catholic Biblical Quarterly Monograph Series 10 (Washington, DC: Catholic Biblical Association, 1981). Here I leave out of consideration the more speculative suggestions of scholars who have found James the Just to be important in the scrolls (Eisenman), Jesus to be the Teacher of Righteousness, or the apostle Paul the Wicked Priest (Teicher).

30. The texts have been published, translated and analyzed by Carol Newsom, *Songs of the Sabbath Sacrifice: A Critical Edition,* Harvard Semitic Studies 27 (Atlanta: Scholars Press, 1985); see her comments on pp. 37, 133, 144. See also Fitzmyer, "The Qumran Scrolls and the New Testament," pp. 618–619. Some caution is in order because Melchizedek's name is never fully preserved in any of the fragmentary remains of these manuscripts.

31. Josephus (*The Jewish War* 2.8,3 [sec. 122]) and Pliny the Elder (*Natural History* 5.15) also refer to the community property of the Essenes.

32. There is a dittography (unintentional repetition of letters or words while copying) in lines 5–6.

33. Translation of Lawrence Schiffman, *The Eschatological Community of the Dead Sea Scrolls: A Study of the Rule of the Congregation,* SBL Monograph Series 38 (Atlanta: Scholars Press, 1989), pp. 53–55.

34. Ibid., p. 67.

35. An early and important study of this parallel is Karl Georg Kuhn's "The Lord's Supper and the Communal Meal at Qumran" in Stendahl, ed., *The Scrolls and the New Testament,* pp. 65–93.

36. For a brief and precise presentation of the evidence and bibliography for this debate, see Fitzmyer, *The Dead Sea Scrolls: Major Publications and Tools for Study,* Sources for Biblical Study 20 (Atlanta: Scholars Press, rev. ed. 1990), pp. 180–186.

37. Annie Jaubert, *The Date of the Last Supper* (Staten Island, NY: Alba House, 1965).

38. Fitzmyer, "The Qumran Scrolls and the New Testament," p. 617. The text has been given the siglum 4QpsDan [pseudo-Daniel] A^a (4Q246) and dates from the last third of the first century B.C. See Fitzmyer, "The Contribution of Qumran Aramaic to the Study of the New Testament," in his *A Wandering Aramean: Collected Aramaic Essays,* SBL Monograph Series 25 (Missoula, MT: Scholars Press, 1979), pp. 90–94, 102–107, for more detail (originally published in *New Testament Studies* 20 [1973–1974], pp. 382–407). See also Chapter 15.

39. See Fitzmyer, "The Contribution of Qumran Aramaic," p. 98.

40. Karl Elliger, *Studien zum Habakuk-Kommentar vom Töten Meer* (Beiträge zur historischen Theologie 15; Tübingen: J.C.B. Mohr [Paul Siebeck], 1953) pp. 150–164. The wording of the assumptions given here is a paraphrase of what he wrote.

41. Joel 2:28 (3:1 in Hebrew).

42. Josephus, *The Jewish War* 2.8,10–11; sec. 153–154. Josephus also notes their belief in the immortality of the soul in his *Antiquities of the Jews* 18.1,5; sec. 18.

43. Hippolytus, *Refutation of All Heresies* 9.27,1.

44. If so, we would conclude that Josephus distorted Essene beliefs, as he does Pharisaic beliefs about the resurrection, in order to appeal to the tastes of his larger, Greek-reading audience, to whom it may have seemed peculiar.

45. Émile Puech, "Les Esséniens et la vie future," *Le Monde de la Bible* 4 (1978), pp. 38–40. The quotation is my translation of his French rendering (p. 40). The text in question is apparently 4Q521 (so García-Martínez, "Lista de MSS procedentes de Qumran," p. 210).

46. Josephus reports that Herod favored the Essenes (*Antiquities of the Jews* 15.10,4 [sec. 372]). See Yigael Yadin, "The Temple Scroll—The Longest and Most Recently Discovered Dead Sea Scroll," *Biblical Archaeology Review,* September/October 1984, p. 48.

47. See the discussion in Vermes, *The Dead Sea Scrolls,* p. 220.

48. The name "Bethusians" is often suspected of being a reference to the Essenes.

CHAPTER 16.

WAS JOHN THE BAPTIST AN ESSENE?

1. Josephus, *Antiquities of the Jews,* 18:119.

2. Ibid., 18:116–7.

3. Josephus, *The Jewish War,* 2:120.

4. Josephus, *Antiquities of the Jews,* 18:117.

5. Ibid., 18:118.

6. Josephus, *The Jewish War*, 1:78–80, 2:112–113; *Antiquities of the Jews*, 15:-371–379.

CHAPTER 17.
NEW LIGHT ON THE PHARISEES

1. See Chapter 3. Cf. also L. H. Schiffman, "Confessionalism and the Study of the Dead Sea Scrolls," *Jewish Studies* 31 (1991), pp. 3–14.
2. For a comprehensive discussion of this entire period, see Schiffman, *From Text to Tradition, A History of Second Temple and Rabbinic Judaism* (Hoboken, NJ: Ktav, 1991).
3. See J. Neusner, *From Politics to Piety, the Emergence of Pharisaic Judaism* (Englewood, NJ: Prentice Hall, 1973).
4. Note that Avot 1:1 ascribes this notion to "the men of the Great Assembly," the last of which is said to have lived c. 250 B.C.E.
5. See Schiffman, *The Halakhah at Qumran* (Leiden: E. J. Brill, 1975), pp. 22–32.
6. M. P. Horgan, *Pesharim: Qumran Interpretations of Biblical Books*, CBQ Monograph Series 8 (Washington, DC: Catholic Biblical Association, 1979), pp. 160–162.
7. For bibliography, see Horgan, *Pesharem*, p. 184.
8. B. Z. Wacholder, "A Qumran Attack on Oral Exegesis? The Phrase *'asher be-talmud shegaram* in 4Q Pesher Nahum," *Revue de Qumran* 5 (1964–1966), pp. 575–578.
9. F. M. Cross, "The Early History of the Qumran Community," *New Directions in Biblical Archaeology*, ed. D. N. Freedman, J. C. Greenfield (Garden City, NY: Doubleday, 1971), pp. 70–89.
10. See the extremely important article of Y. Sussmann, "The History of Halakha and the Dead Sea Scrolls—Preliminary Observations on *Miqsat Ma'ase Ha-Torah* (4QMMT)" (Hebrew), *Tarbiz* 59 (1989/90), pp. 11–76.
11. Cf. Schiffman, "The Temple Scroll and the Systems of Jewish Law of the Second Temple Period," *Temple Scroll Studies*, ed. G. J. Brooke (Sheffield: JSOT Press, 1989), pp. 245–51 and Schiffman, "*Miqsat Ma'aseh Ha-Torah* and the *Temple Scroll*," *Revue de Qumran* 14 (1990), pp. 435–457.
12. See Chapter 3 and "The New Halakhic Letter (4QMMT) and the Origins of the Dead Sea Sect," *Biblical Archaeologist* 53, no. 2 (June 1990), pp. 64–73.
13. Further evidence of the political role of the Pharisees is found in the scrolls as well, but it will have to remain beyond the scope of this essay. In the scrolls we find evidence of the falling-out which eventually separated the Pharisees from the Hasmonean dynasty as the Hasmoneans became progressively Hellenized. In this respect, the scrolls confirm evidence found in Josephus and rabbinic literature.

CHAPTER 18.
THE MYSTERY OF THE COPPER SCROLL

1. See K. G. Kuhn, "Les rouleaux de cuivre de Qumran," *Revue Biblique* 61 (1954), pp. 193–205.
2. The official publication is J. T. Milik, R. de Vaux, and H.W. Baker, "Le rouleau de cuivre provenant de la grotte 3Q (3Q15)," pp. 201–302 in M. Baillet, J. T. Milik, and R. de Vaux, *Les "Petites Grottes" de Qumran,* Discoveries in the Judaean Desert of Jordan 3 (Oxford: Clarendon Press, 1962). This is hereafter cited as DJD 3.
3. John Allegro, *The Treasure of the Copper Scroll* (Garden City, NY: Doubleday, 1960; 2d edition: 1964).
4. See the extremely negative review of Allegro's book by Roland de Vaux, the chief archaeologist of Qumran and its caves, in *Revue Biblique* 68 (1961), pp. 466–467.
5. The Mishnah is an early rabbinic text assembled in about 200 A.D.
6. DJD 3, p. 282.
7. Milik, DJD 3, p. 262.
8. See, for example, E. Ullendorff, "The Greek Letters of the Copper Scroll," *Vetus Testament* 11 (1961), pp. 227–228.
9. The most vigorous spokesman for this position is Norman Golb. See "The Problem of the Origin and Identification of the Dead Sea Scrolls," *Proceedings of the American Philosophical Society* 124 (1980), pp. 1–24; "Who Hid the Dead Sea Scrolls?" *Biblical Archaeologist* 48 (1985), pp. 68–82.
10. As, for example, in the Mishnaic tractate *Tevul Yom* 4.4.
11. As recognized by Manfred R. Lehmann ("Identification of the Copper Scroll Based on Its Technical Terms," *Revue de Qumran* 6 [1964], pp. 97–105), who cites a Tosefta, *Shevi'it* 7.3,5 and 8.1.
12. Cf. Lehmann, op. cit., pp. 99–100.
13. Lehmann, op. cit., p. 99.
14. An important exception is B. Z. Lurie, *The Copper Scroll from the Judaean Desert* Publications of the Israel Bible Research Society 14 (Jerusalem: Kiryat-Sepher, 1963) (in Hebrew).
15. See F. M. Cross, "Excursus on the Palaeographical Dating of the Copper Document," in DJD 3, pp. 217–221.

CHAPTER 19.
HOW TO CONNECT DEAD SEA SCROLL FRAGMENTS

1. See Andre Lemaire, "Fragments from the Book of Balaam Found at Deir Alla," *Biblical Archaeology Review,* September/October 1985.
2. Texts of phylacteries *(tephillin)* and *mezuzoth* were written on sheets rather than on scrolls. *Tephillin* are black leather boxes containing scriptural passages that are bound on the left hand and on the forehead by black leather

strips and are worn for the morning services on all days of the year except Sabbaths and scriptural holy days. See the article by L. I Rabinowitz, "Tefellin," in *Encyclopedia Judaica,* vol. 15 (Jerusalem: Keter Publishing House, 1972), cols. 898–904. A *mezuzah* is a parchment scroll affixed to the doorposts of rooms in Jewish homes. See the article by Rabinowitz, "Mezuzah," in *Encyclopedia Judaica,* vol. 11, cols. 1474–1477. In addition, a text known as 4Q Testimonia, consisting of a small collection of quotations, was also written on a sheet, rather than on a scroll. To make a scroll, sheets were sewn (in the case of parchment) or pasted (in the case of papyrus) together.

3. Precisely when the posts were introduced we do not know. But a fragment of a disc presumably attached to a post was found in the synagogue at Ein Gedi, dated to the third to sixth centuries A.D. See Hershel Shanks, *Judaism in Stone* (New York: Harper & Row/Washington, D.C.: Biblical Archaeology Society, 1979), p. 134.

4. Maurice Baillet, *Qumran Grotte 4,* III (4Q 482–520), Discoveries in the Judaean Desert, vol. VII (Oxford, UK: Clarendon Press, 1982).

5. There is, of course, a portion of this scroll, constituted by the fragments 44–59, that stuck together when the remains of this scroll came to the museum. Baillet tried to get to the original order of these fragments (see p. 242 of his edition and plates LXIII–LXV). But his results do not appear to be correct.

CHAPTER 22.
IS THE VATICAN SUPPRESSING
THE DEAD SEA SCROLLS?

1. Michael Baigent and Richard Leigh, *The Dead Sea Scrolls Deception* (London: Jonathan Cape, 1991). To be published in the United States by Summit Books (a subsidiary of Simon and Schuster) in January 1992.

2. The *New Jerome Biblical Commentary* states:

> Catholic critical scholarship from DAS [Divino afflante Spiritu] until 1970 was marked by intensive growth. . . .
> Catholic biblical scholars received official church encouragement through two primary documents, the PBC's [Pontifical Biblical Commission's] "Instruction on the Historical Truth of the Gospels" (1964) and Vatican II's *Dei Verbum* (Dogmatic Constitution on Divine Revelation, 1965). The former document, in particular, recognized that the Gospels consisted of several layers of tradition and thus are not literal or chronological accounts of the life of Jesus. This position confirmed the results of biblical scholarship while setting the stage for further developments in the scientific, critical study of the NT [New Testament] among Catholic biblical scholars. . . .

Catholic NT scholarship increasingly made its own mark in the study of the NT. It succeeded in convincing more intelligent Catholics that the ultraconservative biblical positions of the past were no longer tenable and that the new approaches had values of their own which could feed worship and spirituality. It incorporated the results of scientific NT study into the discussion of issues with dogmatic implications, e.g., the limitations of Jesus' knowledge regarding himself, the future, and the church; qualifications in the reliability of Acts as a guide to how the church historically emerged; the extent of creativity exercised in the formation of the Gospel tradition; the limited historicity of the infancy narratives."

John S. Kselman, S.S., and Ronald D. Witherup, S.S., "Modern New Testament Criticism" (Englewood Cliffs, NJ: Prentice-Hall, 1990), pp. 1142–1143.
3. "Leading Dead Sea Scroll Scholar Denounces Delay," *Biblical Archaeology Review,* March/April 1990.
4. Joseph A. Fitzmyer, "A Visit with M. Jozef Milik," *Biblical Archaeology Review,* July/August 1990.
5. John Allegro, *The Sacred Mushroom and the Cross* (Garden City, NY: Doubleday, 1970).
6. Émile Puech, "Un Hymn Essénien en Partie Retrouve et les Béatitudes," *Revue de Qumran* 13, nos. 49–52 (October 1988).

About the Authors

OTTO BETZ

Formerly professor of New Testament at Chicago Theological Seminary. Taught New Testament and Ancient Judaism at the University of Tübingen. Now retired.

MAGEN BROSHI

Curator of the Shrine of the Book in Jerusalem, where most of the intact Dead Sea Scrolls are kept. Directed archaeological excavations on Mt. Zion and elsewhere in Jerusalem. Member of the Dead Sea Scroll advisory committee of the Israel Antiquities Authority.

FRANK MOORE CROSS

Hancock Professor of Hebrew and Other Oriental Languages, Harvard University. Director of Harvard Semitic Museum. *Canaanite Myth and Hebrew Epic* (Cambridge, MA: Harvard University Press, 1973), *The Ancient Library of Qumran and Modern Biblical Studies* (rev. ed. Grand Rapids, MI: Baker Book House, 1980), and coeditor of *Scrolls from Qumran Cave I* (Jerusalem: Albright Institute of Archaeological Research and Shrine of the Book, 1972). Member of original editing team of Cave 4 texts from Qumran. Former president of the American Schools of Oriental Research and of the Society of Biblical Literature.

HARRY THOMAS FRANK

Formerly professor of Religion at Oberlin College. Staff archaeologist at Tell el-Hesi excavations in Israel. Author of *Discovering the Biblical World* (Maplewood, NJ: Hammond, 1975). Deceased.

RONALD S. HENDEL

Assistant Professor of Religious Studies at Southern Methodist University. Author of *Parallel Themes in the Ugaritic Epic Poems and the Hebrew Bible.* Work in progress: *The Text of Genesis 1–11: Massoretic Text, Samaritan Text, Septuagint, and Qumran.*

AVI KATZMAN

Journalist with *Ha'aretz,* a leading Tel Aviv newspaper.

RAPHAEL LEVY

Writer, newspaperman, film maker, public relations director, and Dead Sea Scrolls buff.

P. KYLE MCCARTER, JR.

William Foxwell Albright Professor of Biblical and Ancient Near Eastern Studies at The Johns Hopkins University. Author of commentaries on I Samuel and II Samuel for the Anchor Bible series. Preparing a new edition and translation of the Copper Scroll from Qumran for Princeton University Press. Formerly president of the American Schools of Oriental Research.

LAWRENCE H. SCHIFFMAN

Professor of Hebrew and Judaic Studies at New York University. Author of *Who Was a Jew? Rabbinic and Halakhic Perspectives on the Jewish-Christian Schism* (Hoboken, NJ: Ktav, 1985), *Text and Tradition, A History of Second Temple and Rabbinic Judaism* (Hoboken, NJ: Ktav, 1990), and editor of *Archaeology and History in the Dead Sea Scrolls* (Sheffield with ASOR, 1990). 1989/90 Fellow of the Institute for Advanced Studies at the Hebrew University of Jerusalem dealing with the Dead Sea Scrolls. Recent recipient of editorial assignment of Cave 4 texts from Qumran.

HERSHEL SHANKS

Founder and editor of *Biblical Archaeology Review* and *Bible Review*. President of The Biblical Archaeology Society, publisher of *A Preliminary Edition of the Unpublished Dead Sea Scrolls—The Hebrew and Aramaic Texts from Cave Four—Fascicle One* (1991) and *A Facsimile Edition of the Dead Sea Scrolls—Volumes I and II* (1991). Author of *The City of David: A Guide to Biblical Jerusalem* (Jerusalem: Bazak, 1973) and *Judaism in Stone: The Archaeology of Ancient Synagogues* (New York: Harper & Row, 1979). Editor of *Ancient Israel: A Short History from Abraham to the Roman Destruction of the Temple* (Englewood Cliffs, N.J.: Prentice-Hall, 1988).

HARTMUT STEGEMANN

Professor of New Testament Science at the University of Göttingen. Director of the Qumran Research Center at the University of Göttingen. Author of numerous articles on Qumran and problems of the historical Jesus. Preparing a dictionary of the nonbiblical Qumran texts.

JAMES C. VANDERKAM

Professor of Old Testament Studies at the University of Notre Dame. Author of *Enoch and the Growth of an Apocalyptic Tradition* (Washington, D.C.: Catholic Biblical Association, 1984) and *The Book of Jubilees* (Leuvan, Belgium: Peeters, 1989). Editor of Jubilees texts from Qumran Cave 4. Chair of the Ancient Manuscripts Committee of the American Schools of Oriental Research.

YIGAEL YADIN

Acquired four Dead Sea Scrolls from Cave 1 for Israel and later the Temple Scroll. Until his death in 1984, he was Israel's leading archaeologist. Directed archaeological excavations at Masada and Hazor. Also led an expedition to search for scrolls in caves by the Dead Sea. Served as head of the Department of Archaeology and later of the Institute of Archaeology of the Hebrew University in Jerusalem. Edited *The Scroll of the War of the Sons of Light against the Sons of Darkness* [the War Scroll from Qumran] (Oxford: Oxford University Press, 1962), *Tefillin from Qumran* (Jerusalem: The Israel Exploration Society and the Shrine of the Book, 1969), and *The Temple Scroll* (Jerusalem: Israel Exploration Society, 1983). Author of *The Message of the Scrolls* (New York: Simon and Schuster, 1957) and popular books on Masada, Hazor, the Bar Kokhba documents, and the Temple Scroll.

Index

Sources and Dates
of Original Articles

Chapter 1: *Biblical Archaeology Review*, December 1975.
Chapter 2: *Biblical Archaeology Review*, March 1977.
Chapter 3: *Bible Review*, October 1990.
Chapter 4: *Bible Review*, April 1991.
Chapter 5: *Biblical Archaeology Review*, September/October 1982.
Chapter 6: *Biblical Archaeology Review*, September/October 1982.
Chapter 7: *Biblical Archaeology Review*, September/October 1984.
Chapter 8: *Biblical Archaeology Review*, November/December 1987.
Chapter 9: *Biblical Archaeology Review*, November/December 1987.
Chapter 10: *Biblical Archaeology Review*, November/December 1987.
Chapter 11: *Bible Review*, Summer 1985.
Chapter 12: *Bible Review*, Fall 1985.
Chapter 13: *Bible Review*, Summer 1987.
Chapter 14: *Bible Review*, December 1991/February 1992.
Chapter 15: *Biblical Archaeology Review*, March/April 1990.
Chapter 16: *Bible Review*, December 1990.
Chapter 17: *Bible Review*, June 1992.
Chapter 18: *Bible Review*, August 1992.
Chapter 19: *Bible Review*, February 1988.
Chapter 20: *Biblical Archaeology Review*, January/February 1991.
Chapter 21: *Biblical Archaeology Review*, March/April 1991.
Chapter 22: *Biblical Archaeology Review*, November/December 1991.

ABOUT THE TYPE

This book was set in Bembo, a typeface based on an
old-style Roman face that was used for Cardinal
Bembo's tract *De Actua* in 1495. Bembo was cut by
Francisco Griffo in the early sixteenth century. The
Lanston Monotype Machine Company of Philadelphia
brought the well-proportioned letter forms of Bembo
to the United States in the 1930s.